GOD
IN DISPUTE

GOD IN DISPUTE

"Conversations"
among
Great Christian
Thinkers

ROGER E. OLSON

Baker Academic
a division of Baker Publishing Group
Grand Rapids, Michigan

Published by Baker Academic
a division of Baker Publishing Group
P.O. Box 6287, Grand Rapids, MI 49516-6287
www.bakeracademic.com

Printed in the United States of America

Library of Congress Cataloging-in-Publication Data

Olson, Roger E.
     God in dispute : "conversations" among great Christian thinkers / Roger E. Olson.
         p.   cm.
     Includes bibliographical references and index.
     ISBN 978-0-8010-3639-2 (pbk. : alk. paper)
     1. Theology, Doctrinal—History. 2. Church history. I. Title.
BT21.3.O46 2009
230.09—dc22   2009016437

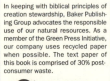

Dedicated to my students,

who have endured and enjoyed these
"conversations" as they were being written

and especially to those who volunteered to play roles
as they performed them in my historical theology classes.

Contents

Introduction

This book rises out of my use of imaginary dialogues in various historical theology courses I have taught over the last three decades. Most of my students have found the practice to be helpful if not delightful. I usually ask one or more students (depending on how many roles are in a dialogue) to play the part of a theologian and use dramatic inflection for emphasis. I began to think that others might enjoy listening in and perhaps using such dialogues in their classes. Yet I've written them so that anyone can benefit from and enjoy them, not just theologians or teachers of theology.

I've carefully chosen the twenty-nine dialogues in this book to represent selected high points of the development of Christian thought over the centuries. Some important thinkers are necessarily neglected. Perhaps a sequel volume can include them.

Each dialogue is preceded by a section called "Setting," which provides information about the thinkers in the conversation and where the imaginary dialogue is supposed to be taking place. Then comes the dialogue itself, followed by "Analysis" that discusses the dialogue and what happened there. Finally, each conversation/chapter ends with suggestions "For Further Reading" to assist readers interested in learning more.

I realize that I have taken fairly large poetic license with thinkers in some of these conversations. I put words into their mouths. When it comes to content, I try to be faithful to their ideas; but when it comes to style, I try to entertain the readers with jokes and jibes, snide remarks and warm, friendly comments. Hopefully the participants in the conversations will come alive and seem quite real.

I believe that a careful reading of this book will deliver a brief course in the history of Christian thought. In each conversation I have tried to include the participants' most important contributions to Christian theology. If you're intrigued, read further in the conversation partners' own writings (mentioned in the text) and secondary sources about the thinker (mentioned in the sections "For Further Reading").

1

Second-Century Critic Celsus Queries Polycarp, Valentinus, and Montanus about the Christian Sect

Setting

Little is known about the personal life of the Roman philosopher Celsus. He may have been a Christian early in life, but by the time he wrote his anti-Christian polemic commonly known as *The True Doctrine* in about 175 or 180, he was Christianity's leading critic in the empire. His knowledge of Christianity was limited, but he seems to have gone to some trouble to find out what Christians believed even if he sometimes got it wrong. In his book he states quite unequivocally that Christians worship Jesus as God, which for him is a mark against them. Contemporary critics of orthodox Christology—belief that Jesus is fully God and fully human—often claim that this doctrine, known as the "hypostatic union," was "invented" by fourth-century Christian bishops under the influence of the half-Christian, half-pagan emperor Constantine. They have obviously never read Celsus or the early church fathers.

It is highly unlikely, if not impossible, that Celsus ever met the early Christian bishop and martyr Polycarp, who was burned at the stake and killed by a dagger in Smyrna in about 155. Nor would he have met or talked to the so-called heretics (considered so by leading Christian bishops of the Roman Empire) Valentinus and Montanus (second century, though their exact dates are unknown). Little is known about either man's personal life or even their teachings, other than from what their more orthodox Christian opponents said about them. Valentinus lived in Rome and led a group of Gnostic Christians,

11

who considered matter evil and denied both the true humanity of Jesus and his bodily resurrection.

Montanus lived in Asia Minor (now Turkey) and led a group of Christians who called their movement "The New Prophecy." They were the extreme charismatics of the middle of the second century. The group believed not only in the supernatural gifts of the Holy Spirit (like contemporary Pentecostals and charismatics) but also that the Holy Spirit spoke through Montanus, and his sayings were considered equal in authority with those of the apostles and their writings.

Scholars looking back at the infancy of the Christian movement often consider Valentinus and Montanus to be archheretics, who led many innocent Christians astray. Polycarp is usually held up as a great representative of orthodox Christianity, who gave up his life rather than bow to the emperor. Like other so-called Apostolic Fathers, he likely knew at least one of the original apostles—probably John.

In this imaginary conversation, Celsus encounters Polycarp, Valentinus, and Montanus on a ship sailing to Rome. He queries them about Christianity for his research, which will lead to the book he plans to write: *The True Doctrine*. The ensuing debate reflects the diversity of Christianity in the second century; Celsus's three new Christian acquaintances agree about little.

In a way, Polycarp, Valentinus, and Montanus respectively represent three impulses within historic Christianity: the orthodox impulse for theological correctness, the Gnostic impulse for higher knowledge and wisdom, and the enthusiastic impulse for transformative experience.

The Conversation

CELSUS: How interesting to find us all together on this Rome-bound ship! You know, I've been preparing a new talk for the Rotary Clubs around the empire. It's about you Christians and what I call "the true doctrine." By that I mean the hybrid of Platonic and Stoic ideas that forms the consensual worldview of sophisticated, educated people throughout our great empire. Compared with that, what you Christians teach seems to be sheer superstition. It's a wonder that anyone could or would believe it—except ignorant people, I suppose. I'm on my way to Rome now to deliver the first draft of my speech to an elite club that includes members of the Roman Senate. Eventually I plan to write a book about the Christian movement, showing that its beliefs are not only false but also pernicious: it leads people away from true philosophy, which forms the basis of our great culture.

POLYCARP: Roman senators, did you say? I hope you'll encourage them to recognize Christianity as a legitimate religion separate from the Jewish religion and to stop persecuting us. I'm on my way to Rome to appeal to its leaders to lift the laws against practicing our faith. I also hope to meet some senators and members of the emperor's household. Back home in Smyrna, where I am the bishop of the Christians and thus their leading minister, we are under tremendous pressure these days. And there's no good reason for it. We're good citizens, and we don't harm anyone, contrary to rumors about eating babies and engaging in incestuous orgies. But it sounds as though you're not going to be our ally, are you?

MONTANUS: Excuse me, Bishop Polycarp, but what do you mean by saying you don't harm anyone? You bishops are constantly criticizing and even condemning our New Prophecy movement as if we weren't authentically Christian, as you think you are. I am, after all, the mouthpiece of the Holy Spirit, and you bishops have no right to persecute me or my followers—no more right than you say the empire has to persecute you and your followers. I'm on my way to Rome to establish a new church there—one that will follow what the Spirit is saying through me today. Our New Prophecy churches are going to spread throughout the empire and sweep away your dead, dry-as-dust bishops' churches.

VALENTINUS: Celsus, don't listen to either one of them! We Gnostics (as some call us) are the true Christians with the higher spiritual wisdom that is in many ways similar to what you call the true doctrine. We're more philosophically minded than the bishop and his followers, and we're certainly more intellectual than fanatics like Montanus and his ilk. Surely you've heard of us! We Gnostics are thriving in Egypt, especially in and around Alexandria, the great cultural capital of the empire. Many wealthy, educated, and highly cultured people attend our meetings. Please tell the Roman senators to regard us as the true Christians. Oh, by the way, I'm on my way to Rome to visit our group there. They meet in several villas around the city and engage in study of higher spiritual wisdom and in meditation.

CELSUS: Now this is a perfect example of what I'm intending to tell my audiences in Rome and around the empire. You Christians can't even agree among yourselves about what you believe! You're divided into many quarreling sects and factions. When you talk, you sound like a bunch of babbling animals fighting over scraps of food! But the glue that holds the empire together is the true doctrine: an ethical-spiritual philosophy based on nature and reason. It's one true doctrine without variations, and it doesn't approve of all kinds of weird, mystical beliefs or authoritative pronouncements of bishops.

POLYCARP: No, you're wrong, Celsus—at least about Christian unity. And, I suspect, one could find many different versions of your precious true doctrine. After all, it is an unstable compound of the teachings of Plato and the Stoics! Tell your audiences that we Christians are united. We do believe the same things. We believe exactly what the apostles taught us. We bishops of the true Christian churches, which we call both "catholic" and "orthodox," are all heirs of the apostles. They appointed us. For example, when I was a boy, I learned Christian truth from Christ's youngest and most beloved disciple, John, who was very old at that time. He was the bishop of the Christians in Ephesus, where I grew up. From him I know exactly what Christ was all about.

These other so-called Christians can't make such a claim of apostolic succession. John warned us against false prophets like Valentinus and Montanus. Valentinus is a false prophet and not a true Christian because he denies that God became flesh in Jesus Christ. Montanus is a false prophet because he claims to be the exclusive mouthpiece of the Holy Spirit and sets his authority over that of the apostles! The apostles left behind a tradition of truth, the rule of faith, which forms the foundation of what true Christians believe and teach. These others are interlopers and false brethren. Don't even listen to them on the subject of Christianity.

MONTANUS: Wait! Listen! I feel the Holy Spirit moving over my vocal cords like a breeze over the strings of a harp. Be quiet. Yes . . . yes . . . listen. "I am the Spirit of God, and I speak through this man. Listen to him. He is my chosen mouthpiece, . . . not the so-called bishops who have led my people astray by imprisoning my Spirit in writings. Here now is true counsel: Do not marry or engage in any lustful thoughts or relationships. Avoid strong drink, and spend most of your time in prayer and waiting for the Savior Jesus to return. Above all, listen to and obey my prophets . . . and prophetesses. Do not quench my Spirit among you. For I am the Lord your God!"

Did you hear that? Celsus, tell the Roman senators that Christ is alive and well and speaks through me and that our New Prophecy movement is the true Christianity. And tell them that we mean no harm to the Roman government. We are just gathering in various places to praise God and wait for Jesus to return. If they do decide to extend peace to Christians, make sure that includes our congregations in Rome and throughout the empire.

VALENTINUS: Celsus, please pay no attention to these men. One is a pompous you-know-what, and the other is a raving religious fanatic. There's no chance that the Roman Senate or the emperor is going to recognize them or their followers as legal and legitimate. Now we Gnostics are different. We're not stuffy, dogmatic, hellfire-and-brimstone preachers like Polycarp and the other bishops. We're not intolerant as they are. We welcome into our circles anyone with special spiritual insight and abilities. Our job as Gnostic teachers is merely to encourage spiritual seekers to search beyond the physical-material realm and find the pure cosmic Christ-spirit that dwells in the temple of the human.

We teach that Christ-wisdom and not some set of dogmas. And what we teach is not so different from what some of your own Greek philosophers teach. Matter is a prison of the soul-spirit. True wisdom comes from above the material realm. This wisdom is knowledge of the inner divinity of the soul-spirit; it is a spark of the divine light and fire from above. Seek that which is above, and you will find it within. Didn't Plato say as much in his allegory of the cave?

CELSUS: Actually, I think you're all nuts. You all agree on one thing that we philosophers find just stupid: that God appeared in a man in the most backwater region of the whole empire, suffered and died on a Roman cross, then rose again, and is the savior of the whole world. No matter how you polish it, that central Christian belief, what you call the "gospel," conflicts with our true doctrine of Greek philosophy. It is simply absurd. God, you see, cannot enter flesh or appear within time or suffer, let alone die! And dead bodies do not rise. Who would want his body after death? All these things are not only mysteries; they're also superstitions. That's what I'll tell my audiences.

POLYCARP: Well, then, Celsus, I don't hold out much hope for changing your mind unless the Spirit of God works in your heart and mind. But I will say this: your "true doctrine" of Greek philosophy is partly right. God is pure spirit, eternal, true, and perfect in every way. But your doctrine goes wrong in thinking that he cannot also take on a human form in order to identify with his wretched human creatures and teach them how to obey God. Jesus Christ is God's Son. I say "is" because Jesus still lives. But he's not all of God that there is. You seem to think that if God became flesh, there would then be no God running the universe. But that's not what we believe. The Logos was who became man in Jesus—God's Word and God's Son. The Father remained in heaven and cannot suffer or die.

VALENTINUS: Um, Celsus, may I say you've got us Gnostic Christians all wrong? We don't believe that God entered into human flesh or suffered or died. And we don't believe that Jesus Christ rose bodily from death. What we believe is what a few of Christ's own disciples learned secretly from him and passed down to us. Christ is a spirit messenger sent from the high and heavenly God, whom Jesus called Father and who is pure Spirit and cannot come into direct contact with matter. After all, matter is not only corrupting; it is also evil.

This redeemer Christ-spirit took over the body of Jesus when he was about thirty years old. Through Jesus, this spirit taught wisdom and then left Jesus just before he died. On the cross Jesus uttered, "Father, into your hands I commit my spirit." That was when the Christ-spirit left Jesus to return to the Father. But the Christ-spirit came back to teach a few of the disciples the secret wisdom that most mortals cannot handle: that the human soul is a spark of God. It has lost its way in the universe and has fallen into bondage to matter. Through prayer, knowledge, and meditation, we can help people release the soul from matter and return to its heavenly home.

MONTANUS: That's the biggest bunch of pseudo-intellectual, spiritual non-sense I've ever heard. Wait, wait . . . I feel something happening. Listen! "I am the Spirit of God speaking through this man. Listen to him. The Spirit says that in these last days many false teachers will come and lead people astray from the truth. These Gnostics are the worst of them. Shun them and don't listen to them. But the bishops aren't much better. Listen only to my mouthpiece and his two prophetesses. Lo, I come quickly, says Christ. Leave all behind and move to Pepuza and await my coming with my people of the New Prophecy." Amen! You heard the Spirit. Valentinus and his followers are false teachers and learners. They do not know the truth.

POLYCARP: Oh, brother! What a bunch of heresy and fanaticism we have here parading as "Christian." Listen, Celsus, you can see for yourself that these men are charlatans. They are not true teachers of Jesus Christ or mouthpieces of the Holy Spirit. The church of Jesus Christ believes exactly what the apostles taught and wrote. We have many of their writings, you see—

MONTANUS (*interrupting Polycarp*): Stop! The Spirit is about to speak again!

POLYCARP (*to Montanus sharply*): Be quiet! Before I smite thy "spirit" on the snout!

MONTANUS (*to Polycarp sharply*): Ah, Brother Polycarp, you seem to have the gift of quenching the Spirit, don't you? I believe the apostle Paul warned against that. Would you chase the Holy Spirit back into the last century and into the writings of the apostles? Why won't you accept that the Spirit still speaks today?

POLYCARP: The Spirit does still speak today, but only through the apostolic teachings as interpreted by the bishops appointed by the apostles or their successors. The true Christian church is where the bishop is.

MONTANUS: No, you're wrong. The true Christian church is where the Spirit is!

VALENTINUS: You're both ignorant of the truth. "Christ" remains above us in the Spirit world; our spirits, our souls, must ascend out of our bodies to unite with his. He "returns" every time one of us achieves a spiritual oneness with him through spiritual disciplines and knowledge. The "Holy Spirit" is the substance of the soul-spirit of humans and is the same in everyone. It doesn't "speak" any more through you, Montanus, than through anyone else who seeks to become one with spirit apart from flesh. And that goes for you too, Polycarp.

(Polycarp and Montanus stand apart and both back away from Valentinus while muttering things like "Nonsense!" and "Heresy!" and "How stupid!" and "Get behind me, Satan!")

CELSUS: Well, I've heard just about enough from all of you. When my book *The True Doctrine* comes out, everyone will know how ignorant you Christians really are. You'd better get your act together and at least decide on what you believe, and it had better be something much closer to the true doctrine of Greek philosophy if you hope for it to catch on among the powerful elite of the empire.

Analysis

Keep in mind that this is an imaginary conversation; it did not take place nor would it have taken place exactly as it is written here. The purpose is to present a composite account of what we think these men believed and might have said to each other. It illustrates the diversity among second-century Christians and the attitude of many of the educated elite of the Roman Empire toward Christianity.

Celsus did not advocate persecution of Christians; he simply ridiculed Christianity as equal to superstition. We know what he wrote from the later church father Origen, who included virtually all of *The True Doctrine* in his book *Contra Celsum* (*Against Celsus*), written in the third century, fifty to seventy-five years after Celsus wrote. We have to trust that Origen quoted it correctly, and there's no reason to suspect otherwise. Celsus probably had knowledge of Christianity about as accurate as most educated Romans who bothered to look into the matter. He might have had even more, because he took the time and trouble to do some research.

Perhaps as a result of Celsus's negative comparisons between Christianity and Greek philosophy, some second- and third-century Christians tried to show that the two are compatible. Among these are the so-called Christian apologists (a category of early church writers) such as Justin Martyr, who was both a Christian teacher and a Greek philosopher. He wrote two *Apologies* (defenses of the faith) to Greek and Roman intellectuals. They are both strongly Hellenistic (influenced by Greek culture and thought). While Justin almost certainly did not know or read Celsus (Justin came somewhat before Celsus), other Christian apologists may have responded to Celsus. Origen certainly did. And Justin used some Greek philosophical concepts to reconcile Christianity with the best of Greek philosophy without merging the two.

Valentinus was one of the Gnostic leaders in the second century; there were many others around the empire. Much of what we know about him comes from the five books of Christian bishop Irenaeus's *Against Heresies*. Irenaeus (ca. 130–ca. 202) studied Gnosticism and refuted it by using some of the arguments that Polycarp employed in our imaginary dialogue. According to Irenaeus, he studied under Polycarp as a boy and therefore was a direct link back to one of the apostles, John the Beloved. If Jesus had secretly passed down Gnostic teachings to a select group of disciples, Irenaeus would have known about it. He said that he never heard about it from Polycarp, who never heard of it from John.

Gnosticism is hard to pin down. In the second century it was like a jungle of ideas, and it spawned a whole library of writings, including Gnostic "gospels" such as the *Gospel of Thomas*. These included alleged sayings of Jesus that supported Gnostic beliefs. The second-century Gnostics were like a shadow of Christianity, and they did not disappear. Under the rule of Emperor Constantine and later Christian political leaders, they simply went underground. Throughout Christian history, Gnostic-like sects secretly passed down what scholars call "esoteric Christianity." Twentieth-century groups such as the Rosicrucians continue this tradition.

The key doctrine (or idea) of the Gnostics, which they all shared in spite of secondary differences, was and is that matter is either evil or somehow the cause of evil. The body, being material, is the seat of sin. Therefore the true God could not have created the material world; it was created by a demented or fallen demiurge, a lesser god. They identified this being with Yahweh and rejected every Jewish element in Christianity. Their antipathy toward matter led them to deny that the heavenly redeemer could have taken on a body or become truly and fully human. Rather, he appeared to be human or used the human body of Jesus as an instrument for teaching the higher wisdom to the chosen few, who were spiritually capable of receiving it. Finally, the Gnostics taught that the inner self or soul of each person is a spark of God that has forgotten its true divinity and needs to be reminded of its origin. Such is the nature of the gnosis, or wisdom, that the Gnostics taught.

Polycarp is generally considered to be one of the Apostolic Fathers; his claim to have known John the Beloved is rarely doubted. He was an important Christian leader in the middle of the second century, which is why he was arrested and executed by Roman officials in Smyrna in 155. Someone wrote about his martyrdom, and that document, known as the *Martyrdom of Polycarp*, is usually considered among the writings of the Apostolic Fathers even though no one knows who wrote it. Polycarp himself wrote little that survives. Only his *Letter to the Philippians* exists. Even though we know little about him, most Christian scholars consider him to be a second-century standard of orthodoxy.

Some scholarly readers of this imaginary conversation may object to its portrayal of Montanus. It's true that later Montanism—the New Prophecy movement after Montanus—may not have been this extreme. But early Christian sources portray Montanus himself and the two prophetesses with him as extreme. Without doubt he considered himself to be an oracle, if not *the* oracle, of God and elevated his own utterances to a level of authority equal to that of the apostles. He does not seem to have taught any heresies about Christ or God; his bad reputation among Christians then and now rests on his claims to have authority and his rejection of the bishops' authority. But apparently he also rejected marriage and advocated a strictly ascetic lifestyle while calling his followers to gather in Pepuza in Asia Minor to await the return of Christ.

Throughout the history of Christian theology, "Montanism" has been used to label Christian groups engaging in prophecy that adds to Scripture. Some have considered Mormonism to be a modern form of Montanism.

All this raises the question that Celsus must have considered: who were the true and authentic Christians of the second century? Obviously there were schisms and divisions among the Christians in the Roman Empire. There was no authority with power to decide which groups were orthodox (theologically correct) and which were heretical (theologically incorrect). There were simply competing claims of Christian authenticity. Every few years some author publishes a book claiming that there was no orthodox Christianity in the second century or until Constantine embraced Christianity and enforced a particular version of it as the only acceptable one in the early fourth century. According to these scholars, then, second-century Christianity was merely a blooming, buzzing confusion of radically divergent theologies.

The simple answer to this suggestion is that lack of an enforcing power does not equal relativism of truth. All the groups claiming Christian authenticity could not have been right, unless one is willing to reduce Christianity to folk religion and mere opinion. But if Christian faith is compatible with anything and everything, it is strictly nothing. Surely some were more right than others in this competition for the soul of Christianity. Conservative Christians have always acknowledged the bishops as orthodox to the exclusion of groups like Montanists and Gnostics. That is not to say that the Montanists and Gnostics were totally wrong about everything; it is only to say that their claims to be the holders of authentic Christianity were dubious at best. It's hard to oppose Polycarp's and Irenaeus's arguments about carrying on the traditions taught to them by the apostles.

Perhaps, however, the churches of the bishops made a mistake by overreacting to Montanism. They tended to quench the spiritual fervor of second-century Christians; thus prophecy, speaking in tongues, and other supernatural gifts of the Spirit gradually disappeared. That's unfortunate but understandable. Even the best modern Pentecostal and charismatic groups have trouble in striking a balance between spiritual enthusiasm and order. The early church chose order to the detriment of spiritual enthusiasm. We can only ask what we would have done differently.

After the setting of this imaginary conversation, Christian bishops such as Irenaeus in Gaul (modern France) worked hard to standardize Christian belief by proving that Gnostic claims were wrong. Bishops in the region around Pepuza excluded the New Prophecy movement. It spread far and wide anyway but was never fully accepted as part of the network of churches led by bishops. It gradually died out as a relatively organized movement.

One can hardly blame Celsus for being confused about Christianity, but we can only wish that he had listened carefully, long and hard, to Polycarp or someone like him. Or perhaps listened to Irenaeus. But Irenaeus was busy writing his five books *Against Heresies* way off in Gaul when Celsus was writing *The True Doctrine* in (probably) Alexandria, Egypt, or Rome.

For Further Reading

The Apostolic Fathers in English. Translated by Michael W. Holmes. 3rd ed. Grand Rapids: Baker Academic, 2006.

Celsus. *On the True Doctrine*. Translated by R. Joseph Hoffmann. New York: Oxford University Press, 1987.

Jonas, Hans. *The Gnostic Religion*. 3rd ed. Boston: Beacon, 2001.

Osborn, Eric. *Irenaeus of Lyons*. Cambridge: Cambridge University Press, 2001.

2

Second-Century Critic Celsus Interviews Tertullian, Irenaeus, and Clement about Christianity

Setting

This imaginary conversation takes place in Rome in about 200, in a room in the Senate House. Celsus (see conversation 1, above) has published his exposé of Christianity, titled *The True Doctrine*, in which he ridicules its adherents as superstitious and ignorant. There he implies that virtually no common ground exists between Christianity and "the true doctrine," by which he means the generally accepted hybrid of Greek philosophy combining aspects of Platonism and Stoicism. After reading his book, one could hardly imagine an "intellectual Christian." That would seem to be an oxymoron.

A committee of the Roman Senate has asked Celsus, a well-known author and speaker, to bring together some leading Christian writers to answer questions about their religious beliefs and especially about the relationship between Christianity and Greco-Roman culture. Remember that then, in about 200, most leaders of the Roman Empire considered something like Celsus's philosophy, the so-called true doctrine, to be the ideological glue holding the empire together. Christianity was spreading so quickly that some Roman senators worried about it undermining the "morals" of society (by which they meant society's common norms).

Such a meeting as this never actually took place. The church father Clement of Alexandria (ca. 150–ca. 215), the principal of the Christian catechetical school (somewhat like a Christian college or seminary today), is not known to have visited Rome. But he could have. He was well traveled. The school in Alexandria, the empire's second-largest and wealthiest city, both economically and culturally, was gaining a reputation even among pagans as a great center of intellectual life. Clement wrote several books explaining Christianity, including his well-known *Stromata* (*Miscellanies*) and *Paedagogus* (*The Instructor*). His treatise *Protrepticus* is also known as *Exhortation to the Greeks*. Clement tried to reconcile the best of Greek philosophy with the best of Christian doctrine. Some argue that he went too far in accommodating Christian thought to Greek philosophy.

Irenaeus (d. ca. 202) was one of ancient Christianity's most influential leaders and thinkers. This church father emigrated with a group of Christians from the western coast of Asia Minor to Gaul, in what today is France. There he became bishop of the churches in and around Lyons. He is sometimes called Irenaeus of Lugdunum (modern Lyons, France) but is best known as Irenaeus of Lyons. In the second half of the second century, he undertook a thorough investigation of the various Gnostic Christian sects. (See the first conversation above for information about Gnosticism. Valentinus, a participant in that conversation, was a leading Gnostic in Rome, and Irenaeus seems to be especially out to refute him and his followers.) Irenaeus published *Against Heresies* in five volumes in approximately 175–185. He died in a persecution of Christians in about 202.

One reason Irenaeus was so influential among Christians was his link to the apostles. During his lifetime there surely was not yet an agreed-upon Christian canon of Scriptures (what would come to be called the New Testament when it was finally compiled and accepted by all Christians). Irenaeus studied the faith under Polycarp (a participant in the first conversation above), who studied it under John the Beloved, Jesus's youngest and longest-lived disciple. So Irenaeus could recall and recount apostolic Christianity as John taught it to Polycarp and as Polycarp taught it to Irenaeus. This was important at a time when Christianity was plagued by false rumors and accusations and by schisms and divisions over the meaning of the gospel.

Tertullian (ca. 160–ca. 225) was a Christian thinker and writer in Carthage, North Africa. He is often considered to be the greatest of the early Latin church fathers even though he was not an ordained clergyman of the church. He was a lawyer who undertook to explain Christianity, at least from his own perspective, to Romans and others. (Carthage was a large metropolitan area and considered as a suburb of Rome even though it lay across the Mediterranean Sea.) Tertullian died of unknown cause in about 225, leaving behind scores of writings on a wide variety of subjects related to Christian belief and living. He is sometimes counted as one of the early Christian apologists because some of his writings appealed to Roman leaders for correct understanding of Christianity. But he also wrote treatises against heretics such as Marcion and Praxeas, both of Rome.

As stated earlier, this conversation is completely imaginary. To the best of our knowledge, none of the participants ever met one another. Doubtless, however, they knew of each other, and if Celsus had tried to bring three great Christian leaders of his time to Rome, he might have chosen these three.

The Conversation

CELSUS: Gentlemen of the Senate, allow me to introduce to you three of the most important scholars of the upstart religion called Christianity, which is sweeping through our empire and causing so much consternation and trouble. I have searched far and wide throughout the empire and have found these three, who are reputed to be true scholars, genuine intellectuals, and also Christians. Yet as you know from my book *The True Doctrine*, that is improbable. How someone can be both an intellectual and a Christian is anyone's guess. Until now I have not thought it possible. You asked me to bring before you the cream of the Christian crop to explain that religion's beliefs and practices and especially how it is not a threat to the peace and unity of the empire. Here they are. I'll ask them questions, and you may judge for yourselves whether their answers are convincing and bring any relief to our concerns.

    Mr. Clement, or should I call you Dr. Clement or Dean Clement? I'd like to start the questioning with you. In your recent books *The Instructor* and *Miscellanies*, you argue that Christianity and Greek philosophy are actually in agreement. That seems counterintuitive at best. Could you please elaborate on that a bit? What do you mean?

CLEMENT: Thank you for inviting me to participate in this meeting, Mr. Celsus. And thanks to you, Roman senators, for granting all three of us safety from prosecution for coming here today. I trust that you'll keep that promise.

    I hope I can shed some light on the true nature of our Christian movement, which is so widely misunderstood in the empire. Like our beloved hero Justin Martyr, who was executed here in Rome for teaching the same things I teach—that Christianity is continuous with and yet superior to the best of Greek philosophy—I believe that Greek philosophy contains a significant portion of the truth. I see it as a preparation for the gospel of Christ, which we Christians believe in and teach and by which we are saved. Greek philosophy is a work of divine providence, preparing Greeks and Romans for Christianity. Just as God led the Jews to Christ by using Moses, so God is using Socrates and Plato to lead gentiles to Christ.

    The Greek philosophers knew that the gods and goddesses of folk religion are not real; they taught their followers to think of the divine source as one, as spiritual, and as moral. They also taught about immortality and judgment after death for deeds done in the bodily life. So we find many excellent truths in Greek philosophy. Our motto in Alexandria is "All truth is God's truth," wherever it may be found. The universal Logos of which the philosophers spoke is known to us as the source of all truth; the Logos became man in Jesus Christ and fulfilled Greek philosophy just as Christ fulfilled Jewish religion.

    So, you see, we Christians in Alexandria regard Greek philosophy as a useful tool for bringing men and women to Christ. (I mention women where others may ignore them because I consider them to be just as spiritually capable of the "true wisdom" as men.) Philosophy also helps us to refine our Christian doctrines and make them more intelligible to educated non-Christians such as yourselves.

CELSUS: Okay, Mr. Tertullian, what do you think of what Clement just said? How do you regard Greek philosophy? I expect that you'll disagree with what he said. After all, I hear that your motto is "What has Athens to do with Jerusalem?" Could you please explain what that means and your attitude regarding the relationship of Christianity to philosophy?

TERTULLIAN: Gladly, Mr. Celsus. But first I'd also like to thank you for giving me this splendid opportunity to appear before the senators and explain the truth about Christianity. I do wish, however, that you had invited only me. Perhaps Bishop Irenaeus too. But Clement here is a dangerous man. He is leading many Christians astray by feeding them a poisonous mixture of the gospel and philosophy. I wouldn't exactly call him a heretic, like Praxeas or Marcion, but I would say that he is setting up the possibility of more heresies because heresies always come from philosophy and the craving to have knowledge outside what is revealed.

Now, don't get me wrong. There are some truths in Greek philosophy. I myself have studied the Stoics and find much good in their teachings. They encourage good moral living and teach one divine source of everything. But like other Greek philosophers, their ideas are quite confused. For example, some of them teach that nature itself is divine and that whatever happens is due to the hand of fate. Therefore, we Christians do not need to rely on such philosophers because whatever is good and right in Greek philosophy may also be found in purer form in our rule of faith. For most Christians, Greek philosophy is a spiritual hindrance; it leads them to crave knowledge of what cannot be known, and it seduces them into heresies.

Now, you asked me to explain my motto "What has Athens to do with Jerusalem?" By Athens I mean the teachings of the philosophers. After all, the Platonic Academy is there. By Jerusalem I mean the doctrines of Christ and the apostles, preserved in our rule of faith. The two are really incompatible with each other even if they vaguely share some ideas. The only good reason for a Christian to study Greek philosophy is to refute its errors, and only mature Christians, such as myself, should do that.

CELSUS: Bishop Irenaeus, would you like to add any word to this discussion? What is your attitude toward Greek philosophy?

IRENAEUS: Well, like Tertullian and Clement, I'd like to thank you for this opportunity to explain the true Christian faith to you and to the senators. I hope we three will not confirm your belief that Christians are all divided into many squabbling sects. Actually, authentic—that is, apostolic—Christianity cannot be divided.

Humbly I claim that as a student of Polycarp I have some special insight into these matters. Jesus's disciple John is our source for authentic, apostolic Christianity. What better source could there be? A direct line of authority flows from Jesus through John through Polycarp to me. Also, I am a bishop of the churches whereas these other men are not even ordained priests or ministers.

Clement is partly right, and so is Tertullian. Clement is correct in stating that the gospel can make use of some Greek concepts. John himself borrowed the idea of the Logos from Greek philosophy and applied it to our Savior Jesus Christ, who, he said, was the Logos of God—the mediator between God and humanity. He is God's very self-expression, equal with God. The apostle Paul also made some use of Greek philosophy when he visited Athens; he quoted Greek poets and referred to the "Unknown God," whose monument still stands there.

But Clement goes too far in his use of Greek philosophy to support Christianity. I especially object to him calling Socrates "a Christian before Christ" and to him comparing Greek philosophy with the Hebrew prophets by referring to Greek philosophy as God's preparation for the coming of Christ and the gospel.

I hate to say this before an intimidating body of Roman senators, but I think Clement actually adapts Greek philosophy more to the gospel than vice versa. So I definitely cut him some slack. He's not a heretic, and his teachings do not necessarily lead to heresy. But I fear for the immature who read him and follow him. Some of them may be seduced into considering Greek philosophy as equal with the gospel itself.

As for Tertullian, I think he simply goes to the opposite extreme. He tends to throw out the baby with the bathwater. "Athens" and "Jerusalem" are not totally opposed to each other. But he's right that wherever they conflict, we Christians must allow the apostolic teachings contained in our rule of faith to trump even the best of Greek thought.

Tertullian is right, however, to warn against the danger of swallowing Greek categories and concepts hook, line, and sinker. For example, I fear that Clement and some of the other Alexandrian Christians are toying with heresy when they talk about Christianity as "true Gnosticism" and about God as incomprehensible and impassible. There's truth in these statements, but there's also error. The great God of Israel and the church is very personal and powerful and exists without body, parts, or passions. But he is not an impersonal principle or a grand idea beyond the world, not like the deity in much contemporary Greek philosophy. One must strike a balance here and not go too far in one direction or another.

CELSUS: Well, Clement, I believe your bishop has thrown down the glove. I'll let you respond in a moment, Tertullian. I see you're chomping at the bit. What do you say by way of response, Clement? Are you teaching near heresy over there in Alexandria?

CLEMENT: No, we most certainly are not. By "true Gnosticism" I do not mean Gnosticism like that of Valentinus or any other heretical sects. I'm borrowing the Gnostics' own terminology: "wisdom." Christians should be and can be the ones with the true wisdom of God, which comes through both philosophy and revelation. But it is not some higher, secret knowledge as the Gnostics claim to possess. A true Gnostic is a Christian who is truly seeking to please God with a life of wisdom and intellect and not indulging in physical pleasures and passions. The true Gnostic rises above the lower nature and lives according to the higher nature—the image of God in him. Like God himself, the true Gnostic lives a life of calm, rational contemplation and self-control. The body no longer controls the true Gnostic. This was the case with our master Jesus; he was ruled entirely by the Logos of God dwelling in him.

TERTULLIAN *(interrupting Clement)*: Wait just a minute, there, Clement. Oh, I'm sorry for interrupting, but someone has to point out how far away from authentic Christianity Clement is straying here. He's treading on dangerous ground. What about God's wrath and judgment against sin? It seems to me that sometimes you Alexandrian Christians water down the gospel too much. You turn it into some kind of mystical, contemplative piety as you encourage people to stare at their navels in a spiritual trance. No, the Christian life is a war, and God is our champion! We are on God's side and must fight with him against all immorality and heresy and paganism; our only weapon is the church's rule of faith, derived not from Greek philosophers but from Jesus and the apostles and prayer.

Your namby-pamby "true Gnosticism" is a barely recognizable, watered-down form of Christianity, and the God you teach is hardly distinguishable from Platonism's highest Being—a great spiritual being uninvolved in our daily lives. I certainly agree with Bishop Irenaeus about these dangers in your teachings.

IRENAEUS *(ignoring Celsus and butting in)*: Excuse me, you two. Let's not give our pagan audience the wrong impression. We Christians are united when it comes to the essence of our faith. We may disagree about details, such as how best to use Greek philosophy and the precise meaning of God's attributes, but when it comes to fighting pernicious heresies, such as Gnosticism, we're together.

But Clement, I wish you would stop using the term "true Gnostic" for your ideal Christian person. It causes confusion. Gnosticism is bad, period. You can't rescue the label by filling it with new content; it's too late for that. Also, your description of the ideal Christian places too much emphasis on reason and contemplation and ascetic living. That just increases the perception that you really do come close to Gnosticism in your theology. You need to root your teachings more in Scripture and the apostles' writings and less in philosophy.

Tertullian, I wish you would keep using your razor-sharp mind and wit to fight heretics like Praxeas and Marcion and lay off the well-meaning, if misled, Alexandrian Christians like Clement here. They mean well even if they sometimes seem to allow philosophy to subvert the gospel. The main thing is that all of us believe in redemption through Jesus Christ and his cross. And we all believe in the incarnation of God's Son, the Logos, in the man Jesus. We share our common faith in his death for the forgiveness of sins and in his resurrection to give us new life and even a share in God's own nature. These things Greek philosophy knows nothing about. Let's keep focused on the good news of Christ's defeat of sin and death and God's gift of immortality through Jesus, our "new Adam."

CELSUS: Bishop Irenaeus, am I interpreting you correctly when I say that you believe there are really two races of people—those like me, who are rooted in that Adam guy, and you Christians, whose source is in the "new Adam," Jesus? Isn't that rather intolerant of you? Are you saying that all but Christians are going to hell?

IRENAEUS: I'm sorry if that sounds intolerant to you, Mr. Celsus. But the gospel is not meant to make people feel comfortable. Humanity's common ancestor, Adam, fell into death by giving in to temptation; and since he was God's appointed head of the human race, all his descendents fell into death with him. They lost the gift of immortality. Christ came in the very same form as Adam and reversed that fall by obeying God. He resisted temptation and thereby gave humanity a new start, a new source, a new head. All who have faith in him and enter into union with him through the church and its sacraments move from Adam's fallen race into Christ's new humanity. We gain life and immortality, a partial participation in God's own nature. So, yes, we believe there are two human races—Christ's and the first Adam's. Everyone belongs to one or the other. You, Mr. Celsus, could gain life and immortality simply by joining us Christians.

TERTULLIAN (butting in): Yes, I quite agree with Irenaeus, although I've never thought about Christ's redemptive work on our behalf quite that way before. Not bad, bishop! But what I want to add is that many who call themselves Christians are not truly of Christ's family. They are worse than pagans because they say they are Christians but deny the essential truths of our rule of faith—the apostolic tradition handed down through men like your teacher Polycarp.

Take Praxeas of Asia, now in Rome, for example. I think some of you in this room have heard of him even though you're not Christians. I said "take Praxeas." Indeed, God will take him away to that place of fire where you all will go when you die. It's because of his blasphemies that he will be punished with you in the flames of hell.

I have spent years refuting his heresies, just as you, Irenaeus, have spent years in refuting the heresies of the Gnostics. Praxeas has accomplished two works of the devil here in Rome. He has crucified God the Father and put the Holy Spirit to flight. In other words, he denies our most holy doctrine of *trinitas*—the triunity of God.

CELSUS *(interrupting)*: Wait a minute, there, Tertullian. I thought you Christians, like the Jews and some of the Greek philosophers, believe in one
God. What's this about a threeness in God?

TERTULLIAN *(continuing)*: We do believe in one God, but we also believe in a
threeness of God. We believe, as the apostles taught, that there are three
distinct "persons" of God, who together make up one God because they
share the same divine substance. The phrase I use for this is *una substantia,
tres persona*, "one divine substance, three distinct persons." One of my
followers said it this way: "one 'what' and three 'whos.'"

Some have claimed that this is too much of a mystery to believe. Well,
to them I say, "I believe it because it is impossible; I proclaim it because
it is absurd!"

Praxeas tries to destroy the mystery of God's triunity by claiming that
Father, Son, and Holy Spirit are not three distinct persons but merely
manifestations of one person who is God. But that means, then, that the
Father was crucified and died on the cross! I call that heresy patripassionism. Some call it modalism. It's nonsense. Only the Son, the Logos
of God, God's Word, was crucified. Jesus was and is the incarnation of
that Word.

CLEMENT: You know, Tertullian, I think you're right about the Trinity. But I don't
think it's absurd. It makes quite a bit of sense, actually. Think about it. If God
is absolutely perfect in every way, as the best of Greek philosophy teaches,
then he cannot directly relate to the world of time and matter. Such a direct
relationship would infect and corrupt his perfect being. God is beyond such
direct involvement in the decay of our world. Certainly he cannot suffer! So
he relates to the world and suffers through the Logos and Spirit. For God to
be God—the divine, providential Creator and Ruler of all things—he must
have his agents through whom he works in the world. They are his right and
left hands, his Word and his Spirit. So your Trinity teaching is actually good
philosophy. There actually are many hints of it in the writings of Plato and
Aristotle as well as in the Hebrew prophets of wisdom.

CELSUS: Bishop Irenaeus, I think you should have the last word here. We're running
out of time. What do you have to say in response to this discussion?

TERTULLIAN *(talking over Irenaeus's first syllable)*: Why should he get the
last word? Just because he's a bishop? The new church I have joined in
Carthage, the New Prophecy, doesn't recognize bishops as anything special.
At least not just because they possess apostolic pedigrees. Our leaders
are filled with the Holy Spirit and exercise the Spirit's gifts, especially
prophecy. The true church is where the Spirit resides and manifests himself
and not necessarily where the bishop rules. We don't hold ordination to
clergy status in high regard. So I don't think Irenaeus should get the final
word here.

CELSUS *(talking directly to Tertullian)*: But you're not in charge here, Tertullian. We faithful Romans are more inclined to accept the authority of

bishops as true spokesmen for the Christians than to accept the authority of prophets. We understand order through hierarchy. So shut up and
sit down.

IRENAEUS *(humbly but firmly)*: Thank you, Mr. Celsus. Order is important to
us Christians as well. I didn't know that Tertullian here had joined that
fanatical sect begun some years ago by the heretic Montanus. I agree
with you that I deserve the last word because Jesus's disciple John speaks
indirectly through me. There's no way to validate the prophets' claims to
truth. My claim is rooted in history.

I agree with much of what Tertullian and Clement have said, but I want
to bring everything back to salvation. I hope the Roman senators here will
grasp its centrality to our Christian faith and message.

Clement and his followers in and around Alexandria seem to focus too
much on the intellect, as if salvation comes through learning and contemplation. While their ideal of detachment from the world is not entirely
wrong, true Christianity also emphasizes God's redemption of the world.
Christ is our teacher; that's true. But his teaching is one aspect and not
the whole of his redemptive work. We are not transformed by wisdom or
knowledge or detachment. We are transformed by the great exchange in
which God took on flesh so that our flesh might take on God's immortality. It is by faith and the Christian sacraments of baptism and Eucharist
that this work of Christ is applied to us.

Tertullian has many good things to say about the Trinity and so forth.
But in his writings, one gathers the impression that for him salvation is
gaining God's favor by holding fast to certain doctrines and shunning
heresies and living a strict, moral life. If Clement's theology is too heavy
on the philosophical and intellectual side, then Tertullian's is too heavy
on the legalistic and moral side. I hope that we Christians can all hold
fast to the true gospel that I received from Polycarp, who received it from
John. That *includes* doctrine and moral living and perhaps contemplation and detachment. But it *revolves* around Christ's life, death, and
resurrection and our participation in his resurrected life by faith and
the sacraments, which our great bishop Ignatius called "the medicine
of immortality."

CELSUS: Well, thank you, Bishop Irenaeus. I didn't understand much of what
you just said, but it is intriguing. Especially that nonsense about our becoming partakers of God's own nature through the peasant Jesus, who
lived and died in that backwater territory called Palestine.

(Speaking to the senators): Next, I'll be interviewing the Roman Christians Marcion and Praxeas. I suspect that you'll hear a different version
of Christianity from them than you've heard here today.

IRENAEUS, TERTULLIAN, AND CLEMENT *(together)*: What? No! Don't listen to
those heretics! They don't represent true Christianity!

Analysis

Like all the other imaginary conversations in this book, this one could not have taken place. There's little evidence that Irenaeus, Tertullian, and Clement (or any two of them) ever met face-to-face. And if they had met, they wouldn't have used English terms such as "One 'what' and three 'whos.'" But they might have used Greek and/or Latin equivalents! Another reason it's unlikely that this conversation would ever have taken place is that Tertullian spoke mostly Latin; Clement and Irenaeus spoke and wrote in Greek (even though Irenaeus in particular was no doubt fluent in Latin).

In spite of the artificialities of the imaginary dialogue, it is meant to represent what church historian Justo González calls the three types of Christian theology (see his revised *Christian Thought Revisited* [Maryknoll, NY: Orbis Books, 1999]). Clement represents the philosophical type, which accents the life of the mind and tends to be somewhat speculative and often contemplative if not mystical. Tertullian represents the legal type, which emphasizes right living according to Christianity interpreted as the new law of God. It tends to be moralistic rather than mystical and often eschews the use of philosophy if not reason in Christian theology. Irenaeus represents the pastoral and biblical type, which underscores the work of Christ for salvation appropriated by faithful participation in the life of the church. These three types do not exclude each other; they overlap and share much common ground. Their differences lie in emphasis more than in substance.

In this conversation each participant reveals something about what he considers to be the heart of true or authentic Christianity. For Clement, typical of the Alexandrian approach, Christianity is primarily about gaining higher knowledge and wisdom, which for him comes through Jesus Christ to the believer through a lifestyle of reason, contemplation, and relative detachment from bodily pleasures. On the surface, this sounds like Gnosticism. And Clement added to the confusion by calling his ideal Christian a "true Gnostic." But it isn't Gnosticism as it has generally come to be understood.

Clement never identified the body or matter in general as evil or as the seat of sin. Like most Greek thinkers, however, he did regard the body as a kind of "drag" on the spirit. And he tended to identify the spirit with the human's higher nature (as opposed to the lower nature, which is the physical body) and with the mind. Further, Clement was not a full-blown Gnostic because he did believe in the bodily resurrection of Jesus and in Jesus's true humanity and divinity. He simply regarded Jesus as a great master teacher who showed his followers how to live rather detached from cares and concerns of the body and the world.

Tertullian's emphasis is on rules, laws, and doctrines. Christians stand out from the crowd. They reject the philosophies that drive non-Christian culture and society. They embrace the apostolic rule of faith or set of doctrines without doubt or question. They believe even if it is absurd. Tertullian and Irenaeus both set forth their own versions of the Christian rule of faith and argued that heretics who deny it have no right to refer to the Scriptures because the rule of faith is the clue to the true meaning of Scripture. For them, the rule of faith centers around the identity of Jesus Christ as God come in the flesh, who suffered and died in his humanity and was raised to give humanity new life. This apostolic tradition, or rule of faith, forms the heart of authentic Christianity, and a Christian is known by holding allegiance to it.

Irenaeus agrees with Tertullian that right doctrine is important, but he adds his own theory of how Christ's life, death, and resurrection saves people who come to him in faith and participate faithfully in the life of the church. That theory is known as (in Greek) *anakephalaiōsis*, or (in English derived from Latin) recapitulation. For Irenaeus, Christ had to be both divine and human in order to save because salvation means recapitulating or "summing up" all of humanity in his obedient life as the new Adam. Only God could do that; so only a human could do it for us.

Thus Christ had to be truly human to be the second Adam and to give the human race a new fountainhead or source of being. He even had to take on the same form as Adam and obey at every point where Adam disobeyed. Since Adam disobeyed in temptation, Christ had to face temptation, and he obeyed, thus reversing Adam's transgression. Since Adam disobeyed at a tree (the tree of the knowledge of good and evil), so Christ had to face a tree of temptation (the cross) and obey.

These three theologians and the types of theology they represent are all orthodox. Even though Tertullian probably joined a Montanist church in Carthage, he is still considered to be a great teacher of early Christians. By the time he joined the New Prophecy, it had probably lost most of the fanaticism that marked its beginnings in Asia Minor. Irenaeus is usually considered to be the first great systematic Christian thinker, and according to some Orthodox Christians, every crucial doctrine of the Christian faith is found in his writings. Clement's reputation among traditional Christians is not as robust as Irenaeus's. His tendencies toward asceticism and his emphasis on salvation through knowledge (although he almost certainly means *sanctification* through knowledge) are often suspected of being too close to Gnosticism for comfort. But that is probably an undeserved rap against him. The objective reader of Clement cannot help but be impressed by his concern for right doctrine, including the incarnation and resurrection, and by his piety.

For Further Reading

Barnes, Timothy David. *Tertullian: A Historical and Literary Study*. New York: Oxford University Press, 1985.

Osborn, Eric. *Clement of Alexandria*. Cambridge: Cambridge University Press, 2005.

———. *Irenaeus of Lyons*. Cambridge: Cambridge University Press, 2001.

3

Second- and Third-Century Leaders Irenaeus, Tertullian, and Clement Discuss Beliefs Necessary to Be a True Christian

Setting

I hope patient readers will bear with one more imaginary dialogue between these three early church fathers. They are so crucial for understanding the whole history of Christian thought and especially the early church and its conflicts. This conversation will be briefer than the previous one, in which they were interviewed by Celsus before the Roman Senate. If you skipped that conversation, you may want to go back and at least skim the "Setting" for conversation 2, where information about each church father can be found.

The scene is inside a public bathhouse in Rome in about 200. These three Christian leaders have come to Rome at the behest of Celsus, critic of Christianity, who interviewed them before a committee of the Roman Senate. After their grueling inquisition, each one needed a bath. In ancient Rome, men bathed together in large public buildings that contained something much like a swimming pool. Their custom was to have conversations as they bathed, and so our three church fathers independently decided to clean up and relax. They find themselves together again under these different circumstances. There's no interviewer and no listening committee. They are free to sit near one another with their feet in the water and discuss their differences.

The Conversation

IRENAEUS: I'd say it's strange to see you two Christian leaders here in one of Rome's public bathhouses except that my mentor Polycarp often told stories about the disciple John in the public bathhouse in Ephesus. According to him, once they carried John in his old age into the bathhouse on a stretcher. As was his custom, he lifted his hand in blessing and said to the people gathered there, "Love one another." But this time, before being lowered into the water, he also shouted out: "Let's get out of here before the roof comes down on us! The heretic Cerinthus is here!" As you probably know, Cerinthus was one of the first Gnostics. John despised Gnosticism and feared the Gnostics because he expected God to hit them with bolts of lightning for their blasphemies.

TERTULLIAN: That's a nice story, Irenaeus. I suspect that it's apocryphal, but it's entertaining anyway. I too am surprised to see you both here. I guess we were subjected to that grilling by Celsus before the Senate so long that we need to cool off in these soothing waters.

CLEMENT: Yes, that's why I'm here. But also, I am hoping to listen in on some of the latest talk about philosophy that goes on in this bathhouse. There are some Stoic philosophers over there talking about the ideal Stoic life as detachment. I think I have something in common with them. But before I go over to listen in and perhaps join their conversation, I'll stay here by you two a little while so we can debrief after our hearing before the Senate. What do you think? Did we come off well?

IRENAEUS: Well, I'm not so concerned about whether we came off well. I'm concerned about whether they now better understand the gospel. I'm not sure, because we each gave somewhat different versions of it. We should have emphasized our common faith more.

TERTULLIAN: Perhaps so, Irenaeus. We do have a lot in common. But it's so much more fun to argue than just to meet as a mutual admiration society. We do have our differences, you know. That's why I've joined the New Prophecy church. I just can't accept the idea that you bishops are always right when your churches are so spiritually dead. To say nothing of being permissive! Whatever happened to the belief that a Christian can sin only once after baptism? I still believe it. Don't you?

CLEMENT: Certainly not. That was just something the author of the *Shepherd of Hermas* wrote to scare immature Christians into obedience. If that were true, we shouldn't baptize anyone until they're dying!

TERTULLIAN: Not a bad idea. But I think we should forbid this silly practice of baptizing babies and children. Some have started doing that. It's a mistake because it's so unlikely that any child can pass through adolescence without sinning more than once! And by the way, it isn't just a silly idea posed by the author of that wonderful tract. It's true.

IRENAEUS: Be that as it may, fellows, let's try to set aside our differences for a while and talk about the state of our Christian churches back home. I'll start. Things are really awful in Gaul; the Romans are persecuting us so much that many Christians are going into hiding. Some have denied the faith altogether. We're not sure what to do with them when the persecution runs its course and they want to come back among us. Some have been put to death for refusing to deny the faith. We call them "martyrs," and we will celebrate their days of death in future years.

But worse than the persecution we suffer from pagans is the infiltration of our churches by heretics. Sometimes when I preach in one of our churches, I see counterfeit Christians, wolves in sheep's clothing, sitting among the faithful. They are there to devour the flock. The worst among them are the Gnostics.

TERTULLIAN: Yes, we have them in Carthage as well. Our local Gnostics think it is okay to sin in the body because the spirit is untouched by the flesh. They sin just to prove how spiritual they are! Their influence is one reason I insist on moral perfection among Christians.

And then there are those who deny the Trinity. They consider Father, Son, and Holy Spirit to be nothing more than masks that God wears. Their error is obvious, and I have argued against it at great length in my writings; yet some still hold on to it. I wonder if Christians will ever understand the triunity of God. The other day one of our teachers was explaining it to young students by using the analogy of water—one substance in three forms: liquid, vapor, and ice. I gave him a good tongue-lashing for implying that the Father was crucified. No matter what we say about the truth, that heresy of modalism just seems to hold on in the minds of simple Christians.

CLEMENT: As you both know, Alexandria is a melting pot of many cultures, philosophies, and religions. So we started a school to train Christians in doctrine, and we invite some non-Christians to come there to study Christianity and philosophy with us. Our most brilliant student is a young Christian named Origen; he will surely make something of himself someday. The only problem is that he keeps trying to get himself killed whenever there's a persecution of Christians. His father died that way, and now Origen thinks he should die as well. His mother hid all his clothes so he couldn't go outside and surrender himself to the authorities. Lately he's been talking about castrating himself. I'm trying to talk him out of it.

Anyway, my main concern is that too many Christians avoid any intellectual understanding of the faith; they revel in feelings and experiences but give little thought to how knowledge and wisdom play into Christian maturity. I try to get Christians to grow up intellectually and take every thought captive to Christ.

TERTULLIAN: Don't you mean you try to get them to grow up and take every thought captive to Plato? Oh, sorry. I forgot. We're supposed to be reporting on our Christian churches back home and not arguing. I'm not sure I can do that, but I'll try.

Clement, I must say your little book *Stromata*, or *Miscellanies*, is selling wonderfully in Latin translation in the Christian bookstore in Carthage. I'm certainly not pleased with it since in it you seem to be advocating a kind of Gnosticism. Yet I admire and respect your passion for strict living that avoids the many pleasures afforded by your eclectic culture.

IRENAEUS: Let's not go over the same ground as we did before the Roman Senate earlier today. I'm glad to hear that the faith is thriving and growing in both of your regions. It is in mine too. Tertullian, I like what you said to the Roman persecutors: "The blood of the martyrs is the seed of the church." Oh, I know you didn't say "of the church," but that's what you meant, right? Besides, the whole sentence wouldn't fit on a chariot bumper sticker. Anyway, it's true. The more the Romans persecute us, the more we grow.

TERTULLIAN: Let's discuss what is necessary to believe to be a Christian. Isn't that a crucial issue we're all facing? In my books I've included what I call the rule of faith. You know what that is. It's my summary of what the apostles taught and what must be believed to be a Christian. Let me quote one of my expressions of it:

"We believe there is only one God, and that he is none other than the creator of the world, who produced all things out of nothing through his own Word, first of all sent forth; that this Word is called his Son, and under the name of God was seen in diverse manners by the patriarchs, heard at all times in the prophets, at last brought down by the Spirit and Power of the Father into the Virgin Mary, was made flesh in her womb, and being born of her, went forth as Jesus Christ; thenceforth he preached the new law and the new promise of the kingdom of heaven, worked miracles; after being crucified, he rose again the third day; then, after ascending into the heavens, he sat down at the right hand of the Father; he sent instead of himself the Power of the Holy Spirit to lead such as believe; he will come with glory to take the saints to the enjoyment of everlasting life and of the heavenly promises, and to condemn the wicked to everlasting fire, after the resurrection of both these classes shall have happened, together with the restoration of their flesh." I wrote that in my book *Prescription against Heretics*. It's in chapter 13.

IRENAEUS: Show-off! Okay, I've also memorized my summary. It's in *Against Heresies*, book 3, chapter 4, verses 1–2. We believe "in one God, the creator of heaven and earth, and all things therein, by means of Christ Jesus, the Son of God; who because of his surpassing love toward his creation, condescended to be born of the virgin, he himself uniting man through himself to God, and having suffered under Pontius Pilate, and rising again, and having been received up in splendor, shall come in glory, the Savior of those who are saved, and the Judge of those who are judged, and sending into eternal fire those who transform the truth and despise his Father and his advent."

TERTULLIAN: I like mine better. It's more detailed. But the substance is the same.

CLEMENT: They're both okay, but I wonder if this whole dogma thing can be taken a little too far. I agree that real Christians must believe certain things, but what about those who are ignorant or who have come to believe the same thing in substance but outside the written or spoken Word? What about the philosophically minded Jew or pagan? Can such a person find Christ through nature? I'm just a little hesitant to sign on to a fixed rule of faith, like both of yours, if that means excluding all who don't know or don't yet believe every jot and tittle of these things.

IRENAEUS: Clement, sooner or later you'll have to define what must be believed to be a Christian and even to be saved. Our faith is not an experience without mental content or verbal confession.

TERTULLIAN: Amen to that!

CLEMENT: I'm not saying that Christianity is without content. In my writings I've made clear what I believe and what all informed and initiated Christians believe. I'm just not as anxious as you two seem to be to draw a circle around "true Christians" and exclude everyone else from having godly faith. After all, as I've said before, Socrates was a type of Christ. Why can't there be pagan virtues and even beliefs that adumbrate, or foreshadow, the fullness of Christ so that pagans can also be in communion with God?

IRENAEUS: Well, perhaps only God knows about that. But our rules of faith are necessary to exclude heretics who call themselves Christians and yet believe something foreign to the apostolic tradition. They even claim to support their brazen heresies with Scripture! I think Tertullian here will agree with me that only those who abide by our rule of faith have a right to use Scripture.

TERTULLIAN: I most certainly do agree, Irenaeus. Clement here seems to be a little wishy-washy about doctrines.

CLEMENT: No, please, don't get me wrong. Doctrines matter. But so does the spiritual path of wisdom, and wisdom includes admitting that we don't yet know everything. True wisdom understands that the Logos of God, whom we know as Jesus Christ, has planted truth in many forms throughout the world. Just because someone doesn't agree with the wording of our rule of faith doesn't mean that person lacks any true knowledge or wisdom.

IRENAEUS: I don't know if we are even communicating here. Your issues seem completely different from ours. We are mainly concerned about combating false gospels and counterfeit forms of Christianity. You seem mainly concerned about finding truth everywhere; your interests are inclusive while ours seem more exclusive.

CLEMENT: I wouldn't exactly say that there's truth everywhere, but wherever it does exist, we Christians should embrace it and make use of it. Perhaps some evil mystery cult lacks any shred of truth. But some of the great philosophers of the Greeks and Romans have spoken much that is true, and surely they can't just be rejected out of hand as having nothing of value because they don't adhere to our rule of faith.

TERTULLIAN: Well, this doesn't seem to be going anywhere, and I'm starting to turn into a prune in this water. Time to get out, go back to my room, and prepare for dinner. I'm having a meal with fellow followers of the New Prophecy here in Rome.

IRENAEUS: I'm still scratching my head over Clement's points. I'm not sure what he's getting at. But I'm afraid that he leaves a door wide open to heresy with his openness to all kinds of truth found in many different places. I know you share that concern, Tertullian.

This evening I plan to meet with two competitors for the office of bishop in a nearby area. I've made several trips to Italy to unite quarreling factions within our catholic and orthodox churches.

CLEMENT: This evening I plan to stay with a group of contemplative philosophers who aren't yet Christians but who have much to teach us. We'll read some essays by Platonic and Stoic philosophers, then some portions of Scripture and the apostles, and then meditate. After that we'll discuss how we can find common ground in universal truth.

TERTULLIAN: Well, you just go and do that, Clement. I can't wish you the best. I can only wish you God's protection from the false teachings of those philosophers.

Analysis

These three typical church fathers (in the sense of representing three types of Christian theology as explained in the analysis of the second conversation) talk about the rule of faith, or *regula fidei*. What must a person believe in order to be Christian and have the right to interpret the Bible? At least Tertullian and Irenaeus believe that people who carry Bibles around door-to-door and evangelize for a cult that teaches false doctrines have no right to call themselves Christians or even to use the Bible. The Bible, they argue, belongs to those who believe the doctrines handed down by the apostles.

Later, the rules of faith came to be called creeds. The most universally accepted one is the Nicene Creed, written at the Council of Nicaea in 325. Its final form comes from the Council of Constantinople, meeting in 381. The Apostles' Creed is a short version of the Nicene Creed even though it has older roots. When Christians talk about "the creed," they generally mean the Nicene Creed (sometimes called the Niceno-Constantinopolitan Creed, after the two ecumenical councils that wrote it). Informally, some people use "creed" for any written confession of faith or doctrinal statement. Yet that's not correct. But Irenaeus's and Tertullian's rules of faith were early statements of faith even though they did not find universal acceptance as did the later Nicene Creed.

The question raised by this conversation is still relevant today. Is there a fundamental cognitive core of Christianity such that anyone who denies any part of it is thereby automatically revealed to be a false Christian? Traditionalists say yes and point out that people can make the Bible say whatever they want it to say. There has to be an official version of its crucial doctrinal content in order to have boundaries around Christian faith. Noncreedalists, such as many in the free churches or believers churches (many Baptists, Mennonites, Evangelical Free, et al.), say no. They don't reject doctrines and may have their statements of faith, but these statements, like early Christian creeds, are considered true only insofar as they express what the Bible says, and they are open to revision.

Tertullian and Irenaeus did not think that their versions of the rule of faith were open to revision. They were convinced that these concise statements of Christian truth came down to them from the apostles. Is that the case? It's difficult to say. It's possible that John wrote one and that it formed the foundation for the others. The authors of the New Testament occasionally present brief confessions of faith, such as the one found in Philippians 2: Christ did not think equality with God a thing to be held on to but emptied himself, taking the form of a servant. (This may have been an early Christian hymn, but even so it also functions as a statement of doctrine.)

Clement did not reject right doctrine, but he was probably somewhat wary of the kind of closed and fixed, rigid statement of faith written and promoted by Tertullian and Irenaeus. He was wary not because he disagreed with the doctrines in them but because he was open to the light of truth wherever it might be found. Further, he regarded authentic Christian faith as a journey and not primarily as a defense of a territory.

No doubt someone familiar with Clement's writings will find something like a rule of faith in them and criticize my portrayal of him as too liberal and open. I don't deny that he would, under the right circumstances, affirm a set of doctrines. But the point is that he was not enamored with fixed, written summaries of the faith to the exclusion of anything and everything that might disagree with them. I think he would be open to revision of doctrines if they turned out to be defective in light of Scripture and reason. He gave reason a high place in his hierarchy of authorities for discovering truth.

Modern-day liberal Christians are often open to revising doctrine in light of modern discoveries and to thinking like Clement. I don't know whether he would view them favorably, but they do seem to share a similar spirit of openness to truth from outside Christian sources. Modern-day fundamentalists are often adamant about correct doctrines and opposed to modernity having any say in what Christians believe, much like Tertullian's stand against paganism and heresy. Irenaeus is a favorite of Eastern Orthodox Christians, but many Protestants like him as well. He seemed to possess a pastoral heart combined with a somewhat speculative mind that was anchored in the Bible.

For Further Reading

See books about these three church fathers listed at the end of the previous conversation.

4

Second- and Third-Century Origen and Tertullian Debate Faith's Relationship to Reason and the Nature of the Eternal Godhead

Setting

If you have read conversations 2 or 3 (or both), you already know about Tertullian. Origen was mentioned in passing as Clement of Alexandria's protégé. If you haven't read either of the two previous conversations and each "Setting," you may want to go back and read them to know more about Tertullian.

Here Tertullian of North Africa, one of the most important Latin church fathers, meets Origen, perhaps the most brilliant and prolific church father. They represent two quite different Christian mentalities about theology. That will become apparent in their dialogue. It is highly unlikely that they ever met; there's no record that they even corresponded with each other even though their lifetimes overlapped. Origen lived from about 185 to about 254. Tertullian lived from about 155 to about 225. This imaginary meeting and conversation takes place in about 220 on a ship in the Mediterranean Sea. At that time Origen was still living in Alexandria, Egypt. Later, in about 230, he moved to Caesarea in Palestine. Tertullian was born in Carthage, practiced law in Rome, then after his conversion near 193, he settled in Carthage. Origen was from Alexandria, spoke Greek, and was steeped in the multicultural, cosmopolitan atmosphere of his home city. As a student of Clement (see conversations 2–3) at the Christian catechetical school and as Clement's successor as principal or dean at that school, he was philosophically oriented.

Origen's life story is amazing. At a young age he felt that he had the gift of martyrdom and tried to turn himself over to the Roman authorities who were persecuting Christians in and around Alexandria. To prevent him from doing so, Origen's mother hid his clothes so he couldn't leave the house. Apparently his father had died in a similar persecution. Later in life he castrated himself (some say by using two bricks). The reasons are not entirely clear, but some scholars speculate that it was to become as much of a martyr as possible in the absence of official persecution of Christians. He may also have struggled with sexual temptations and wanted to live a perfectly celibate life without struggle. In any case, his act was shocking to his bishop, and he had to leave Alexandria and find refuge among Christians at Caesarea in Palestine.

According to Eusebius, Origen wrote many letters and about two thousand distinct treatises. Some are longer than others, but all are substantial. How could he do it? History tells us that he was supported by a wealthy Christian patron named Ambrose (not to be confused with the later Bishop Ambrose of Milan, Augustine's mentor). Ambrose paid for several secretaries to copy down Origen's dictations. The scene was something like this: Origen would dictate a portion of a book to a secretary, who took it down in shorthand; a copyist, man or young woman, expanded the notations in good penmanship; and Origen would go to another secretary to dictate a portion of another book. And so forth. Without doubt Origen was a genius and possessed a photographic memory so that he could "write" several books at once.

Origen's most important books are *First Principles* (*De principiis*) and *Contra Celsum* (*Against Celsus*). The latter book contains almost the entirety of the Roman philosopher's book *The True Doctrine*, which was an attack on Christianity. Origen quotes it extensively and proves it to be a flawed critique of the Christian faith and of Christians. We would not know the content of Celsus's book if not for Origen's direct quoting in *Contra Celsum*, which also contains detailed expositions of Christian beliefs.

First Principles is the first comprehensive exposition of a Christian life- and worldview, including a wide range of Christian doctrines. It is quite philosophically oriented but also contains extensive biblical interpretation. Like his teacher Clement, Origen tried to combine Greek philosophy with biblical teachings and the teachings of the apostles. The latter took priority over the former, but Origen saw no necessary conflict between them except at certain points, such as on the origin of the world. Like other Christian fathers, he believed that the world was created by God ex nihilo, out of nothing; non-Christian Greek thinkers generally taught that the world had always existed or was created out of eternal matter existing alongside the deity as his counterpart.

Origen was a speculative theologian. He saw no problem with trying to answer questions about God, the world, and the soul that find no answers in Scripture. For him, answers could be derived from logic and speculation. If such-and-such is the case, as the Bible and Christian doctrine affirm, then such-and-such must also be the case. The latter such-and-such might be quite distant from anything the Bible or the teaching of the apostles says or even directly implies. An example is Origen's answer as to why God hated Esau and loved Jacob before either one did anything (see Rom. 9). Simple. Like all souls, Jacob's and Esau's souls existed before they were born, and in that preexistence Jacob pleased God and Esau offended God. Origen thought belief in the preexistence of souls, if not the eternality of souls, was both philosophically sound (as taught by Plato and the Platonists) and the only solution to certain biblical enigmas.

Also in *First Principles*, Origen suggests what is known as *apokatastasis*, the ultimate reconciliation of everything. There is some question as to whether he or a later Latin translator of his works included Satan in that ultimate reconciliation. But without question, Origen believed that eventually all humans, if not all creatures, will be reconciled with God and enter into heaven. Today we call this view universalism. Origen based it on the logic of God's perfection and the logic of God's love. If God could lose any of his creatures created in his own image and likeness forever, then he would be a loser. God cannot lose. His desire is to save everyone. Therefore, eventually everyone must be saved. Also, if God loves every one of his human creatures enough to send his Word to die for them, why would he ever give up on any of them?

Origen was not the only church father to advocate universal salvation. The later church father Gregory of Nyssa, one of the Cappadocian fathers, also believed in it and promoted it in his writings. It's ironic that much later the Eastern and Western churches together condemned Origen for this heresy but did not condemn Gregory, who is still considered a great, orthodox teacher of the church. Unlike Gregory, Origen's reputation among Eastern Orthodox and Roman Catholic theologians was tainted for hundreds of years because of his alleged teaching about the final reconciliation of Satan with God.

Tertullian breathed a different theological air. He was anything but a speculative, philosophical thinker; his main goal was to exclude anything and everything that conflicted with or even went beyond the rule of faith, the teachings of the apostles (as he understood those teachings). (See the previous conversation for more about the rule of faith.) Tertullian explored and expounded Christian doctrines and went beyond what had been said before, but never out of speculative interest or inclination. For example, no Christian before Tertullian laid out the basics of the doctrine of the Trinity in as much detail. He contributed the categories of "substance" and "person" to the theological discussion without appealing to Greek philosophy (even if he was indirectly indebted to Stoicism). Tertullian used these categories to explain to Greeks and Romans the Christian idea of the unity and multiplicity of God. But that's a far cry from Origen's speculative method. Tertullian was simply borrowing terms and concepts to explain and express Christian doctrines. Origen, by contrast, was following trajectories of thought that were deeply rooted in philosophy in order to invent new doctrines (even though he did not suggest that everyone must believe all of them).

On a ship sailing the Mediterranean Sea, this imaginary conversation takes place between these two early Christian giants of theology. Both men are familiar with the sea and have traveled it in this way. We won't go so far as to imagine where they are going or from where they have started. Tertullian usually speaks Latin, and Origen usually speaks Greek. But Tertullian can also speak and write Greek, and Origen surely knows some Latin. So such a conversation could take place. Throughout the empire, after all, Greek was the universal language of culture, and Latin was the universal language of law.

The Conversation

TERTULLIAN: Excuse me, young man. Aren't you Origen of Alexandria, the principal of the Christian catechetical school there? I saw you reading Celsus's book against Christianity and taking notes as you read. I heard through the grapevine that Origen is writing a response to *The True Doctrine*, by Celsus. I apologize for interrupting your work, but I wonder if you'd mind sitting and talking for a while. Oh, by the way, I'm Tertullian of Carthage. Perhaps you've heard of me.

ORIGEN: You flatter me by recognizing me and asking so politely if we might have some conversation. I do know who you are. Your reputation as a great defender of the faith is known to virtually every Christian in Alexandria and throughout the eastern part of the empire. You wrote some of your books in Greek, and others have been translated into Greek. Please, sit down. I would be honored to talk with you.

TERTULLIAN: Thanks very much for your gracious acceptance of my overture to dialogue. We Christians should take the time and trouble to talk to each other even when we don't see eye to eye about the most serious matters.

ORIGEN: Oh? What kinds of matters? About what do you think we disagree?

TERTULLIAN: Well, you know, . . . the role of philosophy in theology and all that. I once debated your mentor Clement on that subject. I suspect that you agree with him, and we probably disagree about the same things. Nevertheless, I found him to be a worthy counterpart in debate. I'm sure you will be the same if not better.

ORIGEN: So you enjoy debate, do you? As Christians, shouldn't we first talk about our common faith?

TERTULLIAN: Okay, I guess. But I rather do enjoy polemics more than sweetness and light.

ORIGEN: Ah, but too often polemics shed more heat than light on the subject being debated. I prefer to find our common ground and then move from that to possibly divergent opinions.

TERTULLIAN: *I* certainly don't have any opinions, but I'm sure you do. What I teach is truth.

ORIGEN: I see you're a humble man, Tertullian. But please, let's talk about our agreements first. I'm sure we both believe that in Jesus Christ, God became human, clothing himself in our very flesh in order to die and rise to new life, and that by his life, death, and resurrection we can be taken up into God's very life and given the wonderful gift of immortality. In fact, through him we become something more than mere mortals; we become gods—less than God himself, surely, but partial partakers in God's own immortal life.

TERTULLIAN: I don't necessarily disagree, but that's not how we like to express the gospel in Carthage. For me, the gospel is a new law. It is God's revelation of his will for our obedience. By obeying this new law, we become heirs with Jesus Christ, heirs to God's storehouse of rich blessings, including especially his favor and forgiveness.

ORIGEN: I don't necessarily disagree with that, Tertullian. But for me the gospel transcends mere moralism, with its stress on obedience. For me the gospel is not a new law so much as the revelation of a path to union with God. You seem to dwell much on the gospel as information; I view it as transformation.

TERTULLIAN: Already we're talking about our disagreements, aren't we? It's hard to avoid. But, yes, we agree that salvation, whatever exactly that entails, is through the Word, who through Jesus Christ brings us to God.

ORIGEN: I'd prefer to say that the Word through Jesus Christ brings God to us.

TERTULLIAN: Okay, fine, be mystical about it. I just find legal categories more resonant with what I read in the apostles. Our beloved apostle Paul, for example, emphasized reconciliation with God through repentance and forgiveness, and he never tired of telling his readers how to behave themselves. Paul was a great Christian moralist.

ORIGEN: Yes, there is a moral aspect in the writings of the apostles. But more abundant and impressive is their teaching about our being changed and given immortal life through faith in Christ.

TERTULLIAN: You know, Origen, I think you, like your mentor Clement, have drunk too deeply from the wells of Greek philosophy and that there's more than a touch of mysticism in your writings. Just the other day I was slogging through your book *First Principles*. It just hit the bookstores in Carthage in Latin translation. It reads more like a textbook of philosophy than an account of Christian theology. As I read it, I kept asking myself, "What has Athens to do with Jerusalem?" There's a lot of "Athens" in there!

ORIGEN: Didn't you notice, though, how near the outset I expressed strong disagreement with some important points of Greek philosophy? For example, none of the Greeks ever thought that the world was created out of nothing—ex nihilo, to use your language. They find that idea offensive because it is mysterious. But I teach it in the face of the overwhelming consensus of Greek philosophy and religion. I disagree with Greek thought on many other points as well.

TERTULLIAN: Yes, yes. But it's more in your methods than in your conclusions that I find an inordinate influence of Greek philosophy. In *First Principles*, for example, you don't begin with the Bible or the apostolic witness. You begin with self-evident truths about the world and work from there to what is found in Scripture. Throughout the book you struggle to make Christianity conform to the Greek's understanding of reason. For example, all the Greeks assume that where the reality is, there must also be the corresponding possibility. You work from the reality of the world as we experience it to what must be true to explain it. Occasionally you appeal to Scripture or the teaching of the apostles, but more often than not, you draw your conclusions from observation, logic, and speculation.

ORIGEN: Keep reading, Tertullian. You'll find that I make positive use of Scripture more toward the end of the book than at the beginning. After all, when I wrote that book I had in mind my many non-Christian students; I was trying to explain the Christian faith to them in a way they could follow and understand. If I just jumped right in with supernatural revelation and ignored nature, observation, experience, and logic, most of my non-Christian readers would close the book and walk away. I think you'll have to agree that all of my conclusions are consistent with sound Christian doctrine.

TERTULLIAN: Perhaps. Except for that stuff about universal reconciliation. How can you believe that all will be saved when our Lord Jesus Christ, in whom the Word dwelt, taught so much about hell?

ORIGEN: I believe in hell. I just don't think it can eternally stand over against God. Our God is perfect in power and majesty as well as in goodness. He cannot endure the permanent loss of even one of his human creatures because in the Logos we possess his own image and likeness. God cannot allow a part of himself or even his image to be lost forever. That would show weakness on his part.

TERTULLIAN: See! That's what I'm talking about. You appeal to logic against Scripture. Scripture, including the writings of our apostles, clearly teaches the final judgment of the wicked and their consignment to everlasting punishment in hell. There's no hint of ultimate reconciliation of the damned there. You're just a hopeless optimist, Origen.

ORIGEN: Perhaps. But since our God is a good God who loves his creatures, I think there's good warrant for being optimistic.

TERTULLIAN: And what about your belief in the preexistence of souls? That's so Greek! There's nothing revealed about that.

ORIGEN: Perhaps not. But that doesn't mean it cannot be true. God could not have revealed everything. Surely he expects us, by using our God-given minds, to draw right conclusions from what he has revealed.

TERTULLIAN: Well, maybe. But we shouldn't go searching for truth beyond what is revealed. That just leads to heresy. We should be content with God's revelation.

ORIGEN: Oh, I'm content with what has been revealed. But that doesn't stop my inquiring mind from thinking further along the trajectory of divine revelation to what more must be true. Surely God wants us to use our minds to answer questions not answered in Scripture. You even do that, Tertullian. You have written that even the spirit is made up of highly refined matter. That's a Stoic idea, and it's not revealed in Scripture. By the way, that idea doesn't make sense to me. Matter is a prison of spirit.

TERTULLIAN: I always suspected you of being a bit Gnostic! There it is from your mouth: matter is evil.

ORIGEN: I didn't say that. All I said was that matter imprisons soul or spirit. The body, composed of matter, is a drag on the spirit, which desires to soar back to God, from whence it came.

TERTULLIAN: No, the soul or spirit is a highly refined, ethereal form of matter that is firmly planted in creation and not in heaven.

ORIGEN: Let's change the subject and explore one more idea where we may have some common ground in spite of differences: the nature of our Savior Jesus Christ. Who is he? From where did he come? Of what stuff is he made? In some of your antiheretical writings, you've explored these questions. What say you?

TERTULLIAN: The Lord is a man indwelt by the Spirit of God; he is also the Logos of God, God's own Son, condescending to live humanly among us. He is "one person of two natures," *una persona, duae substantiae*—to use my Latin. I don't know how you'd say that in Greek. So Jesus Christ is one person possessing two substances or natures, divine and human.

ORIGEN *(smiling)*: You know what? That sounds a little philosophical and speculative! Sorry, I just had to say that. Actually, it's not too bad. Personally, however, I like to dwell on the Logos in him. Jesus Christ is the incarnation of the divine Logos of the Father, the mediator between creation and heaven.

TERTULLIAN: Okay, that's not bad, but who and what is this Logos? I know that our beloved apostle John referred to Jesus in this manner in the prologue to his Gospel.

ORIGEN *(interrupting)*: Yes, by the way, John borrowed that idea from Greek philosophy!

TERTULLIAN: Yes, but he filled it with new meaning. And it's also found in Jewish thought. Maybe that's his main source for it.

ORIGEN: I apologize for my rude interruption; please continue.

TERTULLIAN: As I was saying, John did make use of the Logos concept to help explain the deity of Jesus Christ to Hellenistic Jewish and Greek readers. But you seem to take it much further.

ORIGEN: I do, and I don't apologize for it. The Logos concept is tremendously
    helpful in our day to communicate what we believe about the Son of God
    as we find him in Jesus Christ. As I explain in *First Principles* and other
    books, the Logos is a being, eternally begotten of the Father; the Logos is
    the Father's emanation into creation. It is by means of his Logos that the
    Father created everything and now redeems everything. The Father, being
    apart from time and its corruption, cannot enter into the world directly.
    He enters it by means of his Logos, who is like the rays of the sun—not
    the sun itself but offshoots from it.

TERTULLIAN: You say "not the sun itself"? Do you thus deny the deity of our
    Lord?

ORIGEN: Not at all! I worship Jesus Christ as Lord and Savior and also as God
    among us. But it is our task as theologians to explain what we mean by
    "God among us." We don't mean that the eternal Creator, who is above
    all imperfection and decay, became one of us. That would be improper to
    the glory and majesty of the Father, who is aloof from this realm of sin,
    death, and decay. So when we affirm the deity of Jesus Christ, we mean
    that God's own Logos came down to be one of us and live among us in
    order to reveal God to us.

TERTULLIAN: Say more about the Logos in relation to God. Is the Logos actu-
    ally God?

ORIGEN: Yes, but not in the same way that the Father is God. The rays of the
    sun are, in essence, one with the sun. They shoot forth from it. But we
    distinguish them from the sun since they enter our atmosphere and dimin-
    ish in power and glory. So the Logos is God's primary offshoot, forever
    blazing forth in glory toward what is outside God. The Logos is, in effect,
    a second God. God two or God too.

TERTULLIAN: Clever play on words. But one problem remains. As I read
    your book, I noticed that sometimes you equate the Logos with God
    and sometimes you subordinate the Logos to the Father. What's up
    with that?

ORIGEN: On the one hand, the Logos is eternal; therefore the Logos is part of
    God. Whatever is eternal must be divine. But on the other hand, from
    eternity the Logos is descended from God. The difference between the
    Logos and the Father is greater than the difference between the Logos
    and the world.

TERTULLIAN: That sounds very subordinationist. You know what I mean. It
    seems as though you are making the Logos and therefore our master Jesus
    Christ into something less than God and not of God's own substance. If
    that's true, you should stop worshiping him immediately!

ORIGEN: No, no. You don't understand. While the Son or Logos is subordinate
    to the Father, he is also eternal with the Father and therefore equal in
    some ways with the Father. But the inequality lies in his dependence on
    the Father for his being. Even the Logos draws life from the Father and

goes forth from him. The Father is the monarch of heaven, even of the Word and the Spirit, who are his right and left arms.

TERTULLIAN: But I think you lay too much stress on the Word's subordination to the Father. What you leave unclear and is bound to confuse your followers for years to come: how is the Logos equal with the Father and therefore worthy of worship? I foresee a not-too-distant day when your followers will cut the tenuous chord you create between the Father and the Son and simply say bluntly that the Son is not fully or truly God. You'll be partly to blame for that.

ORIGEN: No, I won't take any blame if that happens. They would then have misunderstood my teachings. The Word, Son, Logos is subordinate to the Father but eternally shares in the Father's majesty and glory.

TERTULLIAN: The wind is picking up and rocking this ship. Hmmm, and I wonder if that's one of those infernal pirate ships coming toward us. I think I'll go back to my cabin, wait out the storm, and try to avoid being noticed by the pirates if they board us. You should do the same.

ORIGEN: I think I'll stay on deck for a little longer reading Celsus and taking notes. Our conversation has helped to clarify some things I plan to write in response to his ridiculous accusations about our beliefs.

Analysis

Some of the subjects discussed in this conversation were also covered in the previous two, especially the relationship between Christianity and Greek philosophy. That subject, however, is well worth repeating. Early Christians struggled over it; practically none intended to subvert the gospel with Greek thought, but some scholars have argued that it happened anyway. The great German church historian Adolf von Harnack (1851–1930) built a reputation on advancing the theory that certain early Christians, such as the Alexandrians Clement and Origen, hellenized Christianity. He meant that they accommodated the gospel to Greek thought in order to make it respectable.

The main topic of this conversation, however, is the Logos or Word of God. ("Word" is the common English translation of Logos.) Most Greek philosophers used the concept of the Logos in some way. And in the first chapter of John's Gospel, Logos expresses the preexistence of Christ and his relationship with God. The Alexandrian Jewish exegete and philosopher Philo, who was contemporary with Jesus Christ, used the Logos idea to convey something about God's immanence in the world, and he tended to equate Logos with reason. Although he was Jewish, he was certainly also a Greek thinker. Early Christians in Alexandria were no doubt influenced by him.

Origen's use of the Logos had unintended consequences, and in the above conversation Tertullian fictitiously hints at what they might be. His prediction came true. Here's what happened. About one hundred years after Origen, some

Christians in Alexandria emphasized the subordination of the Logos to the Father and proclaimed that "there was [a time] when the Son was not." Even though Origen clearly affirmed the everlastingness of the Logos, he also affirmed the Logos's subordination to the Father. As will be seen in a later conversation, the Alexandrian presbyter (priest) Arius and his followers taught that Jesus Christ was the incarnation of the Logos/Word of God but not of God. For them, the Logos/Word is not God but a creature—God's first and highest creature.

Origen would have turned over in his grave when Arius and his followers denied the deity of Jesus Christ. Any fair-minded reader of Origen's theology must come to that conclusion. He clearly believed that Jesus Christ is the incarnation of God's Logos/Word, also known as God's Son, and that the Logos is eternally with God the Father. There is no real doubt that Origen affirmed the deity of Christ in this way. For whatever reason, however, Origen also just as strongly denied the full equality of the Logos/Word with the Father. For him, only the Father is the source of divinity, and the Logos/Word, Son of God, derives his divinity from the Father eternally and is most definitely second in power and glory to the Father. Yet according to Origen, the Logos/Word shares the Father's power and glory.

In any case, the point is that Origen seemed a little confused about the Trinity even as he taught it. One can only conclude that he bought into the Greek notion that the supreme being, the source of all things, must be untouched by the imperfections of creation and therefore has to relate to creation through an intermediary being—the Logos. That immediately implies that the Logos is not as metaphysically perfect as the Father. For example, the Father is impassible, incapable of suffering, whereas the Logos can suffer in and through a human body such as Jesus. But this means, then, that the Logos is not quite as perfectly God as the Father is—in spite of Origen's claims. He couldn't make up his mind about the status of the Logos. That led to big trouble in Christian theology later. The Nicene affair over the Trinity is rooted in Origen's ambiguous attitude toward the Logos.

This whole issue of the status of the being who became incarnate in Jesus is still a source of great confusion among Christians. Not long ago a Jehovah's Witness missionary came to my door, and I engaged her in conversation about who Jesus was and is. She admitted that they do not believe he is God, but she said, "Neither does my sister's church, and it's Baptist." I talked with her long enough to believe it. I've met many Christians who can't quite grasp the idea that God himself, in the person of the Logos, his Son, became incarnate. They think they have an exalted view of God, and they attach that solely to the Father. It means that the most perfect God, God Almighty, the Father, cannot really live a human life among us. So whoever did become Jesus Christ was not as much God as the Father. As we'll see, the fourth-century councils of the church declared that to be heresy.

It's ironic that the very same Christians, when asked about the Trinity, usually express some version of modalism—the heresy of Praxeas of Rome, which

Tertullian called patripassionism. But modalism stands in absolute contradiction to their belief that the Son, Jesus, is somehow less God than is the Father. Such folks combine subordinationism with modalism in their folk religious version of Christianity. Maybe we can't blame them. Most of them are untutored in theology (to say nothing of logic!). But Origen, being the great genius he was, should have known better than to equate the Logos with the Father in terms of eternal existence and then put great distance between the Father and the Logos in terms of divinity. A little more than a century later, the church would engage in a decades-long struggle over this issue.

For Further Reading

For suggestions for further reading on Tertullian, see the end of the previous conversation.

Crouzel, Henri. *Origen.* Translated by A. S. Worrell. San Francisco: Harper & Row, 1989.

5

Third-Century Bishop
Cyprian of Carthage Is Interviewed
about the Church and Salvation

Setting

Bishop Cyprian of Carthage receives less attention than he deserves in books about church history and the history of Christian theology. He was a quite influential church leader during a difficult time. The first empirewide persecution occurred during his tenure as bishop in part of North Africa. Cyprian became a bishop in 248/249, served during the terrible persecution of Christians begun by Emperor Decius in 250 and continued at lower intensity by his successors from 251, and died in 258. Cyprian had been a wealthy man, but upon ordination—first as a deacon, next as a priest, then as a bishop—he divested himself of his abundance and gave it to the poor.

The persecution under Decius was unique in that it extended throughout the empire; it was illegal to be a Christian, and persisting in that faith often resulted in death. Many Christians denied Christ under torture and threat of death (including threats against their families), and some even cooperated with the persecuting authorities by providing lists of church members and Christian books.

Cyprian was an extremely popular Christian leader, especially with the poor. He was not popular with all Christians, however. A group of men and women now called the "Confessors" rose up to challenge his authority. These were Christians who had suffered terribly at the hands of the Roman persecutors and had remained steadfast in their faith. Somehow they survived the persecution and were around during Cyprian's tenure as bishop.

The Confessors claimed that they alone had the right to decide which apostates (Christians who denied Christ for any reason, including persecution) could return to the church. They were often extremely strict, requiring repentant apostates to suffer long and hard before being forgiven. (This was not necessarily physical suffering but "doing penance" in service and prayer and self-denial.) Some apostates they would not forgive.

Cyprian eventually opposed the Confessors in this matter. He proclaimed that only the bishop and his appointed agents such as priests could forgive sins such as apostasy. Surely he meant "forgive sins on behalf of God." He began to set up what would later be called the "penitential system," by which gross sinners such as apostates could be readmitted to Christian fellowship and to the sacraments. His requirements were less stringent than that of the Confessors.

Because of this, many Confessors left the bishop's churches and founded separate, stricter, "purer" churches. A later group known to church history as the Donatists may have been the refuge of many Confessors. A group called the Novatians were also restrictive and denied the authority of the bishops to forgive sins. That was in part because they were considered too lenient. The Novatians and later Donatists claimed to be Christians, but they rejected the authority of bishops like Cyprian. They were strongest in Rome and North Africa. They wanted a pure church exclusive of gross sinners, and they had much more stringent requirements for penance and restoration to the church than had Cyprian. In effect, the Donatists and the Confessors divided the church, something that Cyprian believed cannot be done. In other words, in his mind there can only be one true church; a breakaway group may call itself Christian, but it is not really so.

During a particularly violent time of the persecution by Decius, Cyprian fled Carthage and went into the desert, where he hid from the authorities. It might be fair to say there was a "price on his head." At that time he did not think that he had the gift of martyrdom, or at least he did not want to leave his flock without a shepherd. So he wrote numerous treatises and letters and had them smuggled back into Carthage, where they were read in secret meetings of Christians. He also wrote letters to other Christian bishops throughout the empire.

One of his most influential and best-known treatises is *The Unity of the Catholic Church*, in which he argues that the church is in essence one and cannot be divided. There can be only one visible and institutional church, made up of many congregations, and it is characterized by the leadership of a bishop who stands in the apostolic succession. Those who break away and start their own parallel "churches" are no longer Christians. In a famous statement Cyprian said, "Whoever does not have the church as mother cannot have God as father." He was in effect declaring the schismatics to be unsaved because they were not in the one true church.

In another important treatise, *The Lapsed*, Cyprian argued that only the bishop can decide whose sins are forgiven and under what conditions. Cyprian walked a thin line of moderation in this and related matters. The Confessors thought he was too lenient. Cornelius, the bishop of Rome, thought he was too strict. Cornelius would allow baptisms performed by schismatics and heretics to be valid. Cyprian rejected them. Yet his standards for restoration to the church were too lenient for the Confessors.

Cornelius claimed that, as bishop of Rome, he had supreme authority over such matters. His word would trump all other human authorities. This was one step in the long process that ultimately led to the imperial papacy. Cyprian rejected this assertion and considered the bishop of Rome to be the "first among equals." For him, the bishop of Rome, the "pope," was a figurehead leader and without absolute authority. The final word in controversies would be the consensus of all the bishops throughout a region (where a controversy was taking place) or the empire (if it was a universal issue for all Christians).

Cyprian escaped death during the Decian persecution but in 258 died publicly at the hands of a Roman swordsman, in Carthage during the Valerian persecution.

The setting of this conversation is a secret hideout in the North African desert. The date is about 251, during the Decian persecution. Cyprian has heard from Carthage that some church leaders there want to bar the restoration of lapsed Christians once the persecution has ended. He has also heard that some who are suffering under persecution while remaining steadfast in the faith want to decide such matters. Cyprian has been found by an investigative reporter for the *Rome Times*, who wants to publish a profile of this popular but controversial Christian leader, who is in hiding during the persecution of Christians.

The Conversation

REPORTER: Hello there. Bishop Cyprian, I presume? I've been searching all over North Africa for you. You really know how to hide well!

CYPRIAN: Greetings in the name of our Lord and Savior Jesus Christ. I hope Roman soldiers or the emperor's secret agents didn't follow you here! I wouldn't want to leave my little flock in Carthage without their shepherd in this difficult time of persecution.

REPORTER: No, I don't think I was followed. If they tried to follow me, they're probably wandering around the desert in circles. I came here with a Bedouin caravan that dropped me off secretly and kept going. They'll pick me up on their way back to Carthage.

CYPRIAN: You must really want to do a story about me! I'm flattered. But why?

REPORTER: Well, as you probably know, there's quite a bit of controversy about you—both among Christians and non-Christians. The Roman authorities really want to find you and make an example of you. Your prestige is known far and wide because you gave up so much to become a Christian and then a bishop. Some Christians are very upset with you for running away when some of them are being thrown to the lions. I'm sure my readers would like to know how you can justify that.

CYPRIAN: It is not yet my time to die for my Lord. The Christian church is in confusion and turmoil right now. I'm needed to help sustain God's people through this terrible time. I'm not running from persecution; I'm only in concealment for a while. Soon I'll return to my public role as bishop of the thousands of Christians in and around Carthage. In the meantime, I stay in touch with them by secret couriers. I write numerous letters every week and send them to my presbyters—that's our term for priests—and deacons in Carthage. I also write to fellow bishops all over North Africa.

REPORTER: Just before coming here, I was traveling in the eastern part of our great empire—over in Alexandria and Caesarea. There I met the venerable Christian philosopher Origen. What do you think of him and his writings? Do you approve of his philosophical form of Christianity? What drew him to my attention was that a noble lady who is not even a Christian paid him to tutor her in philosophy.

CYPRIAN: I believe he is unduly influenced by the Platonists—those Greek philosophers so numerous in the East. I have concerns about his teachings on the preexistence of souls and universal salvation. Generally speaking, we here in and around Carthage are more interested in unifying the church and preserving its order than in speculating about whether there are three heavens or seven heavens.

REPORTER: So what does that mean?

CYPRIAN: It's just a saying. "How many angels can dance on the head of a pin?" It refers to any useless speculation in philosophy or theology.

REPORTER: Okay. Let's move on. What do you think about maverick Christians closer to home? In my research I've discovered that Christians are deeply divided over several issues. Some want to accept back into the church those who denied Christ under torture, and others want to reject them. Some who are suffering for their faith in Christ are claiming that they should have the authority to decide this issue once the pressure is off.

CYPRIAN: Yes, I've heard reports that back in Carthage and over in Rome some of the so-called Confessors who survived torture by your Roman authorities without ever denying Christ are trying to usurp the power of us bishops. In my letters to them I'm urging them to stop going beyond their boundaries. Only bishops can forgive sins in God's name and restore lapsed Christians to full fellowship. We bishops can delegate that authority to presbyters. But ordinary laypeople, including Confessors—no, they cannot make such weighty spiritual decisions on their own.

REPORTER: Well, what about the new sects of Christians that keep popping up all around? In spite of persecution, they abound. How are we Romans supposed to know who speaks for all Christians or even who the true Christians are?

CYPRIAN: A true Christian is a baptized believer in Jesus Christ who worships under the guidance and authority of a true bishop of Christ's church. A true bishop is one who is ordained in apostolic succession, teaches what has always been taught and believed since the apostles, and is in fellowship with all the other apostolic bishops. Only a bishop can speak for all the Christians under his authority.

REPORTER: Then what about those other Christians? Are they not even Christians if they join one of the many sects who follow someone other than a bishop or who appoint their own, rival bishop?

CYPRIAN: My motto is, "Whoever does not have the church as mother cannot have God as father!" Also, here's another motto I hold: "Outside the church there is no salvation." And by "the church" I mean the original, catholic, and orthodox church led by a line of bishops first appointed by the apostles. These harsh truths are necessary to preserve the unity and integrity of our religion. We must have unity of the faith, and the unity of the faith depends on the visible unity of the church, and the unity of the church depends on the bishops.

REPORTER: But what's to stop other Christians from forming rival churches and having their own bishops?

CYPRIAN: Right now, nothing. Because we are all being persecuted and we have no legal authority to unify the church and exclude heretics and schismatics or stop them from calling their little groups "churches," we have to rely on the power of persuasion. But I predict that someday there will be a Christian emperor, and he will be raised up by God to unify the church and exclude the troublemakers and counterfeit Christians.

REPORTER: A Christian emperor? That's ridiculous. That will never happen!

CYPRIAN: With God all things are possible.

REPORTER: But would you even want that? Can a Roman emperor really be a true Christian? You don't even allow Christians to carry swords, so how could you ever recognize the emperor as a Christian?

CYPRIAN: I'll leave that to God.

REPORTER: Okay, then, let's move on. In Rome there's a bishop named Cornelius, who claims that your view of church organization will not work. He insists that there must be one supreme bishop over all the others, and he claims that that bishop must be the bishop of Rome—in other words, himself. What do you say to that?

CYPRIAN: We are prepared to accept the bishop of Rome as "first among equals," with special honor among the bishops. But he may not rule over the bishops; his edicts depend on our consent. The consensus of all the bishops throughout the empire is the ultimate earthly authority in the church.

REPORTER: If I may change the subject a bit, we in the press keep hearing about a controversy: Who among Christians has the power to decide who is "saved" and how a person becomes saved or forgiven? Would you explain what you bishops think is the right way for a person to become a Christian and—how do you say it?—receive God's favor and share in God's own nature?

CYPRIAN: Well, you see, that's where the controversy between myself and Bishop Cornelius becomes practical. I say that the local bishop of a diocese—that's our term for a region of Christian churches—decides such matters, especially when it gets down to the level of which lapsed Christians may reenter the church and under what conditions. Cornelius says that the bishop of Rome has the final say in such matters and can overrule the local bishop. Certainly we all agree that only God can forgive sins. The issue is one of earthly order: to whom has God delegated the authority to declare sins forgiven?

REPORTER: Okay. That's the political side of the issue. Now, please tell me precisely how a person such as I might become a Christian?

CYPRIAN: It begins with baptism, the "bath of regeneration," or the "laver of saving water." When a person comes to the baptismal font with faith in Christ and true repentance for sins and undergoes water baptism in the name of the Father, Son, and Holy Spirit, that person is automatically saved through the Spirit's work and enters into Christ's family. Whoever is baptized also begins to share in God's own divine being.

REPORTER: But what if afterward that baptized person falls into what you consider sin?

CYPRIAN: Then the bishop, often operating through his instrument the priest, assigns acts of contrition to the person. It's called penance. That's assuming the person wants to be forgiven and restored. We bishops are working together on written guidelines for this. It will be called the "penitential system" and hopefully will be standardized throughout the catholic and orthodox churches.

REPORTER: Can you give me an example? Suppose I'm a baptized Christian who commits adultery. Then I want to be forgiven.

CYPRIAN: I would tell you to spend a month in earnest prayer twice daily and to give significant alms to the poor. I would assign you a deacon or priest who would guide you through the penance process. So long as you do it sincerely and don't give up before the end, you are forgiven. God has given us the bishops, who have the "keys to the kingdom," so that anyone's sins we remit are remitted in heaven.

REPORTER: That's kind of tough, isn't it? I mean, wouldn't a lot of men and some women be doing this all the time? How could they live normal lives?

CYPRIAN: It's nothing compared with what the heretic and schismatic Novatian wants to do with penitent sinners. He wants to exclude most of them or give them extremely harsh, punishing tasks before they can be restored. And he thinks that we bishops don't have the authority to decide such matters. So his followers are establishing counterfeit churches made up only of the so-called pure.

REPORTER: That leads me to ask about schismatic churches such as the
　　Novatians.
CYPRIAN: As I said already, the true church is where the bishop is. And the Spirit
　　of God resides with the bishop. Those who leave cannot take the Spirit
　　of God with them. They cast themselves out of the church by trying to
　　divide it and by leaving it.
REPORTER: Thanks, Bishop Cyprian. Now I see the camels coming, so I have to
　　run and catch my caravan. I'll try to send you a copy of the *Times* when
　　this is published. Stay out of trouble, now.
CYPRIAN: May God go with you and bring you to himself through true sor-
　　row and penitence for your pagan life. I'd be happy to baptize you if you
　　repent!

Analysis

Cyprian's ideas about church authority were not entirely new. But pressing
circumstances forced him to codify them and argue forcefully for them. The
empirewide persecutions of the mid-third century created a set of circumstances
that called for new policies. Cyprian drew on common notions about bishops
and forgiveness and authority, but he stated them in a persuasive way, and his
personal prestige contributed to their wide acceptance among Christians.

One thing that Protestants should note here is Cyprian's commitment to
the unity of the church. He simply could not consider the possibility of more
than one Christian church. Two bishops in the same city? Never. Two or three
or four Christian congregations in the same city that didn't cooperate or have
fellowship? Never. Therefore, when some Christians began to set up their own
rival churches and appoint their own rival bishops, he was horrified and created
such seemingly harsh rules as his statement that without the one, true church
of the bishops, there is no salvation.

Without any doubt Cyprian was not even thinking of the lone Christian
convert off on a desert island or in a cave somewhere. What he had in mind was
the person who consciously and willfully abandons the church of the bishop in
the home city and tries to set up a rival one. That person, according to Cyprian,
is no Christian.

Such notions sound intolerant and even quaint today, especially among Protestants. Protestants have grown used to divisions. Cyprian would be horrified
that there are more than 250 Protestant denominations in the United States.
Most Christians of the past would also be aghast! The Roman Catholic Church
still believes in the visible and institutional unity of the one body of Christ.
They may not agree that outside of it there can be no salvation, but they believe with Cyprian that salvation is uniquely dispensed or experienced within
the life of the one church. The outsiders who call themselves Christians may
be "separated brothers and sisters" at best but only because of some kind

of mysterious union with the Roman Catholic Church. As recently as 2007, Pope Benedict XVI ordered Roman Catholics to stop referring to Protestant assemblies as "churches." Only Roman Catholic churches are true churches. Protestant assemblies are to be seen as "ecclesial communities," another term for parachurch organizations.

Another church body that highly values visible and institutional unity is the Church of England, also known as the Anglican Church. It considers itself catholic. It is the one, universal Christian church of England. By custom, if not law, only Church of England congregations can call themselves "churches" in England. Other congregations are "chapels" or "assemblies." Other Protestant bodies also highly value visible and institutional unity. But at the other end of the spectrum are such bodies as the Baptists, who are divided into at least fifty-seven varieties in North America and don't particularly mind the division. For them, each individual congregation is "the church, the body of Christ." Beyond that, there is no visible and institutional unity of the church. Baptists and other free-church Protestants talk about the invisible unity of the worldwide body of Christ.

Cyprian, like many Christian leaders before and after, tried desperately to hold on to two seemingly incompatible ideals: the visible and institutional unity of the church and the equal partnership of a plurality of bishops leading it. Cornelius, bishop of Rome, saw the problem inherent in that and tried to preserve the church's unity by declaring himself and every bishop of Rome before and after him the sole, supreme authority over the whole church under Christ. Eventually the Western Church, now called Roman Catholic, adopted Cornelius's model in order to preserve unity. The Eastern Orthodox churches to this day embrace Cyprian's model. So does the Church of England, even though the monarch and the archbishop of Canterbury are figureheads of unity.

How is Cyprian relevant to Christians today? At least his concern for Christian unity can speak to divided Protestants. Perhaps Protestants can repent of their apparent love for or at least complacency toward division. After all, Jesus did pray for his disciples' unity in John 17. And he prayed for the unity of all his followers. If we are Christ followers, how can we be content with division? We don't have to go as far as Cyprian in declaring that there is "no salvation outside the church," but perhaps we can acknowledge the church as a means of salvation. The whole idea of strong Christian discipleship outside of and apart from the church is a modern, American notion.

Perhaps Cyprian's most important contribution to church history is his idea that only the bishop can decide whose sins are forgiven and under what circumstances. He reinforced a rather hierarchical model of the church, but he certainly didn't invent it. Early church father Ignatius of Antioch, who was martyred in Rome in about 110, wrote letters in which he elevated the bishop to quite high status and ordered Christians to obey the bishop as they obey Christ himself. Cyprian saw no other way for the bishop to have such authority without the authority to forgive sins or at least decide whose sins are forgiven.

And thus began the detailed penitential system that would grow like a forest into the Middle Ages and against which Martin Luther would rebel in 1517, especially against buying indulgences.

Protestants are definitely uncomfortable with the penitential system of the Roman Catholic Church, which goes back to Cyprian. But have they thrown the baby out with the bathwater? Have they made it too easy to be forgiven so that the average Christian ends up forgiving oneself? What about the Bible's command to confess our sins to one another? We often overreact to something, and in this case we seem to have overreacted to Cyprian. We don't need a penitential system, but perhaps we could use some methods of accountability within the body of Christ.

For Further Reading

Burns, J. Patout, Jr. *Cyprian the Bishop*. New York: Routledge, 2001.
Von Campenhausen, Hans. *The Fathers of the Western Church*. Translated by Manfred Hoffman. Stanford, CA: Stanford University Press, 1964.

6

Fourth-Century Alexandrians
Deacon Athanasius and Presbyter Arius
Are Interviewed about the Council of Nicaea

Setting

In 325 the first Roman emperor to call himself a Christian convened a meeting of all Christian bishops in the empire. They were to come to the town of Nicaea, near where the emperor had just started building his new capital, Constantinople, on the site of an already-existing city, Byzantium. Being a humble fellow, Constantine named the new capital after himself. From that time onward, the Roman emperor would live there and travel occasionally to Rome. Sometimes there were two emperors, one in Rome and one in Constantinople. When Rome fell to barbarian tribes, Constantinople was already the de facto capital of the empire. The "Roman" Empire continued to exist around Constantinople until 1453, when it fell to the Muslims.

The emperor Constantine lived at Nicaea until his new capital was built. He heard rumors that a theological controversy arising out of Alexandria was dividing the empire's Christians. This controversy centered on the status of the Son of God, the Logos, or Word, who became human in Jesus Christ. In other words, it had to do with the status of Jesus Christ vis-à-vis God.

Beginning in about 318/319 in Alexandria, an ambitious presbyter named Arius was challenging the authority of Bishop Alexander by teaching that "there was a time when the Son was not." Bishop Alexander believed strongly in the eternal existence of the Son of God and thus in the deity of Jesus Christ, who was the Son incarnate. Both Arius and Alexander could point back to aspects of the great Alexandrian theologian Origen's theology for support. (See conversation 4 for Origen's ambiguous view of the relationship of the Son of God/ Logos/Word to the Father.)

Arius gathered a following in Alexandria and eventually gained the backing of some bishops in other areas. The controversy among bishops became so heated that Emperor Constantine decided to step in and bring it to a resolution. He ordered all Christian bishops to come to Nicaea in 325 and promised them safe passage. Between 250 and 300 bishops showed up (the number varied during the council as some arrived late and some left early). This was the first ecumenical (universal) council of Christian bishops. Only bishops of the catholic-orthodox church were invited, and Constantine had a lot to say about who was considered to be in that category. Some rival bishops were excluded. From the very beginning, the emperor was meddling in the church's theological business.

The bishops gathered, with Constantine sitting on a throne above them. He declared himself the "thirteenth apostle" and the "bishop of all the bishops." Then someone read a statement about the relationship between the Son and the Father that clearly subordinated the former to the latter and suggested that the Son was not eternal but a creature. A bishop stepped forward, grabbed the scroll from the reader's hands, threw it to the floor, and stomped on it. According to legend, a fistfight broke out among the bishops. Constantine restored order, and the meeting resumed with the determination to write a statement of faith that would clarify the church's teaching about the Son's divinity. It would have the force of law within the church; those who did not sign it would be excluded.

Deacon Athanasius was Bishop Alexander's assistant at the council. He could not vote; only bishops could vote. Presbyter Arius, who instigated the controversy, was not even allowed into the room because he was neither a bishop nor attached to one. But he had his champions among the bishops. Athanasius was only nineteen years old and yet was perceived by many to be extremely precocious in spiritual and theological matters. This interview/conversation is purely imaginary. I have included some statements by both Athanasius and Arius that they would not have made this early. To bring out some of their and their followers' theological differences, I've taken liberties with history and have placed into their mouths things they could only have said or written much later.

By all accounts Athanasius was not a particularly likeable fellow—especially to his heretical foes. Even some of his friends thought he went too far in his rhetoric against heretics. We should remember, however, that he was fighting for what he considered to be the very heart of the Christian faith—the full deity of Jesus Christ, God's Son.

The Conversation

REPORTER: Let's begin the interview with you, Mr. Arius.

ARIUS: Excuse me, but that would be "Father Arius." I am a priest, you know.

ATHANASIUS: You may be for now, but hopefully not for long!

ARIUS: You should be quiet, young man. You're only a deacon, and I'm a presbyter.

ATHANASIUS: As I said—"for now." Our bishop Alexander has removed you from your office once already. I'm sure that the outcome of this council will be your permanent removal and worse. I predict that the emperor will punish you and your followers with exile.

REPORTER (interrupting): Excuse me, gentlemen, but may I ask some questions? As you both well know, our readers in Alexandria are intensely interested in what is happening here. Never before has a controversy among Christians gained the attention of the rulers of the empire. This is a momentous event. So please tell me, Mr. Athanasius, what's going on inside the council chamber?

ATHANASIUS: A bishop who supports Arius, here, stood and read a detailed statement in favor of the Arian heresy about our Lord Jesus Christ. As he read, many bishops and their assistants heckled him, and one finally stepped forward, grabbed the scroll from his hands, and threw it on the floor, stomping on it. A general melee erupted, and the emperor had to force calm on the crowd.

REPORTER: Wow! That must have been quite a sight! Can you give me names of bishops? Who struck whom? Was there bloodshed?

ATHANASIUS: You journalists really like to sensationalize things, don't you? Well, I'm not going to help you. The breach of proper decorum was sad but understandable in light of the horrible heresy that was presented. From here on, I'm sure the deliberations will be calm.

ARIUS: Don't be so sure. The truth always divides. It did in Alexandria, as you know. There was rioting in the streets, and some of my followers were attacked by backers of you and Bishop Alexander.

ATHANASIUS: Well, that wouldn't have happened if you and your followers had not marched through the streets and right past the cathedral, chanting your silly slogans, such as "There was when the Son was not!" You and your disciples are responsible for the riots that ensued.

ARIUS: Hardly! It was you and Bishop Alexander who provoked street violence by trying to remove me from my office as presbyter.

ATHANASIUS: Our bishop had no choice. He gave you every chance to recant, and you refused. He was under tremendous pressure to silence you. He had to do something.

REPORTER: Um, excuse me, but may I return us to the interview? I already know all that stuff. We ran a series about it in the *Tribune-Herald*. I need information about what's going on right now here in Nicaea and what is likely to happen in the future.

ATHANASIUS: Okay, here's something you should write. The gathered bishops have decided to write a creed—a binding statement of Christian belief that all the bishops throughout the world must sign.

REPORTER: Creed? What's that?

ATHANASIUS: It's like a rule of faith only it's very formal, official, and binding. Everything that a person must believe to be a Christian will be in it.

ARIUS: Somehow I doubt that. If things keep going the way you say and I hear, that creed will suppress the truth about the Logos, the Word of God, who became Jesus Christ.

REPORTER: Good, good. That's juicy. Say more, Arius. What is this "truth" of which you speak?

ARIUS: Well, as I've been arguing for years now, the Son of God, also known as the Logos, or Word, became human in Jesus Christ through the Virgin Mary. The very fact that he was begotten proves that he is not God as the Father is God. The Father is eternal God; the Son is his reflection, the first and greatest creature God ever made. To be "born" implies being "made." So obviously the Son of God was made at some time in the past.

ATHANASIUS: That's blasphemy. To call the Son of God a creature! How could a creature save us? How could a creature be the true mediator between humanity and God? And how was the Father "Father" before he created the Word? And if he became Father, then he changed, and we all know that God cannot change. The "birth" of the Son of God must be eternal: he was eternally begotten of the Father.

ARIUS: That doesn't even make sense, Athanasius. Think about it. How can he be the "firstborn among many sons," as Paul says in his Letter to the Romans, if he were eternal God and equal with the Father? And how can the Son be our example for life if he were God? He would have too great an advantage over us: we would be unable to imitate him. Surely he was a creature who conquered temptation even though he could have given in to it. If he were God, he couldn't really be tempted. But he was tempted. And if he were God, being sinless would not be an achievement but a given. If all that is true, then he's no example for us.

ATHANASIUS: You and your supporters, such as Bishop Eusebius of Nicomedia, claim to use the Bible to support your heresy. But as our fathers in the faith knew, the Bible really belongs to those who believe. We who hold fast to the rule of faith as given by the apostles and as handed down to us have the exclusive right to interpret the Bible. And the rule of faith has always affirmed the deity of the Son, who became Jesus through the incarnation.

ARIUS: Not so fast, little deacon. The fathers' rules of faith were not as clear about that matter as you pretend. Think about our great Alexandrian hero Origen. He subordinated the Son to the Father. And he was steeped in the written Word, including the apostles' writings. Origen knew that if the Son is equal with the Father in every dignity, then we have two Gods and God can change. Or we have one divine person with three manifestations. That's what the heretic Sabellius taught: that the Son of God and the Father and the Spirit are but manifestations of the one, hidden God. You see, if you equate the Son with the Father as to their deity, then they are the same "stuff," the same substance. If so, then they are identical. The distinction between the Father and the Son is then collapsed.

ATHANASIUS: That's your and your supporters' big argument, isn't it? I heard Bishop Eusebius saying something like that inside the council chamber. He was arguing with another bishop during a break in the proceedings, and he said that if the council affirms the equality of the Son with the Father, then the heresy of modalism will prevail. We don't agree. Christians have always believed that God is one being of glory and to be worshiped as one, but at the same time there are three who make up that one divine being: Father, Son, and Spirit. The Son proceeds from the Father eternally, and the Spirit is breathed out from the Father eternally.

REPORTER: Well, you'll have to admit, Athanasius, that's rather hard to grasp. Arius's doctrine is easier to understand.

ATHANASIUS: Heresy is always simple; truth is always complex. The very simplicity of Arius's heresy betrays it. The great mystery of the three-in-oneness of God is exploded for the sake of creating a reasonable picture of the Godhead. The trouble is that in this view there is no "Godhead." If Arius is right, as he surely is not, only the Father is truly God, and the Son and Spirit are creatures. That cuts the heart right out of the gospel, which depends on the Son being Savior, which depends on him being both truly human and truly divine.

ARIUS: Now there's a paradox for you. No, let's actually call it what it is: a sheer contradiction! You are asking reasonable people to believe the impossible. How can one being be three beings? Or are you tossing away monotheism in favor of a committee of three gods?

ATHANASIUS: You simpleton! Of course not. We orthodox Christians have always maintained that the Godhead is a mystery and that we must simply confess both the oneness and the threeness of God. But it isn't a contradiction.

REPORTER: How not? It sounds like one to me!

ATHANASIUS: Okay, well, I'm going to let you both in on a little secret. "Off the record," Mr. Reporter!

REPORTER *(putting down his pen and notebook)*: Okay, I guess. Although I'd sure like to share it with our readers.

ATHANASIUS: Well, that's not possible right now. Bishop Alexander and I have been conferring together, and we have come up with a term to describe the relationship of the Son with the Father: *homoousion*.

REPORTER: *Homo* what?

ATHANASIUS: You speak Greek. Figure it out.

ARIUS: It means "of the same substance."

ATHANASIUS: Right. That's what we hope to put into the new creed that will be known throughout the ages as the Nicene Creed or the Formula of Nicaea. It will say that the Son is *homoousios* with the Father and with us—both truly God and truly man.

REPORTER: Okay, I get it. They are exactly the same thing.

ARIUS: There! That's the problem with your new formula, Athanasius. People will think you're saying that the Son and the Father, and by extension the Holy Spirit, are one and the same in every way.

ATHANASIUS: That's what we want it to say, and that's what we hope they'll think it means because that's the truth.

ARIUS: I predict that if you use that word, even if most of the bishops sign it with Constantine sitting right there threatening them if they don't, later there will be hell to pay. People will eventually realize that the council made a heresy to be orthodox!

ATHANASIUS: What heresy?

ARIUS: Modalism, for sure. The heresy of Sabellius and Praxeas. It says that Father and Son and Spirit are but masks worn by the one person: God.

ATHANASIUS: But that's not at all what our formula means! It just means that Father and Son are equal in every way.

ARIUS: But they can't be equal in every way without being the same thing.

ATHANASIUS: They are the same "thing" if by "thing" you mean "substance."

ARIUS: What else could I mean? Thing. Substance. Whatever. *Homoousion* automatically implies sameness in every respect.

ATHANASIUS: No, it doesn't. It means equality as to being. But we are saying that three distinct persons—*hypostaseis* might be the right word here—share equally the divine nature.

ARIUS: So how are they different?

ATHANASIUS: They're not different. They are distinct without difference.

REPORTER: I have to admit that I'm confused. So will my readers be confused.

ATHANASIUS: Remember—you're not supposed to reveal this yet. It's far from a done deal.

ARIUS: You and your bishop and all the others who agree with you are making a mockery of Christianity. People will ridicule that belief in the Godhead. It's full of confusion.

ATHANASIUS: No, your view that the Son is not equal with the Father is full of confusion. But tell me, what term would you prefer?

ARIUS: Hmmm. Perhaps *homoiousion*? "Similar" or "of like substance"?

ATHANASIUS: Yikes! That would say that the Son is not God, that he is not divine.

ARIUS: You still don't get it, deacon. I am not saying that the Son is not divine. He is the first and greatest creation of God and therefore shares in God's own glory. You believe that through Jesus Christ we will all participate in the divine glory, don't you? "Deification," remember? I heard you give a Bible study in Alexandria where you argued that the Son became human so that we might become gods.

ATHANASIUS: Right. But how can we become partakers of the divine nature if the incarnate one with whom we are united by faith through the sacraments is not divine himself? The whole idea of the great exchange, that

God became human so that human might become God, depends on the incarnate one, the Son of God, himself being God.

ARIUS: But if he is God, then he cannot be truly one of us. How can he communicate God's nature to us if he's not one of us? And we know by definition that God cannot suffer. Yet Jesus, the Son, suffered.

ATHANASIUS: I agree that God cannot suffer; that would be improper for the divine. However, that's why Jesus had to be both God and man—so that he could shine in his glory by his divine nature and suffer in weakness in his human nature.

ARIUS: Oh, no! Another mystery that's really a contradiction!

ATHANASIUS: There's no contradiction in the mystery of Christ's two natures. He was one person, the divine Son of God, taking on a human form, clothing himself with flesh, using the body as his instrument.

ARIUS: Well, I agree, except that he wasn't and isn't God himself. He's a divine being, a great heavenly being. But a creature nevertheless.

ATHANASIUS: That is not what the fathers taught us. Go back and read them. They all affirmed the deity of the Son of God.

ARIUS: So do I, deacon. Are you simpleminded or what?

ATHANASIUS: Not at all, ex-presbyter. You have a problem with mystery. You want to rationalize the faith, and you do so only by destroying its central mystery—the incarnation of God. I'm already creating the outline of a book I hope to write someday. The title will be *De incarnatione, On the Incarnation.*

REPORTER: Could I have a peek at that outline?

ATHANASIUS: No, you won't see any of it until it's published.

REPORTER: Rats.

ARIUS: Go ahead and publish it, Athanasius. It will expose your theology for what it is: gobbledygook, nonsense. What you call "mystery" is really just that—nonsense.

ATHANASIUS: Well, I hear the signal that the council is about to reconvene. I'd better go take notes on the proceedings for my bishop. I can't wait to see what's going to happen next. Watch. I'll bet *homoousion* will be written into a creed and everyone will be made to sign it. Arius, you will then be expelled from the church and forced into exile, along with the bishops who support you.

REPORTER: This has been just fascinating. But I'm not sure what to write. I don't think our average reader can swim in these deep theological waters!

Analysis

In this conversation Arius expresses his frustration over the orthodox doctrine of the Trinity being carved out in the council. Several of the 318 bishops agreed with him and thought that equality of being between Father, Son, and Holy

Spirit implied strict identity. To Athanasius, Alexander, and the majority, however, it did not. The council did affirm that the Son of God is *homoousios* with the Father, of the same substance. It preserved the distinctiveness of the three persons by referring to their relationships of origin. The Father is ungenerate, unbegotten. The Son is eternally generated or begotten by the Father. The Spirit proceeds eternally from the Father.

Although the council did not write this into its creed, the bishops who signed the creed were probably thinking of an analogy of the sun and its rays and its heat. This would be used later to explain the equality of being and distinctness of relations of the three persons. The sun is the source of its rays and its heat, but there never was a time when the sun existed without its rays and its heat. The rays and heat of the sun have always gone forth from the sun even as they are not the sun itself. All three, however, are of the same "stuff." So the Son and the Spirit are eternally going forth from their source, the Father. The Father is the "fount of divinity." The council clearly was affirming the monarchy of the Father. But the Son and Spirit share in the Father's divinity by nature. Through salvation we will share it in by grace.

So how exactly are the Son and the Spirit different from the Father? How does this affirmation of their equality of being not equal modalism? After the council, that question would plague the church. Many bishops came to believe that they had unwittingly made modalism to be orthodox! But Athanasius persisted in showing them that such is not the case. Later his friends, the three Cappadocian fathers—Basil the Great, Gregory of Nyssa, and Gregory of Nazianzus—would tidy up the matter with a clear distinction between *ousia*, or substance, and *hypostasis*, or subsistence (which is translated into English as "person"). The fathers of the council, however, made clear that the Father, Son, and Holy Spirit are *not* different, which would imply over-againstness. They exist eternally as one divine being and community without any separation or division. But within that perfect unity are distinctions without difference. The Father does not go forth from anyone. The Son is born of the Father and is therefore dependent on the Father. The Spirit is a spiration, proceeding from the Father, and is therefore also dependent on the Father, but in a different way.

Astute readers will notice that current Western forms of the Nicene Creed say that the Spirit proceeds from the Father *and the Son*. That's a whole other controversy. Suffice it to say now that the Nicene Council did not include that phrase in its creed. It crept in later, much to the dismay of the Eastern churches. Only Latin versions of the creed include *filioque* (and the Son).

The outcome of the council was that Arius was condemned as a heretic. The two bishops who refused to sign the new creed were also banished. All but two signed it, even if some had qualms about it. The resulting creed is what we today know as the Creed of Nicaea, or the Nicene Creed, although the "third article" on the Holy Spirit was added later at the Council of Constantinople in 381. It is technically, then, the Niceno-Constantinopolitan Creed. But who can say all that?

So in effect the Council of Nicaea made official and binding a doctrine of the Trinity that had been presupposed by many Christians since the earliest church fathers. The Latin church father Tertullian had already spelled it out rather clearly in Latin: *una substantia, tres personae*, "one substance, three persons." But many Eastern Christians (and more than half the bishops at Nicaea were Eastern) did not read Latin. Tertullian's formula was largely forgotten. It may have been ignored in part because he joined the New Prophecy church and therefore was widely considered less than a paragon of orthodoxy.

So how can we understand the trinitarian doctrine of the Council of Nicaea and its creed today? A preliminary question might be whether such a council should ever have taken place and whether such a creed should ever have been written. Certainly some Christians have qualms about a ruler such as Constantine convening and directing a meeting of Christian bishops. But it is easier to question it than to explain how it could have happened otherwise. How could this controversy, spreading like wildfire throughout the churches, be settled in any other way? If it weren't for Bishop Alexander, Emperor Constantine, and Deacon Athanasius, we might all be Arians today! And what difference would that make in our faith?

The doctrine of the Trinity might seem abstract and mysterious, but it all centers around the issue of the relationship of the Son of God, Jesus Christ, to God the Father. Are they one? In what sense? Is Jesus divine? How so? The council chose the Greek compound word *homoousion* to answer these questions. It's not a biblical term, but it expresses concisely what the Bible says about Jesus Christ. For example, Jesus went around forgiving people's sins. Who can forgive sins but God? He didn't say, "On God's behalf I forgive you." On many occasions he simply declared, "Your sins are forgiven." That was implicitly a claim to deity. It was either true or blasphemous or the claim of a madman.

Today many people who call themselves Christians express doubts about the deity of Jesus Christ or just outright deny it. Are they, then, Christians? The World Council of Churches requires member organizations to affirm one thing in order to belong: Jesus Christ is God and Savior. It's the church's one universal, binding affirmation across the centuries. Why? Because, as Athanasius never tired of arguing, if Jesus is not God incarnate, our sins are not forgiven, and we are not united with God. What is at stake, then, is salvation.

The Arians and later semi-Arians viewed salvation primarily as a human achievement. That's why they didn't need a divine savior. Jesus was seen as our example of how to live a life pleasing to God. If he couldn't have failed, then he wasn't much of an example for us. One could easily argue against that point, but more importantly for this context, we should note that salvation is not a human achievement but a gift of God's grace and a work of God within us on account of our faith. Without Christ as God, that gift does not seem to be possible. The law proved to be a failure. So God came among us and not only showed us a way but also made that way possible by uniting us with God in his own person and dying to pay the penalty for our sins. (By the way, Athanasius clearly believed in the substitutionary theory of the atonement.)

The Trinity, and especially the deity of Jesus Christ, is no arcane subject without relevance to today. At least not if we understand salvation the way Christians have always understood it, going back to the earliest church fathers. And if Jesus is divine, then there must be more than one "person" (the word has its problems but seems to be unavoidable) in God. "God," then, is a term for either the one divine nature or, perhaps better, the divine community of Father, Son, and Holy Spirit. As a divine community of love, the three persons of God demonstrate to us that all of life is about community; the very image of God within us is a call to live in community even as Father, Son, and Spirit live eternally in community with each other.

Unfortunately, the controversy over the deity of Christ and over the Trinity did not end with the Council of Nicaea. Soon afterward, Emperor Constantine decided that the council had made a mistake and called for subtle but important changes in the creed. Athanasius became bishop of Alexandria and fought hard against the emperor's changes. He suffered five exiles, during which his people held that bishop's position open. Athanasius died not long before the final resolution of the conflict at the Council of Constantinople (381). His friends, the three Cappadocian fathers—Basil, Gregory, and Gregory—carried on his work and greatly influenced the outcome of that second ecumenical council.

For Further Reading

Anatolios, Khaled. *Athanasius*. Oxford: Routledge, 2004.

Pettersen, Alvyn. *Athanasius*. Harrisburg, PA: Morehouse, 1995.

Williams, Rowan. *Arius: Heresy and Tradition*. Grand Rapids: Eerdmans, 2002.

7

The Fourth-Century Cappadocian Fathers Meet to Settle on the Orthodox Doctrine of the Trinity

Setting

Unlike many of the imaginary conversations in this book, this one could have taken place. The three participants knew one another and were quite close. Two of them were even brothers, Basil the Great and Gregory of Nyssa, and Gregory of Nazianzus was their friend. Basil is now called "the Great," though that wasn't his title during his lifetime. He is also known in church history as Basil of Caesarea because he was bishop of that city in Asia Minor. (There were several Caesareas in the Roman Empire; this one is not to be confused with Caesarea in Palestine.)

Basil's younger brother Gregory was bishop of Nyssa, and their friend Gregory was from Nazianzus but for a while served later as bishop of Constantinople, the "new Rome." But that didn't work out for him. These three are called the Cappadocian fathers because they lived and worked in Cappadocia, a central region of Asia Minor, in what is now called Turkey. Athanasius of Alexandria was also their friend, but he died before this imaginary meeting.

These three friends lived through the most heated controversy in early Christian history, the semi-Arian controversy of the fourth century. This was a continuation of the trinitarian controversy that began in Alexandria and was supposed to end with the Council of Nicaea in 325. It did not end there. Emperor Constantine, who considered himself a Christian, vacillated back and forth about the wording of the Nicene Creed. For much of his reign he favored what has come to be called semi-Arianism.

The semi-Arians picked up where Arius left off. Arius (see conversation 6) taught that there was a time when the Son of God did not exist and that he was God's first and greatest creature. In effect, this amounted to a denial of the Son's deity, demoting Jesus Christ to the incarnation of a great heavenly being but not of God. The Council of Nicaea condemned this view and wrote a creed affirming that the Son of God is and always has been *homoousios* with the Father, "of the same substance." After the council, however, Constantine regretted that word and ordered that Arius be reinstated as presbyter in Alexandria. Arius died not long after that.

Athanasius (see conversation 6) became bishop of Alexandria and fought hard to keep the word *homoousion* in the Nicene Creed. But Constantine and then his son Constantius championed an alleged compromise term, *homoiousion*, which means "of a like or similar substance." This pleased a number of Christian bishops who thought the first term mistakenly denied any distinction at all between the Father and the Son. These so-called semi-Arians pressed hard for *homoiousion*, and a decades-long controversy ensued.

The semi-Arians wanted to affirm a very close relationship between the Father and Son so that the Son, who became incarnate as Jesus Christ, could be worshiped as God. However, as Athanasius never tired of pointing out, if he is just of a like or similar substance as the Father, he is not quite God. The semi-Arians wanted to say that the Son, Jesus Christ, is "God too." But Athanasius and then his friends the Cappadocian fathers pointed out that this also amounted to him being "God two," and there cannot be two Gods. (For the scholars who might be reading this, I should say that I'm making up some terms here to explain the nature of this controversy. The semi-Arians and Cappadocians never said exactly "God too" or "God two," but this is a helpful way to explain what they were saying.) They turned the tables on the semi-Arians, who said that affirming the deity of Christ would amount to polytheism, belief in more than one God. Athanasius and the Cappadocians responded that the semi-Arian position amounted to polytheism. And so the argument went on.

The three Cappadocian fathers were amazingly productive and brilliant scholars. They received the best educations possible in their time. Basil and Gregory were tutored by their sister Macrina, who was apparently a very intelligent and educated contemplative Christian. Gregory of Nyssa is widely considered to be the greatest genius of the early church. He was also steeped in Platonic philosophy, which he put to use in his explanations of Christian theology.

Basil the Great (ca. 330–379) wrote many books; among them is his treatise on *The Holy Spirit*, the first entire book on that subject by a Christian author. It played a crucial role in the development of the third article, about the Holy Spirit, added to the Nicene Creed by the Council of Constantinople in 381. There Basil argued against a group of heretics called the Spirit-fighters (or Fighters against the Spirit) that the Holy Spirit is a third distinct person (*hypostasis*) of the Godhead, equal with the Father and the Son.

Gregory of Nyssa (ca. 335–394) wrote many treatises, including *On Not Three Gods*, also known as *To Ablabius* (the recipient). There he explained how it is possible for one being to be three persons and vice versa, using many analogies drawn from nature and history.

Gregory of Nazianzus (329–389) also wrote many books; one that stands out as especially important for our purposes here is his *Five Theological Orations*, in which he criticized the lingering Arianism of some priests in Constantinople and other places and argued for the full-bodied doctrine of the Trinity, which would eventually win the day at the Council of Constantinople over which he presided.

The Cappadocian fathers are not well known among Protestants. That's a shame. They played key roles in the final triumph of the orthodox, which is to say biblical, doctrine of the Trinity. They put their devoted minds to work in the service of truth and fought long and hard against the heresies that would destroy belief in the Trinity. History, especially in the Eastern Orthodox family of churches, has honored Basil with the title "the Great." Gregory of Nazianzus is known as "The Theologian."

Gregory of Nyssa is generally considered to be the brightest of the three Cappadocian lights. His intellect was almost without peer in his time. And he contributed significantly to the development and preservation of orthodoxy. However, because he believed, like Origen before him (see conversation 4) in *apokatastasis*, or ultimate reconciliation (universalism), history has neglected to bestow honorific titles on him.

This imaginary conversation is set in the imperial city Constantinople in 379, just two years before the great Council of Constantinople is to convene. The trinitarian emperor Theodosius has just come to the throne of the empire. Basil will die this year, but he doesn't know that yet.

The Conversation

GREGORY OF NAZIANZUS *(below,* **NAZIANZEN**): Dear Friend Basil! It's so good to see you. Thanks for coming such a distance from Caesarea to my humble little villa here in the capital city. As you can see, I've turned it into a chapel I call Anastasia, Resurrection, the place where the faith will be revived. I preach here often. A few years ago, as you know, a group of Arian priests invaded this place while I was preaching and tried to kill me. A visiting bishop died in the riot, but I am now nicely recovered from my wounds.

BASIL THE GREAT *(below,* **BASIL**): It's good to see you well, my friend. I was afraid you would die after that terrible ordeal. But that can't happen again, thank God. Now that our beloved emperor Theodosius is present here in the capital, our victory is assured. The Arian priests are already on the run or going into hiding.

GREGORY OF NYSSA *(below,* **NYSSEN***)*: Brother Basil and Friend Gregory, how good it is to be here with you. I plan to stay here in Constantinople until and through the great council our emperor has promised to call. We three should work shoulder to shoulder to make sure that the council reaffirms our trinitarian faith and adds the article on the Spirit to the creed.

NAZIANZEN: Okay, so we'd better get down to work. First, let's pray. "Father, Son, and Spirit, most holy Three-in-One, we beseech you for your help in this most difficult task. Our enemies have been strong, but you are proving your great power by putting them finally to flight. Give us the light of your created energies to transform and elevate our minds to understand and explain you better than ever before. May we be deified into the image of your human Son Jesus and, like him, become partakers in your own nature by your grace and mercy. Amen."

Basil, you've done a great job of championing the cause of the Holy Spirit against the Pneumatomachians, those wicked fighters against the Spirit. I've put in my two cents' worth on this subject too. What's our best approach to this whole matter of defending the Trinity?

BASIL: I think analogies really help to convince the majority of people who are easily confused. They need something concrete to hang on to. Their minds don't work well with abstract concepts. Abstractions are good for the educated but not much help for the untutored. They need word pictures.

NYSSEN: Yes, we've all used word pictures in our writings. Let's decide what some of the best ones are.

NAZIANZEN: First, let's make sure we're all on the same page about the abstract concepts we're promoting. We've agreed before that we'll stick together on this, haven't we? Here they are: *ousia* to describe the oneness of God, and *hypostasis* to describe each of the three who are God. Isn't that right? So, if I'm not mistaken, our formula is "one *ousia*, three *hypostaseis*."

BASIL: Right. In spite of all the problems, it's the best we can do. There will never be perfect terms for God.

NYSSEN: I agree. As I've stressed in my writings for many years now, God is ineffable and incomprehensible in his nature. The human mind cannot grasp the infinite. God in himself is beyond knowing. But we can't be silent; we have to use the best concepts and words our philosophy and language give us to say, concisely and precisely, what revelation tells us about God. With all their inadequacies, *ousia* and *hypostasis* are the best we have.

NAZIANZEN: Good. Then we're agreed. But we have to be prepared for the inevitable questions. For example, what Latin term translates our use of *ousia*? Latin-speaking people translate it in different ways, and some of them aren't helpful to our cause. And *hypostasis*. Now there's a difficult one because to Latins who are reading Greek and translating it, *hypos-*

tasis can be a synonym for *ousia*. So to them, we're saying God is "one substance and three substances." We don't want to appear to be talking nonsense.

BASIL: Well, there's no avoiding some ambiguity. We'll just have to surround our terminology with lots of explanation and especially word pictures to illustrate what we mean and clarify what we don't mean.

NYSSEN: Right, brother. So to our Latin-speaking friends, we'll send letters explaining that in Greek, at least in our use of these terms, they don't necessarily mean what they seem to mean to them. Thus *ousia* doesn't mean a physical substance or individual thing. In our use of it, it means any nature or essence that can be shared by several individuals. Like human nature. Several humans share the *ousia* of humanity. And *hypostasis* doesn't mean substance in this case. It means an individual instance, an instantiation, of a substance. It means a subsistence. The Latins should translate it *persona*, "person," even though that too has its problems.

NAZIANZEN: Wouldn't it be nice if we didn't have to go so deep into this and didn't have to use extrabiblical language?

BASIL: That's not our fault, friend. It's the fault of the heretics who have forced this on us by twisting the simple words of Scripture. Our words may be extrabiblical, but they're not unbiblical. They express in other words what Scripture clearly means when it talks about one God and yet ascribes deity to the Son and to the Spirit.

NYSSEN: I think philosophy is a great tool of theology. We shouldn't be at all apologetic about borrowing from it. But we need to make clear our distinctively Christian use of philosophical concepts. We take what is pagan and baptize it as Christian. In the process it becomes transformed.

NAZIANZEN: That's a good way to put it. Let's hope that those looking to us for leadership in developing and defending orthodoxy see it our way. Some of them are quite opposed to using abstract philosophical concepts in theology.

BASIL: Okay, let's get back to our terminology and then to our word pictures. We're agreed, then, that we'll tell the next council that they can safely reaffirm the *homoousion*, that the Son is one substance with the Father, because in this case, if not always, *ousia* means not strict identity but shared nature or essence. It is compatible with individuation. Then, although we don't want to add anything to the creed except the article on the Holy Spirit, we'll explain to the bishops and theologians and to the emperor that in this case *hypostasis* means not substance but an individual example of a substance, and that *persona* is a somewhat adequate translation of that into Latin.

NYSSEN: And let's explain that we say "three persons" not because we want to but because there's no alternative. Let's be sure to stress the oneness of the three so that we don't accidentally imply polytheism.

NAZIANZEN: Perhaps the concept of *perichōrēsis* can help with that. We'll explain that it means coinherence, more than one thing indwelling something else. "Perichoresis" also implies interdependence. The three persons of God inhere in one another and are mutually interdependent. Their life is one and not three. And yet they are three distinct identities.

BASIL: But we must be careful about saying things like "three distinct identities." We don't want to be interpreted as affirming tritheism!

NYSSEN: Nor do we want to be misunderstood as affirming modalism. That could easily happen if we go too far in emphasizing the oneness of the three, whatever they are.

NAZIANZEN: "Whatever they are"? We really are struggling with the right term for the three, aren't we? Should we just stick with *hypostasis* and let the chips fall where they may, but explain what we mean as well as we can?

BASIL: I agree. Let's be careful not to slide in either direction. We could easily overemphasize the oneness too much or the threeness too much. Both are equally important. But let's also remember that divine revelation, especially the writings of the apostles, begins with the three and not the one. We actually know and experience Father, Son, and Holy Spirit. We don't experience and we can't really know the one essence that binds them. And yet we know that it does hold them together.

NYSSEN (*somewhat sarcastically*): Now we've got all that straightened out and glued together! You know, it would be much easier just to be a heretic.

NAZIANZEN: Certainly. That's one thing that marks an idea about God as heresy: it's too easy. We should expect words about God to be complicated and inadequate. We're trying to talk about something—I mean someone—who is beyond knowing.

NYSSEN: Then maybe it would be best if we were just silent.

BASIL: Little brother, you've always had a mystical bent, haven't you?

NAZIANZEN: We have to keep going even if we feel a little uncomfortable about it. The only alternatives are silence, which won't work for the churches, and heresy. So what word pictures most helpfully illustrate our formula "one *ousia* and three *hypostaseis*"?

BASIL: We've all made some use of the analogy of the sun and its emanations or rays and its warmth. There's one substance, that of the sun, but three distinct entities that are inseparably united.

NYSSEN: Does that illustrate the threeness adequately? What about the illustration of the first three people: Adam, Eve, and Seth? Or of three disciples: Peter, James, and John? You've used that too, Brother Basil. In each case we see one substance—humanity—and three distinct persons.

NAZIANZEN: Well, isn't that a little too close to tritheism, belief in three gods? We don't want people to have that picture in their minds when someone says "Trinity."

BASIL: Then what about your illustration of a pile of gold coins, little brother? Imagine a pile of gold coins and think of it as all one substance, gold, but at the same time several instances of the same thing, coins. Likewise, the Trinity is one deity composed of three entities that share it equally.

NYSSEN: Thanks, brother. I do like that illustration. I learned it from our sister Macrina. She's so talented at theology. I wish she weren't a woman so she could join us in this endeavor. Macrina would outshine us all! But, alas, she prefers the contemplative life of a nun.

NAZIANZEN: Your sister is amazing, fellows. Perhaps someday women like her will be able to write theology and speak in public about God. We'd all be better off if that day were now.

BASIL: Yes, but she speaks through us. Both of us learned so much from her, and we continue to learn. She is our primary human teacher. Macrina should really get as much credit for our thoughts as we get.

NYSSEN *(incredulously)*: Credit? Credit? You expect us to get credit? Hah! More likely we'll be chased away from Constantinople with sticks and stones. People are going to say, "You confuse us too much!"

NAZIANZEN: But the emperor is on our side. He'll protect us. Eventually we'll be able to convince the average priests and laypeople. But you're right, Friend Gregory, the laypeople and the priests of Constantinople are all worked up about this matter of the Trinity. At least they're interested in theology! The other day I went to take a bath in the city, and the person who handed me a towel said, "The Son is not equal with the Father." And I don't think he even recognized me!

BASIL: And as I came through the city to this place, I stopped to buy a loaf of bread, and the baker said, "The Father is not greater than the Son." I've never encountered such popular interest in a subtle theological issue before.

NYSSEN: But most of them don't know what they're talking about.

NAZIANZEN *(wryly)*: Do we?

NYSSEN: I guess not, really. Except when we say what God is not. I call such talk apophatic theology: our best language about God is negative, saying what God is not. God is not finite, so he's infinite. God is not capable of suffering, so he is impassible. And so forth.

BASIL: But what about God's omnipotence and omniscience? Surely we can say that he is all-powerful and all-knowing, right?

NAZIANZEN: We're drifting off the subject now, aren't we? Let's get back to it. You two brothers can argue about negative theology later.

NYSSEN: Okay, but I do have answers for my brother's jibes. And I know he isn't serious; he agrees with me. He's just parroting what our critics say.

BASIL: Well, I almost agree with you. But I think you take this negative-theology style a little too far. But we can talk about it later. Right now let's get back to the Trinity.

NAZIANZEN: So what about those analogies? Are they really helpful in communicating the Trinity to the masses?

NYSSEN: What else do we have? We must use them, but we must also explain
that they are simply analogies and not descriptions of God's inner life.
All they say is how one thing can be three things, and how three things
can be one thing. Yet "thing" isn't quite the right word.

BASIL: Right. We need to stick to *ousia* and *hypostasis*. Please. God isn't a
"thing." Such language implies that he is an object. We know better. God
is beyond all that. He's not a thing in the cosmos; he's the living source
of all life and dwells in everything. An object is something determined by
other things; God determines himself.

NAZIANZEN: So let's strategize. What comes next? I'm a little nervous about the
upcoming council even though I'm confident of the emperor's support.
I've been told that I'm going to chair the council. That really scares me.
I'm not cut out for politics and such.

NYSSEN: Hang in there, friend. You'll do fine, and we'll be there to support
you.

Analysis

One of the most ingenious and controversial breakthroughs in the history of
Christian theology is the Cappadocian fathers' distinction between *ousia* and *hypostasis* to express the oneness and threeness of the Trinity. These are Greek words
with fairly broad semantic ranges; they can mean a number of different things.
The Cappadocians make clear, however, that for them *ousia* means substance
and *hypostasis* means subsistence: an individual instantiation of a substance. We
translate *hypostasis* as person in English. But that can be a bit misleading.

The common English phrase for the Trinity is "one substance, three persons."
But a careful reading of the Cappadocians and other church fathers makes it
clear that by *hypostasis* they did not mean what we modern Americans (and
many others) mean by "person." In our modern to postmodern American culture, a person is a differentiated self: a center of consciousness and will set over
against others. That automatically makes people think of a committee when
they hear "three persons." But the Cappadocians would not like a committee
analogy. Committees, as we all know, come together to hash things out and
come to compromises. Most of the time they're no fun to serve on.

The Trinity is no committee of three with the Father as the chairperson and
the Son and Spirit as his subordinates. But neither is it one person with three
masks or outward manifestations. That was the tightrope the Cappadocian
fathers gingerly walked as they worked hard to clarify the doctrine of the Trinity
in preparation for the Council of Constantinople.

Their writings and teachings set the stage for the council. Emperor Theodosius, who succeeded an Arian emperor, favored the Cappadocians' ideas and

appointed Gregory of Nazianzus as chairman of the meeting, knowing full well what he wanted to happen. Theodosius was not a nice emperor. Once he had seven thousand Greeks killed because they were in open rebellion against him. They were lured into an arena to watch a sporting event at Thessalonica, and then Theodosius's troops slaughtered them mercilessly. The influential Bishop Ambrose of Milan, where Theodosius was staying for a few months, barred him from communion until he publicly repented, which he did. But in spite of his questionable faith and character, the emperor did champion the Nicene and orthodox doctrine; he finally routed the Arians and semi-Arians with their *homoiousios* idea.

The Council of Constantinople convened in 381 minus Basil the Great, who died in 379. It affirmed the original Nicene Creed with *homoousion* (of the same substance) to describe the relationship of the Son to the Father, and it added the "third article" to the creed, about the Holy Spirit. Thus was the doctrine of the Trinity complete and made official. Theodosius decreed that bishops and other church leaders who would not abide by it were to be removed from their leadership positions. Arianism and semi-Arianism were all but dead in the Roman Empire. However, they thrived among the so-called barbarian tribes to the north. When the barbarians overthrew the Western Empire and took over Rome, they gradually converted to orthodox Christianity.

The Nicene Creed (officially the Niceno-Constantinopolitan Creed) became the official Christian statement of faith expressing what must be believed by all Christians. It has remained the de facto worldwide Christian statement of faith for more than a millennium. The Apostles' Creed, of unknown origin, is usually viewed as a skeletal version of the Nicene Creed. Or one could say that the Nicene Creed is the fleshed-out version of the Apostles' Creed.

This was not all that the Cappadocian fathers accomplished. But it is without doubt their main accomplishment and contribution to Christianity. One example of another contribution is Gregory of Nazianzus's exposure of a Christian teacher named Apollinaris as a heretic. Apollinaris resided at Constantinople and taught Christians there that Jesus Christ is the incarnation of the eternal and divine Word of God, God's Son and equal with the Father, but not fully human. He believed that the person of the Logos, Word, Son of God, took the place of the rational soul (or mind) in Jesus Christ. So Jesus Christ had a human body, a human soul, but not a human rational soul or mind. His rational soul, mind, or *psyche* was divine and not at all human. Reasons for this will become clear in conversation 8.

Gregory of Nazianzus responded by declaring, "What the Son has not assumed is not saved." In other words, if the Son of God did not take on a human rational soul in the incarnation, that part of humanity is not being renewed. For him, as for all Eastern Christians, the incarnation itself is salvific. It includes the cross and resurrection, but they do not exhaust the incarnation. Simply by virtue of taking on a human nature, the Son of God infused humanity with grace such that all who embrace him by faith begin to be transformed by deification.

So if the Son of God did not take on one part of humanity, that part cannot be transformed by the incarnation.

Gregory of Nazianzus fought brilliantly and effectively against this simplistic heresy. One modern wag has called it the "God-in-a-bod heresy." Today we might look to Luke 2:52: Jesus grew in wisdom and stature and favor with God and humans. How can a person who does not have a human mind grow in wisdom? Another way of asking it: how can a divine mind grow in wisdom? Apparently for a number of reasons, then, it is important to believe that Jesus Christ was and is a whole human and not just partly human.

For Further Reading

Meredith, Anthony. *The Cappadocians.* Crestwood, NY: St. Vladimir's Seminary Press, 1995.

Payne, Robert. *Holy Fire: The Story of the Fathers of the Eastern Church.* Crestwood, NY: St. Vladimir's Seminary Press, 1957, 1997.

8

Prominent Fifth-Century Thinkers
Cyril, Apollinaris, Nestorius, and Eutyches
Discuss the Humanity and Divinity
of Jesus Christ

Setting

An actual meeting between these four important Christian thinkers would have been impossible. Apollinaris died in 390. The other three were roughly contemporary with one another, so a meeting among them was conceivable but unlikely. Followers of Apollinaris were in Constantinople when Cyril, Nestorius, and Eutyches were alive and active. So here I let Apollinaris be the voice of his followers, one of whom may well have met with the latter three if such a meeting took place.

In the first half of the fifth century, Constantinople was the capital of the much-reduced Roman Empire. Barbarian tribes from the north had invaded and conquered the western half of the empire, which included the city of Rome. Whoever was patriarch of Constantinople (like a superbishop) wielded great power and influence over the entire empire. Cities like Antioch and Alexandria envied Constantinople's wealth and power and vied for influence there. Each wanted someone from its own city, or at least associated with it, to be patriarch at the capital. Antioch and Alexandria were rivals even among Christians.

Antioch of Syria, where Jesus's followers were first called Christians, differed from Alexandria in many ways. In theology, Antioch adopted a more historical approach to biblical interpretation, and Alexandria stressed an allegorical approach. Antiochenes emphasized the humanity of Jesus Christ; Alexandrian Christians highlighted his deity. The comparisons oversimplify the situation, but as generalizations they have some validity.

Apollinaris (d. 390) was the bishop of Laodicea in Syria. Sometime before the Council of Constantinople, he proposed a solution to the puzzle of how one person could be both divine and human. With the orthodox party, including the Cappadocian fathers Basil and the two Gregories (see conversation 7), Apollinaris affirmed the true divinity and true humanity of Jesus Christ. He was an opponent of the Arians, who denied the divinity of Christ, and he was a trinitarian. However, during the last stages of the controversy over the Trinity, Apollinaris jumped to the task of trying to explain the humanity and divinity of Jesus Christ when most people were still debating whether Jesus was truly divine.

According to Apollinaris, humans are composed of three distinct parts: body, animal soul (life force?), and rational soul (mind?). He borrowed this tripartite view of the human person from the Platonists. The incarnation of God the Son in Jesus Christ was a replacement of the human rational soul with the Logos, who wielded the body of Jesus as an instrument. By no means, however, did the Logos, the Son of God, actually become human in the sense of living a true human life, including a natural human development. Apollinaris's reasons will be made clear in the conversation. His doctrine of Christ was condemned as heresy by the Council of Constantinople in 381.

Cyril (378–444) was the bishop of Alexandria in Egypt and definitely wanted influence in Constantinople. When his rival Nestorius, who represented the school of Antioch, was elevated to be patriarch of Constantinople, Cyril was furious. So their differences were not solely theological in nature; they were also political. But theology is our main concern here. Cyril believed in and taught the doctrine of the one nature of Jesus Christ, which was common in Alexandria. To most Alexandrians, if Jesus Christ is one person, he must also be of a single nature.

Antiochenes, including Nestorius (ca. 386–ca. 451), believed in the two natures of Jesus Christ. And following the same logic as the Alexandrians, if he is of two natures, he must be in some sense two persons. (Although the language "two persons" was rarely used, it was often implied by Antiochene theologians, as will be seen in the case of Nestorius.) When Nestorius became patriarch of Constantinople, much to Cyril's dismay, he preached that the people must stop calling Mary *Theotokos*, "God-bearer." After all, he argued, God cannot be born. He told them to call her *Christotokos*, "Christ-bearer," because the human nature of Jesus Christ can be born.

All of this debate arose out of legitimate theological concerns: to protect the one person of Jesus Christ (Alexandria), and to protect the distinction between divine and human natures (Antioch). The Alexandrians like Cyril feared that talk of two natures of Jesus Christ would lead to dividing him into two different persons, which would destroy the incarnation. The Antiochenes like

Nestorius feared that talk of one nature would lead to dissolution of Christ's humanity and to a diminishing of the transcendence of God, who cannot be born or die.

When Cyril heard about Nestorius's sermons against using *Theotokos* for Mary, he saw his opportunity not only to make a strong theological point but also to gain influence in Constantinople. He was convinced that Nestorius was a heretic who was denying the deity of Jesus Christ by dividing him into two persons: one human (Jesus) and the other divine (the Logos). He launched an all-out attack on Nestorius that led to him being deposed. By all accounts, Nestorius was not very adept at defending himself politically or theologically.

The ensuing controversy lasted for several decades. A council was called at Ephesus, which became the third ecumenical council in 431. The gathered bishops condemned Nestorius's teaching about the two natures of Jesus Christ because it was expressed in an extreme way that verged on dividing Christ into two persons. That will become apparent in the conversation that follows. In return for condemning Nestorius, however, which some bishops were reluctant to do, Cyril agreed to a formula that included language of "two natures" of Jesus Christ. He did it reluctantly and was later harshly criticized for it by some in his home city. It is almost certain that Cyril had his fingers crossed behind his back as he signed the Formula of Reunion two years after the council.

Once Nestorius was condemned and deposed from his church office, it seemed that the Alexandrians had won the debate—except that their champion Cyril had caved in to pressure to use the language of two natures when talking about the person of Jesus Christ and the incarnation of God in him. During the next two decades Cyril developed further his idea of the incarnation as a "hypostatic union," a union of two natures in one person. For him, the one person of Jesus Christ is the eternal Son of God, the divine Logos, the second person of the Trinity. Through Mary, he took on a human nature without a human person. The humanity of Jesus Christ was "attached," as it were, to the person and nature of God the Son. But it was and is a full human nature; it received its personification from the Son of God.

In Constantinople, meanwhile, a monk by the name of Eutyches (ca. 380–ca. 456) thought he was championing Cyril and the Alexandrian Christology when he declared that in Jesus Christ there is only one nature. For him, the human nature of Christ was swallowed up like a drop of wine in the ocean of his divinity. His critics regarded this as a denial of Christ's true humanity. Cyril died at the height of the controversy over Euytches, and a series of unfortunate political events followed that are embarrassing to recount. Christians acted badly on both sides of the debate. Finally a fourth ecumenical council was called to settle the argument over the makeup of the person of Jesus Christ. It met near Constantinople at Chalcedon in 451 and condemned both Nestorius (again) and Eutyches. Something like Cyril's hypostatic-union doctrine of Jesus Christ was adopted and enshrined in a Definition that would be regarded as an interpretation of the Nicene Creed rather than a new creed.

The Chalcedonian Definition of the person of Jesus Christ set up four fences to protect that doctrine. It said that in him were united two natures "without confusion, without change, without division, without separation." The first two "withouts" were against the Eutychians, who were judged to confuse the two natures of Christ and not keep them distinct. The bishops and theologians of Chalcedon viewed Eutyches's doctrine as presenting in Christ a hybrid of humanity and divinity. But divinity cannot change, so a hybrid is impossible. That model also contradicted Nicaea's doctrine of Christ as truly human and truly divine. For Eutyches and his followers, Christ was neither. The second two "withouts" were against the Nestorians and their sympathizers, who were judged to divide and separate the person of Christ by stressing too much the two natures as somehow in competition with each other.

This imaginary conversation includes all four of the main players in the christological controversy—Apollinaris (who was dead, but we'll pretend not), Cyril, Nestorius, and Eutyches. Cyril died in 444—about halfway between the Council of Ephesus (431) and the Council of Chalcedon (451). So our imaginary conversation will be set in Constantinople in 440. Nestorius has been deposed as patriarch, but he has sneaked back into the capital city to meet secretly with the other three. Cyril has come all the way from Alexandria to set the others straight. Eutyches thinks that he is a follower of Cyril except that he doesn't agree with the latter's signing of the Formula of Reunion, which included language of Christ's having two natures. Only Eutyches actually lives in Constantinople; the others are visiting. All hope to have some influence over the emperor, who will certainly call a new ecumenical council in a few years.

The Conversation

NESTORIUS: Well, well. Imagine the four of us meeting like this! How unlikely. I guess only an emperor could force us into one room to try to settle our differences about the incarnation and the person of our Savior Jesus Christ. I doubt that we'll come to any significant agreement, but we might as well try. I'm still hoping to be exonerated by another council of the bishops. That last one, in 431, was rough on me. I don't think I deserved the treatment I got, and it was largely your doing, Bishop Cyril.

CYRIL: I agree with you, Nestorius, that agreement among us is unlikely. After all, you're the one who started all this fuss by publicly forbidding the faithful from calling Mary *Theotokos*, "God-bearer." You can't go around messing with people's piety that way! Besides, theologically you were plain wrong; if you admit it and recant, maybe you can be restored to the priesthood yet. But never to the exalted office of patriarch that you once held. You should just publicly admit that Mary gave birth to God; to say otherwise—as you did and still do—is to deny the deity of Jesus Christ.

That issue was settled in the last century at the Councils of Nicaea and Constantinople.

NESTORIUS: No, you're wrong, Cyril. I didn't start this fuss. Our friend Apollinaris here did that. I was just trying to clear things up after he muddied the christological waters by claiming that Jesus Christ was half God and half man. I told the good Christian folks of Constantinople to stop referring to Mary as *Theotokos* because that title confuses people. It makes them think that God can be born. We all know better! God is immutable and impassible—as all of our ancestors in the faith well knew. God cannot be born. I told people to call Mary *Christotokos*, "Christ-bearer," because the man Jesus could be born, and he is called the Christ. But his divinity cannot be born.

APOLLINARIS: Wait a minute there, Nestorius. I was just trying to explain what our great church father Athanasius believed about the humanity and divinity of Jesus Christ. Haven't you read him lately? I wasn't inventing some new heresy, as you claim. People wanted to know how one person—Jesus Christ—could be both God and man, as the councils said. So I explained it to them. Jesus Christ was a human body and soul possessed of a divine mind, or rational soul, which was the Logos, the eternal Son of God.

That explains everything about the incarnation. It isn't really so mysterious after all. A body is subject to change and suffering; Jesus's body must have been human. But a mind or intellect is pure thought without change or emotion or decay. Jesus's mind was divine.

EUTYCHES: Excuse me, may I butt in here? You weren't really too far off, Apollinaris. Your only problem was in dividing the person of Jesus Christ into two distinct and separable parts. You made him sound like a "God in a bod!" My proposal also preserves his full and true divinity without dividing him up into parts. He was a hybrid of divine nature and human nature. We all know of hybrids in agriculture. You take two species and wed them so that the offspring are a new species—a "third something." A donkey is a hybrid of a mule and a horse. So Jesus Christ is a hybrid of God's own nature and our nature, yet truly one person.

CYRIL: Um, Eutyches, I hate to say this to such a devout monk as you, but I'm afraid you're a little feebleminded, at least when it comes to theology. I realize that you're just trying to correct Apollinaris and Nestorius; in their own ways, both divide the person of Christ. And I suppose you're trying to build on my own contribution to theology: the doctrine of the hypostatic union. But you should know that divinity and humanity cannot be mixed or mingled. Have you ever put water and oil into a jar and shaken them? What happens? They don't mix or mingle; they separate within the jar. The properties of one are incompatible with the properties of the other. So it is with human nature and divine nature. God is immutable and impassible; humans by nature are changeable and capable of suffering.

Just the other day I heard someone pressing you on this subject, and you said that Jesus's humanity was swallowed up like a drop of wine in the ocean of his deity. In the end, then, you have a partly divine, partly human person whose humanity is meaningless. It was a valiant try on your part, and I respect you for at least insisting on the one person of Jesus Christ against Nestorius and his followers. But I'm afraid your explanation is nearly as bad as his.

NESTORIUS: Now wait a minute! First of all, Apollinaris and I have nothing in common. He really does divide Jesus Christ—into three separable parts, only one of which is divine! His Jesus is not truly human or truly divine. Mine is both. So please don't lump us together. And Eutyches, you're just taking Cyril's Christology to its logical conclusion. After all, Cyril started out by saying that Jesus Christ, our incarnate God-man and Savior, is "out of two natures, one." That sounds an awful lot like what you're saying, so why is he so upset with you? Only under great pressure from the emperor and the patriarchs did Cyril finally confess that Jesus Christ possesses two distinct natures: one human and one divine. But that put him squarely and firmly in my corner. So why isn't he deposed and in exile with me? It's just politics, that's all.

The great councils of the last century wrote a creed that confesses Jesus Christ as truly human and truly divine, one substance with the Father and one with us. Now what is a substance or nature without a person? Obviously the fathers of the councils were saying that Jesus Christ is a composite "person," a corporate personality, two working in harmony together in all things. That's what I taught, and I still don't see why I'm persona non grata here in Constantinople. Why did I have to sneak into the city just to meet with you three?

CYRIL: Hold on there, Nestorius. First of all, Eutyches here is not teaching my view of the person of Jesus Christ. Nor is Apollinaris saying what our great father in the faith Athanasius said a century ago. It's true that at one time I taught that Jesus Christ is "out of two natures, one." But that was to affirm the integrity of his personhood. I saw that you and your friends in Antioch believe that a nature without a person is nothing, so I wanted to make it clear that Jesus Christ is one person and not two. In the Formula of Reunion, when I admitted that he possesses two natures, I made it clear that one of them, the human nature, has no person attached to it. It is *anhypostasis*—without a person except the person of the Son of God, who takes on the human nature and personifies it, if you will, in himself.

Your problem, Nestorius, is that you went too far with the two-natures doctrine of Antioch. You said that both natures are attached to persons so that Jesus Christ is a union of two natures and two persons. How is that an incarnation? It isn't! Your view, as I preached to everyone who would listen, amounts to a fancy, updated adoptionism. You just have the Son of

God adopting a human and entering into a special relationship with him. That doesn't make Jesus into God! It just makes him a man in a special relationship with God. That's heresy!

APOLLINARIS: I'd like to step in here to defend myself. I don't divide the person of Jesus Christ; I keep the person whole and undivided. "Person" is the rational soul, or mind, of a human being. My account of Jesus Christ is nothing at all like Nestorius's view.

CYRIL: Well, your view has already been condemned, Apollinaris, so there's no point in your trying to defend it. Same with you, Nestorius. Constantinople condemned Apollinaris's God-in-a-bod heresy, and Ephesus condemned yours, both for the same reason. Neither one of you understands the truth of Jesus's true divinity and humanity. You, Apollinaris, deny his true humanity. What is a human being without a human rational soul, as you call it, or mind, as I call it? Our great father in the faith Gregory of Nazianzus was right in saying, "Whoever denies that Jesus Christ has a human mind is oneself bereft of mind!"

After all, as Gregory also pointed out, whatever the Logos did not assume in the incarnation is not saved. If Jesus Christ did not have a human mind, our minds have no hope of being redeemed. Nestorius, you admit that Jesus Christ has a human mind, but you divorce it from his deity. In your account of the incarnation, the Son of God did not really assume a human anything! He simply entered into a close friendship with the man. How you can explain that as truly an incarnation is beyond me.

NESTORIUS: It's easy. Try to think with me here, Cyril. The deity and humanity of Christ are two sons: one is the Son of God, and the other is the Son of David. But they work in such close harmony together that to all intents and purposes, they are one. Think of a perfect marriage. After all, the Bible says that two shall become one flesh. And think of Jesus's prayer to the Father for the disciples in John 17: "Make them one even as you and I are one." So the man and the God in Jesus are one just as two human persons can be one, only closer. The Son of God controlled the man so that there was no chance of disagreement or competition or conflict. How can two work as one? Well, think of the sight of two eyes!

EUTYCHES: That's just nonsense and heresy, Nestorius. And some of your followers are still going around Constantinople and spouting that stuff. As much as two eyes cooperate in sight, they're still two eyes. One can do without the other one. But the humanity and divinity of Christ cannot do without each other if we are going to have salvation. Salvation depends on the incarnation, and so long as anyone talks about two natures of Christ, there can be no incarnation. Everything about our salvation depends on Jesus being God.

CYRIL *(interrupting)*: And man! Don't forget that, Eutyches. I know you mean well, but you go too far in defending the divinity. Not only does salvation depend on the deity of Christ; it also depends on his full and true humanity.

EUTYCHES: But, Cyril, even you have had to resort to the concept of *communicatio idiomatum*, the communication of attributes, to explain how the two natures—which you never should have confessed!—can coexist in a single person so that there is a true incarnation. And you say that the divine nature and person communicates divine attributes to the human nature but not vice versa. How is that really different from what I'm saying? I think you're just caving in by compromising with the Antiochenes!

NESTORIUS: I have to agree with Eutyches there, Cyril. You pay lip service to the two natures of Christ, but in the end you collapse them together into one. As with Eutyches, you have the divine nature swallow up the human nature. Only my view secures the distinction between the two natures and the completeness of the two natures.

CYRIL: Well, I'm the only one here who is still a bishop. You, Eutyches, are only a monk. And a bit feebleminded at that. Apollinaris's view can't even be taken seriously; it has no proponents anymore. But it is still a danger among the layfolks, whose minds tend to go that direction unless they are taught differently. Nestorius's view is already heresy according to the Council of Ephesus because it amounts to a kind of adoptionism. Eutyches's view is a type of docetism and will inevitably be condemned as heresy at another council in a few years.

Our only hope of transcending this debate that is tearing the church apart is compromise, and I'm the only one here willing to do that. Alexandria and Antioch must come together here in Constantinople. My hypostatic-union doctrine of the person of Jesus Christ holds together the concerns of each city. Jesus Christ was and is one integral person without division. But he possesses two distinct natures without confusion or mingling. This was the view assumed by the great teachers of the church in the past, and it will win over your heresies in the future. I'm confident of that.

Analysis

Confusing. That's the word many people use to describe this fifth-century debate. Let's see if it can be clarified. Throughout the fourth century a controversy over the Trinity raged throughout the churches of the Roman Empire. Even the emperors became involved. But it was really about the status of Jesus Christ in relation to God and humanity. Some people thought that if he was the Savior of the world, he couldn't really be human because humanity is sinful. How could the Savior be sinful? Also, humans are creatures; how could the Savior be a creature?

Other people thought the Savior of the world could not be completely divine because then he would have a huge advantage over the rest of us. To these people, Jesus's main mission was to give us an example of how to please God with our lives. Therefore, his sinlessness had to be a human achievement and not a foregone conclusion, as it would be if he were God.

Others (and some of the first two groups) simply could not fathom the Trinity. How could one being be three beings? How could a Son be equal with his own Father?

The two fourth-century councils, Nicaea and Constantinople, affirmed the full equality of the Son of God with his Father except that the Son derives his divinity from the Father eternally. The Holy Spirit was affirmed as also equal with the Father and the Son. Both councils adopted the term *homoousion* to describe the equality of the Son with the Father and with us: he is "of the same substance" with the Father and with us.

This raised the question to a fever pitch: how can one being, Jesus Christ, be of the same substance as God and as creatures? Apollinaris was one of the first to step forth and try to answer that. As we have seen, his answer was incomplete at best and heretical at worst simply because it amounted to a denial of Jesus's full and true humanity. If Apollinaris was right, Jesus is not of the same substance as us.

Then came Nestorius, who accepted the idea that Jesus is of the same substance as God and us, but he tried to explain that by appealing to a doctrine of two natures, divine and human. That stirred up Cyril and the Alexandrians because they thought he meant that Jesus Christ is a divided person, really two persons acting together. And the more Nestorius tried to explain himself, the deeper he dug the hole he was getting into. He ended up calling Jesus Christ "two sons" and thereby confirming Cyril's and the Alexandrians' worst fears. So Nestorians preserved the two natures or substances of Christ but only by sacrificing the integrity of his person.

Cyril shied away from talk of two natures of Christ and preferred the Alexandrian language of the incarnation as "out of two natures one." This was his and their way of preserving the unity of Christ's person, but it sacrificed the completeness of the two natures. Eutyches held on to this formula, insisted on Jesus as one-natured, and tended to reduce his humanity to a fiction. Cyril didn't go that far and even compromised with the Antiochenes (but not Nestorius) by using the two-natures language. He ended up affirming what has been called the doctrine of Christ's hypostatic union: two natures united inseparably in one person.

Cyril died before the Council of Chalcedon met in 451. Bishop Leo of Rome (400–461) wrote a letter to Bishop Flavian of Constantinople (d. 449), outlining what he thought the orthodox doctrine of the person of Christ should be. This is one of the most important documents in church history; the Council of Chalcedon largely adopted its language in its Definition. Leo's Christology is not very different from Cyril's and might have received Cyril's affirmation if he had lived that long. The letter, known to church history as *Leo's Tome*, explains the person of Jesus Christ as one person of two natures, divine and human.

So who is the "one person"? Without doubt it is the eternal Son of God, equal with the Father. What are the two natures? Without doubt they are divine and human. The council declared a form of Cyril's hypostatic union to be orthodox, and thus to be believed by all Christians everywhere. But some in Alexandria were unhappy because it condemned Eutyches and his Christology of the one-natured God-human.

The bishops at Chalcedon acknowledged the mystery at the heart of the incarnation; with their Definition they were not trying to "explain" a mystery. They were simply trying to decide what language should be used to express the mystery. The language they settled on was a compromise: from Alexandria came the emphasis on *one person*, and from Antioch came the emphasis on *two natures*. How one person can have two natures is never explained: therein lies the mystery. It would be left for later theologians to explore it and try to explain it further. So long as they stay within the four fences set up by Chalcedon (see the "Setting" section for this conversation), they are within Christian orthodoxy.

For Further Reading

Grillmeier, Aloys. *Christ in Christian Tradition*. Vol. 1, *From the Apostolic Age to Chalcedon (451)*. Translated by John Bowden. Atlanta: John Knox, 1965.

Need, Stephen W. *Truly Divine and Truly Human: The Story of Christ and the Seven Ecumenical Councils*. Peabody, MA: Hendrickson, 2008.

9

Fifth-Century Bishop Augustine of Hippo and British Monk Pelagius Argue about Sin and Salvation

Setting

A public bath is where strangers were most likely to meet in a Roman city. Men went there frequently to bathe; there was nothing necessarily sinister or sexual about these places. Few people in the Roman Empire could afford a private bathing place in their own homes. Even if they could afford it, they often preferred to bathe publicly—at least occasionally—to catch up on the latest gossip, debate politics, or just hear the news. These places were like indoor swimming pools, though in a North African city such as Carthage, they were probably open to the outside.

This imaginary conversation takes place in a large public bath in Carthage. In the early fifth century, Carthage was the largest metropolitan area in North Africa except for Alexandria. In our imagination, Augustine (354–430), Bishop of Hippo, a very influential church leader in his own time and one of the most important Christian thinkers of all time, has traveled to his home city of Carthage to speak to Christians there. He's relaxing in the public bath when his archadversary British monk Pelagius (354–ca. 440) enters. The two find themselves sitting near each other, draped in towels and dangling their feet in the warmed water.

Augustine's life story is known well, partly because of his spiritual biography *Confessions*, which is still read and studied in literature and philosophy classes throughout the world. It is considered a masterpiece of early psychology

because there Augustine explores his subconscious world of drives and motives
from childhood to adulthood. He was raised by a Christian mother, Monica,
and a pagan father. Augustine left the church to study and then teach rhetoric
in Italy. While living in Milan, he came under the influence of the great bishop
and preacher Ambrose and experienced a famous conversion. He reentered the
church and eventually became a bishop in Hippo, in North Africa, against his
will. The people demanded it.

Augustine wrote numerous books on philosophy and theology. He sought
to integrate the relatively new philosophy called Neoplatonism with Christianity. Augustine entered into heated theological and political conflicts with
the Manicheans, a rival religion to Christianity in North Africa, and the Donatists, a schismatic Christian sect. His most enduring legacy for Christian
theology, however, arose out of his debates with Pelagius. Although the two
probably never met (there is some doubt about that), they both wrote theological treatises against each other. Most of them had to do with the natures
of sin and salvation.

From Britain, Pelagius arrived in Rome in the early fifth century and immediately was repulsed by what he considered to be the morally indifferent lifestyles
of Christians there. His own form of Christianity in Britain was extremely
strict morally. While in Rome, he became convinced that part of the blame for
the moral indifference of the Christians was due to Augustine's influence there.
Augustine's prayer, "O God, give what you command, and command what you
will," was popular in Rome. Augustine thought that if a sinful person would
be chaste, God had to give that one the gift of chastity. Augustine reported that
one of his early prayers as a university student in Carthage was, "O God, give
me the gift of chastity, but not yet." As a Christian he believed that people are
too sinful to stop sinning without supernatural assisting grace from God.

Pelagius began to teach a contrary message about sin and salvation. He
taught that every human is born morally neutral and in the same condition as
Adam before the fall, able to sin or not to sin. He denied any inborn condition
of corruption such that a person could not exercise one's will to obey God.
Every person faces the same temptation that Adam and Eve faced: to obey God
or not. The fact that most or all people repeat that fatal disobedience is due to
bad influences around them. Original sin, then, is simply the habit of disobedience, which is deeply ingrained in society. Original sin is a social disease, caught
from parents, friends, and neighbors. It has nothing to do with biology, nor is
it a spiritual fate. One who chooses to sin simply chooses to imitate the sinners
around oneself and is therefore responsible and guilty. According to Pelagius,
one could have done otherwise.

Augustine pounced on Pelagius's doctrine of sin and the implied doctrine
of salvation, as will be seen in the imaginary conversation that follows. He
hounded Pelagius around the Roman Empire, writing letters to every bishop and
influential leader he knew, insisting that they denounce Pelagius. When Pelagius
fled to the eastern part of the empire, where Greek was the dominant language,

Augustine—who never fully mastered speaking, reading, or writing Greek—
wrote to his Latin-speaking friend Jerome, who was translating the Greek Bible
into Latin at Bethlehem, where Jesus was believed to have been born. Jerome
took up Augustine's crusade against Pelagius in the East. Eventually Pelagius
was condemned as a heretic at the Council of Ephesus in 431.

Early in his career as a Christian bishop and theologian, Augustine believed
in free will. He used that idea against the Manicheans, who believed that sin
and evil arise from matter. Instead, Augustine argued, it arises from misuse of
God's good gift of free will. His controversy with Pelagius changed his mind.
Toward the end of his life he denied freedom of the will in favor of bondage
of the will to sin—before and apart from the supernatural assisting grace that
people receive in regeneration. According to Augustine, Adam's condition before
the fall made it "possible not to sin." After the fall Adam and all of us with
him fell into the condition making it "not possible not to sin." Only the Holy
Spirit can restore us to the condition where it is possible not to sin. Pelagius's
emphasis on free will drove Augustine to the point where he believed in and
taught unconditional predestination. If a person is saved by God, it is because
God chose that person. As a reluctant young convert, Augustine experienced
that reality.

Pelagius's main writing explaining his views on sin, free will, and salvation
is *On Nature*, to which Augustine responded with one of his most important
and influential theological treatises: *Nature and Grace*. Clearly, Pelagius thought
the debate was mainly about free will; Augustine thought it was about the grace
of God in salvation.

The following conversation is based on what I imagine Augustine and Pelagius
would have said to each other if they had met unexpectedly in a public bath in
Carthage in about 420.

The Conversation

PELAGIUS: Is that you, Augustine? I have seen only your likeness drawn and never
you in person. I wondered if I might meet you here in Carthage. I see that
the public bath is not too lowly a place for the great bishop of Hippo!

AUGUSTINE: And who might you be, little man? Can it be Pelagius from Britain,
who has recently troubled the Christians in Rome about sin and salvation?
I did not know that you were in Carthage or I might have stayed away, at
least from this public bath!

PELAGIUS: Now, now, dear Augustine, don't get upset. I know you don't favor
my theology, but it won't hurt you to share the warm waters of the public
bath with a heretic. Not that I really confess to being a heretic, you know.
Actually, I suspect that your theology is nearer heresy than mine!

AUGUSTINE: You know that I am writing letters all over the empire—including
the East—alerting bishops and presbyters and theologians such as my dear

friend Jerome in Bethlehem about your heretical teachings. Soon I doubt that there is anywhere you can go where Christians will embrace you. As you know, our own synod or council of bishops met here in Carthage just two years ago to denounce you and your teachings.

PELAGIUS: Well, I'm sorry for that. You don't seem to understand my beliefs at all. And what about your own prayer, "O, Lord, give what you command, and command what you will"? If that isn't heretical, I don't know what is. If people wait to obey God's law until God gives them the gift of obedience, they will never obey. God expects us to use our free will and the moral power he gave us to obey him. What would be the point of all the commands of Scripture if we were unable to keep them?

AUGUSTINE: And therein lies your heresy, Pelagius. You do not understand how depraved humans are. We are incapable of obeying God or even pleasing God without a special infusion of assisting grace to renew our spirits and free our wills from bondage to sin. God's commands in Scripture show us how helpless we are to obey him apart from his grace, and once we are given his grace, his commands show us how to use that grace to please him. But why am I explaining all this to you? You know it all very well. You're just looking for a debate.

PELAGIUS: As for looking for a debate—it seems that you are the one who always wants a dispute. You debated the Manicheans and the Donatists and now me. I think you thrive on controversy! As for this total depravity you speak of—it's nonsense. If that were so, why would Jesus have commanded that we be perfect even as our Father in heaven is perfect? And why would Jesus have ordered the woman caught in adultery, "Go and sin no more"? Throughout Scripture the prophets and apostles constantly command people to avoid sin and obey God; righteousness is something we can accomplish with the aid of God's grace.

AUGUSTINE: Aha! You just said "with the aid of God's grace." Indeed! That's my point. Only with the aid of God's special, supernatural, renewing grace can we avoid sin. So do you admit that by ourselves we cannot avoid sinning?

PELAGIUS: Well, my point is that we are never "by ourselves." God has given each of us a conscience and God's own law. Grace is universal in these. Everyone has some intimation of God's will, and that is due to God's grace. He never leaves any to their own devices but offers righteousness to everyone if they will simply follow the dictates of conscience and obey the law of God.

AUGUSTINE: Wait a minute! So the "grace" whereof you speak is not special or supernatural at all? It's just part of man's natural equipment? How then is it grace?

PELAGIUS: It is special and supernatural grace for us if we sin. Then we need God's special grace for forgiveness. But unless or until we sin, we need only the grace of nature and law. And this is grace because it is a gift from God. God did not have to give us his law or the ability to keep it.

AUGUSTINE: Then you believe it is possible for any person to obey God from life's start until death without any special infusion of supernatural assisting grace?

PELAGIUS: Sure thing! Otherwise why would we be responsible for obedience and be guilty if we disobey? God's commandments imply that we can obey them if we will. That most people disobey them and need the grace of forgiveness says nothing about the possibility of obeying them. We have free will, and God expects us to use it rightly. That's why we're condemned if we do sin—because we could have done otherwise!

AUGUSTINE: I can't express how damnable this heresy is! I am more determined than ever to see you driven out of the church so that you cannot corrupt the gospel with your teachings. You make the grace of God null and void, and you empty the cross of Christ. Scripture is clear that all have sinned and come short of the glory of God! Even infants sinned "in Adam." Haven't you read Paul's Letter to the Romans, which clearly says that we all sinned in Adam?

PELAGIUS: No, I don't think that's what Scripture teaches. It says merely that death passed to all because all sin. Besides, what we're debating here is actual sin, not original sin. Original sin is our misery of being born into a corrupt world. We all tend to sin because the pull of temptation is so great and all our examples are sinful. But there is no necessity in sinning. If we would but resist temptation, we could be sinless.

AUGUSTINE: Incredible! What you say destroys the gospel. The gospel is that Christ died for us all because we are all condemned sinners. "There is none that does good, no not one." Read Romans, man! We are born with the stain and guilt of Adam's rebellion, and we need the grace of baptism to wash it away. Also, we need an infusion of supernatural grace to strengthen our wills so that we do not go on sinning after baptism.

PELAGIUS: I disagree with you about inheriting Adam's guilt or receiving his corruption. We are all born in the same state of nature with which Adam was created: innocent and neutral with regard to sin. We have the same human condition he had before he fell except that now we have many evil examples around us, and we have the wonderful example of Jesus Christ to guide us. But like Adam before he fell, we can either sin or not sin. It's entirely up to us. Otherwise we could hardly be held accountable for sinning.

AUGUSTINE: No, Pelagius. God holds us accountable because we were included in Adam so far as God is concerned. Adam was our source, our representative, our "head." When he rebelled and fell into death and condemnation, we all fell with him. Before he fell, Adam had the power not to sin; after he fell he lost that power. We are born in the condition of Adam after he fell: unable not to sin. And all of humanity is but a "mass of damnation" because of Adam—except for those who are in Christ by baptism and faith.

PELAGIUS: This teaching leads people to be spiritually and morally lazy; they blame their sins on their fallen nature and on Adam. You're responsible for that. Where do you find this teaching about Adam's guilt being ours? The New Testament only says that we are miserable because of the sin of the world and our cooperation with it. But that is not necessary. If we choose rightly, we would not sin.

AUGUSTINE: But our will is fallen and corrupt. Haven't you read in Romans that we are "dead in trespasses and sins"?

PELAGIUS: But that surely is a metaphor. We are not actually dead. There you sit in the warm water of the public bath, very much alive. So Paul must have meant that we are in a state of misery because of the sin of the world around us. Apart from conscience and God's law showing us the way to life abundant, we would be most miserable.

AUGUSTINE: You are twisting the Scriptures, Pelagius. Clearly the prophets and apostles taught that there is no one who does good, no not one! Show me one perfectly obedient human being other than Jesus Christ!

PELAGIUS: The fact that nobody lives a perfectly obedient life does not mean that it is impossible. What I am arguing for is the possibility of obedience even apart from an infusion of supernatural, assisting grace. I'm not claiming that anyone actually does live that way. But they could.

AUGUSTINE: What's the point?

PELAGIUS: It is just this: if we teach that it is impossible to please God apart from a supernatural gift of grace, people will wait until they have that gift to obey God. God expects them to begin obeying him now and not wait for a gift from above other than conscience and God's law. Your theology of total depravity and guilt inherited from Adam is the reason so many Christians are spiritually lazy and immoral.

AUGUSTINE: And your theology will lead people to trust in their own good works rather than in Christ alone; it will lead many other people to hopelessness when they try to live in obedience by themselves and find that they cannot do so. The gospel is that all our goodness comes from God and not at all from ourselves. The apostle Paul asked the Corinthians, "What do you have that you did not receive?"

PELAGIUS: But I agree that all goodness comes from God. Conscience and the law of nature and the law of God are all good gifts from God.

AUGUSTINE: I'm starting to feel like a prune sitting in this water so long while debating with you. I think I'll get out of here before God sends lightning to destroy this building and you in it! Your so-called gospel is little more than Jewish or Stoic moralism. That's not the gospel of Jesus Christ.

Analysis

Before this controversy between Augustine and Pelagius, most theological debate among Christians had to do with the nature of Jesus Christ. Is he truly human? Is he truly divine, equal with God the Father? Is he one person or two melded together in a union of natures and persons? Is he of a single nature or two? These questions were inseparable from questions about the Trinity. Are there three equal persons in God, or just one manifesting himself in three ways? How can three persons be one being? Christian theology entered a new stage with the debate between Augustine and Pelagius. Many Christians, especially in the East, thought more or less like Pelagius, although they may have had a stronger appreciation for human fallenness than he had. But when Pelagius finally reached the East, he found acceptance there, at least at first.

Many other Christians thought much like Augustine about sin, grace, and salvation. Few thought like Augustine about predestination—a view he came to after this conversation would have taken place and as a direct result of wanting to guard against giving humans any crucial role in salvation. Many of Augustine's own followers were horrified by his extreme doctrines of original sin and predestination. They recoiled against his later denial of free will and his strong emphasis on the unconditional sovereignty of God in selecting who would be saved apart from any free decisions or choices they make. But they couldn't stomach Pelagius's denial of original sin either. They have been labeled semi-Pelagians in church history. Yet they might as well be called semi-Augustinians.

What we see in this debate is two extremes. But overall, Augustine won—except for his later doctrine of predestination, which was never officially accepted by the Orthodox or Catholic churches but gained acceptance among some Protestant Reformers of the sixteenth century such as John Calvin. The Eastern Orthodox churches have never fully embraced Augustine's doctrine of original sin. They believe in universal human fallenness, but they tend to identify it more with mortality than with condemnation. Salvation, then, is God's deifying restoration of the image of God and gift of eternal life.

Augustine set the pattern for Western Christian thought that focuses more on legalities: condemnation, forgiveness, reconciliation, and so forth. Most Western Christians came to agree with Augustine that human babies are born guilty if not condemned for Adam's sin, and born so totally corrupted and depraved that they cannot help but sin. It is impossible for them not to sin.

So if babies are born not only depraved but also condemned, what happens when they die? Augustine argued that baptized babies are saved and go to heaven if they die. Unbaptized babies go to a place Augustine called limbo: a state of suspended animation between heaven and hell. It is not a place of suffering, but neither is it the beatific vision of God that saved persons experience in heaven. And why are some people baptized and saved and others are not? Augustine appealed to God's sovereign choice; for him it certainly has nothing to do with the sinner's exercise of goodwill toward God since that is impossible without regenerating grace.

Augustine's account of humanity and of God seems severe except for those who are being saved. For them it is comforting and even relaxing. After all, it's all up to God. But Augustine did believe that Christians have the responsibility and ability to please God with a life of love. One of his mottos was "Love and do as you please." Pelagius would hate that one too! What Augustine meant was that someone who really loves God and one's neighbor will always do the right thing.

Pelagius's account of humanity and God seems sunny and optimistic except for his real claim that people are capable of obeying God perfectly, and God expects them to do it. How hopeful is that, given our helplessness to do the good? And how realistic is it? Who can just decide to obey God and do it without God's special and even supernatural help? If Augustine was too pessimistic about human nature, he was very optimistic about grace. If Pelagius was too optimistic about human nature, he was very pessimistic about the power of Christ and the Holy Spirit to transform a person so that one doesn't need to be told how to please God but does it out of a heart of love. Pelagius was a legalist.

Many people wonder if there is some middle ground between Augustine and Pelagius. During Augustine's own lifetime, some who claimed to admire him developed what has come to be called semi-Pelagianism. What is that, exactly? It is the view that humans, though fallen into a corrupt, sinful condition, have enough moral power to initiate a relationship with God by exercising goodwill toward God. God waits to see that and then responds with saving grace. Humans cannot save themselves, contra Pelagius; but contra Augustine, they can take the first step toward God, and that indeed is what God expects. When God sees the beginning of goodwill in us, he responds with all that a person needs for salvation.

But is semi-Pelagianism a good middle ground between Augustine and Pelagius? The bishops gathered at the Second Council of Orange in 529 didn't think so. They condemned semi-Pelagianism as heresy without endorsing Augustine's strong doctrine of predestination. So Pelagianism and semi-Pelagianism are considered heresies in the history of Christianity. Yet both are rampant in Christian folk religion today. Semi-Pelagianism seems to be the default theology of most laypeople and many pastors. Nevertheless, it ignores the biblical affirmation that nobody seeks after God or does anything good (Rom. 3:10–18). Even the first exercise of goodwill toward God has to be God's gift.

Later, out of the Protestant Reformation came a theology that might be the viable middle ground between Augustine and Pelagius. It was expressed by Dutch theologian Jacob Arminius (d. 1609) and is called Arminianism. According to this view, God gives sinners sufficient "prevenient grace" (grace that goes before salvation and prepares for it) to exercise goodwill toward God. But the initiative is God's, not humans'. People do have free will to respond to God's call, conviction, illumination, and enablement (prevenient grace), but even that free will is a gift of God. God's grace "goes before" and sets the stage, so to speak, for whatever good a person does. Thus the person cannot boast; all glory is God's alone. But a person must cooperate with grace by allowing it to work its transformation in one's life. And people must respond to grace with faith and repentance. Their ability to do so is a gift of God.

I believe Arminianism is the middle ground many people are looking for between Augustine and Pelagius. And it was not completely thought up by Arminius. He built on the ideas of many before him, including the sixteenth-century Catholic reformer Desiderius Erasmus. Some scholars argue that Arminius simply rediscovered and reexpressed the ancient consensus about sin and salvation found in the early church fathers before Augustine. Other critics accuse Arminians of being semi-Pelagian, but that is simply incorrect because Arminius and his followers strongly emphasize the divine initiative in salvation and stress the necessity of God's supernatural, prevenient grace for even the beginning of an exercise of goodwill toward God.

Someone has labeled Pelagius the "reluctant heretic." By no means was he out to destroy the gospel. In some ways his theology is not much worse than some aspects of Augustine's. (For example, Augustine believed that original sin as guilt and corruption is passed down through the generations by sex.) Be that as it may, Pelagius's doctrine of human moral capacity contradicts what the Bible says about sin, grace, Jesus Christ, the atonement, and much else. Though Pelagius did not intend to undermine the gospel with his doctrine, that was its effect. As Augustine never tired of pointing out, if Pelagius is right, then the cross was not necessary. The gospel, however, says that the cross was for the sins of the whole world and not only for those who happen not to obey God. The fact that Christ had to die for everyone proves that everyone is a sinner.

For Further Reading

Rees, B. R. *Pelagius: A Reluctant Heretic*. Rochester, NY: Boydell & Brewer, 1988.

Scott, T. Kermit, *Augustine: His Thought in Context*. Mahwah, NJ: Paulist Press, 1995.

10

Medieval Abbot-Archbishop Anselm of Canterbury and Monk-Philosopher Abelard Debate Faith, Reason, and Atonement

Setting

Anselm of Canterbury (also known as Anselm of Bec, after his monastery in France) and Peter Abelard of Paris are two of the best-known and most-influential medieval theologians. They were also Christian philosophers. During their lifetimes, theology and philosophy were inseparable in European schools and universities. In many ways they represent polar opposites in medieval Christian thought.

Anselm was born in Aosta, Alpine Italy, in 1033 and educated at Normandy, in what is now France. He became the abbot of a monastery at Bec and was part of the wave of Normans who swept into England in the wake of King William's conquest. Anselm became the head of Catholics in England when he was appointed archbishop of Canterbury in 1093. He died in 1109 after a stellar career as a churchman and intellectual defender of the faith. Anselm anticipated objections to classical Christian beliefs long before they were popular and wrote books, using reason to defend Christian doctrine.

Peter Abelard was born in 1079 and died in 1142 after a tumultuous life. At least one secular movie has been made about his life and especially his love affair with the beautiful Héloïse, whom he secretly married against her guardian's wishes. (Actually, the details of her uncle's attitude toward Abelard and their marriage are debatable.) Her uncle hired thugs to break into the philosopher's living quarters and castrate him. Sometime afterward Abelard joined a monastery and Héloïse became a nun. She wrote him numerous love letters, some of which are still read as examples of medieval literature.

Abelard was thirty years old when Anselm died. They almost certainly never met. However, one can imagine them meeting in 1109, not long before Anselm's demise. In this imaginary conversation, Abelard, after fleeing the Inquisition, travels to England, and meets with the archbishop of Canterbury to try to secure his support and perhaps protection. Abelard was fleeing from the wrath of the great Catholic monk and crusade preacher Bernard of Clairvaux, perhaps the most influential Christian of his day. Bernard despised Abelard for daring to question the allegedly settled answers of medieval orthodoxy. Eventually Abelard died on his way to Rome to appeal to the pope. He almost certainly would have been burned at the stake if he had made it there.

Anselm represents a highly orthodox and rationalistic approach to Christian faith. "Rationalist" here does not mean "believe only what can be proved." That's a modern definition of the term. Rather, for Anselm, reason is a tool in the service of faith. One of his mottos was "I believe in order that I may understand." Some have abbreviated that to "faith seeking understanding" and made it a definition of theology.

The best way to illustrate Anselm's rationalism in theology is with his so-called ontological proof of God's existence. Anselm did not think proof was necessary; belief in God can be supported by proof even if it is based on faith. According to Anselm, a definition of God is "the being greater than which none can be conceived." If you can think of a being greater than the one you are calling God, then that greater being would be God. If God is the being greater than which none can be conceived, he must be conceived as existing because to exist is greater than not to exist. (Later philosophers will question that presupposition, but Anselm considered it self-evident.)

Someone who claims to conceive of God but does not believe in God's existence, Anselm argued, is guilty of self-contradiction. A person's very conception of God must include his existence or else there would be a being greater than the one imagined, one who is like that conception but actually existing. In brief, Anselm considered God's existence part of the very definition of God.

Over the centuries Anselm's argument has been much debated. Yet it illustrates his "faith seeking understanding" approach. One begins with faith in God. Then one seeks to add reason to faith. What makes Anselm rationalistic is that he seemed to believe that every major doctrine of the Christian faith is amenable to rational proof.

Abelard was not sure that reason could reach so far in theology. For him, the major theological beliefs of Christianity are beyond proof, and that's a sign of their truth. They are signs of the infinite, transcendent God, whose existence can be doubted just because our minds are so far from God's. Abelard was an extremely popular professor of theology in Paris partly because he was daring and creative. He dared to question the allegedly settled methods and conclusions of medieval Christian thought, and he sought to develop new ways to look at old doctrines such as the Trinity.

One book that got Abelard in trouble with more conservative churchmen such as Bernard of Clairvaux is titled *Sic et Non* (*Yes and No*). Abelard set down the traditional answers of theology and then demonstrated that there is further work to do in clarifying them. A reasonable Christian can look at every major doctrine of Christian faith and say "yes" and "no." In other words, he tried to show that theology's work is never done. No doctrine is final. A popular way to teach theology during his lifetime was to make students study and even memorize the Sentences, traditional affirmations of doctrine. These were considered beyond questioning. Abelard rebelled against this and tried to establish a more open, dialectical method of teaching theology. For that he gained the undying enmity of Bernard and many other defenders of tradition.

Among Anselm's best known and most influential works were *Proslogium* and *Monologium*; the former was written as prayers to God, the latter as logical syllogisms. These are sometimes considered his philosophical treatises since they focus on reason and God. Just as important to Christian theology, however, is *Cur Deus Homo?* (*Why Did God Become a Human Being?*). There Anselm tried to use reason to explain the atonement and the doctrine of the person of Jesus Christ as God incarnate. He overturned a thousand years of thinking about the cross of Jesus Christ and how it saves sinners, putting in its place a new and more rational account of that doctrine. Before Anselm, almost all Christians assumed that Christ died as a ransom paid by God to Satan for the release of humanity. Both Anselm and Abelard considered this beneath God's dignity, but they arrived at very different models of the atonement to replace the old one.

What if Abelard sought and received an audience with the great Catholic churchman Anselm of Canterbury? What would they say to each other? What follows is my best attempt to imagine such a conversation.

The Conversation

ANSELM: So, little man, you've come to me for guidance and advice, have you? Maybe for protection? I understand you've made some powerful enemies in France. What can I do for you?

ABELARD: Thank you so much for giving me this audience, your holiness.

ANSELM: Please. Don't flatter me with sweet words. I know that's not your habit. Your reputation for impertinence has preceded you.

ABELARD: Okay, then, let's talk plainly. I have come here seeking your counsel and protection. I'm being hounded throughout France by our own church's leaders. They misunderstand what I'm all about. I'm not a rebel or a heretic. I just ask questions that other people don't dare to ask.

ANSELM: Then perhaps you should join the undaring. Your lectures to throngs of admiring students in Paris have stirred up a hornets' nest. You have to bear responsibility for that. Then there's that little affair with the cathedral canon's niece. Very improper for a churchman!

ABELARD: Well, I'm not really a churchman. I'm a philosopher.

ANSELM: Rue the day when there should be a difference! Philosophy has always been taught by churchmen; since you teach philosophy, you are automatically a churchman whether you have been ordained or not. You were expected to remain celibate.

ABELARD: But church law doesn't require it.

ANSELM: Custom does, and that's where you fail. You flout the customs of church and society.

ABELARD: I think I've learned my lesson about that particular custom. Now that I'm no longer fully a man!

ANSELM: What happened to you is a shame, but you did bring it on yourself. Rumor has it that you were not only secretly married but also about to abandon your wife!

ABELARD: Untrue. I had no such thoughts. We were temporarily separated to avoid scandal.

ANSELM: Which only created more scandal! But let's get back to your reason for coming here.

ABELARD: You're a great philosopher yourself, Anselm. I've long been an admirer of yours.

ANSELM (*interrupting*): Stop! I don't believe you. Speak plainly.

ABELARD: Okay, okay. We have our differences. But you are a very smart man, and you're well connected in the life of the church throughout Europe. I was hoping you would hear me out and then possibly write a few letters on my behalf.

ANSELM: Possibly. But only if you convince me you're not a heretic.

ABELARD: Right now I'm in the process of writing some books that will prove I'm no heretic. In one of them I'll show that the doctrine of the Trinity is reasonable.

ANSELM: Then why are you so controversial? Perhaps because that other book you're allegedly writing is based on your treatment of the Sentences in your theology seminars?

ABELARD: Yes, I guess so. I plan to call the book *Sic et Non*.

ANSELM: *Yes and No*? What an odd title for a theology book. Why the "no"? Is that aimed at heresies?

ABELARD: Well, not exactly. My concern is that so many teachers of philosophy and theology in our monastery schools and universities treat doctrines as though carved in stone even when the Bible is not so clear about the subject. And then there's reason. And tradition. Our method of simply making students memorize and comment on Sentences without questioning them in any way is contrary to the spirit of reason.

ANSELM: Go on. What's so controversial about *Sic et Non*?

ABELARD: Well, I set down traditional Sentences of theology and then show that each one is amenable to both yes and no. Plenty of proofs can be marshaled for each one, and yet there are reasons to doubt whether their current formulation is the best possible. My intention is simply to show that there is always more to do in theology and that learning theology is not merely a matter of memorizing and praising traditional clichés.

ANSELM: Clichés? You would reduce our Sentences to clichés? Who do you think you are?

ABELARD: Nobody special. But someone has to point out that at least in some cases the emperor has no clothes. What I mean is, some of the Sentences are deeply flawed and in need of reconsideration and reformulation. Theology should not be considered a fortress to be defended but more a pilgrimage to be enjoyed.

ANSELM: So what is one of these sacred doctrines you dare to question?

ABELARD: I think the traditional doctrine of the death of Christ and its atonement for sins needs to be examined and possibly updated.

ANSELM: Hmmm. So do I. But why do I suspect that your way of updating it will be different from mine?

ABELARD: I don't know, but I'm glad to hear that you agree there's something not quite right about our traditional thinking and teaching about Christ's atonement for sins.

ANSELM: So tell me, little man, what is your proposed doctrine of the atonement? And how is it better than what has been believed by all the faithful for a thousand years.

ABELARD: Well, the traditional doctrine says that God gave his Son over to Satan as a ransom so that Satan would let sinful humanity go free.

ANSELM: And what's the problem with that? After all, the New Testament does refer to Christ as a "ransom."

ABELARD: But it doesn't say "to Satan." That's one problem. Surely "ransom" is a metaphor. Why would God have to deal with Satan in that way? The doctrine makes God out to be a counterpart to Satan. He has to make deals with the devil. Surely our God does not have to stoop so low!

ANSELM: Go on.

ABELARD: Furthermore, nowhere does the New Testament say that Christ was a ransom paid to the devil. That's just speculation. And furthermore, the doctrine includes the idea that God tricked Satan. Satan did not know that he could not keep the Son of God because of his glory and power. So he accepted the ransom of God's own Son, handed over sinful humanity to God, and then lost the Son as well. It pictures God as laughing at his trickery.

ANSELM: What's wrong with tricking the devil?

ABELARD: Nothing if it were one of us. But God? Why would God have to trick the devil? The whole doctrine demeans God. It also fails to explain the effect the cross has on us. Surely the Son came to transform us inwardly and not only to play tricks on the devil!

ANSELM: More important, don't you think, is the effect of the cross on God? The problem with the traditional ransom doctrine of the atonement is that it fails to explain why God had to become human and die and how that death reconciles us with God. The key to understanding the cross is reconciliation. The cross was God's sacrifice to make us acceptable to God. The ransom view doesn't even touch that issue.

ABELARD: Right, right. I agree. But more important, the cross is God's great object lesson of his love for us. It changes us by showing us how much God loves us. We are sinners because we are ignorant of God's love; Christ laid down his life and thereby gave us an example of love for one another and for God. When we hear the message of the cross and see Christ crucified before our very eyes, we cannot be indifferent. We must repent and throw ourselves on God's mercy, trusting in his steadfast love.

ANSELM: I'm sure that's true, but is that all the atonement does? Is it only an illustration of God's love?

ABELARD: What more would you have it be? If not the ransom doctrine, then what?

ANSELM: Christ's death paid a debt that we owe to God. Jesus paid the debt in our place. The debt is to God's honor. By sinning, we have dishonored God. We deserve to die, just as a vassal deserves to die when he dishonors his lord. But because God loves us, he gave his Son Jesus to suffer the penalty and pay the price for us. God's honor is thereby restored, and God is able to forgive us when we repent.

ABELARD: Are you suggesting, then, that God cannot forgive us without the bloody sacrifice of Christ's death?

ANSELM: That's right. God's honor is at stake. Our sin robbed him of his honor. God's honor must be satisfied; a satisfaction must be paid. That left God with only two options if he would keep his honor or have it restored. On the one hand he could let us suffer our deserved fate of eternal separation from him. In that way he would show how seriously he takes the offense of sin and his own honor. Or he could pay our penalty himself and thus restore his honor. But the second option costs him the life of his own Son.

ABELARD: I have heard talk that you plan to write a book explaining this view of the atonement.

ANSELM: Yes, it will be based on lectures and sermons that I've been giving occasionally over the years. The title will be a real seller: *Cur Deus Homo?* (*Why Did God Become a Human Being?*). As I have explained it, the atonement makes perfect rational sense of the cross. Everyone can understand why Christ had to die. But even more, it shows why our Lord had to be both God and man at once. Only God could pay the price owed to himself because he has no sin, but a human must pay the price because disobedience and dishonor are human.

ABELARD: Very clever, Anselm. But I see a problem.

ANSELM: Why doesn't that surprise me?

ABELARD: Please, let me explain. I agree that Jesus Christ must be both God and human. He must be God in order to demonstrate God's love, but he must also be a human in order to die to show the depth of God's love. Your view of the atonement makes God seem like a bloodthirsty tyrant who demands a pound of flesh for his honor's sake. It makes God appear petty, like our feudal lords. Surely the main motive of the cross is love and not honor.

ANSELM: You miss the point. The cross is a demonstration of God's love. In the person of the Son, God himself paid the price to satisfy his own honor, and did so out of love.

ABELARD: But you make it appear that God is not already reconciled to sinners in his heart. If God is love, how can he be anything but reconciled already? It is we who need reconciliation, not God. What we need to be reconciled with God is repentance, upon which God immediately forgives. But we won't repent because we fear God. So Christ dies to show that God loves us and is already reconciled to us in his heart. When we see this great example of divine love, we are drawn to God in love and with deep sorrow for our sins.

ANSELM: That's a pretty picture, but it won't do. You ignore two things. God's wrath against sin and our depravity. An object lesson of God's love would do us no good because we are so depraved. The cross changes God's relationship with us so that he can woo us to repent and be reconciled with him. Without the sacrifice of the cross, God cannot even look upon us. While the deepest motive of the cross is love, there is also God's wrath against sin. Your view of the atonement does nothing to account for that. Mine takes in both love and wrath.

ABELARD: But at what cost? You make God unable to forgive without a blood sacrifice. That itself dishonors God! Surely God can forgive whoever and whenever he pleases. And it portrays God as angry and vengeful. Your God is an Old Testament God; mine is the loving Father of our Lord Jesus Christ.

ANSELM: I thought you came here seeking my approval and help. You're just digging yourself into a deeper hole. I consider your doctrine of the atoning death of Christ to be heresy.

ABELARD: Well, I'm sorry to hear that. But I can't accept your support if it costs my integrity. I must speak the truth.

ANSELM: I think our differences go deeper than merely this. We have differing opinions about the cross, although mine isn't mere opinion; yet beneath and behind that lie differing attitudes toward faith and reason. My doctrine of the atonement is rigorously rational; it makes our faith in the cross intelligible—even to a Muslim. Yours is sentimental and almost mystical.

ABELARD: Indeed! Mine is based on faith in a loving God; yours is based on a compulsion to make every belief logical. Surely faith goes deeper than reason. It doesn't go against reason, but it cannot be bound to reason. One of my students suggested that what we believe is suprarational. I agree with him.

ANSELM: Why would that be the case?

ABELARD: Because God's ways are so much higher than our ways and his thoughts so much higher than our thoughts, as the prophet Isaiah says. We cannot make God conform to our logic. That would make him our prisoner. But also, you seem to assume a rational ordering to reality such that God and humans share a similar if not identical logic.

ANSELM: Indeed! How else can we know that what we believe is true?

ABELARD: There's the problem. You don't rely enough on faith. You may begin with faith, but then you make it follow reason. And there is no pattern of logic in reality to which both God and humans are subject. You seem to think that God does or commands things because they are good and right. I say things are good and right because God does or commands them. Your view of reality and reason makes God subject to a cosmic set of universals like truth, beauty, and goodness. I believe that God is no prisoner of anything; he is perfectly free to do what he pleases. If he chooses to forgive without cause or reason or satisfaction, he is free to do it. You imply that God cannot just forgive; he has to satisfy some cosmic justice.

ANSELM: But then you make justice a chimera—a mirage, an illusion. And you make the ways of God completely untraceable.

ABELARD: Except by faith alone.

ANSELM: But tell me this, little man: If you are right so that God is not bound by anything, and if there is no cosmic order to which God himself is bound, how can we trust that God will be faithful to his promises? If you're right, then it's conceivable that God may simply decide, willy-nilly, to declare repentance to be cause for eternal death rather than for eternal life, as he promised.

ABELARD: Ah! That's where faith enters the picture. If you are right, we hardly need to have faith at all. In my view, faith is trust that God will be faithful.

ANSELM: You make faith a risk.

ABELARD: Isn't that the nature of faith? Risk? We risk our lives on God's faithfulness.

ANSELM: Knowing all the while that God could change his mind and hate us rather than love us.

ABELARD: But he won't because he is good.

ANSELM: What is his goodness if not his being bound to keep his promises?

ABELARD: It is his decision to be faithful.

ANSELM: I see that we are not getting anywhere with this. I have better things to do than sit here and debate with a heretic all day. You might as well be on your way, little man. Go back to France and face your fate at the hands of the Inquisition. I won't be able to help you.

ABELARD: That's sad. I thought you'd be amenable to reason. After all, you are so committed to rationality.

Analysis

One can only imagine what these two giants of medieval Christian thought would say to each other. The above is only an educated guess, but it does illustrate their differences. Toward the end of the conversation, one of their most basic differences emerges. Abelard is often considered to be one of the first adherents and expounders of a philosophy called nominalism. (Some scholars would prefer to call his view conceptualism.) Nominalism arose more to public view and debate later, with theologian and philosopher William of Ockham (ca. 1288–ca. 1348), who, like Abelard, had to flee the Inquisition.

Nominalism faces off against realism. In this context "realism" has a specific, technical meaning. It doesn't mean the tame form of pessimism that we all call realism. In this context of medieval philosophy, realism is the view that universals like truth, beauty, and goodness have some kind of real existence. They are not merely terms or concepts. They are transcendent realities that make individual things or acts more or less true, beautiful, or good. We have some kind of implicit knowledge of these universals, and at our best we are able to say, "This is more beautiful than that," because "this" conforms more closely to the universal "beauty" than "that" does. You may have heard it said that beauty is in the eye of the beholder. A philosophical realist rejects that. Beauty is not subjective. Nor is truth. Nor is justice. These things have objective existence and serve as the patterns by which things are judged.

Anselm was clearly a realist. In a nominalist mode, Abelard believed that universals are only terms or concepts. We organize the world around us with universals. We see several things that have something in common, and we call that commonality "beauty" or "justice." But there are no transcendent realities of "beauty" or "justice."

It's hard to say how far Abelard took this or how consistent he was with it. But nominalism of some kind and to some degree was presupposed by his theological investigations. A realist like Anselm would see nominalism as pernicious because it undermines cosmic order and our ability to use reason to trace it. And nominalism means that humans have no "human nature" since God has no "divine nature." That means, according to a realist, that God is arbitrary in his decisions and actions. He is sheer will and power and can do whatever he wants to do without any limits or structure. A nominalist like Abelard would consider that an advantage of nominalism, but a realist fears it because it calls into question our ability to trust God to be faithful.

So the most basic philosophical difference between the two antagonists might be realism versus nominalism with regard to universals. The controversy over nominalism continued throughout the Middle Ages and into the Reformation. Martin Luther was a nominalist, as were many Protestants of the sixteenth century. Eventually the Roman Catholic church condemned nominalism as a heresy because it undermined traditional Catholic doctrines about the church and the Eucharist (Lord's Supper). But perhaps the main problem with nominalism is its tendency to slip into relativism. If universals have no real existence outside the mind, how do we support belief in absolutes? The only other option is appeal to divine commands. But what if God, having no eternal nature or character, decides to change his commands? Are God's decrees even absolute if not rooted eternally and absolutely in God's nature and character?

Anselm's and Abelard's doctrines of the atonement stand in stark contrast to each other. Anyone who reads Abelard will observe, however, that he occasionally allowed an objective element of the atonement to creep in. He did acknowledge that on the cross and by his obedient death, Jesus won merits for us before the Father. For the most part, however, he insisted that the atonement is a moral example. This is often called the subjective theory of the atonement, and it has become extremely popular, especially among liberal Protestant theologians in the twentieth and twenty-first centuries. Anselm's satisfaction theory, as it has come to be known, was picked up and given a slight modification by John Calvin during the Reformation. Calvin's version has come to be called the penal substitutionary theory. The "price" Christ paid to the Father's honor was simply changed to a punishment that Christ suffered to satisfy divine justice. This is the most popular doctrine of the atonement among conservative Protestants. The Catholic church still officially holds to something like Anselm's doctrine.

How is the Anselm-versus-Abelard debate relevant to today? On the one hand, Abelard was something of a freethinker in a time when freethinking, especially in theology, could get a person burned at the stake. Christians who fancy themselves to be open-minded consider him to be a hero. But did Abelard put his feet on a slippery slope that inevitably led toward subjective and relativist doctrine? On the other hand, Anselm is often considered to be a hero by strongly objective, absolutist, and traditionalist Christians. But did he close his mind to fresh ways of looking at doctrine even in the light of Scripture? Was he such a staunch defender of the traditional faith that out of hand he rejected any new approaches such as Abelard's? Well, that can't be entirely the case. Conservatives who admire Anselm might want to consider his revolution in the doctrine of the atonement. His doctrine might be considered conservative today, but in his own time it was radical because it overturned a thousand years of Christian belief about Christ's death and its effect on human salvation.

Wouldn't a hybrid of Anselm and Abelard make an interesting animal? We could call it open-minded traditionalism: Moderate realism without Platonic idealism of the forms (universals as conceived by Plato in ancient Greek philosophy). An objective-subjective view of the atonement, where Christ's death really does have an effect on God but also works as an example for humans.

For Further Reading

Brower, Jeffrey E., and Kevin Guilfoy. *The Cambridge Companion to Abelard.* Cambridge: Cambridge University Press, 2004.

Evans, G. R. *Anselm of Canterbury.* Reprint, New York: Continuum, 2005.

11

Medieval Scholastic Philosopher-Theologian Thomas Aquinas and Tree-Hugger Francis of Assisi Enthuse on How to Know God

Setting

Francis of Assisi was born in Italy in 1181 or 1182 and died in Italy in 1226, the year after Thomas Aquinas was born, in 1225 in Sicily. Thomas died in 1274. So they could not possibly have met during their earthly lives. Thus this imaginary conversation assumes an ethereal appearance of Francis to Thomas some years after Francis's death. Such appearances of the dead to the living are not unheard of: credible examples have happened. Scripture recounts the prophet Samuel's appearance to King Saul when he went to visit the medium at Endor. Moses and Elijah appeared with Jesus on the Mount of Transfiguration. In modern times, Bible translator J. B. Phillips tells of being visited and encouraged by the spirit of C. S. Lewis after the latter's bodily demise.

Yet there is no evidence that such a meeting between the ghost of Francis and the living Thomas ever happened. It's just a literary device, based on the story of Lewis's appearing to Phillips. Here, Thomas is at a monastery in the Alps, brooding over the controversy he has caused in the European Catholic universities. (Phillips was brooding over his temporary inability to work on his translation of the New Testament.) The new Aristotelian philosophy was sweeping European universities, and Thomas was trying to integrate it with Christian theology.

For more than a millennium, Plato's philosophy was theology's main conversation partner. Some Christian leaders feared that Thomas was laying the groundwork for a complete reversal of the traditional ordering of faith and reason. The "reason" part of theology was turning to Aristotle's philosophy: in 1100–1270 his works were entering Europe in Latin translation, via the Muslims in Spain. At least according to some of his critics, Thomas was proposing a new approach to Christian theology in which faith does not seek understanding so much as understanding (philosophy) decides what faith can know and believe.

Be that as it may, what Thomas did do was establish room for a natural theology, drawn largely from Aristotle's philosophy and independent of revealed theology. For example, according to Thomas, even the most sinful person can use one's reason to know that God exists, the soul is immortal, and the basic laws of morality are sound. One does not have to be a Christian to know these things. There are proofs of the existence of God drawn from experience of the world. Thomas's proofs are drawn partly from Aristotle. But Aristotle's god was a far cry from the God of Abraham, Isaac, and Jacob. If Thomas noticed that, it didn't seem to affect his theology as much as his critics would like.

Thomas may have been controversial during this lifetime, but later he would be named the Angelic Doctor by the Catholic hierarchy, and his theology would become the norm for all Catholic thought. Every Catholic theologian in good standing with the church is some kind of Thomist. Catholic thinkers have expended a great deal of energy in trying to interpret Thomas, who was second only to Augustine in prolific theological writing.

Thomas was a friar of the relatively new Dominican order; these friars were called the "poor preachers" because as mendicants they lived from donations and specialized in preaching. In the cities they often lived together in houses. Though in some ways similar to monks and monasteries, friars and their orders are somewhat different. Like many affluent Europeans, Thomas's family considered the Dominicans to be a cult. When Thomas first joined the order, his family kidnapped him and tried to convince him to leave it. He refused and eventually lived with the Dominicans in Paris, where he taught at the university.

Francis started his own order, called the Little Brothers. Later they would be known as the Franciscans and, like the Dominicans, they still exist throughout the world as a very influential order of friars. The Franciscans took a vow of poverty, and their approach to Christian theology differed greatly from the Dominicans. For centuries these two orders were locked in tension and sometimes even conflict—but not during Francis's or Thomas's lifetimes.

Francis was also born to a wealthy Italian family, but he came to reject all wealth and even material possessions beyond what is necessary to live. He built a small chapel in a wilderness area and lived there. He was a poet and a preacher of poverty, simplicity, and spirituality. Eventually a group of followers gathered around him, and his order was granted official status by the pope. By the time of his death, however, the order was large and flourishing and losing its early spirit of poverty and simplicity. Francis died somewhat disillusioned by the direction his followers were taking.

Without any doubt Thomas and Francis are two of the best-known and most-beloved figures in the history of Christianity: Thomas for his intellect, and Francis for his love of nature, including especially animals. There was a revival of interest in both men during the second half of the twentieth century. A feature film titled *Brother Sun, Sister Moon* (1972) was based on the life of Francis. Statues of Francis adorn millions of gardens around the world. His canticles are widely read and discussed as classics of spirituality. Thomas and Francis are famous examples of medieval Christianity, but are polar opposites in many ways. Thomas was an intellectual and almost the model of an ivory-tower thinker. Francis was a mystic and practitioner of spirituality.

This imaginary conversation is set in a monastery in the Alps—halfway between Francis's home at Assisi, Italy, and Thomas's home in Paris. It is 1274, early in the year Thomas died and forty-eight years after Francis died.

The Conversation

FRANCIS: Blessings, Brother Thomas. I see you look discouraged. Why?

THOMAS (*shocked*): What? Who is that? I thought I was alone in this tiny cell. You surprised me. How did you get in here?

FRANCIS: Dear, dear Brother Thomas. I'm sure you've seen portraits of me, although I never really wanted such made. God sent me here from paradise to encourage you and also perhaps provide a few words of correction for your path. I'm Francis of Assisi.

THOMAS: Indeed I have heard of you. Now that the light is a little better, I see the resemblance to your portraits. As is almost always the case with visions, you certainly look better now than then! You have a certain glow about you.

FRANCIS: We all have that in paradise, Brother Thomas. Someday, perhaps soon, you'll have it as well.

THOMAS: Soon? What's that supposed to mean?

FRANCIS: Oops. I wasn't supposed to say that. I still struggle with even passive deception. I guess that's partly why they're calling me "saint" down here.

THOMAS: I must admit that I'm startled by your appearance here. I've heard of apparitions and such, but I've never experienced one before. Are you real?

FRANCIS: As real as you are—and more!

THOMAS: Well, you're right. I am discouraged. I've spent most of my life trying to help the church cope with the new knowledge flooding in from the Muslim world, and they keep criticizing me. Word is that one or two bishops and maybe even archbishops want me subjected to the Inquisition. And what for? What have I done to deserve that?

FRANCIS: I also suffered persecution from the church. Like Israel of old, the church does not always value its prophets during their lifetimes. But since I passed on into paradise, most of the church leaders have come to revere my cause. I admit that some of my followers have become too radical, even to the point of burning palaces and churches. But they didn't get that from me! Anyway, I'm here to talk to you and not to talk about myself. Just know that you're not alone. Being criticized says nothing about whether you're right or wrong.

THOMAS: I know, I know. But it still hurts. I wish they would just leave me alone and let me do my work.

FRANCIS: And what is your most important work, Brother Thomas?

THOMAS: Writing books of theology and apologetics. Surely you know that. I've written many volumes of such. My life's project is to show the compatibility between science and faith. Theology should not stay the same forever; it needs to take into account new knowledge, and the new knowledge we must adjust to now is Aristotle's philosophy, which has been forgotten for so long. It's a wonderful handmaid to theology.

FRANCIS: Ah, yes. Philosophy, the handmaid to theology, which we call the "queen of the sciences." Theology a science? It seems to me that theology is more of an art than a science.

THOMAS: Well, when I say that theology is a science, I mean "science" in the sense of a method of acquiring knowledge that is orderly and reasonable. And the knowledge acquired is systematic and coherent. During my whole career I've been striving for that: a theology that is completely coherent, where every piece fits with every other piece into a consistent, interlocking whole.

FRANCIS: Like one of our great Gothic cathedrals, right?

THOMAS: Exactly! Good analogy.

FRANCIS: But what about the personal presence of God within the soul and within nature? Don't you think it's just as important if not more important than intellectual understanding of God?

THOMAS: I'm sure it is important, but that hasn't been my gift. And there is a great need for intellectual understanding of the faith today. The infidels—I mean the Muslims of Spain—are putting pressure on our church throughout Europe. They have magnificent universities that are discovering all kinds of knowledge. If we don't compete with them on their level, Christianity will be the poorer for it.

FRANCIS: Right, right. But God instructed me to tell you to add heart to your head. In other words, you could use a dose of contemplation of God in nature added to your cognitive speculations.

THOMAS: That's strange. I've worked hard to prove God's existence and attributes from observation of nature. My work on natural theology is bearing fruit with those who need reasons to believe.

FRANCIS: That's all well and good. But you use nature as a tool in the service of philosophy and theology. How about just communing with nature and finding God in the connections between your soul and the souls in nature?

THOMAS: I'm afraid I don't even quite know what you mean.

FRANCIS: I believe every animal and every plant has a soul in some sense. They are not just material things, objects to be used like tools. We can and should discover God in them as the source of their life and ours. Have you ever tried talking to the birds?

THOMAS: I heard that you preached to the birds. How strange! I'm afraid I don't know anything about that.

FRANCIS: And they talked back to me. It was wordless communication, a kind of communion more than cognition.

THOMAS: And to what benefit?

FRANCIS: Love. It's all about the love of God for all of nature, including us. We are also part of nature. We increase in love as we feel the love of God for everything. I discovered that alone out in the wilderness, just sitting and letting my five senses absorb the work of God.

THOMAS: And what did you say to the birds when you preached to them?

FRANCIS: I told them how much God loves them, but I didn't use words.

THOMAS: Preaching without words! How novel. I don't think I get it.

FRANCIS: Later, let's complete a little exercise in contemplation. We'll open all the windows and let the smells and sounds of nature come wafting through the room while we just sit and meditate on God's great love for all things.

THOMAS: Fine. Later. But I don't think I'm going to be very good at that.

FRANCIS: But first, let's talk about the controversy swirling around your work. You've published two multivolume sets of theological reflections: *Summa theologiae* and *Summa contra gentiles*—a summary of all theological knowledge systematically ordered and a summary of the arguments against unbelievers. God appreciates the effort you've put into these. But don't you think there might be some validity to the criticism that you begin with reason and then move to faith? How can a person without faith even begin to understand who God is and what God expects of us?

THOMAS: You talk a lot about nature, Francis. So let me tell you something about nature and grace. I believe that nature, including our own human nature and reasoning ability, was not severely damaged by Adam's fall. We are born with original sin, but also with minds capable of grasping the truth about God revealed in nature. Even rank sinners can know, for example, that God exists and grasp something about God's nature. Such natural knowledge of God serves as a vestibule, if you will, to the sanctuary of supernaturally revealed knowledge, which we can receive only through faith.

For example, that God exists can be proved through reason. There must be a first cause of everything. Otherwise there would be nothing. Whatever might not exist, and that includes all creatures, would cease to exist, given enough time, without an uncaused cause. So there must be a great cosmic first cause and unmoved mover to explain the existence of the world and its orderliness. Grace is not required to prove this. But God graciously reveals who he is as Father, Son, and Holy Spirit.

Reason alone cannot discover this. It requires faith. But what we know of God through reason and what we know of God through faith do not contradict each other. Grace, the realm above nature, does not contradict nature but elevates and fulfills it. The prime mover of the universe comes to be known as the Blessed Trinity when we add faith to reason.

FRANCIS: But there's a problem in that scheme, Brother Thomas. The moment you separate any true knowledge of God from grace and hand it over to nature alone, you run the risk of it taking on a life of its own apart from the faith and teaching of the church. It seems that your discussion of God in natural theology is so controlled by Aristotle's logic and metaphysics that your discussion of God as he is revealed in Scripture is also guided, if not controlled, by that philosophy.

Don't you think the God of Abraham, Isaac, and Jacob, the God of the birds and trees, is too personal to be proved in a syllogism or dissected in a lecture? How can someone really come to know Father, Son, and Holy Spirit in such a way that conforms to the constraints of philosophy?

THOMAS: Are you suggesting that I allow philosophy to be more than a hand-maid to theology? Are you claiming that my natural theology controls my accounts of supernaturally revealed truths?

FRANCIS: Uh, yes, I think you're grasping it now. But even more, please allow me to suggest that your whole distinction between what is "natural" and what is "supernatural" is dubious. Is anything in God's good creation merely natural, devoid of the supernatural presence of God? And is any miracle of God above and outside of nature? Don't you risk locking God out of nature and making nature an autonomous sphere of reality, where God is absent?

THOMAS: I wouldn't put it quite that way. For me, and for many of my colleagues in the universities of Europe, "nature" designates observable, physical reality. God is not absent from it, but its workings are everywhere and at all times the same. "Supernature" designates the reality above nature, where God dwells in his glory and power, and where the mind of humanity cannot go without being supernaturally aided and elevated. To illustrate: I can prove God's existence to anyone with working mental capacities and five senses. But I can't prove that this God is triune. To know that requires supernatural revelation and faith.

FRANCIS: Lurking within that scheme is too great a divorce between the ordinary and the extraordinary, between nature and grace. Nature is charged with the glory of God. Even nature is supernatural, to borrow your term. The whole world is one great miracle. Everything is both natural and supernatural at once, so those categories don't really help.

THOMAS: Well, let me strike back. Doesn't your view risk pantheism, where God and nature are so intermingled that they become one?

FRANCIS: No, but I'd rather have pantheism than view nature as a realm independent of God, where God has to break in from the outside to work there.

THOMAS: Ah, but the budding sciences in our universities will never burst into full bloom if we treat nature as divine. We must dedivinize nature if we are to study it and handle it rationally. So long as your mystical and almost pantheistic view of nature prevails, science will never get off the ground.

FRANCIS: So, let me see if I understand you correctly. You are saying that the only real value nature has for theology is providing proof of the existence of God as the first cause, the prime mover. And that nature is so much like a machine that the unaided human mind can study it and conclude from it that God is its creator. But nature is not the temple of God or God's personal activity. And if we want to know God as personal Father and Savior, we have to turn away from nature to supernatural revelation and have faith.

THOMAS: Good! You're getting it. That's quite right. That's what people need today. They need an appeal to reason and then to faith.

FRANCIS: Aren't you afraid that eventually people following your line of reasoning will just say, "If natural knowledge of God is what everyone can have without supernatural revelation or faith, then let's just rest content with natural knowledge of God"? They'll take everything you place in the realm of grace and faith and relegate it to private opinion.

THOMAS: And what's your alternative?

FRANCIS: We should begin with faith in a personal God known through our communion with his presence and handiwork in nature, then move onward to greater understanding of this God through revelation. Faith seeking understanding. I believe in order that I may understand. You imply that we must understand in order to have faith. You place unaided reason and nature devoid of God's personal presence too much to the fore in your theology. Why begin with nature when we have revelation?

THOMAS: Because we need to lay a foundation for Christian faith in reason so that when rational skepticism arises, we are prepared to show that the God we know and worship is provable.

FRANCIS: But the God we know and worship is Father, Son, and Holy Spirit. So all your proofs yield no true knowledge of the God we know and worship, do they? How does that help the skeptic know the true God, then? You are just proving an idol to him.

THOMAS: No, because through reason alone I show the skeptic that our God, the one whose existence has been proved, is the God of the Bible. He is immutable, all-powerful, incapable of suffering, simple and not compound in substance, and so forth. These attributes are both biblical and rational.

FRANCIS: "Simple and not compound in substance"? Where is that in the Bible? You might be right, but that seems more like a philosophical description of

God than a biblical or spiritual one. Your God sounds a lot like Aristotle's
Actus Purus, pure actuality without potentiality.

THOMAS: That's right! Our God is the one that Aristotle's philosophy aimed at
proving. God is perfect. Perfection is incapable of change. A change must
be either for better or worse, but God is already perfect and therefore cannot be improved or impoverished. What is already perfect cannot change.
Therefore, God is pure actuality without potentiality and is immutable
and impassible.

FRANCIS: Sounds good—as a syllogism. But what does this immutable and
impassible God have to do with the God of Jesus Christ and of the Bible?
I've come to warn you, Thomas, that although you've done much good
for God's cause on earth, your love for philosophy and the authority you
grant philosophy in theology are dangerous.

THOMAS: Uh-oh. God sent you to tell me that? Maybe it's time for that contemplation exercise you mentioned earlier.

FRANCIS: Yes, it's time. Let's open all the windows and sit here in silent meditation. Ask God to fill your heart with love for nature and show you his
presence in all things.

*(The warble of birds and the rustle of trees in the breeze wafts through the
windows.)*

FRANCIS: So now what do you have to say, Brother Thomas?

THOMAS: All that I have written appears to be as much straw after the things
that have been revealed to me.

FRANCIS: Good! Then my work here is done. Peace be with you!

Analysis

The last saying of Thomas Aquinas in the imaginary conversation is not invented; this is what he actually said near the end of his life. Nobody knows for
sure what he meant. Apparently he had some kind of mystical experience of
God that made all his theological work pale in comparison to what was revealed
there. Without doubt Francis of Assisi would applaud.

Nothing in this imaginary conversation should be taken as implying that
Thomas Aquinas was opposed to personal and mystical experiences of God,
even in nature. Nor should anything be interpreted as implying that Francis
was opposed to the life of the mind when it serves God. By no means. However,
each partner in the conversation placed his life's emphasis in a different place.
Thomas understood his calling and mission to be primarily intellectual and
even philosophical. The ascendency of Aristotle's newly discovered and freshly
translated philosophy in Christian Europe presented a challenge to Christian
thought. Thomas was all about trying to reconcile the two. Some of his critics
thought little of the effort; some even rejected it as heretical.

In his reasoning, for example, Thomas agreed with Aristotle on it being conceivable that the world, meaning the universe, has always existed. He didn't think that creation, even in the Christian sense, depended on a temporal beginning. This came into play as he tried to establish God's existence by arguing from causation. He realized that his argument could be undermined if someone insisted, with Aristotle, that there is no definite beginning to the universe. So he agreed to assume that to be the case and then proceeded to construct an argument for nontemporal ultimate causation of the universe. In other words, the universe as a whole is finite and therefore does not explain itself; its explanation requires a first cause, ontologically if not temporally. There must be a Being that is uncaused in order for there to be a finite, caused universe. But some of his critics accused him of heresy for even agreeing that it might be possible that the world has no beginning.

During his lifetime Francis was controversial and even afterward because of his challenge to the church's wealth and earthly power. He demonstrated a Christian life that is fully spiritual and even authoritative, yet without the trappings of power and wealth. His example was such a contrast to the extreme luxury and power of the church hierarchy that at first church officials sought to marginalize him or even ruin him, and then they tried to co-opt him by bringing his order of poor brothers within the church's framework.

Francis taught that the true spiritual person lives as Jesus did: unattached to worldly possessions and power. He was a romanticist long before the Romantic movement of the late eighteenth and early nineteenth centuries. For him, the good life is one lived among the animals and plants and a few like-minded Christian friends, a life spent in prayer and contemplation. In today's terms, he was as Christian tree hugger.

Thomas and Francis would have talked about so many things in such a conversation. I chose to focus here on what would likely be their main point of disagreement. They shared the Catholic faith; neither one rejected or even questioned any major doctrine of Christian orthodoxy. (Even as he argued that the world might be eternal, Thomas confessed *creatio ex nihilo*, creation out of nothing.) But Thomas took a new turn in Christian philosophy and theology. Nobody before him divided reality into two complementary realms, nature and grace, quite as he did.

Yes, the faith always affirmed that grace is above nature and cannot be compelled by nature. Grace is sheer gift from God. But Thomas introduced the concept of the supernatural (a modern term for it) by dividing knowledge into two distinct realms: knowledge of God by reason and nature alone, and knowledge of God by faith and supernatural revelation. Before him the only view was some version of faith seeking understanding. Thomas made the turn toward understanding seeking faith. The realm of nature and reason began to float away, as it were, from its traditional grounding in the grace of creation and faith.

One critique of Thomas's theology has frequently arisen among Protestants. The rap is that Thomas set the stage for the coming of secularism by making nature relatively independent of God and knowable by reason apart from faith. He dedivinized nature. That's also how the modern physical sciences took off: nature gradually became a realm of dependable laws discoverable by reason apart from faith. That's good, but for theology it may have negative unintended consequences.

Natural theology, the attempt to know God by reason alone through nature alone (not "in" nature but "through" nature), may fail as science's discovery of natural laws becomes comprehensive. Also, natural theology opens the door to finding God through culture as well as through the physical environment. In the twentieth century the German Nazis convinced Christians in Germany that their movement was a new revelation of God in German culture.

Francis's critique is much simpler. He just thinks that nature is thoroughly infused with the presence of God in all things and that immediate experience of God there is far superior to rational proofs or arguments. Natural theology turns nature into an object. Nature is alive. It is a place of worship, not a laboratory or lecture hall. And God is best known through immediate experience of a mystical sort.

Thomas represents the intellectual, rational side of Christianity. Francis represents the contemplative, mystical side of Christianity. As with Anselm and Abelard (conversation 10), wouldn't a hybrid of both be interesting and perhaps beneficial?

For Further Reading

Davies, Brian. *The Thought of Thomas Aquinas*. Oxford: Oxford University Press, 1993.

House, Adrian. *Francis of Assisi: A Revolutionary Life*. New York: Hidden-Spring, 2001.

12

Sixteenth-Century Bucer Convenes Luther, Karlstadt, Erasmus, Zwingli, Grebel, Calvin, and Servetus on Church Reform

Setting

The sixteenth-century Reformation was carried out by a diverse and even motley crew of churchmen and theologians. In this imaginary conversation, seven major leaders meet to discuss how best to reform Christendom or the Christian churches. These seven represent all the major divisions in Reformation times—Lutheran, radical, Catholic, Reformed, Anabaptist, and antitrinitarian rationalist.

Martin Bucer was a Reformed theologian of Strasbourg, which now lies in France, with Germany just across the Rhine. It has been French and German at different times in its eventful history. Bucer was dismayed by the divisions among Protestants and wanted Luther and Zwingli—the first two great Protestant reformers—to patch up their differences and unite Protestantism. That didn't happen. When Luther and Zwingli met in Marburg to try to agree on the Lord's Supper, a major bone of contention between them, things only grew worse.

In this imaginary conversation Bucer has called these seven reformers together in a castle on the Rhine near Strasbourg. As the conversation will reveal, this couldn't have happened. But as in the case of many of these imaginary conversations, the reader is again asked to suspend credulity in order to learn something and be entertained.

And now about the participants: In 1483 Martin Luther was born in Saxony, in what is now Germany; he died in 1546. For a while he was a monk and a professor of New Testament and theology at the University of Wittenberg. In 1517 he began his public career as a reformer of the church by nailing his Ninety-five Theses, propositions for debate, to the cathedral door in Wittenberg. That created a furor that lasted for decades. He was excommunicated by the pope in 1521, but many churches throughout central Europe left the Roman Catholic Church with him.

Luther's story is so familiar that it hardly needs elaboration here. But readers unfamiliar with it should view the movie *Luther* (2003) and/or read one of the many books about his life. There are also numerous more-or-less reliable Web sites devoted to the subject.

Luther could be a harsh debate partner. In matters about which he cared deeply, and they were many, he brooked no disagreement from fellow reformers (to say nothing about Catholics and skeptics!). One of his favorite terms for theological enemies was "pig theologian." But such name-calling was common in that era. One of Luther's mottos was "Peace if possible, but truth at any cost." He was uncompromising about his beliefs and about the right way to reform Christendom.

Andreas Karlstadt (or Carlstadt; 1486–1541) was Luther's professor when he was a student at Wittenberg. He was a well-known and highly respected theologian who threw his lot in with the young reformer after they became colleagues. But while Luther was in hiding from the emperor, who wanted him arrested and perhaps killed, Karlstadt led the Reformation in Saxony and took it in a radical direction. He wanted to destroy every remnant of the old Catholic order and even supported the peasants in their bloody revolt against their feudal lords. Luther rebuked him, and they went their separate ways. Karlstadt is generally considered to be the most outstanding and influential of the radical reformers of the sixteenth century.

Desiderius Erasmus (1466–1536), also known as Erasmus of Rotterdam, was a Catholic reformer. He never broke away from the church even when its leaders harshly criticized him and even threatened him. He was widely considered to be the most respected scholar in Europe during his mature life. Luther reviled him because of his refusal to support the Protestant cause. Yet Erasmus did lend some moral support to the Protestant Reformation. Luther and Erasmus debated the issue of predestination and free will, with Luther stringently defending predestination and Erasmus just as passionately defending free will.

Ulrich Zwingli (1484–1531) was Luther's counterpart in the Swiss Reformation. To this day many Swiss Protestants consider him to be the real catalyst of the Protestant movement. He stripped the Zurich churches of Catholic trappings and outlawed the Mass. Zwingli and Luther debated the presence of Christ in the Lord's Supper and went their separate ways over that and other matters. Zwingli was a chaplain of the Protestant Swiss army and was killed in battle while defending Zurich against Catholic invasion. Luther's response to the news of Zwingli's death was harsh: "Serves him right for carrying a sword into battle as a priest and for holding false views of the Lord's Supper."

Conrad Grebel (1498–1526) was one of Zwingli's protégés in Zurich, but he wanted to go further with reforms. Zwingli moved slowly in order to keep the city council on his side, but Grebel and his friend Felix Manz decided to break away from the official reforms and abolish infant baptism. They baptized themselves as believers (by pouring) and taught their followers to refuse baptism to infants. They wanted to purify the Swiss churches of all Catholic elements and restore the New Testament church in all its simplicity. They opposed state churches and therefore are often lumped together with militant reformers. Actually, they were the first Anabaptists and rejected use of the sword.

John Calvin (1509–1564), born in France, is the most widely known Protestant reformer who was working in Switzerland. He is generally considered the true father of the Reformed branch of Protestantism, which includes Presbyterians. He wrote (in Latin, then translated into his native French) the first Protestant systematic theology, *Institutes of the Christian Religion* (1536; last ed., 1559); it is still widely read and discussed. Calvin is revered by most Reformed Protestants, and many call themselves "Calvinists." He emphasized the sovereignty of God in a fairly extreme way, including unconditional foreordination, or predestination, of individuals to heaven and hell. Calvin really did not do or believe much that cannot be found in Luther and/or Zwingli, but his influence on English-speaking Protestants has been incalculable. He was the chief pastor of Geneva, in the French-speaking area of Switzerland.

Michael Servetus (1511–1553) was an antitrinitarian radical reformer from Spain, who kept trying to convince John Calvin of the truth of his (Servetus's) beliefs, which Calvin regarded as heresies. Calvin warned him not to come to Geneva, but he went there anyway. Calvin saw him and had him arrested by the city council. Servetus was condemned to death at the stake. Calvin tried to persuade the council to commute the sentence to death by beheading, but to no avail. Servetus's execution in Geneva is considered to be one of the worst blemishes on the face of the Reformation. But Calvin and other reformers (to say nothing of Catholics!) despised Servetus and regarded his influence as poisonous. There is no excuse for what happened to him, but one has to remember that this was the custom of the times, and Protestant leaders feared that his heresies, including denial of the deity of Christ, would be blamed on all Protestants.

So these are our seven reformers. Learn about their distinct ideas from their own voices in this imaginary conversation.

The Conversation

LUTHER: Gentlemen . . . well, I use that term loosely . . . we have been brought together by our friend and fellow reformer Martin Bucer of Strasbourg, who is always trying to unify our Reformation movement. Remember that we have all taken a vow of secrecy about this meeting; nobody but Bucer and the seven of us know where we are at this moment. Nobody would even believe that we are meeting like this, and I'm only here to try once more to get all of you to join me in my recovery of the gospel—in what I call our "evangelical" movement, which is also catholic even though not Roman Catholic.

KARLSTADT: Martin, I've only come here at the behest of our peace-loving friend Bucer and with the hope that you might finally see the error of your ways and continue further down the path of reform with me and my fellow radical reformers—we whom you quite ungenerously call fanatics, *die Schwärmer*, as if we are vermin.

ERASMUS: If I might chime in here and add to that: Luther, once you divide the church, the kind of revolutionary and rebellious overthrowing of the whole social order promoted by Karlstadt and his like is inevitable. Yes, the Roman Church needs reform, but reform must come within and not by dividing the body of Christ or destroying the whole order of society.

ZWINGLI: Gentlemen, gentlemen, let's keep this dialogue civil and respectful, okay? Otherwise nothing is going to be accomplished here. Luther, you are both too radical and too conservative, if I may dare such a criticism. I mean it in a most constructive way. In my opinion, your reforms in Saxony and other parts of Germany are right and good even if they divide the church. But your harsh words against me and other reformers who sympathize with you and look up to you as a leader only serve to undermine our Protestant cause. Calling those who dare to disagree with you "pig theologians" is completely uncalled for. Your rhetoric is too rank.

However, you don't go far enough in your reforms; you still believe that Christ is bodily present in the Lord's Supper—which you still call the Eucharist!—and you allow unbiblical traditions to continue in worship. I say, away with any ceremony or symbol that is not commanded in the New Testament!

GREBEL: Father Zwingli, it seems that you are the proverbial pot calling the kettle black! Talk about refusing to go all the way in restoring the New Testament church! You claim to reject extrabiblical traditions in the churches, but you hold on to infant baptism, and you allow the city council of Zurich to control the course of the reformation of the church. Why don't you become consistent and reject infant baptism, which is completely unbiblical, and baptize only those who voluntarily convert to Christ by means of conscious repentance and mature faith?

SERVETUS: And you, Grebel, what about you and your Anabaptist brothers and sisters? Do you go all the way in reforming the church? No, you don't. You and these other would-be reformers hold on to the Nicene Creed, which is riddled with Greek philosophical terms and concepts; you insist on preaching that horrible doctrine of the Trinity and the unique deity of Jesus Christ and his substitutionary atonement. We reformers of the churches must follow reason as well as Scripture as we cut down the human traditions that have accumulated around the simple gospel that Jesus preached.

CALVIN: Servetus, if you ever come to Geneva, you'd better wear a disguise. If I or any other pastor or member of the city council sees you in our godly city, you'll be arrested and burned at the stake! You're no true reformer. You're a rationalist who would destroy the gospel by robbing it of all majesty and mystery. You're not even a Christian. Why don't you go to Poland? That's where the radical reformer Faustus Socinus is establishing a Unitarian church, which we all reject as totally false. That's where you belong. And eventually you and they will be cut down by the emperor, with the help of both Protestants and Catholics!

KARLSTADT: Come, come, Brother Calvin! Calm yourself. Yes, Servetus is a heretic and a troubler of the churches, but he and all other heretics should be free to argue their point of view without hindrance from church or state. After all, many in our empire consider you to be a heretic as well! How are you different from those of the Catholic Inquisition, who would burn you at the stake if they could get their hands on you?

We are all equal in God's sight, which is not to say that all opinions are equal. But all should have an equal right to worship in their own way without interference. I believe that true reformation will come only when church and state are entirely separate and when the state is run by the poor people, not by the rich and powerful.

CALVIN: You'd better stay away from Geneva too, Karlstadt. More than a few of your radical reforming colleagues are already in our city's jail.

LUTHER: Stop quarreling, people. All that is really needful or helpful is for all of you to agree with me! Not because I'm someone special, but because God has called me to raise up his church from the ashes of Roman Christianity. The princes of the empire have endorsed me and my method of reform. So long as you all continue to quibble and quarrel, there will be no united Protestant movement, and eventually we'll be so divided that the Roman antichrist and his false prophet, the great beast who is the emperor, will crush us.

ERASMUS: And who appointed you as the dictator, Luther? Oh, excuse me, your God is the all-determining, all-controlling dictator of the universe, who causes even sin and evil—the "hidden God," who cannot stand to give his creatures even one iota of free will lest he be opposed. So you think you can create yourself in the image of your "God" and crush all opposition, don't you? To all of you I say this: stop your bickering and quarreling about the petty details of Christianity and join me in reforming the church according to what I call "the philosophy of Christ," which is simply doing what Jesus would do in every life situation.

If all Christians stopped trusting in relics and popes and ceased quarreling and fighting about abstract doctrines and pointy-headed theological arguments like how many angels can dance on the head of a pin and started loving their neighbors as Christ loves us, then the church and the empire would experience true reform.

ZWINGLI: Ah, Erasmus, there's your humanism raising its ugly head. We all owe you a great debt of gratitude for providing us with an authoritative Greek edition of the New Testament so that we can make accurate translations of the Bible into our own languages. But we cannot congratulate you for watering down doctrine to the lowest common denominator: striving to be like Jesus. Yes, that's good and right, but there's more to Christianity than that.

We must think the right thoughts about God, including that he is all-controlling such that his providential sovereignty reigns over everything. And we do not say that in order to be "dictators," as you suggest; we say it because philosophy and the Bible teach it. If God were not all-controlling, he would not be God.

GREBEL: Zwingli, you're both right and wrong in your response to Erasmus. First, we should all be greatly appreciative of Erasmus's leadership. As someone has said, he laid the egg that Luther—and the rest of us—hatched. He was condemning and ridiculing relics and indulgences long before Luther nailed his Ninety-five Theses to the cathedral door in Wittenberg. You're right to question Erasmus's lack of interest in correct doctrine, but you're wrong to suggest that correct doctrine must include the all-determining sovereignty of God. Our God is not some great cosmic emperor or puppet master; he is our loving, gracious, and merciful Father, who shows us his loving heart in our friend and brother Jesus.

And Erasmus, you're right to say that what's really important is a life of following and imitating Jesus, but your idea of what that entails is faulty. We Anabaptists are becoming his disciples even unto death; as Jesus suffered, we also gladly suffer persecution from enemies. Being Christ's disciple means walking a path of costly grace, in close communion with other disciples, sharing all things in common as in the early church.

SERVETUS: Yes, Grebel, you and I certainly see eye to eye on these matters. Neither one of us considers the abstract doctrines and creeds of Christendom or the rulings of so-called Christian emperors of any weight. What is important is being Christ's disciples even unto death. Martyrdom. That's the "baptism of blood" we all may suffer for the sake of truth. And we agree about baptism; people without reasoning capability should not be baptized; how can they know what they are doing? But you and your Anabaptist sibs are too timid, Grebel. Go further than before in your critique of traditional Christian doctrine and practice. Not only is God not a cosmic dictator, as Luther, Zwingli, and Calvin would have him be; he also is not a three-headed monstrosity, as in the traditional doctrine of the Trinity. You Anabaptists haven't shaken that off yet!

CALVIN: Oh, the barking of mad dogs goes on and drives me crazy! You cannot overturn one word of the gospel or of the creeds by yelping and baying constantly at the great doctrines of the faith. What I see is this: you four—Karlstadt, Grebel, Erasmus, and Servetus—have all drunk too deeply at the wells of Renaissance humanism! You overthrow authority for personal liberty. You don't take seriously enough the total depravity of humans. Without the supernatural power of the Word and the Spirit, we humans can know nothing of God truly; the human mind apart from faith is nothing but a factory of idols!

And by "faith" I mean submission to God's Word, Scripture, which declares quite clearly that we are nothing more than pond scum—unless we are God's elect and given the Spirit of God to rightly interpret God's Word, in submission to the authorities that God has put over us, including especially the chief pastors of our cities.

LUTHER: Well said, Master Calvin! Except that you have broken away from God's appointed rulers yourself by establishing Geneva as an independent city-republic. You drove out the prince-bishop. Isn't that rebellion against God's established order?

KARLSTADT: Yes, Calvin, and what about the priesthood of ordinary Christian believers? You rule Geneva as if it were your private estate! The city council cowers at your bellowing messages from your mighty pulpit in what once was a Roman Catholic cathedral. Tear down all the idols, including stained-glass windows, elevated pulpits, and persecution of so-called heretics. All Christians are equal—in the state as well as in the church!

ERASMUS: Calvin, you're the worst of this whole bunch. I've lived in exile in Switzerland for many years now. Fortunately not in your medieval city of Geneva, where people can't even play cards or laugh on Sunday! If you really believed in the Word and the Spirit and in reason and true Christian piety, you'd encourage lively dissent and debate in your city and in your church. Yet like the pope in Rome, you squelch that before it can even begin. And when you can't answer your critics, you just call them "barking dogs" and drop the conversation; you don't even try to answer their questions—such as how God can be righteous and good yet foreordain and render certain the fall of humanity into sin and degradation!

GREBEL: Well, I guess it's my turn since we're going in order here. Personally, I think all of you except maybe Karlstadt and perhaps Servetus are servants of the mighty and powerful elites of society. You talk a good talk about reform, but the New Testament takes a backseat to preserving tradition and order in society. And some of you call on the civil leaders of society to enforce your opinions and persecute those who disagree with you. Calvin and the rest of you magisterial reformers, take off your robes, climb down from your pulpits, and sit in a circle as one of Christ's contemporary disciples; learn from Christ through the voices of the ordinary and simple folks. Erasmus, as much as we Anabaptists have learned from you about civility and peace—you have rightly condemned all wars as unjust—you still talk and act high and mighty; you still defend the corrupt church and empire.

SERVETUS: I agree with Grebel about all of that, even if he doesn't want my support. But true reform will come only when the likes of Calvin turn to reason alongside the Word and the Spirit as they determine what truth is. This whole notion that God foreordains people to hell for his own glory is not only morally repugnant but also stupid. What kind of God would that be? How could we tell the difference between that God and the devil? Whatever Scripture passages such as Romans 9 mean, they cannot mean such divine cruelty. Reason says so, and we must always submit to reason.

CALVIN: I think I'll leave and go home to Geneva now. But I'm going to stop by Strasbourg and report on the failure of this dialogue to my friend and mentor Bucer. I know he will be disappointed, but I warned him that men and women of such different faith commitments cannot walk together. Luther, I can walk with you and support you in every way except having bishops and believing in the Lord's bodily presence in the Supper. Christ is now in heaven and not in, with, and under the bread and wine all over the world at once. By arguing for consubstantiation—your weaker alternative to transubstantiation—you diminish the reality of Christ's humanity. He is still human and therefore localized in heaven and not ubiquitous, as you claim. What would be a ubiquitous human being?

Zwingli, the one thing we've all been conveniently ignoring this day is that you sit here among us as a ghost. I don't know how Bucer pulled that off, but if Samuel could appear to Saul after he was dead, I guess God can bring you back from death to grace us with your presence. I have no criticism of your theology except that you went too far from the Catholics and Luther in rejecting any presence of Christ in the Lord's Supper. The meal is much more than a memorial or symbol reminding us of Christ's death; it is a real sacrament in which the Holy Spirit nourishes our souls.

The rest of you—well, I don't even want to be in the same room with you anymore. Good-bye and good luck, but I can't say "Go with God" because you're false brethren and not true Christians at all. And don't come to Geneva! You know what fate awaits you there!

ERASMUS: Well, that was a rather imperious exit! But I'm not surprised; Calvin is so sure of the rightness of his own opinions that he can't even stand to be in the presence of those who dare to question them. The sun is beginning to set, and we don't have enough candles to carry on all night, so let's wrap this up. I'm afraid Calvin is right; we aren't going to agree on how to reform the church, and there's no hope of forming a united front against Rome. But I'm the only Catholic here, so I'd like to know why the rest of you who consider yourselves Protestants in some sense cannot unite. I've heard some of your quarrels, but what's really lying underneath all those seemingly petty differences?

LUTHER: That's obvious, isn't it? All these other would-be reformers want to throw the baby of tradition out with the bathwater of Roman Catholic heresies. There's no need to do that. If we want the princes to support us against Rome, we must not threaten the whole social order or the whole structure of the church. And we must, must! retain the sacramental grace of baptism and the Eucharist combined with faith. The great creeds and these sacraments are cornerstones of our faith and must not be tossed out along with rubble from the flying buttresses of medieval Christendom.

KARLSTADT: I remember when you talked otherwise, Brother Martin! When you were my student at the university in Wittenberg, you were the most radical of all. But you changed when the peasants revolted against their feudal lords; you sided with the lords and betrayed your poor followers, who looked to you for liberation. True reform must be an ongoing, never-ending revolution in church and society. Until the kingdom of God arrives, we will never be done with pulling down the strongholds of tradition and power and human authority.

ZWINGLI: Well, even if I am just a ghost here, I can still raise my voice to say that Luther doesn't go far enough in reforming the church and Karlstadt goes too far. But most important of all, we cannot unite because Luther insists on keeping the remnants of the old Catholic sacramental system. He believes that in the Lord's Supper we actually eat the flesh and drink the blood of Christ. That's superstition and completely contrary to the Bible.

GREBEL: Well, I think I've made my position clear by now. I agree with Zwingli about the Lord's Supper but not about baptism. Just as he thinks that Luther has not gone far enough with his reforms, I think Zwingli has not gone far enough. A baby simply cannot have faith. And to compare baptism to circumcision under the old covenant is absurd. The church should be a gathered group of committed disciples who announce their faith to the world by consciously undergoing water baptism as adults. The church will never be sufficiently reformed so long as everyone baptized as an infant is considered part of it.

SERVETUS: You're all too timid. The Lord's Supper is only a symbol—yes. Baptism should only be given to adults—yes. But ancient doctrines like the Trinity and the two natures of Jesus Christ in one person fly in the face of reason. How can we argue that only adults should be baptized because baptism requires a rational understanding of salvation and then insist that people sacrifice their intellects by embracing such irrational doctrines as those?

ERASMUS: You know what I think? I think you're all a bunch of nominalists, each in your own way. And nominalism is a disease that will eventually result in complete relativism, a situation where every Christian is one's own church. Luther, your nominalism is obvious. You think God can even do evil. Karlstadt, your nominalism appears in your opposition to all order and your extreme individualism, which makes every Christian equal.

Zwingli—why am I talking to a ghost?—your nominalism shows up in your view of God—like Luther's. You think of God in terms of sheer freedom and power as if God could do whatever he wants to do regardless of right and wrong. Your God could change his mind and decide tomorrow that the elect are really the reprobate and that salvation is not by faith but by works! You may not talk like Luther about a hidden God, but your God is just as scary as his! How can we trust a God without an unchanging and unchangeable nature and character?

Grebel, your nominalism is like Karlstadt's. You think of the church as just an aggregate of individuals rather than something real apart from the people who are in it. The result will be anarchy in the church just as the result of Karlstadt's nominalism will be anarchy in the empire.

And Servetus, I don't even know what to say about your nominalism except that it is vulgarized. You babble on about reason all the time, but your writings are impossible to understand. But like Karlstadt and Grebel, your nominalism is apparent in your reduction of the church to individuals and even to one individual. Your Christians are just a bunch of isolated monads, self-contained and separate, struggling on their own to figure out the great mysteries of life and religion. I predict that eventually your approach will win over all the others. Why? Because the drift of society today, largely because of Luther, is toward rebellion against authority and tradition—in spite of what he says.

Four hundred years from now, if not earlier, the church will hardly exist. Every person will be their own church, following their own "reason." The whole idea of a universal Christendom holding together church and society will die away. The result will be chaos and anarchy.

Analysis

The great sixteenth-century Reformation was anything but a united movement. The seven participants in this imaginary conversation represent main divisions of the church at the time: Catholic (Erasmus), Lutheran (Luther), Reformed (Zwingli and Calvin), trinitarian radical (Karlstadt), Anabaptist (Grebel), and antitrinitarian rationalist (Servetus). The category "Radical Reformation" often includes all the nonmagisterial Protestants. "Magisterial" indicates cooperation with the state; "nonmagisterial" indicates refusal to cooperate with the state in matters of church life.

Catholic reformers like Erasmus, whose influence helped to bring about the Catholic Reformation (or the Counter-Reformation) in the middle of the sixteenth century, could not stomach division of the church. For them, whatever the Catholic Church's faults and flaws may be, it is the one true church and cannot be divided. Whoever leaves it to start a new church leaves the true church behind. The "new church" is no real church at all. Protestants who do not understand the Roman Catholic doctrine of the oneness of the church cannot hope to grasp the Catholic antipathy to Luther and the whole Protestant movement. Also, as the conversation reveals, Catholics look at splintered Protestantism as the inevitable result of nominalism. (For more about nominalism, see conversation 10, including the introductory "Setting" and concluding "Analysis" sections.)

All the non-Catholic reformers shared just a few basic beliefs in common: salvation is by grace through faith alone and without works, Scripture stands above all church traditions, and every true Christian is a priest unto God and requires no human mediator to commune with God. But the Protestants and Radical Reformers disagreed even on these basic principles. The Anabaptists, for example, believed that the magisterial Reformers like Luther, Zwingli, and Calvin did not take Scripture seriously enough as above all church traditions because they retained some of the developments of theology and worship after the New Testament church. Zwingli, for example, seemed to have doubts about infant baptism but held on to it to please the Zurich city council.

A momentous change swept though European Christianity with the Reformations of the sixteenth century. Nothing would ever be the same again. The medieval synthesis of church and state was dissolved. The unity of Christianity was shattered. The door was open to radical rejection of authority. Cultural, social, and political revolutions followed the theological changes.

Followers of the seven reformers of this conversation can be found today. Yet many of them have no idea that they are replicating these men's ideas and practices. Nevertheless, Lutherans all know who Luther was and revere him as a great hero if not a saint. But one has to wonder what Luther would think of most churches that go by his name today. Zwingli and Calvin have followers throughout the world in the World Alliance of Reformed Churches—an umbrella group of scores of denominations that look back to those Swiss Reformers as the great heroes of the Reformation.

Liberation theologians and radical Christians of all kinds have considered Karlstadt to be a model of real reform that doesn't stop with theology; this reform extends into social and political praxis, levels authorities, and gives power to the people. Free churches that value separation of church and state, and believers churches that limit membership to true believers—these churches look back to Grebel and Anabaptists like him with respect. Unitarians and liberal Protestants often remember Servetus as a martyr for rational religion. But to a large extent, the laypeople have forgotten these heroes of the past even as they carry on their traditions.

For Further Reading

George, Timothy. *Theology of the Reformers.* Nashville: Broadman, 1988.

Lindberg, Carter, ed. *The Reformation Theologians.* Oxford: Blackwell, 2002.

13

Reformer Luther and Roman Catholic Theologian Eck Dispute the Nature of Salvation, Grace, Faith, and Justification

Setting

Luther (see conversation 12 for information about him) faced many adversaries but none as formidable as his Catholic nemesis Johann Eck of Ingolstadt. Eck had many titles, including professor of theology and chancellor at the University of Ingolstadt and canon of Eichstadt. He is generally regarded as the chief defender of ultracatholicism and opponent of Protestantism during the Reformation.

Eck was born in 1486 and died in 1543. He traveled widely and was well known by the pope and the emperor. Eck was a prolific writer, lecturer, and expert debater. By all accounts he was a child prodigy and entered university at the age of twelve. Eck was a tenacious if not brilliant polemicist. According to his critics, he was obsessed with defeating Protestantism and especially Luther, and he did not hesitate to use invectives in his attacks. In other words, he was Luther's rhetorical equal.

Eck was well connected, to say the least. Not only was he personally acquainted with the pope and the emperor, both of whom bestowed honors on him; he also knew many leading Protestants. He was future Anabaptist leader Balthasar Hubmaier's mentor during the latter's student days at university. Later he would viciously attack his former protégé as a heretic. He publicly debated Luther at Leipzig and also contended with Karlstadt, Zwingli (see conversation 12), and Luther's right-hand man Melanchthon. Eck was critical of Erasmus (see conversation 12) and virtually every other Renaissance humanist, reformer, and anyone the Catholic church suspected of heresy.

As part of the Catholic Inquisition, one of Eck's jobs was to go around Europe, seeking out church leaders and others who were any threat to Catholic traditionalism. And yet he was also a reformer himself. He played a key role in laying the foundation for the reforming Council of Trent. But his reforms had nothing to do with theology; he only aimed them at removing corruption from the church.

Without doubt Eck thus was one of the leading Catholic theologians during the Reformation era, perhaps the leading one. And he was an ultracatholic: he sought to defend the most conservative, traditional positions of the church. Many Catholics during his lifetime favored Conciliarism, the practice of ruling the church by councils rather than unrestrained papal authority. He fought that and defended papal supremacy.

Eck wrote numerous theological treatises, but the most important one for our purposes here was a four-volume collection of writings against Luther titled *Opera contra Ludderum* (1530–1535).

The height of Eck's anti-Lutheran campaign was his twenty-three-day disputation with Luther at the University of Leipzig in 1519. It followed a debate with Karlstadt that lasted several days. After that, the Catholic apologist lobbied the pope, emperor, and anyone else who would listen to excommunicate Luther and treat him as an outlaw. Some speculate that he was so humiliated by Luther's victory during the debate that he had a personal grudge against the reformer. Others defend Eck and argue that his campaign against Luther was not personal but purely theological. Given the virulent nature of his attacks on Luther, however, it seems unlikely that the campaign was strictly professional.

In Eck's defense, it would only be fair to say that toward the end of his life he seems to have moderated his anti-Protestantism somewhat. At least it was enough to engage in dialogues with Melanchthon and other Protestant leaders about the possibility of Protestant-Catholic compromise. Those talks led nowhere, and eventually war broke out between Catholic and Protestant states of the empire.

This imaginary conversation between Eck and Luther is set in a beer hall's back room, in a tiny village halfway between Augsburg, where the 1530 Diet (parliament of the empire) was meeting to try to resolve the Catholic-Protestant dispute, and Coburg, where Luther was directing the Protestants as they held their ground against the emperor and the Catholic princes. Luther could not enter Augsburg because the emperor had declared him an outlaw; he could go only where he could receive the protection of a Protestant prince. In theory, Eck could go anywhere, but he was unwelcome in most Protestant territories.

The Conversation

LUTHER: Welcome to my favorite little pub, Canon Eck. I would say *Guten Tag!* but that would imply some kind of good wishes. I really can't wish you well. All over Europe you are persecuting our brothers and sisters now that you've been appointed an inquisitor. Surely you're ashamed of yourself, aren't you?

ECK: I think you know better than that, destroyer of the faith. I've only come here to meet with you because our beloved emperor has some vague hope of settling this controversy and avoiding civil war within the empire. One word from you would go far toward peace.

LUTHER: As I always say, "Peace if possible, but truth at any cost!"

ECK: Well, let's cut the small talk and get right to the point. One question still ought to bother you a great deal. Who do you think you are to go against more than a thousand years of church teaching and order and against the spiritual and secular authorities that God has appointed over this Holy Roman Empire?

LUTHER: First, let's be clear that this empire is neither holy, nor Roman, nor even an empire! It's a patchwork quilt of three hundred principalities, electorates, dukedoms, and free cities. An empire? Please! What does Saxony have to do with Savoy? Second, it's unnatural that Christians in Germany should be ruled by a tyrant of the church in Italy. Third, tradition cannot stand up against the Word of God and reason. The church you defend is no longer the church of Jesus Christ because of the human traditions it has embraced and put above Christ himself.

ECK: I'm sure I already know which ones you mean, but please . . . explain further.

LUTHER: Above all else is the tradition of basing salvation on good works. That totally contradicts the gospel preached by Paul in the New Testament, where salvation is a free gift and not of works. Look at Ephesians 2:8 and 9.

ECK: But you forget, Luther, that Jesus himself handed the keys of the kingdom to Peter, so only his successors, the bishops of Rome, have the right to interpret Scripture. For more than a thousand years they have interpreted it as saying that salvation is a gift that must be merited by good works as well as faith. Haven't you read the Epistle of James lately?

LUTHER: James. James. Yes . . . James is in our New Testament, but it is an epistle of straw. There is no spiritual nourishment in it.

ECK: Then you would kick it out of the Bible as you're doing to thirteen books of the Old Testament that you call the Apocrypha?

LUTHER: No, but only because James was probably Jesus's brother. Yet we don't preach out of it. James contradicts Paul, and Paul in Romans especially promotes Christ.

ECK: You keep forgetting, Luther, that Scripture was selected and canonized by the church; that process is part of tradition. As our early church fathers declared against the heretics of their day, the Bible belongs to the church and not to heretics. You contradict yourself when you place the Bible above venerable church tradition because the Bible grows out of tradition.

LUTHER: No, the Bible is inspired by God. All the church fathers did was recognize the writings that are inspired; then they placed themselves and us under those inspired writings. Your Roman Church, which is no true church at all, has stood above Scripture and twisted it like a wax nose to suit your own countenance.

ECK: You are completely wrong, Luther. You obviously care nothing about the church of Jesus Christ and its traditions. Paul himself told his followers to keep the traditions he handed over to them. So they handed those traditions over to their followers and so on, right down to today. This faith is the only thing that keeps the church unified. You are destroying that unity and with it the body of Christ. And you have set yourself over both Scripture and church tradition. One man—you—over all else. How arrogant!

LUTHER: No, it is not just "one man over all else." It's the Word of God and reason over all else. I don't despise or reject tradition so long as it conforms with the Word of God. But so many Catholic traditions do not, so they must be rejected. I already mentioned one example. If you want more, I can list ninety-five of them.

ECK: Clever. But listen, Luther, the ones you call *die Schwärmer*, the fanatics, Anabaptists and other radicals, accuse you of holding on to unbiblical traditions such as infant baptism. Are you being consistent? You reject the parts of tradition you don't like but retain and even insist on those you like.

LUTHER: Not at all, Eck. I can give strong biblical support for every aspect of tradition that I uphold against the fanatics. Infant baptism is grounded in the biblical practice of circumcision and in Jesus's own admonition to let the little children come to him and forbid them not. The only thing wrong with infant baptism is your Catholic belief that it automatically saves a child apart from faith. There is no salvation without faith.

ECK: And how can a child have faith?

LUTHER: Prove to me that a child cannot have faith! Hah! Besides, if faith is trust, as we believe, then who is more trusting than a child? Also, the faith of the parents stands in for the child's faith until his confirmation.

ECK: And I can give similar support to every aspect of Catholic tradition. Just as infant baptism isn't explicitly taught in the Bible but is nevertheless biblical, so papal authority is biblical. Jesus gave Peter the keys to his kingdom and said that he would build his church on him.

LUTHER: That's not at all what Jesus meant. The "rock" on which he would build his church is Peter's confession of Christ as the Son of God.

ECK: You see, Christians disagree about many things, and people can make the Bible say whatever they want it to say. Just look at the antitrinitarian reformers. Without an authoritative magisterium to interpret the Bible, there will be chaos and anarchy in the churches. Every person will be their own pope.

LUTHER: Better that than one person in Rome forcing people to agree with his interpretation when it is against the plain meaning of Scripture and unreasonable. Besides, Scripture interprets itself. We need no special spiritual authority to interpret Scripture. Its meaning is plain.

ECK: You delude yourself, Luther. You simply want to be the pope, and you can't be, so you try to enforce your interpretation on everyone else. After all, you have urged the Protestant princes of Germany to hunt down and arrest the ones you call fanatics.

LUTHER: Well, we're getting nowhere with this. Let's probe right to the heart of our disagreement: salvation by grace alone through faith alone and without works. That's the gospel. Your church's so-called gospel is false because you lay a heavy burden on people, telling them to earn their salvation. That flies in the face of the whole New Testament. According to Paul, justification is free and given by God's grace alone to those who, like Abraham, trust him.

ECK: You're wrong about this also, Luther. Nowhere does the Bible say that salvation is "by faith alone." By faith, yes. But not "by faith alone."

LUTHER: But it does say "not of works!" What's left but faith?

ECK: Paul was referring to the works of the law, not good works of love, which are required for salvation.

LUTHER: What's the difference? You have turned the gospel into a new law by adding "works of love" to grace and faith. You even talk about people having to merit their salvation. What's that if not earning it by works of the law?

ECK: You clearly don't understand our meaning of "merit," which you should understand because you were a monk and a professor of Catholic theology.

LUTHER: I was never a professor of Catholic theology; I was a professor of Scripture and truth.

ECK: Whatever. You know that by "merit" we mean a gift of God within a person that causes one to do good works that please God. Whatever good we have, including good works, is from God.

LUTHER: So you say. But in practice you deny that by requiring people to suffer for their sins. You rob Jesus Christ's cross of its merit by saying that people must receive merits through suffering, doing penance.

ECK: And you make God's great salvation cheap by saying that people can just wave a magic wand of so-called faith and avoid suffering for their sins.

LUTHER: It's not people who wave your so-called magic wand. It's God. God has every right to simply forgive whomever he wishes to forgive and on any basis. He says he forgives for Christ's sake without requiring suffering or working. Go back and read Romans. Every single chapter says that in some way.

ECK: But Romans has to be read and interpreted in the context of all of Scripture. There Paul was simply trying to correct the mistaken impression held by many Christians that they had to keep the Jewish law in order to be saved. Things like circumcision and observance of Saturday as the Sabbath. And kosher preparation of food.

LUTHER: How much different or better is your Catholic church's detailed and impossible system of penance for those who confess their sins? You make people go on pilgrimages that they cannot afford and walk miles on their knees to shrines and fast for days.

ECK: Only for their own spiritual improvement.

LUTHER: No, you demand deeds of penance only because you don't really believe the gospel, which is that only faith counts for anything with God. And even faith is a gift of God. We sinners have nothing to offer God to make him be pleased with us. God's only pleasure is in Christ's death on our behalf, which is Christ's obedience to the Father. He graciously and freely includes us in that favor when we empty ourselves of all claims to righteousness and admit that we have nothing but Christ to offer God.

ECK: Admit it, Luther; you're an antinomian! An enemy of law. An anarchist. You would allow people to live horrible, sinful lives without shame or punishment. You are exactly the kind of person that Paul referred to when he mockingly asked if we should sin more so that grace may abound. You give permission for sinning if not encouragement for that.

LUTHER: Wrong, Eck. Haven't you read my sermon on "Two Kinds of Righteousness"? God not only freely accounts us as righteous for Christ's sake when we have faith; he also transforms us inwardly so that we want to please him with our lives—not by doing useless penance but by loving our neighbors as ourselves.

ECK: And what if we don't love?

LUTHER: Then we prove that we have not been justified.

ECK: How is that different from what we say?

LUTHER: Because you say that our justification, our being considered righteous by God, is merited by our good works. I say that our good works, our works of love, do not merit anything but flow freely from a heart that is grateful for what Christ has done.

ECK: You make good works unnecessary.

LUTHER: Yes, unnecessary for salvation. But they are necessary as evidence of justification. On the contrary, you make faith unnecessary. According to your doctrine, the sacraments of baptism and the Lord's Supper automatically convey grace into a person until salvation comes ex opere operato, simply from going through the sacramental motions, with or without faith.

ECK: Making their efficacy depend on faith makes faith a work, doesn't it?

LUTHER: I know you expect me to say "Touché," but I won't. You're so far off that I'm hopeless about helping you to understand. No, faith is never a work. It is simply accepting the grace of God without works. But faith is necessary because otherwise grace cannot be received.

ECK: So you do believe in free will after all, do you? I thought you rejected free will in favor of unconditional predestination in your debate with the humanist Erasmus. Now you sound as though grace must be freely received by faith.

LUTHER: No, again you have no understanding of the gospel. Faith itself is a gift of God unconditionally bestowed on sinners, usually at baptism.

ECK: Which sinners? All? Some? How does God decide?

LUTHER: Now you're trying to peer into the mysteries of God's mind. We can't know how God decides whom to elect; all we can know is that election is his sovereign choice, and he is righteous and good whatever he does.

ECK: So how do you decide who is elect?

LUTHER: Baptism is the surest sign at the beginning. Then comes Christian living as believers act out love for God and neighbor.

ECK: So you think we have no free will at all, do you? How can someone be responsible for one's sins without free will?

LUTHER: People have free will in all kinds of trivial matters but not in spiritual matters. We are all in bondage to sin until Christ frees us to live for him. Sinners are responsible for their sins because they want to sin.

ECK: But could they do otherwise?

LUTHER: No.

ECK: That's nonsense. Even the worst sinner is still capable of doing some good things.

LUTHER: No, the gospel tells us that all our good works are as filthy rags in God's sight because they fall so far short of the perfection of Christ.

ECK: So a person who saves a little old lady from being run down by a wild horse is sinning?

LUTHER: Absolutely.

ECK: What can one say to that except "ludicrous!"

LUTHER: Eck, your whole doctrine of salvation is Pelagian. You make salvation into cooperation between the goodwill of a sinner freely directed toward God and God's mercy. The Bible says that no one does good, not even one.

ECK: Again, taken out of context.

LUTHER: Wrong, again. But you're hopelessly and helplessly lost in the darkness of works righteousness, and I can't help you unless God takes over and transforms your heart and mind as he did mine in the tower at Wittenberg when I was studying Romans. My prescription for you is to study Romans with an open mind and let God speak to you through it.

ECK: And my prescription to you is to read James with an open mind and let God speak to you through that!

Analysis

I must admit to having taken some license with the words of both Eck and Luther. What I've tried to do is express their distinctive voices rather than their exact words. That's more or less true in all these imaginary conversations. To some extent, Eck here represents the standard Catholic arguments and points of view, especially during the Reformation era. Today, in the twenty-first century, Catholics and Protestants have reached certain agreements that would have been unthinkable then. Notice, for example, that both Eck and Luther value good works and faith even though they don't grasp that agreement; they magnify their differences rather than look for common ground. Unfortunately that is all too common in theological controversies.

But what does Eck mean by "faith," and what does Luther mean by "good works"? Well, for Eck faith means "faithfulness" to the traditions of the church and to doing works of love (giving alms, doing penance, etc.). This looks like works righteousness to Luther. By "good works" Luther means works of love done through the believer by God's transforming grace and as a result of justification. To Eck this sounds like antinomianism, being opposed to law and doing whatever seems right to oneself.

Whenever Eck mentions merit, Luther overlooks the fact that even for Eck, merit is only possible because of God's gifts such as the sacraments. It doesn't mean "earning" one's salvation. But then, why use the language of merit, which always automatically implies something earned? That would be Luther's question. Whenever Luther mentions faith alone, Eck assumes that he means salvation is totally without works of love. But to Luther and all his followers, there's a difference between saying that salvation comes apart from works and saying that it comes without works. Works form no basis for God's approval; that is something we receive because of Christ and our embrace of him in simple trust. Yet real faith, simple trust that receives God's grace, is always accompanied by works of love. But such faith produces works; works do not produce faith.

Throughout the second half of the twentieth century (as a result of Vatican II) and into the twenty-first century, Catholics have largely abandoned the spirit of Eck and tried to engage Protestants with a hermeneutic of charity, in a spirit of openness to understand. Many Protestants have reciprocated. The result is tremendous ecumenical agreement that still falls far short of shared communion. The Catholic bishops of Germany have agreed that the Augsburg Confession, the basic statement of faith of all Lutherans worldwide, is orthodox. The German Lutheran bishops have agreed that at its best the Catholic doctrine of justification is biblical and not a different gospel. Various statements of agreement about justification have been issued in Europe and America by Catholics and even evangelical Protestant Christians.

One has to wonder what the results might have been if Eck had listened more charitably to Luther and vice versa. But the tenor of the times was against that. The issues were not purely theological; politics played a role in the religious debates and controversies. The Catholic church, as led by the pope and the emperor, could not allow a lowly German monk to correct it. That would show weakness at a time when it was already weakening. The German princes who supported Luther could not compromise with Rome and the emperor without risking being subject to tyranny. They wanted freedom from taxes imposed by the church and by the emperor. Luther provided a way for them to be Christian without being Roman Catholic.

Today the differences between Eck and Luther may not seem as important as then. But they still exist and they still matter. The gulf might be narrower, but it is still there. Two principles still divide even the most ecumenically minded Catholics and the most ecumenically minded Protestants: religious authority and salvation. For Catholics, extrabiblical tradition, including the pope's and the council's declarations of doctrine, still stand as authoritative for all true Christians. The fact that many do not recognize them as true does nothing to lessen their truth and their authority. Every good Christian ought to believe that Mary was born without original sin, a dogma promulgated by the Catholic Church in modern times but, so it is claimed, always believed by the faithful. Protestants reject any dogmas not clearly implied by the Bible and refuse to recognize any human as especially spiritually equipped to impose a one and only right interpretation of the Bible on every Christian.

Protestants still believe (however they behave) that no part of salvation can be earned. They disagree among themselves about free will (something that Catholics believe in), but they all agree that good works do not compel grace: grace cannot be bought, earned, or merited. Grace is God's free gift, God's unmerited favor for Christ's sake. The only condition is faith, which includes repentance and trust in Christ alone for salvation. Righteousness is imputed even if it is also imparted. In other words, even if God plants righteousness inside a person, the righteousness that forms the basis for one's salvation is accounted to the person by God because of Christ. Thus it is always an "alien righteousness" (Luther's term) and never the person's rightful possession.

Catholics still have great trouble in accepting this doctrine because they see it as a legal fiction. God would be dishonest to declare someone righteous when they are not at all really righteous. Rather, according to Catholic theology, God makes someone truly righteous (at least in part) and then declares them just as righteous as they really are. That process continues into purgatory because most people die while not yet inwardly righteous and therefore not fit for heaven.

Do these differences still matter? Yes. From a Protestant perspective, the Catholic doctrines of tradition and salvation create tremendous difficulties. For example, what do you do with a church hierarchy that has the sole right to interpret Scripture and dictate faith and practice but has become corrupt? If you stand up to it as Luther did when he publicly condemned the sale of indulgences, you automatically break faith with the church. In the New Testament, Paul stood up to Peter at Antioch (Gal. 2) and criticized him for refusing to eat with gentiles. That sets a precedent for all later Christians: no matter how revered a leader may be, he is always subject to truth, and Christian truth comes from God's Word, Scripture.

Also, from a Protestant perspective, the Catholic doctrine of salvation inevitably implies that one must earn part of salvation by doing good works. No amount of explanation can justify the use of "merit" in connection with human salvation (other than Christ's merits); it automatically implies something earned. Making justification gradual and progressive implies that it can be lost by mere neglect. Is that what the New Testament affirms? Or can nothing separate us from the love of God in Christ Jesus?

What should have happened at the end of Eck's and Luther's conversation is their shaking hands, agreeing to disagree in love, and going back to their separate churches. Then they should have looked for ways they could cooperate in endeavors for the kingdom of God, such as helping the poor. That's what Catholics and Protestants do today. Hopefully.

For Further Reading

Pelikan, Jaroslav. *The Christian Tradition*. Vol. 4, *Reformation of Church and Dogma*. Chicago: University of Chicago Press, 1984.

14

Reformers Luther, Hubmaier, Zwingli, and Calvin Debate the Lord's Supper and Baptism

Setting

Those who have read previous conversations will already be familiar with Martin Luther, Ulrich Zwingli, and John Calvin (see esp. conversation 12). For those who have not read the relevant earlier conversations or their "Setting," a brief description of these Reformers will be given here.

Luther surely was the main catalyst for the Protestant Reformation of the sixteenth century. He was born in 1483 and died in 1546, in what is now Germany. He was a monk and professor of theology at the University of Wittenberg. On October 31, 1517, he nailed his Ninety-five Theses to the cathedral door in Wittenberg, asking for debate among scholars; this act set off the Protestant Reformation. He was excommunicated by the pope in 1521 and went on to lead the Protestant churches of the Holy Roman Empire until his death. Luther did not always get along well with people, especially defenders of the traditional Catholic theology, against which he revolted, and other Reformers with whom he disagreed.

Ulrich Zwingli (1484–1531) was the reformer of Zurich in Switzerland. He carried out reforms much as Luther did in Germany and died in a battle to defend Zurich against Catholic invaders. He is often considered to be the founder of the Reformed branch of Protestantism, whose best-known theologian was the younger John Calvin in Geneva. Reformed Protestantism emphasizes the sovereignty of God and goes further than Lutheranism in rejecting Catholic traditions. Like Luther, Zwingli had little use for Protestant reformers who didn't agree with him about things like the sacraments. He was a cautious reformer, always reforming the church only at a pace acceptable to the city council. The first Anabaptists who rejected infant baptism as a holdover from the Catholic Church were his more radical followers. He reacted harshly against them, even to the point of encouraging the city council to arrest, torture, and execute them.

John Calvin (1509–1564) was the chief pastor of the city of Geneva and led it out of its Catholic past into its Protestant future. He is better known than Zwingli but really did not add much new teaching to him. He did disagree with Zwingli about the Lord's Supper. Calvin provided the Reformed branch of Protestantism with its first and lasting system of theology—the *Institutes of the Christian Religion* (1536; last ed., 1559). Like Zwingli he harshly persecuted radical reformers such as the Anabaptists and even condoned the burning of radical reformer Michael Servetus. Calvin's legacy, especially among Reformed Protestants, is very much alive and well. Many, if not most, Reformed Protestants in the English-speaking world call themselves Calvinists.

Balthasar Hubmaier has not yet appeared in an imaginary conversation. He was born in about 1480 and died in 1528. His death was an especially violent one, at the hands of the Catholic authorities in Vienna, where he ended his career as an Anabaptist leader. Hubmaier was a highly regarded Catholic scholar and churchman and served as head priest of the cathedral of Regensburg in Germany.

In about 1521 Hubmaier left Regensburg for Waldshut in Breisgau, at a ford of the Rhine and near Switzerland; the town was in Hapsburg (Austrian, Catholic) territory and now lies in Germany. There he became first a Lutheran and then an Anabaptist; he led his Catholic congregation into the waters of believers baptism. Hubmaier encouraged them not to have their children baptized but to let them decide whether to be baptized when they were old enough to understand the sacrament.

Hubmaier went to Zurich to debate with Zwingli about baptism. There he was arrested and tortured. He recanted his views on baptism at the behest of Zwingli but later recanted his recantation. After that he and his wife spent years fleeing both Catholic and Protestant authorities. They settled for a while in Nikolsburg in Moravia (today's Czech Republic), where a Protestant church predating Luther's Reformation existed. It was founded by followers of the Reformer Jan Hus, who was burned at the stake in 1415. The Czech Brethren still exists and may hold rightful claim to being the oldest Protestant denomination. Luther was called the "Saxon Hus" by his enemies because he repeated many of the Moravian's ideas.

In Nikolsburg, Hubmaier and his wife and their followers found a measure of toleration and freedom from persecution. The area became a refuge for Anabaptists. As many as twelve thousand of them settled there from all over Europe. During his time in Nikolsburg, Hubmaier wrote numerous treatises explaining and defending Anabaptist beliefs and practices. He became well known throughout Europe as the main proponent of the Anabaptist movement.

The Anabaptist movement began in Zurich in about 1525 with followers of Zwingli who rejected infant baptism and alliances between the church and the state. The label "Anabaptist" means "rebaptizers" and was applied to them by their enemies. Eventually they came to accept it for themselves. Another label for the earliest ones is Swiss Brethren. The Anabaptists largely agreed with Luther, Zwingli, and Calvin about justification by faith alone apart from works, but they placed more emphasis on discipleship, including nonattachment to material possessions. They were considered abusers of children because they withheld baptism from infants.

Eventually a single leader of most Anabaptists in Europe emerged in the person of Menno Simons (1496–1561) who operated mainly out of the Netherlands. His followers came to be called Mennonites and exist today as the largest body of Anabaptists in the world.

Hubmaier and his wife traveled back to Waldshut and were caught and taken to Vienna to stand trial for heresy. He was burned at the stake after being tortured on the rack, and she was thrown into the river, with a rock tied around her neck. Drowning (another baptism?) was considered an appropriate punishment for Anabaptists. But the parallel doesn't exactly work because Anabaptists baptized by pouring rather than immersion. Baptism by immersion came later, with the English Baptists of the seventeenth century.

During the sixteenth century, European Protestants were deeply divided. One of the major bones of contention was the sacraments. They couldn't agree on the meaning of baptism or the Lord's Supper. To this day those disagreements remain major causes of Protestant division.

This imaginary conversation is set in the city of Marburg in 1528—the year of Hubmaier's death. Philipp, the prince of Hesse, invited Luther, Zwingli, and a number of other Protestant Reformers to his castle in Marburg in 1529 to try to settle their differences. The so-called Marburg Colloquy turned into a debate between Luther and Zwingli over the nature of the Lord's Supper. Both left unreconciled and angry. Here we'll pretend that Luther, Zwingli, Hubmaier, and a quite young Calvin meet a year earlier in Marburg to discuss the sacraments. Philipp has asked Luther and Zwingli to come back a year later for a more official discussion.

It's doubtful that Hubmaier would even be invited to such a meeting, so we'll have to imagine that he heard about it and just showed up in disguise among the small audience of theological students and priests. He came to make sure that the Anabaptist point of view on baptism was heard and well represented.

Another difficulty with this setting is the youth of John Calvin, who would have been only nineteen years old in 1528. He was a student in France, first of theology at Paris and then of law at Orléans. But by all accounts he was a child prodigy and by this time may well have been capable of entering into such a conversation with the more mature Reformers. We'll have to pretend that by age

nineteen he had already joined the Protestant movement in his heart and mind
even if not publicly. Certainly he wouldn't have been invited to participate in
such a discussion at that age, so he too is imagined as sitting among the listen-
ers to Luther and Zwingli and then joining in to offer an alternative view of
baptism and the Lord's Supper.

The Conversation

LUTHER: So, Master Zwingli, we meet at last. Thanks to our mutual friends
Martin Bucer of Strasbourg and Prince Philipp of Hesse, in whose castle
we meet. I welcome you and pray that you will see the light regarding the
blessed sacraments of baptism and the Lord's Supper. It's important that
we agree so that our evangelical churches can enter into full fellowship
with each other.

ZWINGLI: It's good to finally meet you also, Brother Luther. And the members
of this small audience of theological students and priests. I hope and pray
that they will recognize what I say about these sacraments as God's truth
and institute these doctrines in their home churches.

LUTHER: Your words don't sound very promising, Ulrich. Are you so closed-
minded to truth that might come through others?

ZWINGLI: No more than you are, Martin. In fact, no, not at all. My mind is
fully open and submitted to the Word of God. But I am not biased toward
your theology because of your greater reputation throughout Europe. You
see, I was already reforming the churches in and around Zurich when you
were just beginning your work of reforming the church in Saxony.

LUTHER: Oh, really? Isn't it interesting that you abolished the Mass in Zurich
only in 1525, when I had already fully reformed the church in Wittenberg
and throughout Saxony and other territories of our empire? Maybe you
read some of my writings about these matters such as my treatise *The
Babylonian Captivity of the Church*, in which I discuss the Mass and why
it is an abomination?

ZWINGLI: No, not really. I mean, yes, I did read it later. But it had no influence
on me except to confirm what I was already doing.

LUTHER *(making a sarcastic sound)*: Humph! Somehow I doubt it. You mimic
my reforms poorly, especially with regard to the Lord's Supper. You learned
from me the evils of the Catholic Mass but went too far. You threw the
baby out with the bathwater and replaced the real presence of Christ in
the sacrament with a real absence of Christ!

ZWINGLI: I'm not sure you're fully informed, Martin. That's one reason I came
here—to set you straight about my doctrines of the sacraments and hopefully
persuade you to continue with your reform of the church by throwing out all
Catholic elements of the sacraments. You still hold on to Catholic notions of
baptism and the Lord's Supper. What kind of halfway reform is that?

LUTHER: Not so, not so! You are wrong about me, Ulrich. Now listen carefully and learn. First, about baptism. The New Testament clearly supports infant baptism, as I'm sure you will agree, when it records our Lord as saying "Let the little children come to me; do not stop them; for it is to such as these that the kingdom of God belongs."

HUBMAIER (*quietly mumbling from the audience*): No, no, no. Not so at all. That's not right. Wrong, wrong, wrong!

LUTHER: What? Who is that mumbling among the spectators? Now, look, you're just here to listen and learn and not to contribute to this discussion. So shut up!

HUBMAIER (*stepping forth from the audience and approaching the table where Luther and Zwingli sit*): Excuse me, Martin and Ulrich. Perhaps you recognize me if I remove my disguise.

LUTHER AND ZWINGLI (*in unison*): Hubmaier!

ZWINGLI: What are you doing here? I thought you were in hiding over in Moravia with the rest of the heretics and fanatics!

LUTHER: Well, I must say you're bold, Balthasar! I guess you know how peace-loving our patron Philipp is and took the chance that he wouldn't have you arrested because there are so many Anabaptists swarming around in this area.

ZWINGLI: You'd better not come to Zurich again, Hubmaier, or you'll get the same treatment as last time or worse! You recanted your heretical beliefs about baptism and then, like a coward, took back your recantation.

HUBMAIER: Both of you are not only wrong about baptism but also about the right of the church and state to persecute good Christians because of their dissenting beliefs. God did not give either the church or the state the sword to punish people for their beliefs. And how ironic that you hunt down and torture and kill so-called heretics when you know very well that the Catholic authorities would do the same to you if they could catch you.

LUTHER: You're wrong. God did give the sword to the magistrates of this world to smite the heretics, who would lead good folks right into hell.

HUBMAIER: So then, do you think the kingdom of God can be brought about with violence? Jesus mocked such nonsense.

LUTHER: No, not the kingdom of God. But the kingdom of this world is also established by God to protect the innocent from evildoers. And God has given princes like Philipp here the sword to defend the order of society, including right doctrine.

ZWINGLI: I don't know about princes, with all apologies to Philipp, but God certainly works through our city council in Zurich to maintain order. Haven't you read Romans 13, man?

HUBMAIER: I think you totally distort that passage; it's not about obeying the state but about voluntarily subordinating oneself to it. Yet the state is not the kingdom of God, and we followers of Christ must be citizens of the kingdom of God first and foremost. You claim to be Christians, but you ignore Jesus's teachings in the Sermon on the Mount. "Blessed are the peacemakers. . . ."

LUTHER: I see our patron Prince Philipp wants us to include you in this discussion. So, with Ulrich's permission, I'll allow it. Sit down and be civil. Hopefully our words will sink in and bring you to repentance for your fanatical heresies.

ZWINGLI *(to Luther)*: So, as you were saying before being so rudely interrupted, infant baptism is ordained of God and supported by the gospels. I agree.

HUBMAIER: Well, I don't agree. Both of you argue that faith is a requirement for salvation. What possible good can baptism do a child? An infant cannot have faith or understand what is being done in baptism. Baptism is an act of commitment and not a means of grace. Neither one of you takes faith seriously enough. You pay it lip service, but then you go back on your beliefs when it comes to baptism. Baptizing a baby is like a pub putting out a sign saying "good wine" before the harvest of grapes is even in! It's presumptuous at best.

LUTHER: Nonsense. Withholding baptism from infants is making a work of the law out of baptism. Baptism saves precisely because it is a gift of God and not a human work. Whom better to baptize than an infant if salvation is totally a gift of God and not at all a reward for good behavior? Plus, who is more likely to have faith than a child? A child trusts. And that is what faith is—trust. Besides, the faith of the parents and the church stand in for the faith of the child until the child later confirms the baptism with faith.

ZWINGLI: That's right, Balthasar. I agree with Luther about this. Just as Israel circumcised babies to signify their inclusion in the covenant people of God, so the church baptizes them to signify their inclusion in it, the new people of God. Without baptism a child is excluded from both church and society. While children may be saved by God's mercy, they will not be given the great gifts of grace that come with being fully within God's family as they grow up.

HUBMAIER: What are you talking about? Children are automatically within God's family because they haven't sinned yet. God does not impute sin to a child for Christ's sake. Read Romans 5. Paul clearly says there that by his death Christ set aside the guilt of Adam's sin for everyone. A child gets no more benefit out of a little water on the forehead than from a little wine in the mouth. You don't give baptized infants the wine of communion, do you? No, because they can't possibly understand it. And they don't need it. But you're so inconsistent. If babies can benefit from baptism without understanding, why not give them the Lord's Supper like the Eastern church does?

LUTHER: You're a child abuser, Balthasar. By denying children the sacrament of baptism, you deny them citizenship in the empire as well as the benefits of membership in the body of Christ. You might even cause a child to go to hell because you refuse him baptism. It's safer to baptize children even if we believe that God will have mercy on unbaptized babies.

ZWINGLI: Now, Martin, you sound very inconsistent. I hate to side with Balthasar here, but he actually learned these things from me when he first became a Christian at Waldshut. He's right that unbaptized babies cannot be damned. I can't even imagine where you get such ideas. They're just downright medieval.

HUBMAIER *(muttering to himself)*: Look who's talking!

ZWINGLI *(trying to ignore Hubmaier)*: All infants are born forgiven by the work of Christ. None who die go to perdition. But that's no reason to deny them baptism! Baptism does not save, but it does insert the child into the covenant that God has with his people.

HUBMAIER: Then why not just go out and grab every baby in sight, including Jewish babies, and baptize them? For you, Martin, they would then be more likely to go to heaven if they die. For you, Ulrich, they would then be blessed by the covenant.

LUTHER: You speak nonsense, Balthasar. Only children of Christians can be baptized.

ZWINGLI: But why, Martin? You don't have the answer, but I do. In your view all children should be baptized to save them from the fires of hell. In my view only children of Christians should be baptized because God establishes his covenant with families.

LUTHER: I didn't say all unbaptized children go to hell.

HUBMAIER: But you imply it. And you, Ulrich, are also inconsistent. Why baptize female babies if baptism is the Christian form of circumcision? The parallel breaks down.

ZWINGLI: Our time is limited. We'd better talk about the Lord's Supper because soon our prince's supper will be ready for us. Luther, you are only halfway reformed when you talk about the Lord's Supper. You seem to agree with the Catholics about transubstantiation—a doctrine full of idolatry.

LUTHER: No, I do not believe in that horrible Catholic doctrine. The wine and the bread remain just that: wine and bread. They do not magically change into the body and blood of Christ. The Catholic Church teaches that only because it believes Christ is resacrificed every time the Mass is observed. And that denies the once-for-all nature of Christ's death for us.

ZWINGLI: But you do believe that we actually chew and swallow Christ's body and blood, don't you?

LUTHER: Yes, without doubt. That's what Christ himself said at the Last Supper: This is my body, and this is my blood.

ZWINGLI: But he could not have meant that literally! He was standing right there in front of them.

LUTHER: He meant it of their future observance of the Supper. He would be with them in, with, and under the elements of bread and wine.

ZWINGLI: How gross! How disgusting! You make us cannibals, eating Christ!

LUTHER: And you empty the Lord's Supper of all benefit by making Christ absent from it.

HUBMAIER: Now I'll have to come to my tormenter's defense, Martin. As much as that pains me, Ulrich is right. You ought to just give up all vestiges of Catholic doctrine, including the real, bodily presence of Christ in the sacrament. You take the Bible too literally sometimes.

ZWINGLI: I don't need or want your help, heretic. What are you doing here, anyway? Martin, you are wrong to think that the body of Christ can be everywhere at once, as you imply by teaching that it is in, with, and under the elements in the Lord's Supper. You dissipate the humanity of the risen Christ by making his body ubiquitous. Jesus Christ is sitting at the right hand of God the Father in heaven. He is present with us through his Spirit, but not bodily.

CALVIN (standing up among the audience): Excuse me, Mr. Zwingli. I hate to interrupt, but I have a thought about this. You're right that Christ is bodily in heaven, but why can't the Spirit of God bring him here among us as we partake of the bread and wine? Don't you risk emptying the sacrament of its mystery by removing Christ's body too much from it?

LUTHER: I don't know who you are, young man, but you're on the right track there. Keep thinking that way, and you'll end up where I am on this important subject.

CALVIN: No, although I respect you very much, Mr. Luther, I have to disagree when you say that Christ is in, with, and under the elements of bread and wine. You make the sacrament too physical and magical. But I also disagree with Mr. Zwingli. He makes the sacrament too ordinary and mundane. There is mystery in the Lord's Supper. Christ is present by his Spirit. But he is also present bodily and not only through a mediator.

ZWINGLI (to Calvin): Who are you, anyway?

CALVIN: My name is John Calvin, and I am from France. But I very much want to participate in the Reformation of the church throughout Europe. Hopefully we can break the stranglehold that the Catholic church has on France and reform the church there just as you gentlemen are doing in Germany and Switzerland.

LUTHER: Well, you're a young whippersnapper to stand up from the audience and interrupt us. So sit down and listen!

ZWINGLI: No, no, I think he has something good to say. But I can't wrap my mind around the idea that Christ is still incarnate and also able to be bodily present in many places at once. How does that work, young man?

CALVIN: I can't explain it. And I don't believe that Christ's body is everywhere at once, as Luther does.

LUTHER: See! Your youth prevents you from understanding me. I did not say that Christ's body is everywhere at once. I said his body is able to be anywhere, as is possible because of the communication of attributes taught by our church father Cyril of Alexandria. By virtue of his resurrection and glorification, Christ's body is not limited by space.

CALVIN: Well, even that goes too far. Jesus is human, and a human cannot be in two places at once—except as the Holy Spirit miraculously makes Christ present among us here and there. And that is what happens when, by faith, we partake of the Lord's Supper.

HUBMAIER: Aha! "By faith." Yes, that's the most important thing that's been said here this afternoon. Both baptism and the Lord's Supper require faith. Not faith in magic, but faith in Christ's sacrifice for us. When we partake of the Lord's Supper in faith, we are mysteriously brought together with Christ, in union with him by the Holy Spirit. But there's nothing magical or mysterious happening. The Spirit lifts our spirits up to heavenly places and brings us into encounter with the living Christ.

ZWINGLI: No, no, no! The Lord's Supper is a memorial meal. It symbolizes Christ's death just as our baptism in water symbolizes our dying with Christ in conversion.

HUBMAIER: But, but . . .

ZWINGLI: Be quiet, Balthasar. I know you're going to say that the sign must follow the reality. I disagree. The sign of baptism can come before the reality it symbolizes. Why not?

HUBMAIER: Because there's nothing yet to symbolize, and if you baptize unregenerate children, they may grow up thinking that they are already converted by baptism and may never repent and confess faith in Christ for themselves.

LUTHER: I thought you said that children are already saved! Now are you calling them "unregenerate"?

HUBMAIER: See, this is where you and Zwingli and I assume that this young student Calvin gets it all wrong. There's a difference between being innocent and being regenerate. A baby is born innocent of all sin because of Christ, whose death has set aside humanity's guilt from Adam's sin. But a baby is not yet regenerate. Regeneration is when a person repents of sin, has faith in Christ, and sets one's feet on a new path of life by the power of the Spirit of God. A baby cannot do that.

ZWINGLI: I agree with you that infants cannot be regenerate, but I think that happens at confirmation, after older children begin to understand the faith.

LUTHER: And I say it happens at baptism. People are born again by the water and the Word at baptism.

HUBMAIER: But I thought you wrote that in the tower at Wittenberg, as you read Paul's Epistle to the Romans, you felt "born again." Weren't you already "born again" when you were baptized?

ZWINGLI: Ha! Caught in a contradiction by a heretic! Serves you right, Martin.

LUTHER: Well, it's almost time for dinner now. I smell the venison roasting in the kitchen below us. And I could use a good stiff beer. Young man Calvin, would you like to go down to the pub in town and have a drink with me while we talk about predestination? You, Zwingli, will hopefully see the light and change your mind about the sacraments by next year, when we meet here for our official colloquy.

Analysis

By all accounts Luther did love his beer. And he hated heretics and fanatics. He also tended to use epithets for everyone who disagreed with him. But that was the tenor of the times; today we expect civility even in the face of atrocity, to say nothing of heresy!

During the sixteenth century the Protestants were all over the map on the sacraments. The one view they all eschewed was the Catholic doctrine of transubstantiation. That's the idea that in the Mass the bread and wine actually turn into the substance of Christ's flesh and blood while retaining the "accidents" or appearance of bread and wine. Luther trusted his senses too much for that, but he did want to take the New Testament literally where Christ says, "Those who eat my flesh and drink my blood abide in me, and I in them" (John 6:56). So he developed what has come to be called the consubstantiation view of the Lord's Supper, as held by most Lutherans around the world. In this view, Christ's risen and glorified body is literally in, with, and under the bread and wine in the Lord's Supper so that the believer is actually eating Christ's flesh and drinking his blood with the elements. This is Luther's version of the real presence of Christ in the Supper.

Zwingli considered this only a hair's breadth from the Catholic doctrine and rejected it mainly on the ground that it contradicts the incarnation. If Christ is really incarnate and therefore human, his body is localized somewhere in heaven. We may not know exactly what that means or where that is (most modern people say it's a "dimension"), but we can be sure that Christ is not bodily everywhere at once. That's completely inconsistent with being a human. So the argument between Zwingli and Luther over the Lord's Supper is really about Christology.

In Zwingli's doctrine the Lord's Supper is a powerful memorial meal that reminds us of Christ's sacrifice and proclaims his second coming. There is no bodily presence of Christ, and believers do not in any sense eat Christ. This is called the Zwinglian view of the Lord's Supper and has become the doctrine of most of the free churches, including Baptists. Naturally, Zwingli interpreted John 6:56 and similar passages figuratively.

Hubmaier agreed with Zwingli about the Lord's Supper, as do all Anabaptists today. But Calvin wasn't satisfied with either Luther's interpretation of the sacrament or Zwingli's. He wanted to take the Bible seriously about Christ's real presence both among the people and with the elements in the sacrament taken by faith. But he had to appeal to mystery because he agreed with Zwingli against Luther that Christ's body is localized in heaven and is not ubiquitous. For him, then, the Spirit is the key to the real presence of Christ in the Lord's Supper. The Holy Spirit unites believers with Christ when they participate in the Supper with faith. There is a real union taking place by the power and presence of the Holy Spirit.

And in some mysterious way, it is possible to say that believers eat Christ when they take in the elements of bread and wine. But it is a spiritual eating and not a physical eating. Who can blame critics for scratching their heads and wondering what this means? But Calvin and his followers would just say, "It's a mystery," and urge people not to rationalize it.

Luther considered baptism to be a real sacrament that brings regeneration to the child when faith is present. It does not work apart from faith, as held in Catholic theology. But when pressed by his critics about the infant's faith, he had to fall back on tradition. Luther was simply not willing to toss aside fifteen hundred years of Christian teaching about baptism. His critics accused him of being inconsistent and reforming only halfway when it came to the sacraments.

Zwingli and Calvin rather much agreed about baptism. For them, and the entire Reformed tradition of Protestantism, baptism is parallel with circumcision. Baptism marks the new covenant, circumcision the old covenant. But both usher the child into God's covenant with his people. A baptized child is automatically considered saved, though only God knows for sure who are the elect.

Hubmaier and all the Anabaptists with him rejected infant baptism in favor of believers baptism. They consider the magisterial reformers' grip on infant baptism as sure evidence of Catholicism's undying legacy among them. The magisterial leaders only halfway reformed the church by keeping infant baptism. But the deeper logic of Hubmaier's rejection of infant baptism is his doctrine of personal salvation, which requires a personal, conscious decision to repent, amend life, and dedicate oneself entirely to Christ. While growing up, children baptized as infants assume that they possess salvation and never feel the need to repent and believe. That is why magisterial Protestant churches are full of unbelievers who grew up in the church. Hubmaier wanted a church composed only of true Christian believers and disciples of Christ.

For him, believers baptism is the foundation of church discipline, and without discipline there is no true church. When people agree to be baptized, they agree to submit to the discipline of the church in case of sin. Hubmaier advocated putting Christians who sin under the ban, which means that other Christians, even family members, do not speak to such persons until they repent.

Although the passions of the sixteenth century have largely died away, Protestantism is still divided over these issues. Underlying the differences are very serious theological commitments at variance with one another. What one believes about Christ's presence in the Lord's Supper or about who should be baptized should certainly depend on what one believes about the incarnation and salvation.

For Further Reading

Mabry, Eddie. *Balthasar Hubmaier's Understanding of Faith*. Lanham, MD: University Press of America, 1998.

McGrath, Alister. *Reformation Thought: An Introduction*. London: Blackwell, 1999.

Pipkin, H. Wayne, and John Howard Yoder, trans. and eds. *Balthasar Hubmaier: Theologian of Anabaptism*. Scottdale, PA: Herald Press, 1989.

Wallace, Ronald S. *Calvin's Doctrine of Word and Sacrament*. Grand Rapids: Eerdmans, 1957.

15

Sixteenth-Century Reformer Calvin and Seventeenth-Century Theologian Arminius Contest Divergent Views of Salvation

Setting

Imagine John Calvin, the great Reformer of Geneva and leading theologian of the Reformed branch of Protestantism, meeting Jacob Arminius as he wakes up in paradise after dying of consumption (tuberculosis) in 1609—exactly one century after Calvin was born. Arminius was born just four years before Calvin died in 1564. So they were hardly contemporaries. But Arminius was the best-known adversary of the Calvinism of his day in Holland, even though he expressed great appreciation for the Genevan Reformer he never met.

Readers who are not familiar with Calvin should read about him in the "Setting" for conversation 12. Suffice it to say here that he was one of the main Protestant Reformers and is regarded by Protestants in the Reformed family of churches as perhaps the greatest Reformer of all. He is best known for his strong emphasis on the absolute sovereignty of God, including unconditional predestination of people to either heaven or hell.

Jacob Arminius studied theology in Geneva under Calvin's successor there, Theodore Beza (1519–1605). Beza systematized Calvin's theology in a scholastic manner that some critics argue was inconsistent with his mentor's approach to theology. In other words, Beza tried to answer questions Calvin left unanswered, issues Calvin likely would have relegated to the realm of mystery. Arminius did not buy into all of Beza's theology, but he was a good-enough student for the

Geneva theologian to recommend him to the consistory of the leading Reformed church in Amsterdam, where he became pastor.

Later Arminius became professor of theology at the Reformed University of Leiden, where he fell into controversy with the other theology professor, Franciscus Gomarus (1563–1641). Gomarus accused Arminius of teaching heresy because Arminius did not believe in unconditional election. Arminius believed in free will and taught that a person must cooperate with God's grace in order to be saved. By cooperation, however, he did not mean, as Gomarus charged, contributing to salvation by good works. That would be semi-Pelagianism if not outright Pelagianism (see conversation 9).

Arminius wrote numerous theological treatises, mostly defending his theology against false accusations (e.g., that it amounted to the Roman Catholic doctrine of salvation) and explaining it to all kinds of interlocutors. His best-known and perhaps clearest explanation of his theology is *Declaration of Sentiments* (written in 1608), which can be found together with his other writings in a three-volume *Works of James Arminius* (Baker Books, 1999). ("James" is the Anglicized form of Jacob.) There and elsewhere the Dutch minister and theologian developed a non-Calvinist but Reformed theology of salvation that includes total depravity but also prevenient grace. These concepts and their place in his theology will become clear in the conversation.

Arminius died at the peak of the controversy over his theology. His followers wrote up a document expressing the main tenets of their theology and called it the Remonstrance. They came to be known as the Remonstrants, which is really just another word for Protestants. They were the protesters against the high Calvinism of the Netherlands in their time. The Remonstrants were brought to trial by the Reformed churches of the United Provinces (the official name of the Netherlands then) in 1618/19. The council that tried them for heresy is known as the Synod of Dort because it met in the city of Dordrecht (English: Dordt/Dort).

The political ruler of the United Provinces was Prince Maurice of Nassau, who favored the Calvinist party. Calvinist theologians came to the synod from all over Europe. The Remonstrants were not allowed to defend themselves, were condemned as heretics, and were banished from their positions as ministers and theologians. Some were forced into exile, and at least one was beheaded.

In 1625 Prince Maurice died, and a new ruler, more sympathetic to dissenting religious groups, allowed the Remonstrants back into the United Provinces. They founded a Remonstrant seminary that still exists in Amsterdam. A Dutch denomination called The Remonstrant Brotherhood is a full charter member of the World Alliance of Reformed Churches (much to the chagrin of extremely conservative Calvinists, especially in America, who still consider Arminianism as theologically not Reformed).

This imaginary conversation is meant to illustrate the main differences between Calvin and Arminius. Since their lifetimes overlapped only four years, we have to imagine them meeting in heaven. Readers are asked to suspend credulity to make this work. But who is to say it couldn't have happened this way?

The Conversation

ARMINIUS: Hello! Where am I? This place is so beautiful. It reminds me of the gorgeous fields of tulips in my homeland, Holland. And yet there's something different . . .

CALVIN: My dear Doctor Arminius, you're not dreaming or waking from sleep; you're in heaven. Isn't this what you expected?

ARMINIUS: Oh, so I died of my consumption, did I? Actually, I do feel much better now. I can breathe so much easier. But, pray tell, who are you? You look familiar. I think I saw portraits of you in Switzerland when I studied there in Geneva. Aren't you—?

CALVIN: That's right, Arminius. I'm John Calvin. You studied in Geneva under my protégé and hand-picked successor as chief pastor and principal of the Genevan Academy, our seminary. His name was Theodore Beza. You remember him, don't you?

ARMINIUS: Yes, yes, I do remember him. And now I remember that there was a large portrait of you hanging in the lecture hall and also one in Beza's office. But you died long before I did. Why are you greeting me just inside the pearly gates?

CALVIN: Well, it certainly wasn't my idea! I was shocked and horrified when I heard how you were contradicting my teachings and the teachings of my protégé, your mentor, and of all our Reformed professors.

ARMINIUS: I'm somewhat surprised to learn that up here you have such knowledge of happenings on earth! Most of us down there don't think you folks up here are paying attention to us. But now that I know you were watching, may I ask if my writings and teachings caused you to reconsider any of your ideas? For example, your ideas about predestination?

CALVIN: We'll talk about that in a little while. Let me first explain why we're having this unexpected and rather awkward meeting. Some time ago I was in misery over your heresies and how you were leading so many of our Reformed people astray with them. Then as I was praising God for the marvelous way in which he uses error to further his own purposes, God appointed me to talk with you as soon as you arrived here. I'm to show you the ropes of heaven, so to speak, and dialogue with you about our theological differences. God didn't explain why; he just said to do it.

ARMINIUS: Well, perhaps he thought you might learn something from me.

CALVIN: That would surprise me very much, but since arriving here many years ago, I've grown used to surprises. Things aren't exactly as I had expected them to be. For example, I saw an angel teaching the archheretic Servetus about the Trinity. He looked as surprised to see me as I was to see him. Eventually the angel brought us together, and we reconciled. I apologized to him for my part in his burning at the stake.

ARMINIUS: So even Servetus is one of God's elect! That is surprising. But I always did suspect that God's mercy might be much wider than most of us Protestant theologians thought. I certainly hoped so. Thanks for confirming it for me.

CALVIN: You might be surprised to know that your old nemesis Franciscus Gomarus is destined to be here when he expires. He virtually danced on your grave the other day. And you didn't seem to think he was much of a Christian.

ARMINIUS: I never said that! I only said that his behavior toward those of us who disagreed with him was indecent and that his views of predestination were extreme. I couldn't find some of what he dogmatically asserted in your writings. And yet he claimed to be your follower.

CALVIN: Yes, yes. I am a bit disappointed in his extreme views and ways of expressing them. But that's only since I learned a greater portion of the truth here. No doubt when Gomarus arrives, he also will be taught how small and puny our earthly concepts of God and his ways are. And you might be interested to know that, according to rumor, God is going to appoint you to be his greeter at the pearly gates. Like Servetus and me, you and Gomarus will learn to get along with each other once you see that both of you had a portion of the truth and both of you were only partially right in what you taught.

ARMINIUS: I can't say that I'm looking forward to that. He lied so terribly about me when he tried to have me deposed from my chair of theology at the University of Leiden. He was most ungenerous.

CALVIN: Well, but you weren't exactly nice in some of your responses to him! You wrote that his God—and mine—is not only the worst sinner of all but also the only sinner!

ARMINIUS: But that was just an admission of how I saw things. After all, if he and you are right, then sin and evil are planned and wrought by God. God is the author of sin and evil. I don't see any way to let God off the hook. If your theology is correct, then God is to blame for all the evil and suffering in the world because he is the all-determining reality.

CALVIN: Absolutely not! If you read me carefully, you know that I repeatedly denied that God is to blame for sin and evil! Only sinners are guilty, even when they disobey God because he compelled them to sin.

ARMINIUS: That just doesn't make sense. You and all your followers said that, but it's impossible. How can God compel sinners to disobedience and be untouched by the guilt of it, and the sinners be the only guilty ones?

CALVIN: I think you know the answer. You were a good student, so Beza says. Surely you know that we say a single act foreordained and rendered certain by God can be both sin and not sin. It is not sin for God who foreordained it and rendered it certain, but it is sin for the person who commits the act even if one could not do otherwise. Why? Because the sin is always chiefly in the desires, motives, and intentions, not just in the physical or mental act itself. All events are foreordained by God for his pleasure and glory; everything serves a higher and greater purpose than itself.

The sinner commits the evil act out of a motive that is sinful, such as selfishness or hatred. That's what makes it wrong. God foreordains and renders the act certain because it is necessary for the fullest possible manifestation of his own glory. For example, murder is wrong for the creature because God has declared it so and because murder is always committed out of some evil motive. But God is not stained by the guilt of the murder he foreordains because he is not subject to any law and because he can bring good out of that act.

ARMINIUS: So, what you have written and now assumed is that God is the creator and providential ruler of all things and that nothing happens without his foreordination. Also, everything that happens is foreordained for his glory, right? And as our church father Augustine said, the only evil thing is an evil will, so evil is only in the intentions and motives of the heart and not at all in the mental decisions and physical acts. And God is not the author of sin and evil because, even though he foreordains and renders certain every mental and physical act, including ones that are sinful, he is not the author of the sin itself because that is in the evil intention of the creature's heart. The mental and physical acts themselves are good because they serve God's higher purpose of glorifying himself.

CALVIN: Yes, that's certainly true.

ARMINIUS: Well, then, from where did the first evil intention come? If you say "from the creature's self," you make a huge exception to God's all-determining power and governance of everything. That would make a creature autonomous, which is exactly what you seek to avoid. But if you say "from God," you undermine your whole attempt to release God from authorship of sin and evil, for if any evil intention comes from God, we are back to God being the ultimate and perhaps only sinner!

CALVIN: We just have to leave some things to mystery. The origin of the first evil intention is a mystery hidden from us. Surely it was not from God, but neither could it have been completely apart from God's will and power. So all that is left is a mystery.

ARMINIUS: I don't think you're allowed to do that, Calvin. It looks like more than a mystery. It sounds to me like a sheer contradiction! You have said that God is the all-ruling power and that nothing exists that isn't foreordained and in some sense caused by him. Then you except evil wills and intentions. Don't evil wills and intentions exist? Aren't they necessarily, then, from God?

CALVIN: You're forgetting that our great church father Augustine taught us that evil is not something but is the absence of the good. So, no, evil wills and intentions do not "exist" in the usual sense. They are not things, nor do they have being. They are privations of the good.

ARMINIUS: But that doesn't answer my question: from where do they come? Even a privation of the good has to begin somewhere and with something. Did God foreordain and render evil intentions certain or not? That's the question, and it remains even if you define evil as the absence of the good. Even absence exists. Think of darkness, for example. It is only the absence of light, but it exists as the absence of light.

CALVIN: Now you're being obstinate. I don't think you can answer your own question. From where do you think evil comes?

ARMINIUS: From the misuse of creaturely free will.

CALVIN: Then you admit that you do not regard God as the all-determining power and as sovereign Lord and ruler over all?

ARMINIUS: I believe that God is sovereign over his own sovereignty and rules over his own rulership. God can limit himself to make room for creatures' freedom, giving them free range even to oppose his perfect will.

CALVIN: Then you say that God can create another creator beside himself: the self-determining creature.

ARMINIUS: Not at all. The gift of free will is from God, and the creature cannot use it rightly or wrongly without God's permission. But God did not foreordain sin or evil and does not compel creatures to disobedience.

CALVIN: You think you let God off the hook with that device, but in fact you also make God responsible for sin and evil by appealing to his permission.

ARMINIUS: No more than a teacher is responsible if a student fails because he allows it.

CALVIN: But what if the teacher could stop the student from failing and doesn't?

ARMINIUS: The only way a teacher can guarantee that a student will not fail is by giving him too much help so that he does not have any alternative but to pass. That would require the teacher giving the answers to the student, which is unjust.

CALVIN: So you believe that God is a distant deity, watching us do our best but not helping us?

ARMINIUS: Not at all! God is like a good parent, constantly helping the children to do their best but allowing them to make mistakes, especially as they mature and take on more self-reliance and responsibility. God is like a good teacher, offering both challenge and support but not doing the work of learning for the students.

CALVIN: Well, at the end of the day, your God is too small! He can't guarantee the triumph of his will. He's not very glorious. I was about to say "in my opinion," but what I say is biblically true. It's not a matter of differing opinions. You are simply not honoring God or the Bible with your teaching about a human's autonomy and ability to thwart God's will.

ARMINIUS: I'm sure we could go on forever arguing about God's providence, but let's turn to a related subject: predestination. As you know, I came to oppose your teaching—and the teachings of your followers—about God's unconditional election of some to salvation and reprobation of others to eternal damnation. The God of Jesus Christ would not do that. He is a God of love and not of hate.

CALVIN: Absolutely, he is a God of love and not of hate. He loves the elect. But he's also a God of justice. He leaves the reprobates to their deserved damnation. God is not obligated to save anyone! What a merciful God we have that he chooses to save some out of the mass of perdition that is fallen humanity.

ARMINIUS: But wait a minute! Didn't you imply earlier and write in your *Institutes of the Christian Religion* that even the fall of humanity into sin with Adam does not land outside the all-determining and foreordaining will and power of God? So if God foreordained and rendered the fall certain, the "mass of perdition" hardly "deserves" damnation. Who deserves damnation for doing what they could not avoid doing? What kind of God would foreordain the fall of his creatures into damnable sin and then hold them accountable and even guilty and deserving of eternal torment in hell? And if God is a God of love and justice, as you affirm, then why wouldn't he save everybody if he could? And why couldn't he? And doesn't Peter's Second Letter tell us that God is "not wanting any to perish, but all to come to repentance"?

CALVIN: Ah, you are peering into the depths of God's hidden will. Yes, God wants everyone to be saved. But for his full glory to be revealed, it's not possible. His justice toward sinners shown through wrath must also be manifested. Hell is necessary for the full glory of God. As one of my faithful followers (was it Beza himself?) said, "Those suffering in the flames of hell for eternity can at least take comfort in the fact that they are there for the greater glory of God." Yes, it's a terrible decree of God that creates hell and foreordains some to be there. But to say otherwise is to rob God of his full glory and imply that all people deserve better!

ARMINIUS: Don't you believe in God's goodness and love? Your God sounds harsh and self-centered. Where's his compassion?

CALVIN: I do believe that God is good. He is the very standard of goodness itself! Any goodness in a creature is but a dim reflection of God's perfect goodness. But God's goodness isn't the same as ours, and whatever God does is good by definition. How can anything done by the highest and greatest being be less than good?

ARMINIUS: In your account of God's "goodness," the term loses all meaning. There's no analogy between our understanding of goodness and the goodness of God. But then what's the point of calling it "good"?

CALVIN: It all goes back to God's revelation of himself in the Word taught to us by the Spirit. Even when we can't understand, we have to believe what is revealed. And the Spirit helps us; only through the inner testimony of the Holy Spirit can we truly grasp the goodness of God. If from a merely human perspective God doesn't seem perfectly good, that's because people project our goodness onto God. We have to learn from God himself what his goodness means. And what the Word and Spirit teach us is that whatever God does is good.

ARMINIUS: Well, your belief about God removes him from all understanding. Even the written Word has to be comprehensible; it can't be so mysterious that no one knows what its words mean! I agree that the Spirit must teach us that the Bible is God's Word, and without the Spirit we cannot truly understand the Bible. But if with the Spirit's help two people cannot agree on what simple words like "good" and "love" mean, all things become obscure.

CALVIN: I'm not sure you even have the Spirit to help you! But, then, I'm not your judge. Only God is. Yet I am a judge of theology, and yours stinks! I apologize for the colloquial language, but even in my *Institutes*, I sometimes had to rely on strong language to correct skeptics.

ARMINIUS: Yes, I know. You said that those who persisted in questioning your account of God's justice are like barking dogs.

CALVIN: Well . . . ?

ARMINIUS: As with God's providence, it appears that we're getting nowhere in our discussion of God's predestination to salvation.

CALVIN: But you haven't even explained what you believe about that very important doctrine! I think I know what your view is, but let me hear it straight from you. Sometimes hearing it said aloud reveals its inner absurdity.

ARMINIUS: God is the electing God, and his election, which surely is the same as predestination, is first and foremost of Jesus Christ to be the mediator between God and humanity. Second, God's election is of the church, as it was of Israel. God elects to have a people called by his name. Finally, election, or predestination, refers to God's foreknowledge of believers. God predestines all who believe to be saved and become part of God's elect people. And he foreknows who will freely choose to become part of God's elect people. Finally, God's purpose in it all is to show his love by means of grace and mercy.

CALVIN: That's a cute but sentimental notion of election and predestination. It hardly does justice to God's glory or human sinfulness. It implies that God is conditioned by our choices. It puts humanity over God. And it implies that we are not totally depraved, contradicting Paul in Romans 3. There the apostle says that no one seeks after God. Unless God unconditionally elects and irresistibly calls humans, they have no chance of repenting and being saved because they are, as the apostle says, dead in trespasses and sins.

ARMINIUS: I agree that by oneself no person seeks after God, let alone finds God. But God gives people prevenient grace to assist them. Prevenient grace enables free will and is resistible.

CALVIN: What's the point of this extrabiblical concept of prevenient grace?

ARMINIUS: Scripture everywhere assumes it even if it doesn't name it. On the one hand, Scripture says that God alone saves; fallen humans have no spiritual power even to initiate their own salvation. The heresy of semi-Pelagianism is something I reject. God, not humans, initiates salvation.

On the other hand, Scripture calls people to decide to respond to God's call and makes them responsible for their choices.

How can people be responsible if they are not free? Why would God call people who cannot freely respond? "Prevenient grace" is a biblical concept even if the phrase is not found in Scripture. The concept of the Trinity isn't spelled out in the Bible, but only that doctrine makes sense of all that Scripture says about God; likewise, prevenient grace isn't spelled out in Scripture, but without it Scripture makes no sense.

CALVIN: Well, I and my followers also believe in prevenient grace even if we don't call it that. But we follow Scripture by believing that it is irresistible. When God calls a person inwardly to salvation, that person must be saved. The outward call comes to many, but the inward call—which is a portion of prevenient grace—is given only to the elect, who must respond yes to God. God graciously bends their wills to such a saving response.

ARMINIUS: Answer me this, Calvin: if God could save everyone but doesn't do so, what kind of God is he? In your theology God could save everyone because salvation is unconditional and irresistible. So why wouldn't a loving God save everyone rather than just some?

CALVIN: I think we have already covered some of this. God's chief purpose in creation is to glorify himself, and his full glory can be achieved and revealed only if all of his attributes are manifested. God's wrath against sin and sinners is necessary for his full glorification.

ARMINIUS: You undermine the power of the cross, then. Wasn't the cross a sufficient revelation of God's wrath against sin? Why would more be necessary?

CALVIN: Well, apparently it wasn't sufficient.

ARMINIUS: Aha! There's the Achilles' heel of your theology, Calvin! It implies that the cross was an incomplete and insufficient revelation of God's wrath, which it wasn't. The just punishment for the sins of all people was laid on Christ. What more could God do to reveal his justice and wrath?

CALVIN: Then how do you account for hell? If the cross sufficiently revealed the glory of God and if the deserved punishment of all people was laid on Jesus there, then why would hell be necessary? It wouldn't be! Your view, Arminius, inevitably leads to universalism, the heresy that all will be saved.

ARMINIUS: No, your theology actually leads inevitably to universalism—if one really believes in God's goodness. A truly good God would elect everyone to salvation! And hell isn't strictly necessary at all. It's truly tragic because it is so unnecessary. The cross declared a universal amnesty for all sinners, but sinners must accept it to inherit heaven. Many do not and instead choose hell. Hell, then, is where God allows evil people to go because they reject his grace.

CALVIN: Well, Arminius, I don't know that we've come close to learning from each other. Our views of God's sovereignty over history and salvation seem irreconcilable. But when God appointed me to talk with you, he said that if we couldn't agree, he would appoint an archangel to teach both of us. So let's just go and find that archangel.

Analysis

There are many more differences between Calvin's and Arminius's theologies than could possibly be included in such a brief conversation. But to the surprise of both Calvinists and Arminians, the two theologians also shared much common theological ground. For example, as is clear in the conversation and in his writings, Arminius believed in total depravity—that every person born into this world except Jesus Christ is completely helpless to do anything spiritually good or even to exercise goodwill toward God apart from God's supernatural, prevenient grace.

They differed about whether prevenient grace is resistible or irresistible. Calvin thought it was irresistible, as do all his followers. Arminius thought it was resistible. For him, people do not have "free will" with regard to salvation, but the Holy Spirit gives them the gift of "freed will" through prevenient grace. This is the grace that convicts, calls, illumines, and enables sinners who hear the gospel to repent and believe. Without it they would never respond to God in faith.

Arminius also believed in God's sovereignty, but he rejected any account of divine providence that would make God the cause of sin or evil. For him, sin and evil are not part of God's plan or purpose, but God works in spite of them to bring about good. Arminius feared that Calvinism made God to be the author of sin and evil, and he could not stomach that. The main contention between Arminius and the Calvinists of his day, if not Calvin himself, was the character of God. Arminius was all about preserving and protecting the good character of God as loving, merciful, and compassionate. He could not see how an all-determining God who foreordains sin and evil could have that character.

Arminius also believed in predestination. After all, it's a good biblical term! But he defined it as God's foreknowledge of which persons would respond to the gospel with faith.

The debate between Arminius and his followers and the followers of Calvin has waxed and waned over the years. Eighteenth-century revivalist and founder of Methodism John Wesley (1703–1791) was a passionate Arminian; his friend and fellow Great Awakening revivalist George Whitefield (1714–1770) was an equally passionate Calvinist. The two eventually had a falling out over their theological differences, but they reconciled, and Wesley preached a laudatory sermon at Whitefield's funeral.

The Arminian-Calvinist debate waned somewhat during the last half of the nineteenth century and first half of the twentieth century as evangelicals banded together to oppose liberalism in their denominations. They put aside their differences over predestination and free will (really over the character of God) to present a united front to the watching world. But then, in the last decades of the twentieth century and into the twenty-first century, another round of the debate heated up among evangelical Protestants.

Does it matter? Do these differences really deserve the attention they often receive? Knowledgeable persons on both sides of the divide will say yes, because at stake are not secondary issues such as free will but actually the character of God. Calvinists view God's glory primarily as his sovereignty and power. Arminians view God's glory primarily as his love. Both surely contain some truth. The difference lies in how each side of God's nature and character is stressed. Calvinists do not deny God's love, but they qualify it. For example, some of them say that God loves all people in some ways but only some people in all ways. Arminians do not deny God's sovereignty and power, but they qualify them. For example, some of them say that God limits himself so that he does not even know what free creatures will do with their free will until they make their decisions (open theism). The extremes on both sides tend to fuel the fires of debate and controversy.

For Further Reading

Bangs, Carl. *Arminius: A Study in the Dutch Reformation.* Nashville: Abingdon, 1973.

Klooster, Fred H. *Calvin's Doctrine of Predestination.* Grand Rapids: Baker Academic, 1977.

Olson, Roger. *Arminian Theology: Myths and Realities.* Downers Grove, IL: InterVarsity, 2006.

16

Eighteenth-Century Evangelical Revivalists-Theologians Wesley and Edwards Compare Differing Views of Salvation

Setting

As the reader can tell, I find imagining what great Christian thinkers would say to each other in heaven fun. So I like to use that device when the conversation partners could not possibly have met during their earthly lives. Over the years my students have also enjoyed imagining this setting with me. I can only hope readers will forgive me for using it so often and realize that it's difficult to conceive of any other imaginary setting in cases where two or more people could not have met before death.

John Wesley and Jonathan Edwards were born the same year: 1703. Edwards died from a smallpox inoculation shortly after becoming president of the College of New Jersey (now Princeton University) in 1758. Wesley lived much longer, dying in 1791. Both were eminent religious leaders during their lifetimes and in their respective countries.

John Wesley was one of the two leaders of the British Great Awakening in England. The other was his friend George Whitefield (1714–1770). Both men preached to large crowds, often outdoors. They were considered fanatics by their more dignified Church of England critics. The derisive term then was "enthusiast." Neither man set out to stir up emotions, but emotional outbursts often occurred while they preached.

Wesley set up conventicles (small religious groups) whose members came to be known as Methodists. The movement was intended as a renewal movement within the established church, but in spite of Wesley's intentions, it turned into a denomination separate from the Church of England. That was especially true in America, beginning with the Revolutionary War. Wesley thus was the founder of the worldwide Methodist movement, with many branches and offshoots, including many Holiness and Pentecostal churches.

The Methodist founder wrote numerous sermons, commentaries, and essays but never a system of theology. He was a self-identified Arminian in theology (see conversation 15) and believed in human free will as a gift of God's prevenient grace. His friend and fellow evangelist Whitefield was an ardent Calvinist. So was Jonathan Edwards.

Edwards pastored the Congregational church of Northampton, Massachusetts. From his pulpit he led the Great Awakening of New England in the 1730s and 1740s and wrote an account of it called *A Faithful Narrative of a Surprising Work of God* (1737). He wrote numerous sermons, essays, and articles, often promoting his own version of Puritan Calvinism.

Edwards did not found any denomination or movement, but his preaching, along with that of Whitefield, who visited America several times, revived and enlivened many churches, including Congregational and Presbyterian and, surprisingly, Baptist. Many people converted during the Great Awakening in America became Baptists, which helped that denomination to grow into one of the country's largest.

Most people know of Edwards only as the fire-and-brimstone Puritan preacher of the sermon "Sinners in the Hands of an Angry God" (1741), included in many high school and college textbooks. Yet Edwards was a philosopher as well as a preacher and theologian. He was highly educated in the latest philosophical and scientific movements and was influenced by the empiricism of John Locke (1632–1704). By all accounts his sermons, including "Sinners," were delivered in an unemotional style even if they had an emotional impact on their audiences.

Wesley and Edwards never met, although they knew of each other through their mutual friend Whitefield and news accounts of their respective revivals. They were separated by "the big pond"—the Atlantic Ocean—that presented a great obstacle to casual acquaintance. Wesley had served as an Anglican pastor in Georgia early in his ministry (1736–1737) but did not return to America. Edwards did not travel to England even though he was a British subject. (The North American colonies were still under British rule during his lifetime.) In spite of being far apart geographically, they are often paired with each other in accounts of British and American church history as the two fathers of the evangelical movement. What many people call "evangelicalism" in England and America began out of the Great Awakenings, with the emotional conversions of thousands of souls.

Many of the fissures in American evangelicalism are products of the different theological styles of the movement's two fathers. Though both believed in radical conversion and a personal relationship with Jesus Christ, they differed about subjects such as the sovereignty of God. Edwards believed that whatever happens, God foreordains it and renders it certain for his glory. Even sin and evil are foreordained by God, even though God is not the author of sin and evil. (This dual claim sounded like a contradiction to Edwards's Arminian critics.)

It would be difficult to imagine a Christian thinker more obsessed with God's glory and power and control over all things than Edwards. In at least one of his writings, he argued that God creates the whole world out of nothing at every moment. Thus, whatever is happening is God's intention and serves his glory.

According to Wesley, God gives people free will, and much that is happening in the world, such as sin, is not according to God's foreordained plan or purpose. The moral evil and perhaps much of the natural evil in the world is the result of the fall of Adam and Eve and our replication of that disobedience in our own lives. God is a God of love and mercy, who offers salvation to everyone. Edwards did not agree; as a good Calvinist, he believed that Christ died only for the elect, and others do not have any opportunity to be saved. Wesley abhorred the Calvinist doctrine of predestination and wrote a biting treatise *Predestination Calmly Considered* (1752), which is not calm at all. For a while it created a rift between friends Wesley and Whitefield.

One can only imagine what Edwards and Wesley might say to each other in heaven. Here I offer my best educated guess.

The Conversation

WESLEY *(confused)*: Uh, where am I? I was lying there on my bed and suffering, surrounded by my family and friends; then, the next thing I know, I'm waking up here. Is this some kind of hospital or something? Wait! This is too beautiful for a hospital. What happened? Did I die? Is this paradise?

EDWARDS: Yes, Brother Wesley, you died and this is paradise. Welcome! Believe me, I know how you feel. I had just moved to Princeton, New Jersey, to become president of the college there when I came down with smallpox. I got it from that new thing they call a vaccine; it was supposed to keep me from catching the pox but instead gave it to me! Like you, I was suffering and then, suddenly, no more! I was here in this beautiful place of gardens and bright light (though there's no sun) and mansions.

WESLEY: Why, you must be that New Englander Jonathan Edwards, of whom my friend George Whitefield spoke so often and so highly. I heard of your demise across the Atlantic. Such a tragedy. But then, here you are and here I am, and this seems like a much nicer place than either London or Princeton, right?

EDWARDS: Yes, yes. But because of your Arminian heresy, I must admit that I was a little surprised when an angel told me that you were coming here. I was afraid that belief might prevent you from being one of God's elect. I guess God must have had a purpose in his great plan to glorify himself even for your damnable folly about free will and your nearly blasphemous tirades against our Reformed theology, which after all is but a transcript of the gospel.

WESLEY: "Damnable folly"? You mean the great truth of God's free grace offered to all? I always did think that you and friend Whitefield misunderstood my Arminianism. Like so many other Puritans, you confused it with Arianism and all kinds of horrible heresies. But Arminianism certainly is not a heresy; it's simply gospel truth. Your Calvinism is nearer heresy. In fact, it approaches blasphemy by calling God's good character into question. What kind of God would create sinners and then angrily hold them over the yawning abyss of hell for doing what he foreordained them to do?

EDWARDS: You distort my doctrine of God, Wesley. Like all good Calvinists, I taught the love of God. By nature God is benevolent to all beings, yet to himself first. His glory is the highest aim of himself and every other being.

WESLEY: The love of God you claim to teach is a love that makes the blood run cold. How can love foreordain humans, created in God's image, to eternal suffering in hell?

EDWARDS: That's easy to understand. God's love is first and foremost love of his own glory.

WESLEY: And I say that kind of glory makes the skin crawl!

EDWARDS: Well, I understand that soon we are to have an audience with the Almighty himself, and he is going to clear up this controversy between us. I've heard angels whispering that God is neither a Calvinist nor an Arminian and that before admitting us into the rapturous joys of paradise, he is going to chide us both for quarreling about this so heatedly. I guess that means there's some truth to purgatory. I've been waiting here for you for several decades. I can't say that it's been unpleasant, but it's not exactly the fullness of heavenly bliss, either.

WESLEY: Since we're going to get the straight truth about this controversy over predestination and free will right from God himself, perhaps we should spend our time in talking over other matters now. Say, you seemed to be quite well-read in our British philosophers. Whitefield told me that you were constantly reading the likes of John Locke and Isaac Newton. I myself have found some value in reason, but those empiricists didn't do much for our Christian endeavors, did they?

EDWARDS: Actually, I found them to be great allies in opposing the rising tide of Arminianism in New England. That thing others call "free will" is uncaused and not an experienced thing at all. It is quite incompatible with both Scripture and the best of modern philosophy.

WESLEY: Well, I really don't think Locke would agree with you there. He was a firm believer in the freedom of the individual. But look, let's talk about our basis for what we believed and taught as reformers of our respective church traditions. To what great authority did you appeal in your writings and teachings? As you perhaps know, I added experience to our Anglican trilateral authority of Scripture, tradition, and reason. Some may call this my "quadrilateral." My Methodist ministers and teachers explain that anyone who uses all four sources and norms correctly will always go right theologically—with God's help, of course.

EDWARDS: I found reason to be of some help in my theology—especially for tearing down the strongholds of heresy and false religion. But my one and only authority for all faith and practice was Holy Scripture, inspired by the Holy Spirit and illumined to our understanding by that same Spirit of God. Tradition at best is a tool of interpretation of Scripture. I always considered our Westminster Confession of Faith and Westminster Shorter Catechism to be of great value in teaching confirmation classes.

Experience is a wax nose that any knave can twist to suit one's own countenance. I don't trust it. Religious affections are not experiences, however. The affections of persons are directed to what they love. God rules over our faculties through affections. Only the person whose affections are governed by God's Spirit can know and please God.

WESLEY: I can't disagree with that, but I do think that the great tradition of Christian teaching going back to the church fathers is indispensible for correct interpretation of Scripture. So is reason, by which I mean logic, and experience. By "experience" I mean the faithful and Spirit-filled worship by the church, such as we had in our Methodist classes.

EDWARDS: Brother Wesley—I can now call you brother since you are here in paradise—I've always wanted to ask you something about your theology. How could you believe that Christians arrive at "sinless perfection" before death? Even the great apostle Paul did not claim to be sinless or perfect. Hadn't you read Romans 7? Did you think that you reached perfection on earth? I certainly never met anyone, even among the elect, who attained perfection.

WESLEY: Brother Edwards, I tried so hard to explain what I meant and did not mean by "Christian perfection." I guess my explanations never reached you. I would have thought that our mutual friend Whitefield would have conveyed my true meaning to you. I have never said that any person, except Christ himself, attains absolute perfection in this life. But I did say and I still believe that we are called to holiness and enabled by God to be perfect, even as our heavenly Father is perfect. Jesus said so in his Sermon on the Mount. And by God's Sprit within us and even before paradise, we can attain a state where we no longer struggle daily against the flesh but always act automatically out of love. Though even the entirely sanctified do make mistakes of judgment, that's not the same as sin.

EDWARDS: This too reeks of folly, Brother Wesley, just like your Arminian theology, which is closer to Roman doctrine than to authentic Christianity. Who can be perfect when still in the body and still on the earth?

WESLEY: Jesus was perfect. Adam and Eve were perfect before they fell. And Enoch of old was said to have "walked with God." You do not give the Holy Spirit enough credit, Brother Edwards. The Spirit of God can so regenerate the heart of persons that they pass from being dominated by the flesh to having abundant life in the Spirit while still in earthly tents. I do not understand how you could believe that regeneration is such a supernatural work of God's grace that totally transforms a person yet deny the possibility of perfection of heart. If God is the sole agent in such a transformation, as you admit, why would he never so renew and transform a person so as to root out all sin and evil from his life?

EDWARDS: Well, perhaps the Almighty One will enlighten us about this as well. Let's make a list of things to ask him when the gates to his throne room open for us and we are ushered in. But I'm sure he will agree with me.

WESLEY: Let's also ask him about those strange manifestations that overtook so many repentant people in our revival meetings. You know . . . Whitefield told me they happened while he preached and also while you preached. People fell on the floor or writhed on the ground in sorrow and anguish of soul for their sins. Some howled or even barked like dogs. Others fell into deep trances or even lost consciousness. What was that all about? I never understood it.

EDWARDS: Ah, yes. I too would like to know what to make of those manifestations. I wrote two books about those revivals, and in one of them, *Religious Affections*, I explored the proper criteria for distinguishing between the emotional manifestations that are of God and thus are true and those that are not of God and thus are false. I argued that whenever the emotions do not result in benevolence toward all beings—God and other humans especially—they are false. I told my congregation to get up off the floor and pay the Indians for the land they stole from them. They proved that their emotions were false by refusing to do it and even expelling me from my pulpit!

WESLEY: I also proclaimed changed behavior shown in love as the test of true emotions. My converts all over England helped to save the kingdom from an upheaval such as the French experienced in their bloody revolution. They did this by rising above their social circumstances, showing forth God's work in their lives, and working hard for God and for their neighbors.

EDWARDS: One last question, Brother Wesley. Just before we go into the holy of holies to meet our Lord, may I ask you whether you truly believed in our cardinal doctrine of justification by grace alone through faith alone? Even Brother Whitefield was known to doubt your orthodoxy on that point. And as you know, the great English hymn writer Augustus Toplady questioned your salvation, and so did many others among the brethren in Britain. Did you teach salvation by works, as some of them said?

WESLEY: It grieves me to hear that anyone doubts my orthodoxy on that or any other question. Indeed I did teach that God alone saves us, and only by a gift of grace received through faith alone. But I did and I still do question the notion of "alien righteousness," which teaches that we are always sinners and righteous at the same time throughout our Christian lives. I believe that when God justifies sinners on account of their faith in Christ, he forgives their sins and requires no further works. Christ has done all the work for us. But! He does not leave them alone in their flesh and merely "impute" righteousness to their account in some heavenly ledger. No. God imparts Christ to forgiven persons. He fills them with the Holy Spirit and renews them inwardly so that they are new creatures with new affections. They no longer want to sin but only to please God with works of love.

I believe in and taught justification by grace through faith alone, apart from works of the law but not without works. "Without works" sounds as though God doesn't transform us into people who love to please him. So, to answer you briefly, I taught sanctification just as fervently as justification, and that's why some Reformed and Lutheran scholars doubted my Protestant credentials.

EDWARDS: Another question for our Lord: write it down. "Was Luther right about *simul justus et peccator*?" Are Christians saved by God's grace always "righteous and sinners at the same time"? Or are they transformed into righteous people by the grace that brings them forgiveness? I always held to Luther's view, but at the same time I preached that the elect can be identified by the signs of grace in their lives, such as benevolence toward all beings. Maybe we're not as far apart as I thought—except for that perfection business.

WESLEY: I have the list of questions for the Almighty right here. Now I see an angel beckoning us. May it be into God's presence? Shall we go and receive our answers?

EDWARDS: Yea, verily, let's go.

Analysis

Surely a conversation between two great Christian thinkers like Edwards and Wesley would be much longer and deeper than this! I tremble at the injustice I have done them. Both were men of tremendous spiritual maturity and theological acumen. Both impacted their cultures in ways that still reverberate long after most people have forgotten them. Edwards may have been a Calvinist, but inadvertently, perhaps, he contributed to American individualism by his heavy emphasis on the individual's encounter with the living God, which requires no mediation except through Christ and the Spirit. The Great Awakening, of which Edwards was America's most influential preacher and apologist (against rationalist skeptics), left an indelible stamp on American Christianity. Revivalism became a normal part of it.

Wesley shaped British and especially English society in powerful ways. His converts almost always rose out of poverty and joined the swelling ranks of the middle class. Some historians have suggested that his fifty-years-plus ministry in England saved it from a bloodbath like the French Revolution. His followers adopted the idea that people need no spiritual hierarchy such as the Church of England to relate to God. The individual, though uneducated and perhaps poor, can experience God's love and understand God's Word just as well as a bishop, if not better.

These two giants of early modern Protestant Christianity shared a great deal of common ground. But Wesley was often accused of rejecting (1) the doctrine of justification by grace alone through faith alone and (2) the doctrine of *sola scriptura*, Scripture as the authoritative source and norm for Christian belief above all others. These were and are vicious calumnies. A fair reading of Wesley's sermons and essays reveals that he held dearly to both doctrines while trying to avoid their extremes.

Both men were assailed by critics as fanatics and rabble-rousers. Edwards especially rose to the challenge and proved them wrong. He demonstrated greater intellectual power than all of his critics, who mostly sat in Boston and reviled the Great Awakening. His treatises *Freedom of the Will* (1754) and *The End for Which God Created the World* (1765) shine as great stars in the galaxy of Christian scholarship. Most of his critics' writings have been long forgotten.

It's a shame that most people know of Edwards only because of his sermon "Sinners in the Hands of an Angry God" (1741). One has to wonder if that was chosen for students to read by the intellectual and spiritual descendents of his Boston critics, to smear his reputation. Much better would be to have students read his *The Nature of True Virtue* (1765), widely regarded as one of his greatest philosophical works.

Edwards's legacy lives on in many ways, but nowhere more visibly than in the works of some early twenty-first-century Reformed preachers and writers. One notable Baptist preacher and author styles himself after Edwards and is proud to say that he simply restates Edwards's theology for a contemporary audience. His books have attracted thousands upon thousands of young readers, who are getting a large dose of Edwards's divine determinism without knowing it.

Nevertheless, there are a few flaws in Edwards's otherwise wonderfully erudite thoughts about God. One is his absolute denial of libertarian freedom (ability to do otherwise than one does) as irrational. This was one of his arguments against Arminianism. Such a free decision is, Edwards argued, uncaused, and an uncaused effect is illogical. The problem is that he believed God to be free and not determined. But if freedom to do otherwise is illogical, then even God cannot be said to possess it. Edwards would agree. He never adequately explained how this is not a contradiction.

Wesley's theology was carried on largely by Methodists. But during the nineteenth century some of them believed that the original passion and fervor of his revivals was dying out in Methodism, so they started rival religious movements that emphasized emotion and sanctification. The so-called Holiness churches of America (such as Church of the Nazarene) claim to be more faithful to Wesley's theology than many in the mainline Methodist churches. They still believe in entire sanctification or "Christian perfection." But like Wesley, they qualify it so as to account for mistakes and sins of omission still besetting even the most sanctified people.

Edwards emphasized God's glory at the expense of God's love. Wesley emphasized God's love at the expense of his glory. At least thus say their critics. There may be some truth in these claims. It greatly depends on what one means by "glory." Wesley believed that God glorifies himself by saving as many as possible. His love is his glory. And his love is not first and foremost self-love but love for others.

In spite of vast areas of agreement in this pairing, the Gods they preach seem quite different. One wag has said that it is virtually impossible to tell the difference between Edwards's God and the devil, except that Edwards's God only wants *some* people to go to hell (for his glory), and the devil wants *everyone* to go to hell. Edwards's defenders are offended by such attacks on his theology. For them, hell is necessary for God's full self-glorification because all of God's attributes must be displayed without prejudice to any. Hell is necessary as the manifestation of God's justice and wrath. Wesley's followers reply that the cross of Jesus was a sufficient manifestation of God's justice and wrath poured out on sin. Hell is not strictly necessary, but it is the "painful refuge" that God provides for those who reject his mercy.

How can two such different accounts of God coexist within the same family of faith? Only uneasily. Many of the tensions in evangelical Christianity can be traced to this deep fissure at the very beginning of the movement.

For Further Reading

Cherry, Conrad. *The Theology of Jonathan Edwards*. Bloomington: Indiana University Press, 1966.

Collins, Kenneth J. *The Theology of John Wesley: Holy Love and the Shape of Grace*. Nashville: Abingdon, 2007.

17

Eighteenth-Century Irish Deist Toland and English Evangelist Wesley Debate Faith and Reason, God and Miracles

Setting

The two historical figures in this imaginary conversation probably never met even though they lived in the same kingdom and their lifetimes overlapped a few years. Some readers may wonder why I occasionally use the device of a supernatural visitation as the setting for a conversation. But there are only a few possibilities in such cases. Sometimes I have the characters conversing in heaven (or paradise). In this case and one or two others, I have one of the characters visit the other one as a ghost or apparition. By "ghost" I simply mean the appearing of a deceased person to another. There seem to be biblical precedents for this.

The spirit of the dead prophet Samuel appeared to King Saul when he consulted the "witch of Endor" (really a medium). Moses and Elijah appeared with Jesus on the Mount of Transfiguration. As I mentioned in the preface to an earlier conversation, C. S. Lewis after his death appeared to Bible translator J. B. Phillips. Here, then, I use this device to bring the deceased philosopher John Toland into conversation with the living evangelist John Wesley. It may stretch some readers' imaginations, but I can only ask them to play along. After all, these are imaginary conversations.

John Toland was a renowned Irish philosopher who lived from 1670 to 1722. So controversial were some of his views that the public hangman in Dublin burned copies of one of his books at the behest of the Irish parliament. He was a public intellectual and iconoclast who loved to challenge what he considered to be irrational beliefs and superstitious practices. A convert from Catholicism to Protestantism, he spared neither religious party his scorn when they insisted on abject surrender to what he considered to be absurd beliefs.

Toland's best-known and most-controversial work was *Christianity not Mysterious*, with the subtitle *A treatise showing that there is nothing in the gospel contrary to reason nor above it and that no Christian doctrine can be properly call'd a mystery*. It was published in 1696 and publicly burned in Dublin in 1697. Many scholars regard it as the first salvo in the great deism controversy that shook Great Britain throughout the eighteenth century. Toland's follower Matthew Tindal (1657–1733) picked up where his master left off in *Christianity as Old as the Creation* (1730). Tindal went much further than Toland in criticizing organized Christianity and limiting the scope of valid religious belief to the natural and rational. Both Toland and Tindal profoundly influenced the founding fathers of the American republic, and none more than Thomas Jefferson.

Deism is usually thought of as belief in an absentee landlord God or a clockmaker God, who created the universe, built natural laws in it, and then went away or watches from a distance without ever interfering. That is a high-school-curriculum caricature of deism. Like all caricatures, it contains some truth. But neither Toland nor Tindal nor any other leading deist of the eighteenth century believed that God is totally removed or uninvolved in the world. In fact, some scholars argue that their view of God verged closer to pantheism than to the popular image of deism.

I have chosen Toland for this conversation because he presents such an interesting counterpoint to John Wesley's evangelical Christianity. (See conversation 16 for more about Wesley.) Wesley was only nineteen years old when Toland died and was just beginning his studies at Oxford University. Without any doubt he heard about Toland, and he may even have read *Christianity not Mysterious*. But nobody really believes that they met. However, it is fascinating to imagine what two of the eighteenth century's most influential men would have said to each other. Both left a profound impact on British and American religion and society, which thereby also influenced the world.

Toland was an Enlightenment figure; he elevated reason to the highest position possible as a criterion for belief. He tried to reform church and society by using reason. Toland found it necessary to use reason to criticize and even ridicule certain commonly held beliefs. When he said that Christianity is not mysterious or contrary to reason, he did not mean what a modern evangelical apologist for Christianity might mean. He was only interested in revising Christianity to conform to secular reason.

Thus Toland was a rationalist. But he was not, as some have claimed, an atheist or even an agnostic. He believed in God and considered himself to be a Christian. He was baptized into the Roman Catholic Church and later converted to Protestantism. But he saw no conflict between true Christianity and reason or natural law. He actually thought that holding on to irrational traditions and dogmas was the surest way to doom Christianity to defeat in a world increasingly ruled by science and philosophy.

Yet, unlike a conservative Christian apologist, he did not begin with belief in traditional Christianity, including dogmas such as the Trinity, and then seek to demonstrate how reason could be used to support belief. Instead, he began with faith in reason and then tried to show how only what is consistent with it should be considered truly Christian. The "essence" of Christianity, then, was whatever did not conflict with reason as Toland conceived it.

During Toland's lifetime there were laws against blasphemy in Great Britain. Only a few years before the publication of Toland's book, a nineteen-year-old university student was hanged for publicly questioning the existence of God. One has to keep that in mind when reading Toland. He attacks Catholic doctrines such as transubstantiation as irrational. He was safe in doing so since, according to British law, blasphemy did not include criticizing or rejecting distinctively Catholic beliefs. He probably counted on astute readers drawing a straight line between his criticism of transubstantiation and certain Protestant doctrines. One has to wonder what he thought of the doctrine of the Trinity even though he never explicitly addressed it.

Toland attacked belief in mysteries. Any doctrine claimed to be mysterious and believed against reason or even above reason was suspect in Toland's mind. He was careful to define what he meant by "mystery." Much of his book is taken up with that cause. But at least, if church or society insisted on belief in something acknowledged to be mysterious, Toland opposed that. If it could be shown not to be really mysterious, fine. But insofar as the doctrine is really mysterious and not conformable to reason, it is not to be believed. Out the window thus went many cherished doctrines and dogmas of the Christian faith. Or at least so thought Toland and especially his followers, who were less threatened by blasphemy laws as they gradually dwindled to the status of ancient relics during the eighteenth-century Enlightenment in Europe.

Wesley was a quite different sort of person from Toland. Like the Irish philosopher, he valued reason, but he did not think of it as a straitjacket into which divine revelation must be squeezed. A reasonable interpretation of Scripture— yes. But to begin with reason and then hack away at Scripture, as he surely thought Toland did, would be anathema to him. For Wesley, reason is at best a tool to be used in the service of faith. For Toland, reason is a canon for deciding what faith can believe. Wesley did not revel in mysteries or miracles, but neither did he discard them. Toland was extremely skeptical of miracles and rejected mysteries.

Both claimed to belong to the same church, the Church of England. They represented two different wings of that church in the eighteenth century and afterward: the rationalist and liberal wing, and the evangelical wing. Many of Toland's followers eventually left the Church of England for the new Unitarian movement, founded in London in the late eighteenth century. Many of Wesley's followers eventually left the Church of England to start Methodist chapels and, in America, revivalist churches.

The setting of this imaginary conversation is Wesley's bedroom in his three-story home in London. It is a dark and stormy night (I couldn't resist that) in 1790, one year before Wesley's death. By all accounts Wesley was a somewhat depressed and disillusioned man in his last years. His marriage had failed. His attempts to keep the Methodist movement within the Church of England were increasingly futile. Many of his high hopes for the complete reform of church and society were being dashed.

During this time he wrote to a friend that he had never believed in God. This surely was his confession of lack of absolute faith in God rather than an expression of atheism. Wesley set higher than humanly possible standards for himself and others. He once wrote that he did not see how someone could claim to be a Christian who did not rise at four every morning and pray for two hours.

Wesley is tossing and turning on his bed, trying to sleep. Suddenly there's a strange glow in the room, but not emanating from the fireplace. He sits up, rubs his eyes, and looks around. In a corner of the bed chamber, he sees a ghostly figure sitting in an armchair.

The Conversation

WESLEY: Who are you, man? What are you doing in my bedchamber at this time of night? How did you get in? Stand back! I'll get out of bed, open the window, and call the night watchman to come and throw you out!

TOLAND: Don't bother, Mr. Wesley; he wouldn't even see me. Only you can see me. I'm here on a mission from a mighty being in the other world. He sent me here to talk some sense into your head before it's too late.

WESLEY *(rubbing his eyes harder and squinting to see the figure better)*: Aren't you . . . ? Yes, I've seen your portrait and bust several times. Can it be you, John Toland? Am I dreaming?

TOLAND: No, I'm not a figment of your imagination, Mr. Wesley. I'm really here. Let's say as a ghost. I've come back from the afterlife to bring you hope and encouragement.

WESLEY: But are you really John Toland? Or someone who looks like him? Wait! I'll go and get my copy of *Christianity not Mysterious*. His picture is on the frontispiece.

TOLAND: No need to do that. Yes, it is I.

WESLEY: But why are you here? How can you possibly offer me encouragement? We have nothing in common.

TOLAND: Ah, but that's not true. You speak highly of reason. You cherish philosophy. For a revivalist, you are extremely well-read and well informed about the latest discoveries of science and philosophy. Why, you even have my book in your library! Think of it! The public hangman burns it in the city square, but John Wesley has his own copy of it!

WESLEY: Well, I also have copies of the works of Cicero and Plotinus and even the archheretic Faustus Socinus. I like to know what the enemy is up to. Is it perhaps the Enemy who sent you here tonight to taunt me? Do I smell smoke?

TOLAND: That's just the fireplace embers, Mr. Wesley. No, no, no. I'm not here to taunt you but to teach you. Who sent me is irrelevant. Truth is truth, whatever its source. And reason is its measure. Come, let's reason together.

WESLEY: I'm not sure I believe you are really John Toland. I've never heard of a phantom coming up from below to haunt good Christians. I think you're a familiar spirit, a demon pretending to be the spirit of a deceased human. In the biblical story, the witch of Endor was surprised when the prophet Samuel appeared to her and King Saul because she expected it to be one of her familiar spirits. What witch has called you from the abyss to come here?

TOLAND: Come, come. Who says I've come "from below"? And who says you're a "good Christian"? Recently, haven't you been somewhat doubtful about that? Be that as it may, be assured I'm not a familiar spirit. I'm really John Toland.

WESLEY: Well, I still think that maybe you're just a piece of spoiled fish I ate last night that's been keeping my stomach upset ever since. But since you're not going away, I'll play along. What have you come to tell me?

TOLAND: Wonderful! You're ready to listen. My master and I have the highest hopes for you. I've come to convince you that reason should guide you and all of your followers as well. Reason is the rule of all thought, especially in our enlightened age. Religion is no exception. Just think of all the wars and martyrdoms that have arisen from belief in mysterious doctrines based on tradition and enforced under pain of death or exile. You have thousands upon thousands of followers. And you have so little time left here. I beg you to heed what I have to say and teach your followers to use their God-given reason to measure truth.

WESLEY: But I do urge them to be reasonable, as I am reasonable. I have never embraced or promoted superstition or even blind faith. Reason is one of my four sources and norms for theological understanding: divine revelation, tradition, reason, and experience.

TOLAND: Yes, yes, we know that. But in practice you place reason in the service of faith in revelation and love of tradition. And for you and your disciples, experience is as much an authority as reason. Now you must place reason first. I'm not asking you to discard revelation or tradition, but you must use reason to discern what in them is worthy of assent.

WESLEY: I'll respond by quoting the great French philosopher and mathematician Pascal: "The heart has its reasons, of which reason knows nothing. . . . Is it by reason that you love yourself?"

TOLAND: Ah, Pascal, poor fellow! He was such a reasonable man, except in religious matters, where he ran to embrace mysteries.

WESLEY: As should all good Christians. Mystery lies at the heart of our faith!

TOLAND: No, no, no, my good fellow! Mystery is a sure sign of error. There is nothing mysterious about the true doctrines of our Christian faith. Those that are truly mysterious cannot be part of our true Christian faith.

WESLEY: By that saying you empty our faith of everything supernatural and distinctive. You cut the heart out of it. You kill it.

TOLAND: Wrong, Mr. Wesley. Rather, *you* kill it by making it mysterious, which is the same as making it untrue—at least so far as we can tell. A mystery is precisely what cannot be known.

WESLEY: Are we talking the same language? What do you mean by "mystery"? I mean a truth that would never be known or even guessed at if it were not for supernatural revelation from God. For example, the Trinity is a mystery because philosophy and science cannot deliver it, prove it, or disprove it. It is a truth revealed.

TOLAND: No, no, no! That's not what mystery means. A mystery is something unintelligible that is believed as ordered by some authority but really is against all reason or above reason.

WESLEY: Wait! There's a difference between "against reason" and "above reason." The Trinity is above reason but not against reason.

TOLAND: How can there be a difference? Whatever is "above reason" is naturally against reason.

WESLEY: And what do you means by "reason"? Proof? How can the Trinity be proved or disproved? If by reason you mean proof, then religion is dead.

TOLAND: Except natural religion.

WESLEY: Okay, except natural religion. But your natural religion is worthless except in philosophy. How can you worship what is purely natural?

TOLAND: Natural religion is the set of beliefs that all rational humans hold. Its doctrines are based on nature and reason and not on revelation.

WESLEY: Let's get back to mystery. So what do you mean by "mystery"?

TOLAND: "Mystery" has two senses. One is something unknowable without revelation and not yet revealed. The other is something revealed but contrary to reason. Neither has any place in our modern Christianity.

WESLEY: Give me an example.

TOLAND: Well, I can't give an example of the first sense of mystery because it hasn't been revealed yet. But let's imagine a hypothetical cure for pneumonia. It hasn't been discovered yet, so it's still a mystery. It has no place in science except as a hope and stimulus for research. In religion, let's imagine an attribute of God not yet revealed. It's a mystery, so it has no place in religion. As for an example of the second sense of mystery, how about the Catholic dogma of transubstantiation? It is supposedly revealed, but it certainly is unintelligible. It involves a sheer contradiction. The bread is supposed to be really the body of Christ, and the wine is supposed to be really the blood of Christ. But it goes against all sense.

WESLEY: I agree that transubstantiation is unintelligible. The Catholics talk about mysteries all the time. Is it only their mysteries that you oppose?

TOLAND: Well, during my life I had to restrict my public criticisms to those. Otherwise I would have gone to that place from which I have just come much more quickly. But now that I'm free from fear of the public executioner, I can say that I also oppose some Protestant dogmas insofar as they are mysterious.

WESLEY: Examples, please.

TOLAND: Well, how about the Trinity? Can you explain it? Can you make it intelligible? Doesn't it involve a contradiction? Isn't it illogical? If so, it is a mystery in the second sense and thus not to be believed.

WESLEY: Aha! I always suspected that you harbored such disbelief.

TOLAND: But what is your defense? How is it believable?

WESLEY: It is divinely revealed in God's Word. Therefore faith accepts it even if it seems unintelligible. But to tell the truth, I don't think it requires a sacrifice of reason. It is not against reason but above reason.

TOLAND: Oh, no, not that cavil again. "Above reason"? What does that even mean? As I wrote in my magnum opus: "Whosoever reveals anything, that is, whosoever tells us something we did not know before, his words must be intelligible, and the matter possible. This Rule holds good, let God or man be the revealer." That's the thesis of my whole life's work. "Above reason" is simply another way of saying "unintelligible" and "impossible."

WESLEY: Even if that were so, I reject your approach to faith and reason. One is not required to sacrifice reason to believe in the Trinity or any other revealed doctrine; one is only required to suspend suspicion and disbelief and skepticism and accept as true something that reason by itself could never know or even guess at.

TOLAND: Nonsense. But let's talk about your elevation of feelings in religion. Don't you base much of what you believe on your "warm heart" rather than your head?

WESLEY: It's true that my heart was strangely warmed. On the evening of May 24, 1738, in the Aldersgate Steet chapel, I knew for the first time that my sins were forgiven and God was my Savior. Without that experience of God speaking to my heart, I would never have come to a living faith as I have.

TOLAND: But a warm heart is no substitute for a warm mind, is it? In this enlightened age, surely religion must be based more on mental knowledge than on feelings. I predict that your movement is doomed to die unless it shifts from feelings to reason.

WESLEY: There is no necessary conflict between feelings and reason. But faith seeks understanding, not the other way around. You put the cart before the horse by making faith the servant of reason. The mind of a fallen person is corrupted by sin. Only the Spirit of God can free the mind from the shackles of selfishness and disobedience to God and make it able to understand divine truths. But those truths do not contradict reason even if they transcend it.

TOLAND: So we're back to that, are we? Suprarational beliefs. Just another term for superstition and magic.

WESLEY: To you, perhaps. But that's because you do not have the Spirit of God. Would you now kneel with me in this room and pray that God will enlighten your mind with his Spirit so that you can discern the Word of God and be saved?

TOLAND: Saved? Saved? What talk is that? You're such an optimist, Wesley. Do you believe that even after death someone can be saved? And what makes you think that I'm not saved?

WESLEY: Your heart is not warm. You have no sense of the divine. You would convince me to use fallen reason to undermine belief in God's Word. And yes, I believe that God is always willing to save someone.

TOLAND: You're wrong again, Mr. Wesley. I don't want to use "fallen reason" to undermine God's Word. All I want is for you to show me how belief in the Trinity, for example, is reasonable. If you can show me its reasonableness, I will accept it.

WESLEY: But your "reasonableness" and mine are not the same thing. I have the inner testimony of the Spirit of God that elevates my reason to accept mysteries such as the Trinity. I see no contradiction in the doctrine of the Trinity as you do, because of your rebellious mind.

TOLAND: Look, reason is reason; logic is logic. "Three-in-one and one-in-three" is gibberish. It's a contradiction. It can't be believed at all.

WESLEY: Well, I see that you don't really understand the doctrine of the Trinity. It isn't just belief in "three-in-one and one-in-three." It's belief in Father, Son, and Holy Spirit as one divine being in three distinct persons.

TOLAND: Same thing. It's still a mystery. There's no example of that in our experience of nature.

WESLEY: There doesn't have to be. God is God and not part of nature. God transcends nature. But there's no logical contradiction in "one substance and three persons."

TOLAND: Well, we're getting nowhere with this. That's too bad. I wonder what my master will do when I report back to him how little I'm achieving here.

WESLEY: And who is your master?

TOLAND: I'm not supposed to say his name.

WESLEY: I'll bet!

TOLAND: Let's talk finally about miracles. You believe in them, don't you?

WESLEY: What do you mean by "miracle"?

TOLAND: What everyone means by it. An event that violates a known law of nature and has no natural explanation.

WESLEY: Like a free decision of the mind and will?

TOLAND: What?

WESLEY: Well, every time you make a free decision and exercise your will freely, you are putting into effect something that has no natural cause. Or else it wouldn't be free, would it?

TOLAND: Well, that's not what most people mean by "miracle."

WESLEY: And since when did you care what most people think?

TOLAND: Anyway, you believe in dead bodies coming back to life, don't you?

WESLEY: If the Word of God reports it, yes.

TOLAND: But now we know, because of Sir Isaac Newton, that there are mathematically describable laws that govern everything. That rather surely rules out miracles.

WESLEY: No, it doesn't. Sir Isaac believed in miracles.

TOLAND: Well, he just hadn't thought through all the ramifications of his discoveries.

WESLEY: I reject the whole framework within which you define miracles. A miracle is simply an unusual and wonderful act of God that goes against the normal course of things. God is the author of nature and can easily suspend its normal workings to act supernaturally. I don't see how you can believe in God and not believe in miracles. A God who can't do miracles is hardly worthy of being called God.

TOLAND: What if God and nature are coextensive so that nature is like a glove and God is the hand? Then there would be no need of any miracle except the one great miracle that is nature.

WESLEY: But that would rob our faith of its very foundation: the resurrection of Jesus Christ. Your hand-in-the-glove analogy cannot account for that. No, nature is God's handiwork and not his glove. But he can work within nature or around nature or against nature as he wishes.

TOLAND: That attitude will doom your movement, Wesley. The Enlightenment is against it. Science depends on uniformity of nature. Miracles go against science.

WESLEY: Not at all. Science can go right on studying natural laws and the events governed by them while religion recognizes some real events not governed by natural laws. The two do not have to collide if they keep within their confines. But you would make religion a slave of science.

TOLAND: Well, that's not exactly the way I'd put it. But the two have to cooperate, and that will never happen until religion gives up belief in things that go against the spirit of science.

WESLEY: Well, enough of this. I'm ready to go back to bed and sleep. You've encouraged me, alright. I now see that the path I've taken of faith founded on feelings is right. If your way is the only alternative, people will flee from it to the safety of belief in God's Word. Go back where you came from.

TOLAND (desperately, pleading): No, please, I like it better here. It's cool here and . . .

Analysis

Some readers may think that I have judged Toland too harshly. Let me assure them that I do not claim to have any knowledge about his afterlife whereabouts. Notice that I did not have him mention either Satan or hell. I suspect, however, that if a ghostly Toland did appear to Wesley, the latter would suspect that he had not come from heaven!

Readers cannot be blamed if they wonder whether Toland and Wesley were totally disagreeing with each other. After all, Toland never does come right out and reject the Trinity or the resurrection of Jesus or any other dogma of the faith. But he raises questions about them and asks for reasons to believe in them. It isn't so much that he demands proof as that he demands intelligibility. Apparently he's willing to believe something based on revelation (or so he says), but not if it is unintelligible, and not if it goes against logic and thus involves a contradiction.

Even Wesley is not completely sure they are totally disagreeing about everything. They both value reason. They both accept mystery in some sense. While Toland seems to be rejecting mystery, he really only rejects it insofar as it requires belief in anything illogical or strictly absurd. However, when he gives the example of the Catholic doctrine of transubstantiation, one has to wonder. Is that doctrine really logically absurd? Well, certainly not if one accepts Aristotelian metaphysics, on which it is based.

Aristotle distinguished between the "accidents," or outer properties of a thing, and its "substance," or often unobserved inner reality. The doctrine of transubstantiation says only that the inner substance of the bread and wine change in the Mass; the accidents or outward properties that are sensed by the five senses remain the same. Is that a logical contradiction? Not really. And one has to believe that Toland knew that. So when he gives transubstantiation as the paradigm for an impossible mystery, one has to wonder if he really means that only illogical beliefs are to be rejected.

The deepest difference between Toland and Wesley was probably over the human faculties that apprehend truth. Toland elevated reason above all else without completely rejecting faith or feelings. Wesley elevated the heart above all else without rejecting reason. Wesley's approach to religious belief is a version of the classical Augustinian "faith seeking understanding." Faith, founded on the inner testimony of the Holy Spirit, comes first. Then reason seeks to understand or make intelligible what is believed by faith. The problem is that many religious believers of all kinds believe by blind faith based on feelings. Wesley knew that, and so he appealed to tradition and reason as well as revelation and feelings. For him, the four sources and norms working together yield right Christian belief. But for Wesley the quadrilateral (revelation/Scripture, tradition, reason, and experience) is not an equilateral. Scripture stands above tradition, reason, and experience.

Toland probably would accept the quadrilateral (although he might have problems with experience insofar as that means feelings) but place reason above

Scripture and tradition, and certainly above experience. It's not that reason itself yields all religious knowledge, although Toland certainly moved in the direction of natural religion, but it is the judge of all religious truth claims. One is not allowed to appeal to revelation or Scripture or tradition or experience over, against, or above reason.

American religion is deeply influenced by both Toland and Wesley. Several of the founding fathers of the republic were deists of Toland's stripe or strongly influenced by deism. Thomas Jefferson was certainly a disciple of Toland and of Matthew Tindal. He used his own reason to cut the New Testament into pieces and paste together the parts he considered reasonable, to create *The Life and Morals of Jesus of Nazareth*, later called *The Jefferson Bible*. Completed in 1819, it was first published in 1903 and 1904, long after his death in 1826.

Even today, American civil religion is a form of deism. Americans want their political leaders to be God-fearing men and women, but their public faith should be quite general and reasonable. We don't want fanatics in the White House. But at the grassroots level, every denomination is pietistic if not revivalistic (unless they work hard at not being so).

The spirit of Toland is alive and well in liberal Protestant thought although there is a good dose of feelings in it as well. But reason is the prime guidance mechanism for Protestant liberals. In Toland's case reason means logic but also Enlightenment philosophy. That's true of most liberal Protestants also. But even some conservative Christian groups are influenced by Toland and deism. Many of them eschew miracles except in "Bible times" or on the "mission field." This is a compromise with the Enlightenment.

The spirit of Wesley is also alive and well in mostly evangelical Protestant thought although there is a good dose of reason in it as well. The garden-variety evangelical Christian is sure that the heart should lead the head in religious matters. But there are also many rationalistic apologists among evangelical scholars.

Studying Toland and Wesley helps us to understand this mixture in American religious life. As different as these men were, their legacies are alive and well and sometimes sitting uncomfortably close together in the same pew.

For Further Reading

Daniel, Stephen Hartley. *John Toland: His Methods, Manners, and Mind*. Montreal: McGill-Queens University Press, 1984.

Rack, Henry D. *Reasonable Enthusiast: John Wesley and the Rise of Methodism*. Nashville: Abingdon, 1989.

18

Enlightenment Philosophers Locke, Kant, and Hegel Deal with Issues Impinging on Christian Theology

Setting

Some readers may wonder whether John Locke, Immanuel Kant, and Georg W. F. Hegel were really "great Christian thinkers" (as in this book's subtitle). Their philosophical influences on modern theology were nevertheless profound. And they all claimed to be Christians and were members of Christian churches.

Some may also wonder whether Kant and Hegel count as "Enlightenment" thinkers. Locke does, to be sure. But Kant and Hegel? Well, much depends on how one defines "the Enlightenment." It was a cultural movement driven by advances in science and philosophy that revolutionized the Western world, beginning in about 1650 and especially flourishing in the eighteenth century. When the Enlightenment ended is a much-debated question. For our purposes here, however, it is virtually coextensive with modernity, and modernity lives on even as it is being challenged by postmodernity.

The hallmark of the Enlightenment was trust in reason over tradition. Certainly that is not dead. Kant questioned the limits of reason without in any way abandoning reason as the primary guiding source and norm for all thought, including religion. His book *Religion within the Limits of Reason Alone* (1783) was and remains a classic of Enlightenment philosophy of religion. And his essay "What Is Enlightenment?" (1784) is still read in college courses as the model of modern, Enlightenment-inspired thought.

Someone challenging Hegel's Enlightenment credentials might have a better case. Yet Hegel certainly elevated reason, interpreted as logic, to the highest level of authority in his philosophy of religion.

All three philosophers influenced Christian and especially Protestant theology throughout the nineteenth and twentieth centuries. Locke was the catalyst behind deism. John Toland, perhaps the greatest Christian deist of all (see conversation 17), stood on Locke's shoulders, as did Matthew Tindal and Thomas Jefferson. Kant has been called the Protestant philosopher even though many of his ideas and arguments undermined traditional Christian beliefs. His influence on liberal Protestant theology in the nineteenth century and then on neoorthodox (Barthian) theology in the twentieth century is incalculable. Hegel's influence on Protestant theology and especially on liberal theology has been immeasurable. Process theology is one example of a type of theology that has built on Hegel's speculative ideas about God.

John Locke was born in 1632 and died in 1704. He lived most of his life in England although he fled to Holland for a few years when he was implicated in a political plot. He was a renowned philosopher and physician who wrote numerous essays, including *An Essay concerning Human Understanding* (1689), considered to be a masterpiece of early Enlightenment philosophy. There and in other writings, he developed what has come to be called empiricism, the idea that all knowledge is derived from the five senses and that there are no innate ideas. This was a major impetus to the rise of modern science. He was also a political thinker who advocated classical liberalism: the basic human rights and freedoms of individuals. His book *The Reasonableness of Christianity* (1695) is considered a forerunner of deism and especially of Toland's work.

Immanuel Kant was born in Königsberg, capital of East Prussia (now Kaliningrad, Russia), in 1724 and died there in 1804, one century after Locke's death. He never traveled more than a hundred miles from his home city. By all accounts Kant was obsessive-compulsive as an eccentric university professor. His magnum opus was *A Critique of Pure Reason* (1781; 2nd ed., 1787), in which he tried to show that the human mind is active in shaping data received through the five senses. Therefore, he argued, we can have no knowledge of things in themselves but only of things as they appear to us. Kant said that he found it necessary to destroy reason (in religion) in order to make room for faith. His critiques of the traditional proofs of the existence of God are often considered conclusive.

G. W. F. Hegel was born in 1770 and died in 1831. He taught philosophy at several German universities before ending his career at the University of Berlin, where he was decorated by the king of Prussia for his service to the state. Hegel thought that the Prussian state was the "end of history," by which he meant the culmination of all the conflicts of history and the highest achievement possible in terms of a social order.

More important for our purposes, he wrote the massive *Lectures on the Philosophy of Religion* (1832, with lectures of 1827), in which he applied his ideas to religion, ideas about Absolute Spirit as the dynamic force of history. Hegel believed that God is immanent within human history and, in some sense, evolving along with human culture. He denied Kant's distinction between knowing and being. Hegel taught that God, the highest being of all, comes to self-realization through human discovery of God.

These thumbnail sketches cannot begin to do justice to these three great philosophers' contributions. Suffice it to say that without them, modern theology would not be what it has been. Like Plato and Aristotle earlier, these three philosophers became modern theology's primary conversation partners, for better or worse.

Readers may wonder if I believe in purgatory. Well, here it is just a literary device. In Catholic theology, purgatory is a vestibule to heaven and lets people's spiritual development continue until they are prepared to enter into God's presence. At least in modern Catholic thought, it is not usually pictured as fire and brimstone or even punishment. Some Catholic thinkers prefer to picture it is as some kind of school or therapy. These changes in the idea of purgatory make it much more acceptable to me and many other Protestants. It makes some sense to believe that at least some people of God are so far off in their thinking about God that they must be reprogrammed, as it were, to enjoy heaven. I'm not ready to embrace any idea of purgatory, but I find it a useful device for imagining a meeting between these three Christian thinkers.

The Conversation

KANT: Well, well. Fancy meeting you two here. You, John Locke, have been here longer than I! And you, Georg Hegel, will be here longer than either one of us. Let me take this opportunity to say how proud I am that I was right about rewards and punishments after death. This isn't exactly what I expected, but I did argue that for ethics to be objective, there has to be a place where doing one's duty is rewarded with happiness. That certainly isn't true in the physical world on earth!

HEGEL: You always were rather proud, Immanuel. But I must chime in here to say that I too was right about something. Well, many things. But here I'll just mention the great union with God that awaits us as we faithfully wait and learn here in purgatory. We surely are already united with God, but we don't realize it. Someday we'll all understand that Absolute Spirit is the march of human history upward toward greater harmonies.

LOCKE: Well, we have yet to see about that, Georg Hegel. I don't know where you get all that metaphysical mumbo jumbo about God and the world, and we don't yet know exactly what heaven will be like. I seriously doubt that we'll "realize" our oneness with Absolute Spirit or God. And we can't really know anything about it until we experience it with our five senses.

KANT: Your empiricism of knowledge derived only from the five senses was too limited, Locke. Your follower David Hume came along and demonstrated that our senses can and often do deceive us. For example, he argued that since we cannot experience cause and effect with our senses, we can't know if they are real. All we can do is suppose cause and effect. But now that we're in the Enlightenment, that doesn't count as real knowledge, right?

HEGEL: Gentlemen! Let's not fight. We have so much in common. After all, we're all Enlightenment thinkers. None of the "tradition is truth" stuff. But Locke, I agree with Kant that your theory of knowledge is far too limited. There are just so many things we need to know and surely can know beyond our sense experience.

KANT: *Jawohl*, Herr Hegel! So we agree against Locke that there must be knowledge beyond the five sense.

LOCKE: So, do you two want to gang up on me now? Just remember that my philosophy was the foundation of modern science. And it opened the door to a more reasonable Christianity, which is not mysterious. You both seem to miss that as "knowledge" I included necessary deductions from sense experience. If an idea is required by sense experience, then it also counts as knowledge. But it has to be rooted in sense experience and has to be reasonable.

HEGEL: Well, that's still too limiting. And it rests on too great a distinction between the knowing subject and the known object. We can never really gain true knowledge of the most important subjects, such as the soul and God, unless we overcome that subject/object distinction and think of all reality as in some sense one Great Subject: God.

KANT: There you go with your metaphysical mumbo jumbo again, Hegel. And Locke, your theory of knowledge, though a big step in the right direction, is still full of problems. It's a step in the right direction because it frees science and religion from the shackles of tradition. If our sense experience contradicts what has always been taught by the church, we have to stop believing what has always been taught and go with our sense experience and what can be derived from it.

LOCKE: Well, thank you, Herr Kant, for at least acknowledging my great contribution to the Enlightenment.

KANT: But! Hume devastated your theory of knowledge. Sense experience can never yield knowledge of things in themselves. It can yield knowledge only of things as we experience them. I picked up that distinction from Hume and showed that it is true but unimportant. All we really need to know are things as they appear to us. We shouldn't even be interested in things in themselves. But! I know what you're thinking, Locke. What knowledge can we have beyond sense experience if we are limited to knowing things as they appear to us? Well, as I argued, we can know that our minds shape and unify and unite the things we know by our five senses.

For example, causation may not be real "out there" in the world of things in themselves, but we can be sure that causation will be "real" in our experience because that category of the understanding called "causation" organizes things into the cause-and-effect relationship. So we can't know things in themselves because our minds shape and organize every signal that comes in through the five senses. But we can know more than just the things we experience with our five senses. We can know the categories of the understanding that shape our sense experiences such as cause and effect, and time. But these may be only in our minds.

HEGEL: What utter nonsense! How are we going to learn about the answers to life's ultimate questions if we can't know things in themselves? The whole realm of Spirit lies beyond our sense experience. And God cannot be a thing-as-it-appears; God is only God if he is a thing-in-himself. Your epistemology makes knowledge of God impossible.

KANT: Well, that's why I said, "I have destroyed reason in order to make room for faith." Yet I meant that to apply only to religion. You're right that we can't have "knowledge" of God, but we can have faith in God.

LOCKE: But think of the implications of that! You're putting a huge wall between "faith" and "knowledge." Where do you think that will inevitably lead? To secularism, that's what.

HEGEL: Kant, I agree with Locke. We can't divorce faith from reason. We have to have a reasonable religion that doesn't rely on blind faith.

KANT: At least you should know, Herr Hegel, that I agree. I wrote a book called *Religion within the Limits of Reason Alone*, didn't I? There I explained that true religion isn't about knowledge of some invisible, spiritual reality. True religion is about ethics: doing one's duty. Jesus is our guide in that. That's why we should continue to hold him in high esteem even if we no longer consider him to be God incarnate.

HEGEL: That's not enough to sustain a vital religious life. We need to know God-in-himself and not just God-as-he-appears-to-us. That's why I corrected your theory of knowledge and showed that there is no real subject-object distinction. At its best, reason brings us to God as Absolute Spirit, the "world soul," the Whole that is greater than the sum of its parts.

LOCKE: Excuse me, gentlemen, but you both make things way, way too complicated. Religion is indeed about ethics, but that doesn't mean we have no knowledge of God. Our five senses show us that there must be a God to explain the world. God is the creator and sustainer of the world. Reason can tell us that. Maybe not much else, but at least that.

KANT: Our five senses often deceive us, and there's no way we can know for sure that what we are experiencing is objectively real. The thing-in-itself only appears to us; thus our experience is only of the thing-as-it-appears-to-us. But that doesn't have to concern us. We can be satisfied with only knowing things as they appear to us. Things in themselves are unknowable and unimportant.

HEGEL: *Das ist alles Käse,* which for you, Locke, means "That's just cheese!" You're talking rubbish! Religion is all about knowing God intellectually and spiritually. And our reason puts us in touch with God, who is "in and for himself" and "in and for us." A reasonable person, observing history as a whole, will come to the conclusion that a Spirit—Absolute Spirit—is unfolding through human culture and that this Spirit is immanent within everything. Spirit is the synthesis of opposites: thesis and antithesis. The Spirit's goal is unity and harmony.

LOCKE: I can't believe what you two have done with my simple, straightforward empiricism. You've destroyed it. I was trying to establish a natural religion and show that Christianity—rightly interpreted—is the zenith of human search for God. All I wanted to do is bypass the traditions of the churches and show that we don't need revelation or an inspired book. All we need are our five senses and logic.

KANT: Well, Locke, you were naive. I presented a critique of reason, your kind of reason. Reason, knowledge, lies only within the realm of appearances and not ineffable things. Therefore religion must be stripped of all metaphysical nonsense about things in themselves and reduced to what's really important about religion: ethics.

HEGEL: Kant, if Locke is naive, you're crazy! The human spirit craves union with God, and logic shows that we are already united with God. We just need to realize it. Religion is really about coming to understand the dynamic, evolving presence of Absolute Spirit, God, in and through universal history. The reason we can't know things in themselves is that there are no things in themselves. All things are interconnected. Reason shows it.

LOCKE: I think we're going around in circles here, fellows. What do you each think of Jesus Christ? You're Christians, right? So talk about Jesus Christ. I saw him as the Messiah, by which I meant the ultimate teacher of truth, the model of humanity.

KANT: I saw him as the ultimate doer of his duty, the one who shows us the ideal ethical life.

HEGEL: I saw him as the ideal representation of the ultimate truth of "Godmanhood": unity between God and humanity.

Analysis

Confused? Don't feel lonely. Anyone listening in on a conversation between these three great thinkers would feel confused. Think of it this way. One of the great causes of the Enlightenment was to define what constitutes "knowledge." Does tradition count as knowledge? If so, then why does tradition so often turn out to be wrong? That was a special problem after Galileo proved that the church's traditional belief in the earth-centered solar system was wrong. Church authorities tried to silence him. Eventually, however, the church's credibility suffered a severe blow. Then came many others. So the Enlightenment asked about knowledge. What must be the case in order for something to constitute knowledge?

There were two main Enlightenment approaches to answering this question: rationalism and empiricism. The leading rationalist was French philosopher René Descartes (1596–1650), who posited that humans possess innate ideas and that knowledge is discovery and exploitation of those. But more important, he claimed that knowledge is a priori: it precedes sense experience. Knowledge is what the mind finds necessary to believe and is based on logic. And knowledge begins with doubt. Try to doubt everything and see what cannot be doubted. If something cannot be doubted, it counts as knowledge. Descartes famously said, "*Cogito, ergo sum.* I think, therefore I am." He could not doubt his own existence. From his own doubtless existence, Descartes deduced the existence of God and much more. Rationalism, then, is the strain of Enlightenment thought that emphasizes the role of logic in knowledge and tends to set sense experience aside as uncertain.

Locke was the leading proponent of empiricism, which denied the existence of innate ideas and relied on sense experience for knowledge. Yet not any and every sense experience counts as knowledge because we all know that our senses can deceive us. But some sense experiences can be trusted, and that is especially true when they can be replicated by others.

Both rationalists and empiricists agreed that tradition did not count as knowledge. Just because something has always been believed does not make it knowledge. At best, tradition can be opinion or belief, but not knowledge. At worst, tradition may embody superstition. Rationalists and empiricists rejected the appeal to authority outside the self. Just because a theologian or priest or pope or king declares something does not make it true. It has to be tested. For Descartes and his followers, if a truth claim can be doubted, it doesn't count as knowledge. If you want others to accept your truth claim as knowledge, you'd better be able to show how it is necessarily supported by some a priori truth of reason, such as your own existence.

Empiricists reject as knowledge any truth claims that have no empirical grounding in sense experience. And the sense experience cannot be esoteric, sensed only by a few special people. It has to be universally possible, and that can be shown only through duplication of the experience for others.

Rationalists like Descartes tried to prove God's existence through the ontological argument that was first proposed by the medieval theologian Anselm of Canterbury (see conversation 10). God's existence cannot be doubted because the very concept of God as the being greater than which none can be conceived, or as the most perfect being, necessarily includes God's existence. A being that exists is greater than one that does not exist, so the being greater than which none can be conceived must be conceived as existing.

Empiricists like Locke tried to prove God's existence through cosmological or teleological arguments. God's existence is necessary to explain the world as we experience it. The universe is finite, so it must have a first cause that is not itself caused. It is orderly, so it must have been designed by an all-powerful mind. And so forth and so on.

Scottish skeptical philosopher David Hume (1711–1776) did not consider God to be an item of knowledge because, he argued, the so-called proofs of God's existence are flawed. Kant agreed with Hume about that, but he argued that belief in God counts as knowledge because God is necessary to account for universal moral and ethical experience. Yet the "God" that Kant considered to be an item of knowledge was not God-in-himself but only God as he appears to us in our moral experience. He reduced religion to morality and ethics.

Hegel was determined to rescue religion from the ravages of the Enlightenment by demonstrating that God is known. But the God of Hegel is not in any way an object like a chair or a planet. God is known because he is the horizon of all knowing. Human knowledge itself presupposes an ultimate unity called Absolute Spirit, which sublates, or transcends, necessary opposites (thesis and antithesis). But knowledge of God is not the result of a syllogism or argument; it is already present within all knowing. And as we uncover our knowledge of God as Absolute Spirit through self-realization, God comes to our self-awareness. Hegel tried to wipe away the whole subject-object dualism assumed by most Enlightenment thinkers before him. But the cost was a depersonalized and immanent God, indistinguishable from the mighty march of the human spirit through the history of culture.

Still confused? Don't worry about it. Some scholars think Hegel is beyond understanding. Kant is only a little less difficult, and Locke is fairly easy, but that's the problem. His philosophy is too easy.

So what is the relevance of these three philosophers to Christian life and thought today? They're still quite alive and influential, especially in Western Protestant thought. Take Kant, for example. One of his major contributions, if you can call it that, is a divorce between facts and values, or between knowledge and faith. One often hears people say, "You have facts, but I have faith"; or "My faith isn't affected by facts." Christianity is often reduced to faith understood as values: right and wrong. Good Christians are any who live a certain kind of good life, whatever their beliefs may be. And religious beliefs are treated as opinions, not facts.

In many Christian or church-related universities, this dualism between faith and fact, or between values and knowledge, appears everywhere. The whole idea of integrating faith and learning often brings howls of protest from Kantian professors in many disciplines. They want their Christian faith left out of the laboratory and classroom, and the results of their research left out of their devotional and church lives.

It would be tempting to say that Locke, Kant, Hegel, and the whole troupe of Enlightenment philosophers affected only liberal Protestants. These philosophers certainly were accepted by the liberals, and some after them even regarded them as rescuers of Christianity in the modern age. They made it possible to be an intellectually fulfilled Christian. But at what cost? Such "Christianity" is often so negotiated (harmonized) with modernity as to be barely recognizable. But not only liberal Protestants are influenced by these philosophers. How many conservative Protestant churches really believe that miracles happen today? "Oh, that's premodern stuff," we may hear. A popular way of accommodating to modernity while keeping traditional beliefs alive is to relegate miracles to "Bible times" and maybe "the mission fields."

One would think that Pentecostal Christians would be the last group affected by the Enlightenment. (I know about this from firsthand experience of growing up and being educated in Pentecostalism.) But a hallmark belief of Pentecostals is speaking in tongues as the "initial, physical evidence" of the infilling of the Holy Spirit. Why does there have to be an "initial, physical evidence"? Could the Enlightenment's obsession with knowledge drawn from observable experience lie behind this?

Especially conservative evangelical Christians would like to think that they are immune to the influences of Enlightenment figures like Locke, Kant, and Hegel, but such is not the case. Together they form the cultural and philosophical environment in which we live and move and have our being. It's better to be aware of this and decide what to do about it based on real knowledge of it, not based just on hearsay, rather than stick our heads in the sand and pretend that we are not touched by it.

For Further Reading

Byrne, James M. *Religion and the Enlightenment*. Louisville: Westminster John Knox, 1997.

Kolb, David, ed. *New Perspectives on Hegel's Philosophy of Religion*. Stony Brook: State University of New York Press, 1992.

Reardon, Bernard M. G. *Kant as Philosophical Theologian*. Totowa, NJ: Barnes & Noble, 1988.

Yolton, John, ed. *John Locke: Problems and Perspectives*. Cambridge: Cambridge University Press, 1969.

19

Father of Modern Theology Schleiermacher and Philosophers Kant and Hegel Debate the Essence of Religion and Christianity

Setting

Once again I find it necessary to stretch the reader's imagination in order to bring these three great Christian thinkers together. If you read conversation 18, you're already familiar with philosophers Kant and Hegel, who discussed theology with Enlightenment thinker John Locke in purgatory. Enter Friedrich Schleiermacher to take Locke's place. Apparently Locke served his time in purgatory and entered heaven. After all, he did die a century before the others. I apologize in advance to readers who are put off by such playfulness. I don't claim to have any knowledge of where any of these men were or are after death. Here purgatory is just a literary device. Imagine with me what they might say if they met with one another after death.

Philosophers Kant and Hegel were two of the three partners in dialogue in conversation 18. Look at the "Setting" portion there to find information about them. Suffice it to say here that they were late Enlightenment thinkers and wrote philosophies of religion that included revisions of classical Christianity in light of modern thought and culture. For Kant, true religion and authentic Christianity are matters of doing one's duty. He reduced religion to ethics. God is beyond knowing, although it is necessary to posit God's existence for the sake of objective right and wrong. Hegel reacted against Kant. He believed that Kant had sacrificed too much in the process of trying to rescue religion and Christianity from the acids of modernity. Hegel suggested that God is the

"Absolute Spirit," or (to use Ralph Waldo Emerson's phrase) the "Oversoul" of the universe coming to self-realization in and through the evolution of human culture. For him, religion is about achieving union with God through a dialectical process of thesis, antithesis, and synthesis. A great idea brings about its opposite, and then the two are reconciled in a higher synthesis in which both are taken up and at the same time transcended.

Unlike Kant and Hegel, Friedrich Schleiermacher was not a philosopher but a theologian. Yet he is often considered to be a quite philosophical theologian. Kant and Hegel were quite theological philosophers. In 1768 Schleiermacher was born in Breslau, Silesia (then in Prussia; now Wroclaw, Poland); he died in Berlin in 1834. During his lifetime Schleiermacher achieved fame for several accomplishments. He translated the works of Plato into German. He was a renowned socialite and promoted the Romantic movement in German art and culture.

Schleiermacher was a founder of the University of Berlin and pastored a large church in that city for years. He was considered a great preacher. He published numerous books of philosophy and theology, including his two best-known works: *On Religion: Speeches to Its Cultured Despisers* and *The Christian Faith*. The latter book is usually placed in the same category as John Calvin's *Institutes of the Christian Religion* and Thomas Aquinas's *Summa theologiae*. It is a landmark in the history of Christian thought.

He grew up in a very religious home, where Pietism had a strong influence. Pietism was a movement within the Lutheran and Reformed churches in Germany that tried to reintroduce feeling into religion. It spread from Germany to many parts of Europe and North America and then around the world. The young Schleiermacher attended the University of Halle, which by then had abandoned Pietism and adopted a rationalist spirit. There he read the philosophy of Kant and began to rebel against the conservatism of his religious upbringing. His father protested, and the student famously wrote to him that he was still a pietist, only of a "higher order."

Schleiermacher was attracted to the Romantic movement in German culture, which tried to take the Enlightenment's rationalism and balance it with an emphasis on emotion. The connection with his pietist upbringing is obvious. Yet romanticist emotion was not necessarily religious at all. In Berlin, Schleiermacher taught theology, pastored, and frequented salons where romanticists engaged in sophisticated conversation, despising religion because they associated it with dry dogma, tradition, and ceremony. The pietists hated "dead orthodoxy." The romanticists hated dead heresy. But their hatred of dead heresy did not drive them to orthodoxy or anything religious.

He wrote *On Religion: Speeches to Its Cultured Despisers* (1799) to convince his romanticist friends that they were already religious, whether they knew it or not. Schleiermacher argued that religion is not about dogma or systems of ideas or ceremonies or tradition. It is about feeling: a particular kind of feeling that Schleiermacher called *Gefühl*. That German word has no precise English translation but usually is taken to mean "feeling," "emotion." Better, however, would be something like "wonder" or "awe." It's not a sensation like a chill running up and down the spine. It's not a feeling as in charismatic devotion and worship. It is a "feeling" like one has while looking at a beautiful sunset and sensing beauty in a special way that goes beyond the beauty of a pretty girl or handsome boy.

According to Schleiermacher, the essence of religion is this "feeling of being utterly dependent" on something or someone infinite. Everyone has it even if they're not consciously aware of it. It is a necessary condition of being personal in a human way or human in a personal way. This feeling is an innate sense of the divine even if it doesn't result in membership in any organized religion. For Schleiermacher, all concepts are foreign to religion. And yet concepts inevitably arise from the feeling of utter dependence. So do religious forms of life such as churches. But at best these are secondary to the feeling or "God-consciousness."

Later Schleiermacher wrote his magnum opus *The Christian Faith* (2 vols., 1821–1822). There he tried to show the intimate connection between the essence of Christianity and the universal feeling of absolute dependence. For him, Christianity is the highest expression of this God-consciousness, and its power is mediated to Christians by Jesus Christ, who possessed an unbroken consciousness of God. Jesus was unique in that, unlike other men and women, his God-consciousness was whole and controlled his life. According to Schleiermacher, his deity was the strength of his God-consciousness, which constituted a veritable existence of God in him. But according to this liberal German professor, there was no preexistence of Christ. He also downplayed the doctrine of the Trinity, relegating it to an afterthought in his theological system because he could not discover its relationship to God-consciousness.

Schleiermacher is usually considered to be the first truly liberal Christian theologian. There were liberal Protestants before him, but most of them joined the Unitarian church movement in the late eighteenth and early nineteenth centuries. Schleiermacher tried to show that one can hold to the essence of Christian faith and join it with modernity, without sacrificing one to the other. In the process he gladly let go of doctrinal formulas he considered to be outdated. For him, every doctrine is relative to its cultural setting and is always open to revision.

In this conversation Schleiermacher joins Kant and Hegel in purgatory just after Locke leaves them for heaven.

The Conversation

HEGEL: Well, well, if it isn't Friedrich Ernst Daniel Schleiermacher! Come here, my boy. Sit down. I have so many things to enlighten you about theology. You were teaching theology at Berlin while I was there as professor of philosophy. Our paths crossed too little, I must say. But finally here we are so that I can talk and you can listen.

KANT: This is Schleiermacher? The author of those awful lectures about religion? A few years before my earthly demise, I read them under the title . . . let's see . . . oh, yes . . . *On Religion: Speeches to Its Cultured Despisers.* I wrote my own little book on religion titled *Religion within the Limits of Reason Alone.* I don't think we agreed very much. I hope I can join this conversation and instruct you, Schleiermacher. Don't do all the talking, Hegel.

SCHLEIERMACHER: Please, gentlemen! Allow me to introduce myself to you, Herr Kant. Yes, I am the author of *On Religion: Speeches to Its Cultured Despisers.* I'm sorry you didn't find my lectures about religion to your liking. But then, I don't think you ever did grasp or appreciate our Romantic movement. As for you, Herr Hegel, we did meet in Berlin. Our paths crossed many times. As I remember, once when the faculty was marching from the university to the cathedral and we were side by side in our fine academic regalia, you were muttering something under your breath at me. What was it? I think I heard you say, "If you're right about religion being a feeling of utter dependence, then my dog is the most religious being in the world."

HEGEL: Yes, I did say that, didn't I? Quite humorous, wouldn't you say? Oh, you still don't think so? Good fellow, we have to learn to laugh at ourselves here. What else is there to do?

KANT: What do you mean, what else is there to do? At least I've been going to my classes and learning where I went wrong in my philosophy. You keep skipping yours. That's why you'll be here for a long time.

SCHLEIERMACHER: Herr Hegel, I didn't see the humor in your quip then or now. There's nothing funny about God-consciousness. And you well know that a dog cannot have it. It's a uniquely human capacity, a big part of the image of God in us that sets us apart from the animals. Besides, I don't think you'd especially appreciate it if I remarked that your "Absolute Spirit" is absolutely only in your own mind.

HEGEL: That's not very funny. Listen, young fellow—

SCHLEIERMACHER *(interrupting)*: What do you mean, "young fellow"? We're almost the same age.

HEGEL: Yes, but I've been here three years longer. You just arrived, so here you're just a "young fellow." Anyway, as I was about to say before I was so rudely interrupted, Absolute Spirit is no laughing matter. Making a joke about it is nearly blasphemous. Absolute Spirit is God, you know.

SCHLEIERMACHER: No, it's more like an idol of your own invention. I can also call God the Absolute Spirit, but not in your sense. You reduce God to an evolving Great Idea that comes to expression as humans discover themselves in history. You almost reduce God to history.

KANT: Gentlemen, please! Let's talk about something constructive. How about something basic? Each of us addressed our contemporary intellectuals and tried to explain the true essence of being Christian. So many enlightened people of Europe thought Christianity was a thing of the past, something to be kicked into the dustbin of history. Think of the French philosopher Voltaire. I don't think he ever did really understand Christianity because he confused it with the nonsense spouted by the French clerics of his day. Let's start with you, Schleiermacher. As the newest arrival in this place, you win the privilege of instructing us about the true inner essence of Christianity.

HEGEL: Why should he get to go first? Theology isn't even a science! And he just fed off of philosophy. I should go first because my philosophy was the culmination, the end point of all philosophy. I summed it all up and put the period at the end of human intellectual life.

KANT: Oh, dear. Have you lost your mind? That's absurd. As my undergraduate students would say, what have you been smoking?

HEGEL: You should agree with me that the Prussian state is the end of history. In it are resolved all the conflicts and contradictions of cultures, politics, and societies. And my philosophy is what undergirds it. Even our beloved King Friedrich Wilhelm III recognized my genius and gave me an award for my service to the Prussian state.

SCHLEIERMACHER: Well, I'll accept our eldest conversation partner's invitation to go first. Friedrich Wilhelm liked me a lot too and gave me an award for my lifelong service to Prussia. I encouraged national resistance to Napoleon when he invaded our beloved country. My father was a chaplain in the Prussian army, you know. Anyway, I believe the essence of Christianity is like the kernel within the husk; the husk must be stripped away so that we can find the nutritious kernel hidden within it. That was my whole project: to explain how so many doctrinal formulations of the past were like the dry husk. They have to be stripped away and the kernel of truth discovered within.

KANT: Yes, yes, my boy. What is that kernel of truth?

SCHLEIERMACHER: If you read my speeches on religion, you already know. The kernel is *Gefühl*—

HEGEL *(interrupting sarcastically)*: Is that what you put in your furnace to heat your house? Fuel!

SCHLEIERMACHER: Please, allow me to continue. You'll have your turn. You know very well what *Gefühl* is. It's the profound sense within the soul that one is utterly dependent on the infinite. It is what some mystics have called "cosmic awe": an awareness that cannot be brought fully to expression in words, awareness that one is a tiny part of the whole and that the whole is greater than the sum of its parts. All religion is based on that feeling. Christianity is the religion in which redemption, the healing of God-consciousness, is mediated to the individual by Jesus Christ, who was fully God-conscious. So the essence of Christianity is God-consciousness redeemed and made whole through the mediation of Jesus as Savior.

KANT: That's it? That's it? Please! Where is duty in your scheme, Schleiermacher? What about ethics? Jesus was first and foremost an ethical teacher. He demonstrated to his followers and to us how to live the good life, which is a life of duty.

HEGEL *(parroting Kant to Kant)*: That's it? That's it? Religion is all about duty? You suck all the life out of religion, Immanuel. You make it a drag, especially when you define duty as doing what's right when you don't want to do it. If you want to do it, it isn't praiseworthy. Right? Boy, is your philosophy of religion sad! And to top it all off, you make knowledge of God impossible by placing God in the "numinous" realm.

SCHLEIERMACHER: Kant, I'll have to agree with Hegel, as much as it pains me to do so. Just as you were awakened from your dogmatic slumbers by reading Hume, so I was awakened from my pious slumbers by reading you at Halle. But eventually I came to realize that your philosophy is incomplete at best. You can't reduce religion and especially Christianity to ethics or morality. Your religion is a vague moral theism centered on reluctantly doing one's duty according to the categorical imperative: "Treat all persons as ends in themselves and not as a means to an end." That falls far short of Christ's Golden Rule: "In everything do to others as you would have them do to you."

KANT: I don't see the big difference. Whoever treats all others as ends in themselves and not as means to an end would be fulfilling the Golden Rule. Besides, as you know very well, that's not the only or even the best formulation of my categorical imperative. I like this version best: "Always act on the principle that you could will to be universalized." That's the only really rational rule of life, and if everyone did it, the world would be a utopia. And that's what Christ taught us with his Golden Rule, which is simply a form of my categorical imperative.

HEGEL: As I said earlier, Kant, you suck the very life out of religion by reducing it to ethics. And Schleiermacher, you fluff it up with air by making it all about feelings. Religion in our age must be rational. My basic maxim is, "The real is the rational, and the rational is the real." That's the only way we can know the real—if it's rational. And our best clue to what's real, ultimately real, is the pattern of reason, the way human thought works. The real, the rational, is the necessary sublation of thesis and antithesis.

In human thought, including religion, a great idea arises. It is always met by its opposite. The two collide until a third idea arises that takes the best of both and leaves behind the worst of both. The third is the synthesis, the union of opposites. This dialectical process is real and rational. What seems irrational is unreal. So the necessary pattern of unfolding thought is being itself. What is known as true and what is real cannot be separated. For knowledge to occur, subject and object must be one. Religion is simply a set of myths that express the philosophical truths within this process.

SCHLEIERMACHER: See! You are more of a reductionist than either one of us, Hegel. You reduce religion to philosophy! That's exactly what I opposed. If you had your way, our faculties of theology in the universities would be branches of the departments of philosophy, and churches would just be places where people gather to celebrate the symbolic expressions of philosophical ideas.

KANT: He's right, Hegel. Religion is more than philosophy. And what's "real" is beyond knowing. All we have access to are things as they appear to us; we have no knowledge of things in themselves. When it comes to religion, I had to destroy knowledge in order to make room for faith. Faith and knowledge are two different things. The only thing that bridges the two is ethics. We know from our moral experience that there are absolutes of right and wrong. Reason delivers the categorical imperatives by which we must live the good life. But faith is what gives us the motive, the drive to live according to the categorical imperatives.

HEGEL: It sounds to me as though you too would reduce religion to philosophy, Kant. But what's wrong with that? We both agree with most of our cultured contemporaries that religion is just a bunch of symbols of philosophical truths. Take the incarnation, for example. That God became a human through a union of two natures is just a symbolic way of expressing the philosophical truth of the union of opposites. God and humanity cannot ultimately be separated or opposed. At bottom they are always already united. The doctrine of the incarnation is simply religion's way of bringing this truth to expression.

Also, take the cross of Jesus Christ and Good Friday. I showed how the cross on Good Friday is simply a religious, symbolic expression of the philosophical truth of what I called the "speculative Good Friday": God's crucifixion on the cross of the world. There the infinite enters into the finite.

SCHLEIERMACHER: You see! Hegel, you reduce religion and even Christianity to philosophy. And bad philosophy at that! Your "God" is not worthy of worship. He or It is certainly neither transcendent nor personal nor sovereign. Your God is a great cosmic Idea. What's Christian about that? It sounds more pantheistic and pagan to me.

KANT: I have to agree with our young pastor friend, here, Hegel. Your God is impersonal and vague.

HEGEL: Wait just a minute there, Kant. Isn't that kind of like the pot calling the kettle black? Your God is so transcendent that he's unknowable. I was never sure you even believed in God. You just argued that we must posit the idea of God to account for objective morality. Your "God" is more just an idea than mine is!

SCHLEIERMACHER: And therein lies the problem of philosophers trying to do theology. You can't do theology, especially Christian theology, without revelation. Both of you quite naturally ignore revelation. Philosophy has no use for revelation. But Christianity is based on it. The revelation of God in Jesus Christ is the very soul of Christianity.

KANT: But, my boy! Revelation? You sound like a supernaturalist. I thought you were trying to make Christianity comport with the modern age of science and reason.

HEGEL: Yes, you do sound like a fanatic there, Schleiermacher. I guess it must be your pietist background coming to the surface.

SCHLEIERMACHER: Wait just a minute! Are you two forgetting where we are? You both died and yet survived. If this isn't supernatural and revelatory, I don't know what is!

KANT: You make a good point, my boy. But so far we haven't received any blinding revelation here.

SCHLEIERMACHER: But you will. Why do you think you're here?

HEGEL: I've been wondering that myself.

KANT: I always said that there's a life after death. I just didn't believe in blinding revelations or miracles on earth. The world is ruled by ironclad natural laws. But heaven, which is surely where we will go next, if we pass our classes, is where happiness is the reward for earthly virtue. On earth, happiness was not correlated with living a virtuous life of doing one's duty.

SCHLEIERMACHER: Well, I don't know about you two, but I expect to meet my Savior Jesus Christ here or after here in paradise. He was my Redeemer in life, and now I want to show him my God-consciousness because he is its source.

HEGEL: Are you going to pull it out of your ear?

KANT *(to Hegel)*: Will you never quit with the cutesy quips?

SCHLEIERMACHER: No, I'll just give Christ whatever rewards I'm offered for whatever I achieved on earth because any good that I did was because of him.

HEGEL: If you actually get to meet this man Jesus, who by the way was a great philosopher in his lifetime on earth, maybe he'll chide you for your heresies. Every traditional Christian theologian on earth condemned you as a "maker of veils," which is what your name literally means. You veiled the truth behind your flowery heresies.

KANT: I too am looking forward to meeting Jesus. I didn't encounter him in any way through the church services on earth. How boring and dull and old-fashioned. I rarely went to church. Real church was helping a little old lady across the street, especially when I didn't want to because I was late for lunch. When I meet Jesus, I'm going to thank him for being our perfect model of living according to our moral duty and for teaching us the best way to be human. No one surpassed him in doing that.

SCHLEIERMACHER: I'm looking at my schedule of classes here. It's time for me to go to "covenant group," whatever that is. I guess it must be some kind of pietist conventicle. Then after covenant group comes a class called "Orthodoxy 101." Hmmm. I wonder what that will be like.

Analysis

Like every conversation in this book, much of this one is tongue in cheek. I have no idea if Hegel would be funny or sarcastic in purgatory! Yet he really did say that if Schleiermacher is right about religion being a feeling of utter dependence, then his dog is the most religious being on earth. That's rather funny in a sarcastic way. But I hope the reader was able to discern the ideas behind the banter.

Liberal Protestant theology really began with Schleiermacher. He was the first person paid to be a professor of theology who consciously set out to reconcile Christianity with modernity and vice versa. And what makes him liberal is that he allowed modernity to become more than a cultural context for updating Christianity. For him, modernity was a criterion of truth for revising Christianity. And his way of revising it was to discover the kernel of truth within the Christian religion, which forms its enduring essence. Not surprisingly, that kernel of truth turns out to be something untouchable by modern science. No scientific discovery can undermine *Gefühl*. It's immune to the acids of modernity. Other things can go, but God-consciousness remains intact no matter what science says.

The liberal movement in Protestant theology, beginning with Schleiermacher, was an attempt to trim traditional Christianity to something that science could not disprove or even touch. Beginning with Galileo, traditional Christian orthodoxy kept losing every battle it engaged in with science. Many people in the early nineteenth century thought that science had rather much destroyed religion, including Christianity.

Kant tried to rescue Christianity by reducing it to ethics. Christianity is about what ought to be and not at all about what is. So science cannot touch it. Schleiermacher tried to rescue Christianity by reducing it to feeling. Christianity is about a kind of mystical experience. Science cannot touch it. Hegel tried to rescue Christianity by reducing it to a set of symbols expressing philosophical truths. Christianity is really about the great ideas of philosophical idealism. Science cannot touch it. But Kant and Hegel were philosophers. They could say whatever they wanted to, and it didn't necessarily affect the churches.

On the contrary, Schleiermacher was a "prince of the church." He was a renowned preacher, a hero of culture, a teacher of theology. And he gained many enemies by saying that the physical sciences could not touch the heart of Christianity. Why? Because that seemed to remove Christianity from the realm of objectivity and put it into the realm of subjectivity. It seemed to reduce its importance in the real world.

Critics of liberal theology have accused it of two things. First, it was so anxious not to be kicked into the ditch by modernity that it jumped into the ditch to avoid the pain of being kicked there. In other words, liberal theology rather much gutted Christianity of everything distinctive about it and reduced it to something easy to ignore. Culture could go its merry way while Christians gazed at their navels in mystical experiences of cosmic piety.

Second, liberal theology subjectivized and relativized doctrine so much that Christianity was virtually emptied of objective cognitive content. That was certainly not Schleiermacher's intention, but critics say it was the unintended consequence of his whole project. What happened to the doctrine of the Trinity? Because he couldn't base it on God-consciousness, Schleiermacher relegated it to an appendix in his theology.

Beginning with Schleiermacher, then, liberal Protestant theology opened the door to a kind of subjectivized, relativized, individualized Christianity, cut off from the real world of science, politics, and culture. Yet liberal Protestant ministers and theologians surely still jumped into the political arena from time to time—as we'll see in the conversation that includes Walter Rauschenbusch, a leading early twentieth-century liberal Protestant theologian associated with the social gospel movement. But what solid ground did they have to stand on? Once the Bible was reduced to a book of ethics robbed of any supernatural authority, what was their basis?

Conservative Christians blame Schleiermacher for much that is wrong with modern Christian theology. But we should not overlook his pious intentions. He was a God-fearing, a Jesus-loving, and in his way, a Bible-believing Christian. He died while praying and taking the sacrament of Holy Communion. His Christ-centered preaching swayed the masses in Berlin. It's more what his disciples did with his theology that concerns astute critics of liberal theology.

A century after Schleiermacher, the great Swiss theologian Karl Barth, a participant with Schleiermacher in a later conversation, quipped that Schleiermacher thought it possible to talk about God by talking about humanity in a loud voice. Well, what Schleiermacher did do was to begin a trend of doing theology "from below," from human experience, rather than "from above," from divine revelation. He didn't throw revelation out, but he found it within the human rather than in a supernatural word from beyond human experience.

For Further Reading

For books about Kant and Hegel, see "For Further Reading" at the end of conversation 18.

Gerrish, Brian. *A Prince of the Church: Schleiermacher and the Beginnings of Modern Theology*. Eugene, OR: Wipf & Stock, 2001.

20

Theologians Liberal Rauschenbusch and Conservative Machen Argue about True Christianity, the Bible, Evolution, and Doctrine

Setting

Two of America's most influential Christian thinkers, professors, and writers of the early twentieth century were the Baptist Walter Rauschenbusch and the Presbyterian John Gresham Machen. They couldn't have been more different. Rauschenbusch was a pioneer in the movement of liberal Protestant theology into America; Machen was a leader of the growing conservative and fundamentalist backlash against liberalism in the denominations and seminaries.

At the outset it's important to cleanse minds of stereotypes of "liberal" and "fundamentalist." These terms have taken on new meanings in the later twentieth and early twenty-first centuries. One could even say that they've lost all meaning through popular misuse. By no means was Rauschenbusch a radical skeptic or iconoclast; his interest lay in reforming the churches of America to become more socially aware and progressive. In his personal life he was, by all accounts, a quite pious, God-fearing, Bible-believing, Jesus-loving Baptist. Some might quarrel with the "Bible-believing part," but he certainly thought that he believed the Bible. He just didn't take it as literally as someone like Machen did.

Machen was far from the stereotypical fundamentalist. The fundamentalist movement was just beginning in the early part of the twentieth century as a reaction against liberal theology and higher criticism of the Bible. Machen was a real scholar who studied theology in Germany under some of the top biblical and theological professors there. He taught New Testament at Princeton Theological Seminary and wrote scholarly books on a variety of subjects related to the Bible and theology. He smoked cigars and drank sherry. Machen was an intellectual. He just happened to believe that liberal theology, including the likes of Rauschenbusch, was dragging the churches down into oblivion.

Rauschenbusch was born into the home of a German immigrant pastor in 1861. He died in 1918. His father had been a Lutheran minister, but soon after arriving in the United States, he became a Baptist. Both he and his son taught theology in the German department of Baptist-related Rochester Theological Seminary. Late nineteenth-century Rochester, New York, was a hotbed of the progressive movement for social change in America. Among other activists, Susan B. Anthony lived there.

The younger Rauschenbusch pastored a Baptist church in the Hell's Kitchen neighborhood of New York City and left there convinced that the churches were failing to care for the poor. As a professor at Rochester Seminary, he embarked on a campaign to abolish the laissez-faire capitalism of America and institute redistribution of wealth. He wrote a number of best-selling books, including *Christianizing the Social Order* (1912) and *A Theology for the Social Gospel* (1917). He came to be recognized as the leading voice of the progressive social gospel movement in America.

Machen was born into a wealthy family in Baltimore in 1881, and he died in 1937, after a stellar career as a theologian of the churches. He taught New Testament at Princeton and wrote numerous books and articles extolling the literal interpretation of Scripture, defending debated doctrines such as the virgin birth of Christ, and attacking liberal theology. Eventually he left Princeton and the mainline Presbyterian church to found his own conservative seminary and denomination—Westminster Theological Seminary (1929) in Philadelphia and the Presbyterian Church in America (1936; renamed Orthodox Presbyterian Church in 1939).

In America in the early twentieth century, Machen was widely considered as the leading voice of the budding fundamentalist movement. He didn't fit in that well with some of the other fundamentalist leaders. But together they worked to defend and enforce belief in the "fundamentals of the faith" in Protestant seminaries and denominations. Among the fundamentals were the virgin birth and bodily resurrection of Jesus, doctrines under attack by some liberals.

In 1923 Machen published his well-known book *Christianity and Liberalism*, in which he argued that liberal Protestantism is not even Christian. Popular secular columnist Walter Lippmann agreed with Machen and said that liberal Protestants should have the integrity to stop calling their religion and theology "Christian."

For this conversation, Rauschenbusch and Machen meet by accident at Penn Station in New York City in 1917, a year before the former's death, and board a train together. Rauschenbusch is going deaf and has stomach cancer but doesn't know it yet. His book *A Theology for the Social Gospel* has just been published, and Machen has read it. Machen's words are in capital letters here because he has to shout them while Rauschenbusch holds a megaphone to his ear as a hearing aid.

The Conversation

RAUSCHENBUSCH: Hello! Aren't you Professor Machen, of Princeton Seminary? I'm very glad to meet you. Have you by any chance read my last book?

MACHEN: I certainly have.

RAUSCHENBUSCH: Say what? I'm rather hard of hearing these days. I didn't quite make out your answer. Could you speak up, good fellow?

MACHEN: UM, YOU MEAN YOUR *THEOLOGY FOR THE SOCIAL GOS-PEL*? I SAID I HAVE READ IT, AND IT'S QUITE INTERESTING. BUT I'M AFRAID I DON'T SYMPATHIZE MUCH WITH IT.

RAUSCHENBUSCH: Well, well . . . that doesn't surprise me. It's a rather radical reworking of the tradition, isn't it?

MACHEN: I'M NOT SURE I'D EVEN CALL IT THAT! IT'S MORE THAN A MERE REWORKING OF THE TRADITION. IT SEEMS TO ME MORE OF A COMPLETE RECONSTRUCTION.

RAUSCHENBUSCH: Oh, I'm not sure about that. I didn't come right out and deny any crucial doctrines of the Christian faith, did I? I certainly didn't intend to.

MACHEN: NO, BUT YOU CERTAINLY PLAYED DOWN TRADITIONAL CHRISTIAN DOGMAS AND DOCTRINES AND PRESSED THEM INTO THE SERVICE OF YOUR SOCIALIST IDEOLOGY. FOR A BOOK OF THEOLOGY, YOU HAVE LITTLE TO SAY ABOUT THE GREAT THEMES AND DOCTRINES OF THE CHRISTIAN FAITH. THE ONES YOU DO TOUCH ON ARE HARDLY RECOGNIZABLE AFTER YOU RECONSTRUCT THEM. I THINK YOUR BOOK IS A PRIME EXAMPLE OF WHAT THE EUROPEANS CALL "THE MORALIZING OF DOGMA."

RAUSCHENBUSCH: But that's a good thing, isn't it? Don't you want dogmas to be ethically relevant?

MACHEN: WELL, YES, BUT YOU DO MUCH MORE THAN SHOW THEIR ETHICAL RELEVANCE; YOU COMPLETELY RESHAPE THEM TO BE CONSISTENT WITH YOUR SOCIAL AGENDA. YOU'VE PUT THE CART BEFORE THE HORSE. RATHER THAN OUR REVEALED TRUTHS GUIDING ETHICS, YOU HAVE ETHICS DETERMINING THE SHAPE OF DOCTRINAL TRUTH.

RAUSCHENBUSCH: I'm sorry to hear you say that. That wasn't my intention. All I wanted to do is show how our experience of the social transformation toward the kingdom of God sheds light on doctrines. Can you tell me about one doctrine that you judge I mistreated?

MACHEN: WELL, VIRTUALLY EVERY DOCTRINE. BUT LET'S TAKE ORIGINAL SIN AS AN EXAMPLE. YOU REDUCE SIN TO IGNORANCE. AND ITS TRANSMISSION IS BY EXAMPLE RATHER THAN BY REPRODUCTION. I DON'T SEE MUCH DIFFERENCE BETWEEN YOUR DOCTRINE OF ORIGINAL SIN AND PELAGIUS'S TEACHING.

RAUSCHENBUSCH: Oh, my! That is a harsh criticism. Didn't you notice how I wrote about the "kingdom of evil" and the "superpersonal forces of evil" that perpetuate sin in the world? I most certainly do not reduce evil to ignorance; evil is within the fallen and corrupt superpersonal forces such as business and government.

MACHEN: YES, BUT YOU HAVE LITTLE TO SAY ABOUT THE EVIL WITHIN THE HEART OF THE INDIVIDUAL FROM BIRTH. YOUR ACCOUNT OF SIN MAKES SINNERS OUT TO BE VICTIMS MORE THAN CULPABLE PERPETRATORS OF EVIL.

RAUSCHENBUSCH: Yes, I do think we are victims of the superpersonal forces. But we are also guilty insofar as we abuse whatever power we have and thereby perpetuate selfishness in the world.

MACHEN: SO LET'S TALK ABOUT YOUR THEOLOGY, RAUSCHENBUSCH. AT THE CENTER OF EVERYTHING YOU PLACE THE IDEA OF THE KINGDOM OF GOD AS A HISTORICAL REALITY THAT IS COMING BUT NEVER FULLY ARRIVING. IT'S A UTOPIAN IDEAL OF SOCIETY. IT SOUNDS AS THOUGH YOU BELIEVE THAT WE HUMANS CAN CREATE IT.

RAUSCHENBUSCH: I do think that God wants us to be his partners in bringing about his kingdom on earth. Yes. We can't do it without him, and he won't do it without us. The very heartbeat of Christianity must be what Jesus cared most about—his own kingdom, where the oppressed of the earth are blessed. It will be a social order fully Christianized through redistribution of wealth until everyone has equal opportunity to flourish.

MACHEN: BUT JESUS NEVER URGED HIS DISCIPLES TO BECOME POLITICAL. CERTAINLY HE NEVER URGED THEM TO OVERTURN THE SOCIAL ORDER TO BRING IN THE KINGDOM OF GOD. IN JESUS'S TEACHING THE KINGDOM IS IN THE CHURCH AND HIDDEN WITHIN THE WORLD; ITS FULLNESS WILL COME ONLY WHEN HE RETURNS.

RAUSCHENBUSCH: Yes, but that was when Christians had no political power. Now the churches and Christian people have tremendous financial and political power to change society. We would be abdicating our responsibility as disciples of Christ if we did not use that power to transform the world into the kingdom of God. I'm optimistic that, together with God's help, we can abolish oppression, poverty, hopelessness, and war.

MACHEN: YOU ARE TOO OPTIMISTIC, RAUSCHENBUSCH! PEOPLE ARE TOO SINFUL FOR THAT. YES, THE CHURCH CAN DO MUCH GOOD, AND WE ARE RESPONSIBLE TO PROVIDE CHARITY TO THE POOR, BUT WE WILL NEVER CHRISTIANIZE THE SOCIAL ORDER.

RAUSCHENBUSCH: How will we know unless we try? Besides, the social order is always evolving in some direction. We Christians have enough influence in our own country to help it evolve in the right direction—toward a classless society of equals.

MACHEN: THAT SOUNDS VERY MARXIAN!

RAUSCHENBUSCH: I have studied Marx some, and I accept some of his ideas, but certainly not his atheism. Yet I believe that the inner contradictions in capitalism will eventually destroy it.

MACHEN: LET'S TURN OUR CONVERSATION IN A NEW DIRECTION. I'M AFRAID WE'LL NEVER AGREE ABOUT SOCIAL ETHICS BECAUSE I'M A PESSIMIST ABOUT HUMAN NATURE AND YOU'RE AN OPTIMIST. LET'S TALK ABOUT EVOLUTION. IT'S A HOT TOPIC THESE DAYS. WHAT'S YOUR STAND ON EVOLUTION?

RAUSCHENBUSCH: Well, I'm no scientist, but the church always seems to lose when it opposes the best of contemporary science. That's one good reason to moralize dogma, to get away from metaphysics as a foundation for theology. Metaphysics always loses to science. If scientists say that life on earth has evolved, what business is that of ours to contradict them?

MACHEN: IT'S OUR BUSINESS BECAUSE THE BIBLE MAKES IT OUR BUSINESS! ACCORDING TO THE BIBLE, WE ARE SPECIALLY CREATED IN GOD'S OWN IMAGE AND LIKENESS. WE CANNOT HAVE JUST EVOLVED FROM SOME OTHER SPECIES.

RAUSCHENBUSCH: I guess it won't surprise you if I say that I don't take the creation and fall narratives of Genesis literally. And I don't see what biology and spirituality have to do with each other. Our bodies may have evolved through natural selection without that in any way affecting our status as special creatures of God made in his image and likeness. Don't you think God can work through natural processes?

MACHEN: CERTAINLY. NATURAL PROCESSES ARE PART OF GOD'S GENERAL PROVIDENCE. BUT WE HAVE SOULS THAT COULD NOT HAVE SIMPLY EMERGED BIOLOGICALLY.

RAUSCHENBUSCH: You're surely right. But couldn't the Creator have added our souls to our evolved bodies without that in any way interfering with biological evolution? Besides, what do science and theology have to do with each other? Science is about what is; theology is about what ought to be.

MACHEN: HOW VERY RITSCHLIAN OF YOU, RAUSCHENBUSCH. I'VE SUSPECTED ALL ALONG THAT YOU WERE TOO MUCH INFLUENCED BY THAT LIBERAL GERMAN THEOLOGIAN ALBRECHT

RITSCHL, WHO SAID THAT SCIENCE DEALS WITH FACTS WHILE THEOLOGY DEALS WITH VALUES. HOW CONVENIENT. THAT WAY SCIENCE AND THEOLOGY CAN NEVER CONFLICT. I DON'T WANT THEM TO CONFLICT, BUT I'D RATHER LET THEM CONFLICT THAN HAVE THEOLOGY REDUCED TO VALUES AND HAVE "FACTS" GIVEN COMPLETELY OVER TO SCIENCE. THAT TRIVIALIZES THEOLOGY!

RAUSCHENBUSCH: I don't see how. Values are more important than facts. Jesus was concerned primarily with what ought to be, how we ought to live our lives. He didn't go around spouting facts about the world. That's science's business. Jesus was all about teaching us to live according to the kingdom of God, which is a social order, not a natural one.

MACHEN: BUT EVEN A SOCIAL ORDER HAS TO INCLUDE FACTS. COME ON, RAUSCHENBUSCH, EVEN YOU CAN'T TOTALLY DIVORCE FAITH AND VALUES FROM THE REALM OF FACTS.

RAUSCHENBUSCH: I don't divorce them. I just think theology ought to be mostly about values. Let the sciences tell us how nature works. As theologians we don't care. What we care about is the kingdom of God and its coming.

MACHEN: I COULDN'T DISAGREE MORE, RAUSCHENBUSCH! I MEAN, YES, WE DO CARE ABOUT THE KINGDOM OF GOD AND ITS COMING. THE KINGDOM OF GOD IS WITHIN US AND AMONG US. IT IS THE CHURCH OF JESUS CHRIST. AND IT WILL BE COMPLETED WHEN CHRIST RETURNS. BUT THE BIBLE HAS SOMETHING TO SAY ABOUT HOW THE NATURAL ORDER IS STRUCTURED. FOR EXAMPLE, IT HAS TO BE OPEN TO THE SUPERNATURAL BECAUSE THE PROPHETS, JESUS, AND THE APOSTLES DID MANY MIRACLES. OBVIOUSLY, THEN, NATURE CANNOT BE A CLOSED SYSTEM OF CAUSES AND EFFECTS, AS SCIENCE TOO OFTEN TRIES TO SAY IT IS.

RAUSCHENBUSCH: I see our train is slowing down to the station where I get off. Our time is limited. So let's talk about doctrine. It seems to me that you and other fundamentalists are too concerned with doctrine as if Christianity were primarily a set of facts about God. I see Christianity as primarily about transformation and not information. Jesus came to give God a foothold, as it were, within history and in human society. His whole mission was to bring justice through love. Jesus didn't judge people by their beliefs; he judged them by the way they treated others. He taught that whatever people do to the least of society, the poor and the outcast, they do to him. We already are so good at giving the hungry some doctrines to eat. Jesus would have us give them food and then a job and a living wage.

MACHEN: BUT JESUS WAS NO POLITICAL AGITATOR!

RAUSCHENBUSCH: No, but his teaching and example drive us to be political agitators. Neither Jesus nor any of his disciples had political or economic power; today Jesus's disciples do have political and economic power. But the churches aren't telling them what to do with that power. Jesus taught us to love one another and to do unto others as we would have them do unto us. The law of love compels us to create structures of society that drive out the evils of oppression and exploitation and create structures that are truly democratic, where everyone has equal opportunity.

MACHEN: I AGREE THAT LOVE COMPELS US TO GIVE CHARITY TO THE POOR. "SOUP, SOAP, AND SALVATION" IS THE SALVATION ARMY'S MOTTO. I RESPECT THAT. WE SHOULD DO MORE FOR THE POOR. BUT NOWHERE DOES THE BIBLE ENCOURAGE US TO ENGAGE IN POLITICAL REVOLUTIONS.

RAUSCHENBUSCH: How do you think Jesus was perceived by the Romans when he entered Jerusalem triumphantly? And haven't you read his declaration of ministry in Luke 4:18? He said he came to bring good news to the poor and to set the captives free. That sounds quite political to me!

MACHEN: BUT HE SURELY MEANT THE SPIRITUALLY POOR AND THOSE HELD CAPTIVE BY SIN.

RAUSCHENBUSCH: Now who's not taking the Bible literally?

MACHEN: I THOUGHT YOU WANTED TO TALK ABOUT DOCTRINE. YOU RELATIVIZE DOCTRINE TO THE POINT OF OBLIVION. IN YOUR THEOLOGY ALL THAT MATTERS IS SOCIAL JUSTICE. YOU MIGHT BE ABLE TO DERIVE SOME PRINCIPLES OF JUSTICE FROM THE BIBLE, BUT IT IS MUCH MORE ABOUT BELIEF. CLEARLY, GOD WANTS US TO THINK THE RIGHT THOUGHTS ABOUT HIM, AND THAT'S WHY HE GAVE US THE BIBLE. PAUL'S EPISTLES ARE FILLED WITH DOCTRINES TO BE BELIEVED. YOU ARE EMPTY-ING CHRISTIANITY OF DOGMAS BY MORALIZING THEM. YOU TRANSLATE THEM INTO A SOCIOPOLITICAL AGENDA AND LEAVE ASIDE THEIR COGNITIVE CONTENT.

RAUSCHENBUSCH: Again, it's Jesus I care about. And while Paul may have created some dogmas and insisted that early Christians believe them, even he was more concerned with how they lived their lives. First Corinthians 13 is all about love, not about doctrine.

MACHEN: BUT 1 CORINTHIANS 15 IS ALL ABOUT THE RESURRECTION, AND THERE THE APOSTLE ABSOLUTELY INSISTS THAT BELIEF IN THE RESURRECTION OF THE BODY IS CENTRAL TO THE WHOLE GOSPEL. IT CANNOT BE DISCARDED WITHOUT GUTTING THE GOSPEL.

RAUSCHENBUSCH: And I don't discard the resurrection. But neither do I set it up as a code of belief and measure people's Christian faith by how they conceive of the resurrection. You and your fellow fundamentalists do that. You turn the resurrection into a doctrine instead of an event and a hope that compel us to breathe new life into the dead body of politics right now.

Machen: TELL ME THIS, RAUSCHENBUSCH. DO YOU THINK SOMEONE CAN BE A CHRISTIAN WITHOUT BELIEVING IN THE VIRGIN BIRTH?

Rauschenbusch: Did your hero the apostle Paul believe in the virgin birth? He never mentions it. Surely he would have mentioned it if he had believed in it, right?

Machen: HE DIDN'T NEED TO MENTION IT BECAUSE IT WASN'T BEING CHALLENGED.

Rauschenbusch: But he mentioned many things that weren't being challenged. Your explanation of why he never mentions the virgin birth is lame.

Machen: BUT YOU STILL HAVEN'T SAID IF YOU BELIEVE IN IT.

Rauschenbusch: I'm not going to play your little game of heresy hunting and inquisition. By discovering and condemning heresy everywhere, you and your fundamentalist friends are always trying to divert attention away from the poor and oppressed, crying for relief.

Machen: UNFORTUNATELY, HERESY IS EVERYWHERE THESE DAYS! SOMEONE HAS TO POINT IT OUT. YOUR LIBERAL THEOLOGY ISN'T EVEN CHRISTIAN, TO SAY NOTHING OF HERESY. REAL CHRISTIANITY INCLUDES CONFESSION OF THE GREAT CREEDS OF THE FAITH. ITS ENDURING ESSENCE IS DOCTRINE.

Rauschenbusch: No, no, no! It's enduring essence is the kingdom of God. And according to Jesus, the kingdom of God is not a system of beliefs but a way of life. It's putting love into effect through service to others. And today that means reforming the social order so that there is no more poverty and illiteracy and hopelessness. In the book of Acts, Jesus's earliest followers didn't write a creed; they created a cooperative community and shared all things in common; it was an example of love to the world.

Machen: I THINK I KNOW WHAT'S REALLY GOING ON IN YOUR LIBERAL PROJECT OF THEOLOGY. YOU AND YOUR LIBERAL FRIENDS ARE SO AFRAID OF THE SECULAR WORLD CONSIDERING YOU IGNORANT AND OLD-FASHIONED THAT YOU'VE SACRIFICED EVERYTHING IN THE BIBLE AND IN CLASSICAL CHRISTIANITY THAT WOULD OFFEND THEM. YOU'VE REDUCED IT ALL TO WHAT THE LIBERAL ELITE OF THIS WORLD FIND ACCEPTABLE: SOCIALISM. YOUR THEOLOGY IS NOTHING MORE THAN A THINLY DISGUISED SOCIOPOLITICAL IDEOLOGY MASQUERADING AS A CHRISTIAN THEOLOGY.

Rauschenbusch: I didn't think this had to be personal. Why are you attacking me personally? You have no idea what my motives are. But since you started it, I'll respond in kind. You were raised in a wealthy family in Baltimore, which paid your way to attend the best private schools that money could buy. You come from wealth, power, and privilege, and that's all you've known. You feel threatened by the progressive movement that would redistribute some of your family's wealth to give the poor of this world a fighting chance to have even an education.

So you react to my reconstruction of theology with fear, and you fight it with charges of heresy. If you had ever pastored as I did in the poorest neighborhood of our country's largest city, you'd think differently about theology and social reform. Then doctrine wouldn't seem quite as important as saving the social order.

MACHEN: MY FAMILY HAS ALWAYS BEEN GENEROUS TO THE POOR. AND I BELIEVE IN FREE AND EQUAL EDUCATION SO THAT EVERYONE HAS AN EQUAL OPPORTUNITY TO FLOURISH. BUT YOU WANT TO ROB FROM THE RICH TO GIVE TO THE POOR. I FIND THAT NOWHERE IN THE BIBLE. AND THAT'S NOT BE-CAUSE I COME FROM PRIVILEGE; IT'S BECAUSE I'M A BIBLICAL SCHOLAR: IT'S SIMPLY NOT THERE.

RAUSCHENBUSCH: Our train is pulling into the station. In the few minutes we have left, let's talk about God. How do you view God and the world?

MACHEN: YOU KNOW VERY WELL THAT I'M A TRADITIONAL CALVIN-IST, SO I VIEW GOD AS THE SOVEREIGN RULER OF ALL THINGS, WHO FOREORDAINED WHATEVER IS HAPPENING.

RAUSCHENBUSCH: Even this awful and meaningless war in Europe?

MACHEN: EVERYTHING.

RAUSCHENBUSCH: To what end?

MACHEN: FOR HIS GLORY.

RAUSCHENBUSCH: Well, that seems like a very unloving God.

MACHEN: HE LOVES HIS GLORY, AND SO SHOULD WE.

RAUSCHENBUSCH: That's hardly what Jesus showed us about God. Jesus revealed God as our heavenly Father, who loves us and wants the best for all of his children. This war and everything evil in history is due to our human resistance to the kingdom of God. God is sorrowful about it.

MACHEN: THAT'S A PATHETIC GOD THAT YOU BELIEVE IN.

RAUSCHENBUSCH: Yes! You've got it! "Pathetic" means "full of passion." The God of Jesus is passionate about his kingdom, which is a social order ruled by love. The Bible tells us that God is love. His power is his suffering love on the cross. But he calls us to be his partners in bringing about his kingdom by suffering with those who suffer.

MACHEN: YOU MAKE IT SOUND AS THOUGH GOD HIMSELF IS DEPEN-DENT ON THE WORLD.

RAUSCHENBUSCH: In some sense, yes, he is. Our highest good is God's king-dom, but also the kingdom is God's highest good. He has chosen it to be that way. Only when his kingdom comes to fruition in an earthly social order governed by love and structured by justice—only then will God be satisfied.

MACHEN: YOUR GOD SCARES ME; HE DOESN'T SEEM TO BE IN CON-TROL. WHERE'S HOPE IN THAT?

RAUSCHENBUSCH: Your God scares me. He sounds like a tyrant who grasps at glory by controlling everything. Oh, here's our station. I'm getting off here to go to a meeting of the Brotherhood of the Kingdom, an organization of like-minded ministers that I helped to found. We're all about social reform.

MACHEN: I'M GETTING OFF HERE TO ATTEND AN ANTI-EVOLUTION RALLY WHERE MY GOOD FRIEND THE STATESMAN AND FORMER SECRETARY OF STATE WILLIAM JENNINGS BRYAN WILL BE SPEAKING. I DON'T REALLY CARE THAT MUCH ABOUT EVOLUTION, BUT IT WILL GIVE ME A CHANCE TO TALK ABOUT YOU LIBERALS WHO NEED TO BE PURGED FROM OUR CHURCHES AND SEMINARIES.

Analysis

Machen and Rauschenbusch represent two quite moderate wings of their respective theological camps. Machen is often considered a father of the modern fundamentalist movement. Early fundamentalism, of which Machen was a part, was simply an aggressive assertion of Protestant orthodoxy over against what conservatives saw as liberal heresy quickly creeping into the churches and seminaries. But Machen was a far cry from later fundamentalists. He was not anti-intellectual or separatist. In the 1920s he was kicked out of the Presbyterian denomination for starting his own mission board. Machen didn't separate; they separated from him.

After that he started Westminster Theological Seminary and the Orthodox Presbyterian Church. He was a sophisticated, privileged man of society and a true scholar. Machen was appalled when some fundamentalists in the 1920s decreed that premillennialism is one of the fundamentals of the faith. Like many Calvinists, if not most of them, Machen was an amillennialist. He did not believe in a second coming of Christ before his thousand-year earthly rule, when the saints would reign over the world with him. For Machen, the millennium (Rev. 20) is the spiritual rule and reign of Christ in the church.

Rauschenbusch was anything but a radical liberal. Many liberal Protestants were more anxious to reconstruct Christian theology. But what made him liberal was his demotion of doctrine into secondary status below kingdom work, interpreted as social transformation. And he bought into the prevailing Kantian dualism between facts and values, which immunized religion from the ravages of modern science. But he was a warmhearted Christian who genuinely loved Jesus and who never openly denied any fundamental doctrines of orthodox Christianity. He did, however, neglect or even ignore some of them. His *Theology for the Social Gospel* has little to say about the Trinity because he could not think of a way to moralize that dogma into a kingdom idea.

Machen's and Rauschenbusch's different types of Protestantism divided Protestant Christianity in America throughout much of the twentieth century. Conservatives followed Machen in resisting evolution, the social gospel, and doctrinal decline. Liberals followed Rauschenbusch in resisting dogmatism, separatism, and social conservatism. Machen's followers divided up into numerous rival groups, separating from one another over the Bible (e.g., what "inspiration" and "inerrancy" mean) and over church government. Machen's Orthodox Presbyterian Church soon split, with the rival Bible Presbyterian Church labeling it liberal because it was not sufficiently "separated" from the world. Rauschenbusch's followers joined the ecumenical movement and tried to unite mainline Protestant denominations around the lowest common denominators.

Both movements eventually failed. Liberal theology ran out of steam in the 1970s on the heels of the radical countercultural movements of the 1960s, when some liberal theologians declared God to be dead. Liberal theology of Rauschenbusch's type lives on into the twenty-first century but has few passionate proponents. The churches that hold to it are for the most part dying inner-city churches. Fundamentalist theology fragmented and then abandoned the public scene, building a separate culture of Bible colleges, publishing houses, radio stations, and mission organizations. During the 1950s Billy Graham led a group out of separatistic fundamentalism, and they came to be known as "evangelicals." Evangelicalism holds to basically conservative Protestant doctrine, but it is much more open to progressive ideas such as fighting poverty and environmental disasters.

Nevertheless, Machen's and Rauschenbusch's legacies live on in contemporary Christian theology in the conservative and liberal impulses. Conservatives tend to view doctrine as the enduring essence of Christianity; liberals tend to view social transformation as the heartbeat of Christianity.

As with many of these imaginary conversations, one can easily see common ground that the participants overlooked. Must these two styles of Protestantism be so separated? Why do people tend to go to extremes in reaction against something with which they disagree? During the second half of the twentieth century, some Christian thinkers stepped forward to show that the best of the Machen style and the best of the Rauschenbusch style can be united.

For example, evangelical author, speaker, and organizer Tony Campolo of Eastern University in Pennsylvania has worked tirelessly to combine basically conservative doctrinal commitments with passion for social transformation. Fundamentalists relegate him to the "social gospel" category they abhor. Liberals think he is too conservative in his traditional views about abortion and homosexuality. But nobody can deny his conservative theological credentials insofar as he publicly defends orthodox Christian doctrine, and nobody can deny his liberal social views on dealing with poverty.

More and more liberals and evangelicals like Campolo are exploring how these two impulses in modern Protestant Christianity can be united. One has to wonder what Machen and Rauschenbusch would say about this development.

I like to think they'd both be pleased to see this happening after a long period in which their followers divided these two impulses in fairly extreme ways.

For Further Reading

Evans, Christopher H. *The Kingdom Is Always but Coming: A Life of Walter Rauschenbusch*. Grand Rapids: Eerdmans, 2004.

Hart, D. G. *Defending the Faith: J. Gresham Machen and the Crisis of Conservative Protestantism in Modern America*. Phillipsburg, NJ: P&R Publishing, 2001.

21

Twentieth-Century Barth and Brunner Discuss Theological Method with Nineteenth-Century Liberal Schleiermacher

Setting

Once again it is necessary to use the literary device of purgatory, a training place for paradise, or heaven, to bring our theologians into conversation with one another. You've already met Schleiermacher in an earlier imaginary conversation (19). He was the reputed father of modern Christian theology and the father of liberal Protestant theology.

Karl Barth was born in Switzerland in 1886 and died in his home country in 1968. He revolutionized modern theology by reacting against the prevailing liberal Protestantism yet without embracing fundamentalism. He regarded liberal theology as a severe and unnecessary accommodation to modern science and philosophy, but he did not interpret all of the Bible literally or advocate Christian separation from secularism or liberalism. Barth blamed Schleiermacher for the ills of modern Christian thought because, he claimed, Schleiermacher's theology was anthropocentric rather than theocentric. As he put it, Schleiermacher's mistake was trying to talk about God by talking about humanity in a very loud voice.

Barth advocated a theology "from above," which begins not with human religious experience or culture or philosophy but with divine revelation in Jesus Christ, the Bible, and the proclamation of the gospel. His nemesis was any form of natural theology or any attempt at natural knowledge of God. He rejected all proofs of God's existence as leading only to an idol and not to the God of

Abraham, Isaac, and Jacob. Barth believed that theology is a science, but it is a unique science of God, with its own logic appropriate to its object: God. His approach to theology was labeled "dialectical" because he believed that all knowledge of God involves divine-human confrontation and not continuity between God and humanity except in Jesus Christ.

Barth's theology was radically Christocentric. In every doctrine of his massive *Church Dogmatics* (5 vols. in 14, in 1936–1962), he begins with Jesus Christ and requires everything to revolve around him as God's sole, supreme revelation. Even the Bible is subordinate to God's personal revelation in Jesus Christ. The Bible "becomes the Word of God" when it is used by God as the instrument of provoking a decision for or against Jesus Christ. He did not believe in the inerrancy or infallibility of Scripture, but he did believe the Bible is a form of God's Word and the unique instrument of God's revelation of Jesus Christ.

Emil Brunner was also born in Switzerland and died there (1889–1966). Barth taught at Basel, Brunner at Zurich. The two met on several occasions and collaborated on the development of dialectical or "neoorthodox" theology (sometimes also called "theology of crisis"). However, they had a famous falling out over natural theology. This will be the subject of a later conversation (22).

Brunner was not as prolific as Barth, but he was translated into English earlier and became a favorite of British and American theologians who were dissatisfied with liberal thought after World War I. Brunner's systematic theology was published in three volumes under the simple title *Dogmatics* (German, 1946–1960; English, 1950–1979). There he gathered his life's work from such earlier monographs in German as *The Mediator* (1927), *The Divine-Human Encounter* (1938), and *Revelation and Reason* (1941).

He was influenced by the nineteenth-century Danish Christian philosopher Søren Kierkegaard, who reacted against Hegel (see conversations 18 and 19) by underscoring the infinite qualitative difference between God and humanity. Brunner strove to counter liberal theology's immanentism (emphasis on continuity between God and humanity) with a version of Kierkegaard's philosophy combined with twentieth-century Jewish philosopher Martin Buber's theme of the "I-Thou" encounter. For Brunner, following Buber, God is wholly other than humanity, but God and humanity can meet in a gracious encounter initiated by God. For Christian Brunner, this happens normatively through Jesus Christ.

Brunner tried to correct Barth's extreme rejection of natural theology, which he thought resulted in discarding general revelation; instead Brunner offered a modified Christian natural theology (perhaps better called a theology of nature). For him, the human person is created in God's image, which forms a natural point of contact for revelation and relationship with God. This natural point of contact is simply the human capacity to receive and respond to the Word of God. In response, Barth was infuriated by what he saw as Brunner's defection from their dialectical condemnation of natural theology. Barth thought that natural theology is never satisfied to play a minor role in theology. He said that natural theology is like the proverbial camel: if you let its nose under the tent flap, it soon fills the whole tent.

Barth believed that natural theology, "the human search for God" through reason, was responsible for the rise of Nazism within the churches of Germany in the 1930s. Therefore he refused to give it any credence whatever in his theology. He condemned it and began his theology with God's self-revelation in Jesus. For him, there is no natural point of contact between humans and the gospel; the Holy Spirit creates faith in the human heart apart from reason (not against it). Brunner disagreed and argued that the Holy Spirit can use the natural point of contact to spark faith in the hearer of the Word. The Barth-Brunner argument of the 1930s is one of the most famous and infamous in Christian history. It colored much of what happened in later Protestant theology.

Here, in this imaginary conversation, Schleiermacher is waiting for Barth and Brunner to arrive in purgatory, just as Kant and Hegel were earlier waiting for Schleiermacher (see conversation 19). Kant and Hegel have left for heaven, but Schleiermacher, who arrived later, is appointed by God to greet Barth and Brunner and to try to get them to reconcile their differences before they enter into the bliss of heaven.

The Conversation

SCHLEIERMACHER: Okay, gentlemen. God assigned me to bring you two together to iron out your differences about natural theology. Up here, we can't have any of that bickering that went on between you two for years on earth. Now that you both have died, we have this opportunity to work out the differences between you amicably and constructively.

BARTH: You say that God gave you this assignment, Schleiermacher? That hardly seems plausible to me. You're hardly a paragon of theological virtue! I kept a bust of you in my home study and pointed to it and told visitors, "He too was a Christian, you know." But that doesn't mean your theology was ideal. Far from it! You set in motion a new trajectory of doctrinal reflection that led to liberalism and even apostasy!

BRUNNER: May I put a word in here, please? I've been here a bit longer than you, Barth, so let me go first. I've been waiting to say some things to you. I hope this meeting does lead to reconciliation, Barth, but I'm not optimistic. You seem to have the same sharp tongue as there. You're not the big theological boss here, you know. Relax a little, and let's have some friendly conversation.

SCHLEIERMACHER: Exactly, Brunner. That's my feeling as well. So let me gently say to your fellow Swiss citizen that I cannot be held responsible for the excesses of some of my followers any more than you, Barth, are responsible for your disciples' excesses. Some would say you are responsible for that rascal Rudolf Bultmann, who didn't believe in the resurrection of Jesus!

BARTH: I would say touché, Schleiermacher, but the comparison doesn't hold up. Bultmann is more your follower than mine. Yes, he started out with us in the beginnings of what has come to be called "dialectical theology," but soon he departed from us to begin his project of demythologizing the New Testament. For him, as for you, Christianity is all about humans; it is anthropocentric. I say to him what I said to you: "You cannot talk about God by talking about humanity in a very loud voice!"

BRUNNER: Gentlemen, gentlemen, this doesn't seem like a heavenly dialogue. Can't you two just hug and make up? After all, both of you experienced the divine-human encounter, and that's what really matters. Neither one of you presented a theology that is completely biblical or coherent, but that's all behind us (or below us!) now.

BARTH: So Brunner, you are still spouting that stuff about divine-human encounter? You were always the touchy-feely theologian who made everything revolve around experience. In so doing you weren't so different from Schleiermacher here.

BRUNNER: Now that's a low blow! You know I have no sympathies with Schleiermacher's approach to theology or his conclusions. The experience I emphasized as crucial to authentic Christianity and to theology is the I-Thou encounter between God and the individual. It's supernatural. Schleiermacher's God-consciousness experience was something entirely different.

BARTH: Well, they don't look so different from where I sit. Theology must begin with, stay with, and end with the objectively given Word of God, which has three forms: Jesus Christ (who is revelation itself!), the Bible (as the instrument of God's Word), and the church's proclamation of the gospel. There's no experience in that! Other than the experience, if you can call it that, of being grasped and changed by the Word. And that change, I might add, is not an experience; instead, it is a transformed standing before God in Jesus Christ.

SCHLEIERMACHER: Okay, you two. From where I sit you don't sound all that different. You're both supernaturalists. And you both appear to believe in human depravity and an objective salvation that places the Christian in an entirely different status. I was trying to show that Christianity is the absolute religion, the pinnacle and zenith of universal human God-consciousness. Only that way can Christianity be something truly human and not float above our heads like a transcendent cloud that never touches earth.

BRUNNER: Well, let me jump in before Barth does for once. Schleiermacher, you tried to do theology "from below." Well, the course of the next century proved that it can't be done. Your disciples, the liberal theologians, tried to follow in your steps by gaining knowledge of God from examining human experience. But Barth and I discovered that to be a dead end. You never get to the prophetic Word of the Lord by beginning from below. God's

Word, God's message, has to come down to us "from above." Otherwise
we end up talking about, and to ourselves, rather than with God.

BARTH: May I just say that both of you suffered from the same problem. In
spite of all your talk about doing theology from above, Brunner, you
allowed natural theology to sneak back into theology. I thought we had
expelled it permanently. You're like Schleiermacher in that you also take
your cues from nature and culture. After all, if you give even one little
finger to natural theology, it will take over everything.

BRUNNER: I think your critique hits its target in Schleiermacher and his theological offspring, but it hardly touches me. You should know by now that
when I wrote about "natural theology," I didn't mean "human search for
God" through nature, culture, or universal human experience. I simply
meant that we are created in God's image, and therefore we are capable of
hearing and responding to God's Word. It's all about the point of contact
between the Christian gospel and the not-yet-believing natural person.

SCHLEIERMACHER: I don't think of my theological project as "natural theology,"
either. Both of you misunderstood me. Did you even read my work *The
Christian Faith*? There I underscored and emphasized the centrality of
Jesus Christ for our God-consciousness. Our beliefs as Christians are
simply our human attempts to put our experience of God and of Jesus
into words.

BARTH: You may protest all day, Schleiermacher, but we know the truth of
the matter. Whether you were aware of it or not, you allowed modern
culture to shape your entire theology. In fact, I would go so far as to say
you were so afraid of modern science and philosophy that you built an
entire theological system on the shaky foundation of humanity's inner
consciousness of God. It's far too subjective, Schleiermacher. What you
promoted and handed on to the next generation of liberal theologians was
what I call "culture Christianity," a Christianity compromised, negotiated,
harmonized with modernity.

BRUNNER: On this point we stand together, Barth. I agree with you about
Schleiermacher and liberal theology in general. It gave us a "gospel" impos-
sible to preach; it sucked the life out of the gospel and out of theology. And
Barth, you know that I never sympathized with either Schleiermacher or
natural theology. I constructed my whole theological system out of God's
Word, which comes down from above and transforms our lives.

BARTH: And yet you reintroduced natural theology, Brunner. How sad that
you couldn't recognize natural theology as the cause of all the problems
of Christianity.

SCHLEIERMACHER: Okay, well, I don't think we're getting anywhere with this.
So let's turn to another subject: Jesus Christ. Now after this time in purgatory we will meet him face-to-face. In fact, I already have. I assume
that you have also, Barth. You, Brunner, will soon enough. Now we are
finding out how far from reality our puny little thoughts about him were.

But I stand by my idea that what makes Jesus to be God is his unbroken and complete God-consciousness. It constitutes a veritable existence of God in him.

BRUNNER: Well, Schleiermacher, when I do meet him face-to-face, I'm going to tell him that you are not fully converted, even here in heaven! You reduced Jesus to a human prophet. That left the door open for later "prophets" claiming to be God or God's Son. If Jesus is not different in kind from us, then he can't be absolute and unique or be our Savior.

SCHLEIERMACHER: I don't think Jesus was always already different in kind from us; that would remove him too far from our struggles and failures. I'd say he is so different in degree that he becomes different in kind from us. But all that supernatural stuff about preexistence and descent from heaven and literal incarnation—well, that's what we moderns just can't believe.

BARTH: And there's your biggest failing, Schleiermacher. You always did and still do decide what to believe based on what you think modern people can believe. Here I agree with Brunner: the entire gospel is based on Jesus Christ as the objectively given Word of God. And when God reveals something, he reveals himself. His Word, Jesus Christ, is God himself. Otherwise, Jesus Christ would not be the fullest revelation of God.

BRUNNER: I think this is our biggest area of agreement over against Schleiermacher, Barth. He seemed to be Christ-centered, but he really wasn't and isn't. His whole theological project is human-centered and church-centered. You and I agree that God's Word appears like a lightning bolt out of heaven. It can't be the end of human search for God. It is rather God's search for us.

You and I agree, for example, that the Bible, as important as it is, is just paper and ink until and unless God speaks through it. In the moment of divine-human encounter, the Bible "becomes" the Word of God insofar as it brings Jesus Christ to us. The Bible is no "paper pope," as the fundamentalists seem to think. It's not a book of divinely revealed facts. It is the instrument of God's Word to us.

SCHLEIERMACHER: But you two still sound like fundamentalists to me! You're so Bible-centered. For all your claims that the Bible is not a paper pope, you both treat it that way in your theologies. Rarely, if ever, do either one of you acknowledge its cultural conditioning and humanness. For us moderns, the Bible is the classical Christian text, but not an inspired or infallible book.

BARTH: I struggled during my entire career to show that I am no fundamentalist! Many times I said that the Bible could be wrong about anything without that affecting our faith. Brunner said the same thing. But you, Schleiermacher, reduced the Bible to classical literature, and you sliced and diced it any way you wanted in order to make its message acceptable to modern people. Well, its message is never acceptable to anyone. But that's not because it conflicts with modernity; it's because its message conflicts with our thoughts and calls us to absolute obedience to the God who elected us and the Christ who redeemed us.

BRUNNER: I agree with so much of what you say, Barth. But when you mention the "electing God," I become nervous. Now, we both come out of the Reformed tradition, but like every human tradition, it needs correction. Yes, God elects people. Yes, Jesus is the primary object of God's election. But contrary to your imagination, Barth, God elects as his own people only those who freely embrace Jesus Christ in the divine-human encounter, where God meets us and calls us to decision.

BARTH: *Nein!* I cannot accept this weak gospel of God's grace and mercy that would leave some out of salvation. Only Jesus Christ was and is the "reprobate man," bearing wrath, hate, death, judgment for all. He took on our punishment so that all of us can be elect to salvation in him.

BRUNNER: So once again, Barth, you show your liberal colors. Universal salvation is a liberal idea, not a biblical or Christian idea. I think your "purified supralapsarianism" was nothing more than an attempt to reconcile God's love with God's foreordination. You agree with hard-shell Calvinists that God does everything for us in salvation and that if we are saved, it is only because God predestined it. Then you teach universalism to rescue God's reputation! That's so liberal of you, Barth.

SCHLEIERMACHER: Okay, okay, okay. You two go to your separate corners before you come to blows. Barth, I have to agree with Brunner. The universal salvation idea in your theology seems like a foreign object from liberal thinking. But Brunner, how do you work this all out?

BRUNNER: I'm so glad you asked that, Schleiermacher. I believe God limits himself by giving people the ability to resist his grace or cooperate with it. God does all the saving, but whether he saves depends on our free acceptance of his grace and mercy in Jesus. God's predestination is of and for all who freely embrace the gospel. But we know some don't, so universalism is out of consideration if we wish to be truly biblical. The Bible also emphasizes the wrath of God. Neither of you two knew what to do with that!

BARTH: Yes, I did! And I do! The wrath of God against sin was poured out on Jesus Christ on his cross. God took our punishment; he suffered his own wrath as judgment on himself so that we don't have to suffer it.

SCHLEIERMACHER: Well, I guess I have to agree that you two stand over against me on this one. What we do agree on, Barth, is that eventually everyone will be saved. Where I disagree with both of you is this primitive notion of the wrath of God. The wrath of God is nothing other than our own failure of God-consciousness. We feel God as wrathful when we are forgetful of God, but God surely feels no such thing as wrath.

BRUNNER: Let's wrap up this conversation. We just seem to be rehashing our old disagreements on earth. I've signed up for God's Theology 101 class. The Holy Spirit is going to teach it. I'm rather sure I'll agree with everything, but I'm going to go with an open mind, just in case there's something for me to learn.

BARTH: I'm not sure. All truth of any importance is somewhere in my *Church Dogmatics*. I'll just go to the heavenly library and reread it.

SCHLEIERMACHER: I've signed up for the Holy Spirit's class on spiritual formation. I think doctrine is probably irrelevant here. Even on earth it was mostly a necessary evil.

Analysis

Don't be misled by Schleiermacher's final statement about doctrine. He did care about doctrine. He wrote a huge volume of doctrine titled *The Christian Faith*. Yet he regarded doctrine as secondary to religious experience and always open to revision in light of new understandings of reality through the lens of experience. But sometimes he was fairly negative toward doctrine. He said that doctrine is nothing more than the attempt to bring religious experiences to speech and that concepts are all foreign to religion, which is essentially experience.

In this conversation you can see how close and yet how far apart Barth and Brunner were. Compared to Schleiermacher, they were very close. They both eschewed "theology from below" in favor of theology based entirely on supernatural divine revelation, "God's Word," which is first and foremost Jesus Christ and secondarily Scripture. They both believed that theology must be God-centered and that God is wholly other and transcendent to creation, including humanity.

Brunner, however, worried that Barth had made God too transcendent. He also strongly disliked Barth's emphasis on God's sovereignty in salvation. Barth was a Calvinist and called his theology "purified supralapsarianism." Supralapsarianism is the most extreme form of Calvinism, in which God's predestination of people logically precedes creation and the fall. Barth softened that by saying that God predestined Jesus Christ to die for the sins of the world and then elected everyone else to be saved in Christ. For Barth, Jesus Christ was the only reprobate (damned) person because God put on him everyone's sins; he suffered the penalty for all. Brunner saw Barth's peculiar form of soteriology (doctrine of salvation) as a huge concession to both high Calvinism and liberalism.

Brunner's own theology was closer to Arminianism (see conversation 15) although he never admitted such. For most Reformed theologians, Arminianism is still a term of derision largely because they have forgotten what Arminianism really is. Brunner believed that God limits himself so that he does not make every decision for the person. Humans have free will as a gift of God's grace, and they are responsible for their decisions about the law and the gospel. He radically rejected monergism, the doctrine that God is the sole active agent in salvation. To be sure, God does all the saving by his grace, but humans must cooperate with God's initiative by exercising faith.

Barth heard echoes of Schleiermacher in Brunner's theology because Brunner gave some role to humans in their own salvation and claimed that, in the aftermath of the fall, they still possess a relic of the image of God. The problem is that this relic of God's image is a natural point of contact between the gospel and the person. Barth believed this doctrine robbed God of some of his sovereignty in salvation and diminished the role of grace. He also thought that it leaned too close to anthropocentrism in theology, which is the poison that Barth fought against so hard.

So what is the relevance of the Barth-Brunner debate for today? Its echoes still reverberate down the corridors of theology many years later, even though many scholars have concluded that it was wholly unnecessary and largely based on Barth's misunderstanding of Brunner. In the late twentieth century and the early twenty-first century, Christian theologians still debate the role of philosophy and natural knowledge in theology. Barth wanted to expunge them from Christian theology. But that made his thought lean perilously close to fideism: belief on the basis of blind faith without reason.

Among evangelical theologians, Donald Bloesch (b. 1928) advocates a kind of Barthian position while expressing some appreciation for Brunner. In his seven-volume work *Christian Foundations* (1992–2004), Bloesch calls his approach "fideistic revelationism." He bases every doctrine on special revelation, to the neglect of any natural knowledge of God or even natural point of contact for the gospel.

German theologian Jürgen Moltmann (b. 1926) engages extensively with philosophy while eschewing any theology from below. Like Brunner, he believes in a point of contact for the gospel in the human. That is humanity's openness to the future, which connects with God's promises for the final restoration of all things to wholeness. Throughout much of his theological career, he has engaged in dialogue with the philosophy of revisionist German Marxist Ernst Bloch (1885–1977), who in biblical eschatology saw a religious utopianism akin to the future classless society.

Moltmann sees in Bloch a person who recognizes a part of the truth and is a great conversation partner. This openness to secular philosophy and to the theological exploitation of echoes of transcendence in human experience makes Moltmann a contemporary theological cousin of Brunner.

Barth and Brunner were two giants of twentieth-century theology; together they reversed the liberal tide in Protestant theology and recovered a semblance of Christian orthodoxy in the churches. Yet fundamentalists were not satisfied. One even labeled Barth's theology "new modernism." ("Modernism" was the fundamentalists' term for liberal theology.) That was simply wrong. Both Barth and Brunner were mediating theologians; they worked tirelessly to create a third way between Schleiermacher's anthropocentric liberalism and fundamentalist biblical literalism. Many evangelical theologians of the 1960s and afterward were and still are strongly influenced by these two Swiss giants of theology.

For Further Reading

Dorrien, Gary. *The Barthian Revolt in Modern Theology*. Louisville: Westminster John Knox, 2000.

McKim, Mark G. *Emil Brunner*. Lanham, MD: Scarecrow, 1996.

22

Barth and Brunner Contest Their Differences on Natural Theology and Whether All Will Be Saved

Setting

I realize that these two theologians were two of the three conversation partners in the immediately preceding imaginary conversation (21). Here they will debate some of the same subjects. However, this is not sheer repetition. In this conversation they probe deeper into some of their major differences. I thought it worthwhile to have these two giants of modern theology face off without Schleiermacher or anyone else with them.

Karl Barth and Emil Brunner lived only a few miles apart in Switzerland. (See the "Setting" to conversation 21 for dates.) Barth taught theology at the University of Basel, and Brunner at the University of Zurich. They were roughly the same age, and their theological orientations were similar. They cooperated in the formation of what has come to be called "neoorthodoxy," a theological movement against liberal theology that was not fundamentalist. Both considered the Bible to be the supreme source and norm for Christian doctrine while eschewing the conservative Protestant doctrine of biblical inerrancy. Brunner referred to the conservatives' and fundamentalists' biblicism as their having a "paper pope." Barth harshly criticized the doctrine of biblical inerrancy while acknowledging affinities for the doctrine of verbal inspiration.

Here the two Swiss theological giants meet by accident on a train going to Geneva. So this conversation chronologically precedes the previous one. I have found both dialogues useful in my courses on modern and contemporary theology. The one that includes Schleiermacher (21) brings out Barth's and Brunner's sharp differences from liberal thought; this one focuses more on the differences between Barth and Brunner. Some people imagine neoorthodoxy to be a monolithic theological movement; it was not. This imaginary conversation will make that clear.

The Conversation

BARTH: *Guten Morgan*, Herr Professor Brunner! Fancy meeting you on this train to Geneva. What is your business in the great Swiss city of our beloved John Calvin?

BRUNNER: *Ach du Liebe!* You gave me quite a shock there, Herr Doktor Barth! Well, like you, I suppose, I'm going to Geneva for the conference of our Swiss Reformed Church. I hope to convince the ministers and delegates to side with me—and Calvin, of course—in our dispute over "nature and grace."

BARTH: *Nein!* It shall not be. I will show them that your concessions to natural theology, though seemingly innocent, are really just the first steps down the slippery slope toward full-blown liberal theology, and that is what led the German Christians to embrace the Nazi ideology.

BRUNNER: *Mein Gott*, Barth! Don't you ever give up on that? You blame everything bad on natural theology. Even the Holocaust! I agree with you that liberal Protestant theology was and is a poisonous enemy that we who follow the Bible and the Reformers must oppose with all our might. But your antidote to that poison is itself poisonous!

BARTH: Ah, strong words from the little theological gnome of Zurich! Well, I hardly think it worth my time to debate further with you about this. Our minds are probably both already made up. And we think differently about God's revelation and nature. As I have said, we are like the whale and the elephant—both God's creatures but not able to meet.

BRUNNER: I thought you said that about yourself and Rudolf Bultmann!

BARTH: So I did. But it applies to us two as well.

BRUNNER: I would be cut to the quick to discover that you put me in the same category as Bultmann, who tried to demythologize the New Testament and in the process removed the resurrection of our Lord from history.

BARTH: Well, you may not be as bad as that, but if you continue with your nonsense about humanity's natural point of contact for the gospel, you'll end up where he did.

BRUNNER: Yes, yes, you may be right about our being like the whale and the elephant. But I certainly have no sympathy with Bultmann's existentializing of the gospel message. He reduces theology entirely to anthropology. It is all and only about our human self-understanding. But let's talk more about us. Surely even the whale and the elephant can come close together if they are both God's creatures. The elephant can walk a ways into the water, the whale can come near the shore, and they can at least try to communicate.

BARTH: Well, there you go again. You are such an optimist about human nature. That reveals what I have said about you all along. Scratch Brunner, and under the surface of his seemingly evangelical skin lurks liberal flesh and bones. Only God can create agreement with his Word. On our own we fallen humans have no innate capacity for agreement with God's truth. God must create that capacity and the agreement. Dialogue is the liberal way toward truth. God's way is submission to his Word. And God's Word tells us that our minds must be transformed by renewing, a renewing of the mind that comes through obedience. Your lovely little faith in dialogue is faith in human flesh; it is evidence of your anthropocentrism.

BRUNNER: *Noch einmal*, Barth! There you go again, completely distorting my words. As you should know by now, I completely agree with you that only by God's Word and Spirit can fallen humans come to know God truly. It is a miracle wrought by God himself. It is the miracle of faith. But the way you portray humans before and apart from faith makes them as dead men floating in the water. I say they are drowning, but capable of swimming just a little. God throws them the lifesaver of his Word, and because they are created in God's own image, they can swim to that life preserver and be saved from drowning. Natural theology is only recognizing a point of contact in every person for God's Word. It is the capacity for hearing and responding to God's Word. Your theology makes it sound as if all people are dead bodies or logs floating around in the water, and then God comes along in the lifeboat of his Word, resuscitates them without their consent, and drags them sputtering and flailing into his boat of salvation.

BARTH: Your analogy is both good and bad, Brunner. It is good because it shows that you think fallen, depraved, sinful humans are not really "dead in trespasses and sins" after all. They can swim a little! How is that different from both the Roman Catholic and the liberal Protestant heresies of assigning humans some credit for their own salvation? And what if some of your struggling swimmers make it to the shore or into the boat on their own? Then they could boast, couldn't they? So much for Ephesians 2:8 and 9! Your analogy is surely bad because it suggests that my view portrays God as arbitrary and capricious in his saving work. *Nein!* God is a God of mercy and grace. In Jesus Christ, God jumps into the water and saves all the drowning people and dies in the process.

BRUNNER: Aha! There it is! Your heresy of *apokatastasis*—ultimate, universal reconciliation. Barth, you are a closet universalist. I've known it all along. How you can possibly reconcile that with God's Word, I do not know. You accuse me of being liberal! At least I'm not a universalist like you!

BARTH: I've never admitted to teaching universalism or the heresy of *apoka-tastasis*. But, Brunner, let me ask you this: would you be angry at God if he did save everyone?

BRUNNER: Definitely not! That would be God's business. But in his Word he has revealed that not all will be saved. And the Bible often talks about the wrath of God against all unrighteousness. Jesus talked more about hell than anyone else in Scripture! This is a matter of believing the Bible or not believing it. You say you do, but in this case I think your own latent liberalism conditions your thinking. For you, as for all liberal Protestants, hell is nothing but an empty threat. That's not the biblical witness.

BARTH: Well, Brunner, you know my answer to that. "Humanity's 'no' to God can never stand up against God's 'yes' to humanity in Jesus Christ." I wrote that in various forms and many times. If we really take Christ and his cross seriously, then we cannot assign any power or reality to sin, evil, or damnation. They are overcome by God's own self-sacrifice in Jesus Christ. Satan and hell and death and sin are either defeated or they are not. God's Word says they are defeated. Besides, Brunner, your use of the Bible sounds like that "paper pope" you accuse fundamentalists of following. Not everything in the Bible is to be taken as God's Word, you know.

BRUNNER: I just don't see where this line of discussion is getting us. You obviously don't take the Bible as seriously as I do!

BARTH: Well, at least I taught the virgin birth and the empty tomb. You count both as legends.

BRUNNER: You know why I denied them. Not because they are impossible, but because they are not central to the biblical witness, and the earliest witnesses say nothing about them. Your uncritical use of the Bible verges on fundamentalist literalism at times. The virgin birth and empty tomb are not central to the biblical message.

BARTH: I think they are, and I reject your accusation of fundamentalism! You well know that I do not take all of the Bible literally. Remember how I relegated the two creation accounts and the fall story to the category of "saga"? But the virgin birth and empty tomb are entirely different. Jesus's very sinlessness and divinity depend on them. But let's get back to the main point of our discussion. I have never understood how you avoid the terrible mistake of making human thinking and experience the measure of the truth of God's Word. Your point-of-contact theory sounds much like the old liberal religious a priori—something within humans themselves that is the judge of religious truth.

BRUNNER: You know better than that, Barth. I can't believe that you would even make such an unfair assertion. I definitely don't believe in the liberal religious a priori as a norm for the truth of God's Word. Instead, God's Word contradicts all our normal human thoughts about God.

BARTH: But you do talk about a natural theology, don't you? That always leads back to a religious a priori. If we allow even the camel's nose of natural theology into the church's tent, the entire camel will charge in and fill up the tent and drive out truth. That is exactly what happened to the German Christians during the 1930s. First came natural theology, and then on its heels came cultural accommodation, and that led to subverting the gospel to Nazi ideology. The only way to resist such apostasy is to push the camel's nose back out of the tent flap the moment it first appears. You haven't done that.

BRUNNER: I see that you are still unable to distinguish between types of natural theology. By natural theology I do not mean anything like what you mean by it. You hear that phrase, and you start salivating like Pavlov's dog. You become mad and begin running around, biting even your best friends. You don't even wait to hear what is meant by natural theology. All I mean, as I've explained before, is that human beings have within them the image of God, which is a formal capacity for hearing and responding to God's Word. Without that, humans would be animals and not men and women.

BARTH: But why call that "natural theology"? Surely the term implies more than a mere capacity for something. I know you mean more by it than that.

BRUNNER: Well, yes. It includes what we know as conscience, what the great British Christian writer C. S. Lewis spoke of in his *Mere Christianity* as "the law of nature." It is our innate human knowledge of right and wrong. We humans know that we are sinners and in need of grace. That is why we are accountable before God. Haven't you yet read and studied Romans 1 carefully?

BARTH: You know I have. I wrote *Der Römerbrief*, my commentary on Romans, which is said to have fallen "like a bombshell" on the playground of the theologians. Your reference to Romans 1 implies that I have missed Paul's point there. It's supposed to be the biblical proof of general revelation and natural theology. Well, I reject that. In Romans 1 Paul teaches that humans should know God through nature, but they don't. They are guilty before God and in need of redemption because they worship the creature rather than the Creator. Obviously they don't know right from wrong. As for Lewis, I've heard of him. He's Anglican, right? Well, too often those Church of England people buy into Catholic doctrines like natural theology.

BRUNNER: Now stop that! Our own Reformed father in the faith John Calvin interpreted Romans 1 differently than you and more along the lines of Lewis. For Calvin, humans do know right from wrong, but they suppress the truth, and that is why they are guilty and condemned unless they repent. Calvin was absolutely clear in his affirmation of general revelation and a bare natural knowledge of God, called the *sensus divinus*, the inner sense of the divine.

You know, Barth, I'm beginning to agree with Paul Tillich that you throw the gospel, God's Word, at people's heads like a rock. Your attitude is, "Like it or lump it," or as the Germans say, "Eat up, little birdies, or die." You don't recognize any point of contact for the gospel in your fellow humans. At least I allow that they are capable of hearing and understanding the Word of God because they are humans and not beasts.

BARTH: I'm not surprised to hear that you agree with that heretic Tillich. You yourself are headed right in his direction! He has completely discarded the Christian faith. At least once a week I pray for him, that he will yet be saved before he dies. I will begin to pray for you too, Brunner. You may not be a heretic or apostate yet, but this natural theology of yours will seduce many people into humanistic theology and religion. It's a Trojan horse of liberalism, and it must be firmly resisted.

BRUNNER: Ah, at last we reach our destination. There's the train station in Geneva. I'm glad we're here. Don't mention that we talked on the train, okay? I won't mention it to anyone either. There's a young American student in Zurich who wants to become famous for arranging our first face-to-face meeting in many years. Let's let him have that claim to fame, okay? We'll get together at either your home or mine, shake hands, say something about whales and elephants, and smile for the cameras. Then he can go down in history as the American student who brought the two giants of neoorthodoxy back together for one last meeting before they died. Okay?

BARTH: *Ja, ja!*

Analysis

The analysis of the previous conversation (21) contains some remarks pertinent to this one. So this analysis will be fairly brief.

Why do Barth and Brunner deserve attention in a book like this one? Without any doubt their controversy over natural theology represents one of the most significant and bewildering debates in twentieth-century Protestant theology. Many theologians, pastors, and teachers lined up behind either Barth or Brunner. Most of them had sympathies with both. Brunner's *Dogmatics* was used as the basic theology textbook in seminaries for decades. There he continued his debate with Barth by including appendixes to chapters where he specifically named Barth as a near heretic for his apparent embrace of *apokatastasis*.

Some would say that he wrote out of bitterness. Brunner was much better known than Barth in the English-speaking world up until the 1950s, when interest in Barth surpassed interest in Brunner. Once Barth's fame spread, Brunner's influence was largely eclipsed except in seminary classrooms. Even there, however, professors of theology often used Brunner to discuss Barth! Barth is difficult to read; Brunner isn't.

Barth's followers vehemently rejected any natural knowledge of God or even a natural point of contact in the person for the gospel. The gospel comes like a bolt of lightning out of the blue and creates something entirely new in the person—both capacity for faith and faith itself. Barth became extremely popular among moderately Reformed theologians and pastors because he stayed close to Calvin in his emphasis on regeneration preceding conversion. And moderate Reformed theologians liked Barth's revision of Calvin's doctrine of election, which seemed to bring into question God's goodness.

For Barth, God is the all-determining reality, especially in salvation. Together with Calvin, Barth eschewed any hint of synergism. But Barth also eschewed double predestination and affirmed that all persons are elect in Jesus Christ. Brunner interpreted this as universalism; others did not. Barth would not come clean about it. His last word on the subject was that he was not now teaching universalism and never had.

Barth founded a whole school of theology without intending to do so. He often said that he was not the final word, and he hated that his followers formed a theological party based on his writings. In any case, however, his tremendous influence in Europe and especially in North America led to an inflation of special revelation and a neglect if not outright denial of general revelation and natural theology. And it led to a renewal of Calvinism even if it was a revisionist form of Calvinism. Barth also almost single-handedly revived interest in the doctrine of the Trinity after its long eclipse in liberal Protestant thought. It actually is not too much of a stretch to claim that Barth killed classical liberal Protestantism with his bombshell book *Der Römerbrief* and later publications.

Brunner's influence is not as obvious or as much discussed. But hundreds if not thousands of seminary students in the 1950s through the 1980s learned theology from him. Brunner was much more the pietist than Barth. Thus Barth had little use for feelings; he equated religious feelings with Schleiermacher's anthropocentric liberal theology. But Brunner, though he rejected Schleiermacher's God-consciousness as any norm for theology, warmly embraced and promoted the experience of the God-person, or I-Thou, encounter. For him, that encounter is a form of the Word of God. It is itself revelatory.

Yet in spite of all his criticisms of the "paper pope" bibliolatry of fundamentalism, Brunner elevated the Bible to the highest source and norm of theology. But the Bible's purpose is to bring readers and hearers into the divine-human encounter with Jesus Christ. It "becomes the Word of God" in that existential moment when God uses it to speak to the individual or the church.

Brunner's doctrine of general revelation and what he unfortunately called "natural theology" is much closer to Calvin's doctrine than is Barth's. While avoiding the excesses of rationalistic apologetics, it leaves the door open to a kind of apologetic. Every sinner knows oneself as a sinner and is capable of hearing and responding to God's Word. Therefore, there is some common ground between the witness and the person being witnessed to. It is not as if one had merely to preach the gospel and let God do all the convincing. God can convince through the persuasive arguments of the Christian preacher or writer.

Another way of saying this that is hopefully congenial to Brunner's meaning is that deep in the heart and mind of every sinner are life's ultimate questions, which receive no adequate answer except through special revelation. General revelation produces questions and the capacity for understanding the answers. Yet the answers all come from special revelation. But they don't come as something alien. They come and ring true to the open ears of honest inquirers.

A great many evangelical and moderately Reformed theologians and pastors adopted Brunner's position rather than Barth's. Brunner founded no school of theology; there are not "Brunnerians" as there are "Barthians." But his influence seeped into the fabric of late twentieth-century Christian thought and convinced many of the value of a modest apologetic approach to the gospel, combined with a strong belief in the power of the Word of God itself to draw people into encounter with Jesus Christ.

The controversy has died down in the early twenty-first century. Many are forgetting it, but it's worth remembering. Barth had something valuable to say about the dangers of natural theology. Whether the dangerous natural theology he decried was Brunner's is doubtful. Barth overreacted to Brunner. Saying anything good about natural theology in Barth's presence, regardless of what one meant by that term, was like waving a red flag in front of a bull. That wariness or even antipathy to natural theology serves a good purpose. There is no Lord but Jesus Christ, and natural theology cannot yield a relationship with Christ. Natural theology always opens the door, even if only a crack, to let the pure gospel capitulate to culture.

But Brunner also had something valuable to say about the value of a kind of natural theology, or what he termed natural theology: the point of contact for the gospel within every human heart. Humans are hearers of the Word. That's what makes them higher and better than animals. There may be other differences, but there are none that compare in importance with this one. This truth requires every effort to learn about life's ultimate questions in every generation and to express the gospel in a way that addresses those questions, answers them, and invites hearers of the Word into encounter with Jesus Christ in repentance and faith.

For Further Reading

Barth, Karl, and Emil Brunner. *Nature and Grace*. Eugene, OR: Wipf & Stock, 2002.

23

Twentieth-Century Theological Giants Barth and Tillich Discuss Crucial Issues, Christ and Culture

Setting

The basic details of Karl Barth's life and career are laid out in the "Setting" sections of the two previous conversation (21 and 22). He without doubt was one of the most influential Christian thinkers of the twentieth century, and his influence continues into the twenty-first century. In 1962 he made his one trip to the United States, traveling around and giving lectures at various seminaries and universities, including Princeton and Chicago, where he engaged in a panel dialogue with various other theologians.

Paul Tillich (1886–1965) was another giant of theology during the twentieth century. In many ways he was Barth's opposite and counterpart. His theology was a form of "chastened liberalism." He strove to give maximal acknowledgment to the claims of modernity while at the same time avoiding the overly optimistic anthropology of the classical liberal Protestants from Schleiermacher to Rauschenbusch. Tillich was deeply affected by World War I. After the war he embraced existentialism and allowed it to color his approach to Christian theology. Thus for him there is a tragic dimension to human existence, and the individual must confront one's own destiny with free choice and create a self-understanding that transcends what is merely given to oneself by culture and family.

Tillich loved philosophy and gave it a place of eminence in his theology. His "method of correlation" was the attempt to begin with philosophy and then move to theology. Philosophy tells the theologian what questions to answer, and the theologian draws the answers from divine revelation. The answers' contents come from revelation; their form comes from philosophy. Some critics believe that Tillich allowed theology's content to be determined by existentialist philosophy.

His lifetime of theological creativity was summed up in his three-volume *Systematic Theology* (1951, 1957, 1963). He wrote numerous other books as well. In all of his writings, Tillich tried to correlate theology with philosophy while remaining faithful to the basic impulses of divine revelation. Barth radically eschewed philosophical speculation in theology and sought to do Christian theology in a way as uncorrupted by philosophy as possible. Thus the two twentieth-century giants of theology reflected the second-century debates over philosophy and theology between church fathers such as Tertullian and Clement of Alexandria.

Tillich was born in Germany. During World War I he served as a chaplain in the German army. After the war he may have suffered a nervous breakdown. He studied theology and became a professor of theology at German universities. After the Nazis' rise to power in the 1930s, Tillich was shadowed by the Gestapo; he was suspected of being anti-Nazi and subversive to the Nationalist Socialist Party's cause. So Tillich fled Germany to avoid being sent to Dachau, the notorious prison camp where Hitler's opponents were interred, allegedly for their own safety. Tillich found refuge in New York at Union Theological Seminary (1933–1955), a bastion of liberal Protestantism.

His theology is sometimes referred to as "neoliberal" due to the heavy dose of existentialism that makes it somewhat more pessimistic about human nature and what Tillich liked to call the "human predicament." "Neoliberalism" is almost a synonym for liberal theology after World War I. It is also often called "chastened liberalism" (as above). In spite of its more pessimistic cast, it is continuous with the older liberalism that reigned in Protestant scholarly circles from Schleiermacher to Rauschenbusch and, in America, even further. Human experience remains the main source and norm of theology, and it is defined by philosophy and culture rather than by the Bible.

As will be seen, Barth abhorred Tillich's neoliberalism and considered it a tragic accommodation to the spirit of the age. Other critics have argued that one can find virtually every heresy in Tillich's thought. Tillich was not much concerned about these charges and accusations. He considered his vocation to be an apologist to the intellectuals of Europe and America, including university students.

Tillich taught at Union Theological Seminary and then in 1955 was appointed a university professor at Harvard. He spent his last years (from 1962) in retirement at the University of Chicago School of Divinity, teaching theology and being showered with honors as one of the great living theologians. He died in 1965 of heart failure shortly after two so-called "death of God" theologians ("Christian atheists") met with him and told him that they took their inspiration from him. They misunderstood Tillich's saying that "God does not exist." In context, it clearly means that God is not a finite object like other things that exist. God is real, Tillich meant, but does not exist because to "exist" means to stand out apart from other things. God is not "thingy."

Barth could have met Tillich in Chicago in 1962, but there is no record of such a meeting. The two had little use for each other. In a letter to a friend, Barth even questioned Tillich's salvation. However, one has to wonder what they might have said to each other if they had met in Chicago in 1962. In this imaginary conversation a mutual theological friend has arranged for Barth and Tillich to meet secretly in a room in Swift Hall, the main building of the University of Chicago Divinity School.

The Conversation

BARTH: Well, well, well, is that you, Paulus? I'm surprised that you have agreed to meet with me. After all, our programs of theology have taken radically different paths, and sometimes our criticisms of each other's works have become quite personal.

TILLICH: Ah, my dear Professor Barth. We meet at last. Yes, I'm surprised I'm meeting with you here. But our mutual friend is quite persuasive, isn't he? He promised me that he would use nothing but my *Systematic Theology* as the textbook in his theology courses in the seminary where he teaches if I would meet with you.

BARTH: That's interesting! He promised me the same thing! I mean, he promised that he would use only my *Church Dogmatics* if I agreed to meet with you! I'll have to have a little talk with him later tonight.

TILLICH: So, what do you have to say for yourself, Barth? How did you become a fundamentalist? That's what you are, you know. Your theology is hardly any better than these American fundamentalists' theology. You want to drag Protestant theology back into the dark ages before the Enlightenment. So much the worse for Protestant theology; your version of it will simply be ignored by the intellectuals of our society because it requires them to sacrifice their intellects by believing in miracles and such.

BARTH: Ah, that's just your problem, Tillich. You've been so intent on making everything about theology intelligible to the intellectuals with their abstract ways of thinking that you've lost sight of the fact that God's Word communicates truth that transcends philosophy's categories. You spent way too much time and gave too much attention to deliteralizing everything.

TILLICH: But in spite of your fundamentalist leanings, the biblical literalists weren't happy with you because you said that their Bible isn't always to be taken literally and isn't inerrant. Remember your concept of "saga"? You said that the first eleven chapters of Genesis are not to be taken as history but as saga—a concept you never adequately explained.

BARTH: So you acknowledge that I am no fundamentalist, then? *Sehr gut!* Now, at risk of sounding like one, let me explain my concept of saga. You well know that I didn't mean for Genesis not to be taken seriously. And I certainly didn't like the term "myth" since it conveys the idea that something is false. I thought I explained saga quite well. You must have skipped over that part of *Church Dogmatics*.

TILLICH: Who says I read *Church Dogmatics*? Don't flatter yourself.

BARTH: Well, in any case, you should have read it. Then maybe you'd be better prepared to criticize my theology. Saga, as you should know, is narrative telling a story of something that did actually happen in time and space but cannot be described in modern, historical, literal terms. It points to a reality to which we have no definite access and that we cannot really understand. But it is not mere legend or myth.

TILLICH: I really can't see why rescuing Genesis is your concern. It's only important insofar as it tells us something about our own existence, and there's not much of that there unless we regard it as myth.

BARTH: You existentialists are always trying to reduce the biblical message to a message about humanity. Our human predicament and its solution is certainly one part of it, and existentialism can shed some light on the problem. But it has no solution. The solution to our anxiety and temptation to despair is found only in what God has done for us in Jesus Christ.

TILLICH: I don't disagree. I also believe the solution is in Jesus Christ as the symbol of the New Being: the image of a finite person who lives in unbroken relationship with the Ground of Being. In other words, who experiences Godmanhood: the union of God and humanity that reunites essence and existence.

BARTH: I'm not sure if you even understand what you're talking about. "Godmanhood"? That sounds rather pantheistic to me. You did always tend to slide into pantheism or at least panentheism, with its overemphasis on God's immanence. Your God is too abstract, Tillich. He isn't really a person and doesn't really do anything. He's more like an "It"—a principle or force that underlies everything, or a potential for infinitization of the finite. It's all metaphysical mumbo jumbo and has no real resemblance to the gospel. You might make a good philosopher of religion, but not a Christian theologian.

TILLICH: You always were given to strong language about people you disagreed with, Karl. I see that old age hasn't changed that! Have you reconciled fully with Brunner yet? You treated him rather shabbily, as I recall.

BARTH: Don't change the subject, Tillich. But since you ask, yes, Brunner and I have reconciled. We still disagree about some things, but compared to you, we are two peas in a pod! At least he begins his theology with the Word of God and not with philosophy!

TILLICH: That's one of your misconceptions, Barth. There is no escaping philosophy. Theology always begins with philosophy, even when it thinks it does not. Philosophy raises the questions that theology answers. Without philosophy, theology would just be speaking into the wind, and its voice would never be heard.

BARTH: Yes, I know all about your method of correlation, but it would be better called the "method of accommodation" because you allow existential ontology not only to formulate the questions, but also to determine theology's answers. When you say that God is "Being Itself," you can't be relying on God's Word. And that's true especially when you say, "God does not exist." In heaven you're going to find out how real God is. He's not your "Ground of Being." Well, to be more precise, he's more than that. He's personal too. God is high and exalted, and we worship him on a daily basis, together with Jesus, whom we also exalt and adore. You're partly responsible, by the way, for the fact that Thomas Altizer and William Hamilton and some of the other "death of God" theologians can think of themselves as Christians. But they are wrong, and so are you.

TILLICH: I object! I am not responsible for their apostasies. They gave up faith in God on their own and without my help. I believe in God. Maybe not in the same way you believe in God, but in my own way.

BARTH: Well, perhaps, but your "God" is too much a tool for achieving authentic existence, and you strip God of supernatural power; it's easy for others to interpret you as denying God. After all, you did say, "God does not exist." How could you expect people not to react to that one way or another?

TILLICH: I explained that! You know very well I didn't mean to deny God's reality. I simply meant that God is not an object like things that "exist." To "exist" means to stand out from other things separately as a thing. God isn't "thingy." He or It is the power that underlies and gives being to all things. My only concern was to help Christians (and others) grow out of childish notions of God as a "man upstairs" or "good buddy in heaven" and realize that God is the foundation of everything and the power within everything.

BARTH: But you needed to be much more careful and balance that with the idea that God is also personal. You neglect that aspect of God, which is so prominent in Scripture.

TILLICH: I said that God is beyond "personality" and is "suprapersonal" only to avoid any notion of God as humanlike. People tend to anthropomorphize God too much. You do that, Karl, by tying God so closely to the man Jesus that there seems to be no real difference.

BARTH: Oh, no, Tillich, don't pin that "Christomonism" label on me. You should know that I am fully trinitarian!

TILLICH: You talk out of both sides of your mouth about that, Barth. One minute you're talking Trinity, and the next minute you're saying that Jesus Christ is our only source of access to God. And in every doctrine you make the man Jesus as God incarnate to be the center of everything.

BARTH: As we all should. He's God for us, you know. Our only access to the Father and our only knowledge of the Holy Spirit come through him. That's the whole point of the incarnation.

TILLICH: Well, that incarnation business seemed mythological to me. Jesus is the New Being, but he is not God, who is the Ground of Being. Nothing finite can be God nor can the finite contain God.

BARTH: There you go, Tillich. Jesus as the "New Being." Mumbo jumbo. What does that even mean?

TILLICH: Back when the New Testament was being written, they ascribed the label "Christ" to Jesus. He was Jesus the Christ. "Christ" was a title, not a last name, you know. So today I translate that as "New Being." They mean the same thing. In Jesus there appeared within history a human existence not broken or estranged from the Ground of Being, which surely is God. Jesus is not God, but he is one who, unlike others, is not cut off from God. Thus under the conditions of existence, he is the achievement of our true human destiny: Godmanhood, or unity between the finite and the infinite. Through communion with Christ, the rest of us can achieve some degree of redemption, meaning New Being.

BARTH: Listen to yourself, man! That's not biblical language at all. You're turning the gospel of Jesus Christ into a philosophy.

TILLICH: No, I'm not. No philosophy would ever identify a particular being as the manifestation of Being itself in such a unique and unsurpassable way. We only know this because of revelation.

BARTH: And what do you mean by "revelation"?

TILLICH: Anything that has the power to transform is revelatory.

BARTH: Anything? How about the Nazi movement, which invaded the German Christian churches with their swastikas? There was certainly a lot of transformation there!

TILLICH: But not all transformations or revelations are good. Some are evil. The swastika was a powerfully transforming evil symbol. The cross, on the contrary, is a wonderfully transforming good symbol.

BARTH: Why? On what grounds do you decide that one is evil and the other is good if both are revelations?

TILLICH: Because one brings salvation and the other one brings destruction.

BARTH: And how do you define salvation?

TILLICH: Receiving the courage to be in the face of the threat of nonbeing.

BARTH: There it is again! Philosophical mumbo jumbo replacing the gospel. Would you care to explain?

TILLICH: It's the arrival of wise resignation in the face of death and accepting that you are accepted.

BARTH: By whom?

TILLICH: The Ground of Being.

BARTH: And we are back to your impersonal, abstract God, who is more like a great idea or principle than a divine person. How can a person be "accepted" by the Ground of Being?

TILLICH: The important thing is just to accept that you are accepted.

BARTH: Okay, let me ask you this.

TILLICH: Oh, no. Here comes the inquisition!

BARTH: Well, this is a litmus-test question for you and for any panentheist. Can you pray to the Ground of Being?

TILLICH: No. But I meditate on the Ground of Being and my being accepted by . . .

BARTH: . . . It?

TILLICH: I don't think there's any pronoun that does justice to the suprapersonal nature of the Gound of Being.

BARTH: What's clear to me is that you have no conception of the God of Abraham, Isaac, and Jacob or the gospel of Jesus Christ. By the way, you told an interviewer, according to the report, that it wouldn't matter to Christian faith if Jesus never even existed. Put that together with "God does not exist," and you're just asking to be called a heretic!

TILLICH: Once again, you miss my point. I did say that to the interviewer, and I've been saying it to my students and anyone who will listen for years. Someone with the power to transform our lives lived in Palestine in the first century. But if the police records of Nazareth were discovered in a hillside cave near the town, and if it were proved that no one named Jesus of Nazareth lived there, all that would mean is that the man who lived in unbroken relationship with the Ground of Being and not in estrangement from Being Itself would have had another name.

BARTH: So at least you admit there had to be some historical existence of the Christ, what you call the New Being?

TILLICH: *Jawohl!* What his name was doesn't matter. What matters is the impact he had on the disciples and through them on the church and then through the church on us today.

BARTH: And what is that impact?

TILLICH: It is the possibility of New Being.

BARTH: And that comes only through this first-century person, whatever his name was?

TILLICH: Right.

BARTH: But help me understand: was he God incarnate?

TILLICH: We already settled that: no.

BARTH: Then how can he save? Only God can save, right?

TILLICH: He wasn't God, but he was the one person in history who experienced Godmanhood and passed that along to others through their communion with him.

BARTH: Godmanhood! Yes. There it is again. I think you're a pantheist, Tillich.

TILLICH: No. But I am a panentheist. God and the world belong inseparably together.

BARTH: Too much immanence, man. Too much immanence. The God of Abraham, Isaac, and Jacob is the transcendent God of glory, who also condescended to enter into human existence through Jesus Christ, who is the Son of God incarnate.

TILLICH: That's mythology. What I'm saying is the same thing, deliteralized for modern-day intellectuals.

BARTH: But if it should happen to turn out that the man who experienced Godmanhood, the New Being, whatever, was not Jesus, then our faith does not rest on history.

TILLICH: That doesn't follow at all. It rests on a powerful image of the possibility of actually achieving our destiny of union with God, the Ground of our Being.

BARTH: So what you are saying is that the image is what matters, and not the particular person or his history.

TILLICH: But the image is so real and so powerful that it transforms us. Its transforming power points to its historical reality.

BARTH: And the point of all this is?

TILLICH: Well, for one thing, I don't have to wait for the results of historical research or archaeology to arrive to know whether I can still be a Christian. My faith doesn't rest on the details of history but on the powerful image of a particular person who did not suffer the estrangement from God that the rest of us do.

BARTH: Ah, so fear of scientific falsification of traditional Christian belief has driven you to separate faith entirely from facts of history.

TILLICH: Um, that sounds exactly like what some fundamentalists have said about you!

BARTH: Well, they are wrong. Take the resurrection, for example. I have always believed, even if I stated it rather weakly early on, that Jesus rose bodily from the tomb and claimed a new form of existence, fit for heaven. But he was still human, and his body was no longer in the tomb after the resurrection.

TILLICH: Well, that empty tomb stuff scares me. What if the skeleton of Jesus should be discovered in a burial tomb somewhere near Jerusalem? What would become of your faith? Mine would be secure. Because for me, the resurrection was not the resuscitation of a corpse but the rise of faith in the Christ in the hearts of the disciples.

BARTH: That's exactly what Bultmann believes, and he's an infamous heretic.

TILLICH: Well, I rather appreciate him.

BARTH: The apostle Paul wrote an entire chapter on the bodily resurrection of Jesus, in 1 Corinthians 15. He said that if the resurrection did not happen and will not happen to us, then our faith is in vain, and we are of all people most to be pitied.

TILLICH: But I don't deny the resurrection! I simply reinterpret it.

BARTH: You mean you interpret it away.

TILLICH: Say what you will, but your account of faith and history is not that far from mine. You also say that the resurrection is unverifiable by ordinary historical research. For you also it is an event of revelation.

Barth: But I never meant that it didn't happen! I only mean that it is not amenable to proof. At least I believe that it actually happened in time and space.

Tillich: But what difference does it make? All that really matters is that our lives are transformed. The image of the crucified but risen Christ does that even if the history surrounding that image is ambiguous.

Barth: No, you subjectivize faith far too much. You make it depend on an image instead of an objective reality in which God has acted decisively to change the world. That's the gospel, man. God has acted decisively to change the world.

Tillich: You've accused me of talking mumbo jumbo. But what you've just said is certainly mumbo jumbo to almost every university professor, journalist, scientist, and philosopher alive today in the Western world. It is simply impossible for them to believe in your supernatural theology. God acting decisively to change the world? That kind of language cuts right across the scientific reality of the world we now know is true.

Barth: The gospel is a stumbling block to those who do not want to believe. The Word of God does not have to appeal to the rebellious minds of sinners. And when we adapt it to make it appeal, it loses all its savor. Your version of the gospel is so cut down and diced up that it has lost everything unique and appealing in it. It's little more than an existential philosophy with a veneer of Christianity thrown over it.

   I have to go now, Tillich. I am serving on a panel with several American theologians at the Rockefeller Chapel this evening. I know someone is going to ask me to sum up my entire life's work in a sentence. I've been forewarned about that. I wonder what I should say.

Tillich: Given all you've said here to me, I think you could rightly quote the little Sunday school ditty "Jesus loves me, this I know. For the Bible tells me so." That's about how deep your theology is.

Barth: Good idea, Tillich. I know you're being sarcastic, but I think it's a great idea. I'll do that.

Analysis

Barth really did answer that question that way. I've heard it a hundred times as a sermon illustration. I doubted it. So I asked a theologian who was there that evening. He confirmed to me that it really happened. Yet it's very doubtful that Barth got the idea from Tillich, but it's fun to imagine it.

   Barth's theology and Tillich's theology are almost as different as two ideas can possibly be. Like Schleiermacher's theology earlier (see conversations 19 and 21), Tillich's is a theology "from below." Human experience is the starting point and serves as a, if not the, major source and norm for theology. For Tillich, existentialist philosophy is the good luck charm of modern theology;

it serves as more than a conversation partner for theology. It is also a perspective that rescues Christian theology from its ancient form and helps translate it into modern form.

Clearly Tillich thought he was merely translating the gospel into thought forms that modern intellectuals could accept. But critics say that he went beyond translation to transformation of the content of the message itself. In his hands, Barth and other more conservative theologians said, the gospel underwent such a change as to be unrecognizable.

Tillich almost invited accusations of heresy with some of his more extreme theological expressions such as "God does not exist" and "It wouldn't undermine Christian faith if we found out that Jesus never existed." Who would ever guess what he meant? Clearly he was not an atheist, even though some critics have hurled that accusation against him. But he was a panentheist: he thought the world (creation) and God coexist eternally and are interdependent. God's immanence is the keynote of Tillich's theology. And his theology is anything but Christocentric. Clearly he did not mean to deny the appearance of Christ in history, but he detached that from the person of the historical Jesus in an almost Gnostic way.

Barth's keynote was God's transcendence, and his theology was thoroughly Christocentric and even Jesus-centered. He refused to make any distinction or separation between Jesus and Christ. Barth was not an extreme literalist, but he was not afraid of offending modern sensibilities with the scandal of the gospel. And his theological approach was "from above." He began his theological work with the presupposition of the reality of God's Word in history and sought to expunge philosophy from his theology. He may have been affected by existentialism early in his career as a theologian, but after 1932 he made a definite turn in theological method that involved expelling philosophy, including existentialism, from his *Church Dogmatics*.

These two conversation partners are two giants of twentieth-century theology. Barth was the conservative (despite fundamentalist criticisms), and Tillich was the liberal. But Barth was not a traditional conservative; his theology was not merely a repetition of the old Protestant orthodoxy. For Barth, revelation is first and foremost God himself in action. Jesus Christ is the primary form of revelation, with Scripture second, and the proclamation of the gospel in the churches third. But he was a supernaturalist; he believed in miracles and especially the bodily resurrection of Jesus Christ.

Tillich was an antisupernaturalist and stood in continuity with the older liberalism while chastening it with a strong dose of pessimism about the human predicament. He did not believe in inevitable progress, as did the older liberals like Rauschenbusch. But for Tillich, as for them, human experience is a powerful force shaping theology. Barth rejected that anthropocentric approach.

Some readers who know a bit about Tillich's theology may think that I'm being unfair to him by calling him a liberal or neoliberal theologian. After all, he did propose the "method of correlation" that lies behind many of the assertions he made in the imaginary conversation above. For example, if he had time to explain it to Barth, he would have said that God as the Ground of Being is drawn from the method of correlation. According to that method, theology begins with the questions about human existence discovered by philosophy. In Tillich's case, that would be existentialist ontology: the study of the human condition, which turns out to be a predicament.

Next, theology turns to divine revelation for the answers. Then it fits the answers to the questions. Philosophy determines the *form* of the answers while revelation determines their *content*. Or so Tillich said. Like many critics of Tillich, however, I think he allowed philosophy to determine much of the *content* of the answers. And in my opinion, his view of revelation was far too broad. Almost anything could count as divine revelation.

There's some truth to the accusation that Barth tended to throw the gospel at people's heads like a rock, and if it sank in, it was more from force than by persuasion. Perhaps that is hyperbole. But Barth was actively disinterested in apologetics of any kind. He believed that the Holy Spirit creates even the ability to hear and understand and respond to the Word of God.

On the one hand, Barth could have made better use of reason and perhaps even philosophy. On the other hand, Tillich should have been more cautious about the role he allowed philosophy to play in his reconstruction of Christian theology. In the end, his reconstruction amounted to something more like deconstruction. What he built on the ruins of tradition after his deconstruction seems like an entirely different edifice than the historic Christian faith.

For Further Reading

For suggestions on Barth, see "For Further Reading" at the ends of the previous conversations (21 and 22).

Taylor, Mark K., ed. *Paul Tillich: Theologian of the Boundaries*. Minneapolis: Fortress, 1991. This book contains excerpts of Tillich's writings as well as an extended introduction by the editor.

24

Twentieth-Century Ethicists Rauschenbusch, Niebuhr, Gutiérrez, Yoder, and Olasky Dispute the Meaning of Justice

Setting

As with other imaginary conversations, the only way to bring these theologians together is to imagine them meeting in heaven. Two of them are still alive at the time of this writing. I do not claim to know exactly what they would say in such a conversation, whether in this life or in the future. However, I have read their books and talked to them. (I am well acquainted with Marvin Olasky, and Gustavo Gutiérrez has spoken at the seminary where I teach.) The words I put in their mouths are my best educated guess at what they would say to the other conversation participants. My aim here is to be as generous as possible and represent their views faithfully and sympathetically.

Imagine that sometime in the future five great Christian thinkers meet and decide to discuss their passion: social justice. All five have been influential in twentieth-century Christianity, and their influence continues into the twenty-first century. Some of them have made a profound impact on politicians and movers and shakers of business, journalism, and the arts. One in particular has been named by a number of presidential candidates as their favorite Christian theologian. Another one has influenced an entire presidency. One of them wants nothing to do with influencing politics. But all are passionate about understanding the kingdom of God and justice and the social order and how they mix.

All five are also specifically concerned about poverty and consider it a tragedy, especially in a society that is supposedly Christian or where Christians form the majority. All are compassionate toward the poor in spite of holding quite different views about how to alleviate poverty.

Walter Rauschenbusch (1861–1918) was a Baptist minister and professor of church history at Baptist-related Rochester Theological Seminary (see conversation 20). His father was a Lutheran minister who emigrated to the United States and immediately became a Baptist. Walter was a leader in the Progressive Movement for social reform in the early twentieth century and became the best-known and most influential proponent of the social gospel movement.

His main books, all of which sold well and were read by many, include *Christianity and the Social Crisis* (1907), *Christianizing the Social Order* (1912), and *A Theology for the Social Gospel* (1917). In these books and in numerous magazine articles, lectures, and sermons, the German Baptist minister argued for radical changes in the order of society and especially its economic order. Rauschenbusch believed that the gospel of Jesus Christ has direct relevance to the "redemption of the social order" and that a moderate socialism is the path toward that.

Reinhold Niebuhr (1892–1971) was also the son of German immigrants. Like Rauschenbusch, his father was a minister in a predominantly German denomination. He kept the faith of his native land and ministered within a Reformed denomination in the United States. Niebuhr grew up to become the most influential Christian theologian in America in the 1940s and 1950s. He was on the twenty-fifth-anniversary cover of *Time* magazine (March 8, 1948).

Niebuhr wrote massive volumes of theology and Christian ethics such as the two-volume *Nature and Destiny of Man* (1941–1943) and also rather slim, concise books such as *An Interpretation of Christian Ethics* (1935), where he reacted against the social gospel movement of Rauschenbusch and others. Niebuhr was a pessimist about human nature; he believed in original sin without any historical fall. He applied this pessimism to social ethics and became the best-known and most influential promoter of "Christian realism."

Gustavo Gutiérrez (b. 1928) is a Peruvian priest and theologian who is generally considered to be the father of liberation theology. His book *A Theology of Liberation* (Spanish, 1971; English, 1972) is in many ways the "Bible of liberation theology." Like most liberationists, he is not a revolutionary in the militant sense; he does not advocate violence. However, like most liberation theologians of Latin America, he worries that the established churches have supported the rich in their oppression of the poor, and he calls for them to switch sides in the struggle for freedom and equality.

Gutiérrez believes that God has a "preferential option for the poor" and that Christians should identify with the poor in their struggle to live fully human lives, free from lack of life's basic necessities. Ultimately, Christians should strive to abolish poverty and build a socialist utopia on earth that will anticipate the equality of the kingdom of God.

John Howard Yoder (1927–1997) was the most influential Anabaptist (Mennonite) theologian of the twentieth century. His book *The Politics of Jesus* (1972) portrayed Jesus as primarily a social reformer bent on building an alternative social order within the church. He did not think Christians are called to reform or revolutionize the kingdoms of this world, but they are called to live socially cooperative lives of love and mutual submission within the church.

For Yoder, Christianizing the social order means influencing the world outside the church simply by being the church as it was meant to be. He took the Sermon on the Mount literally and refused to water it down or make it a "counsel of perfection" that is unattainable. His teaching and writings went directly against Niebuhr's pessimistic view of humanity. However, Yoder did not think changing the world through social transformation is any of the church's business. He was most hopeful about the possibilities of changing the church.

Although his home is in Texas, Marvin Olasky (b. 1950) is provost of The King's College, New York City, and editor of *World* magazine. He is also the author of numerous books on the subject of "compassionate conservatism," an idea that he developed. One of his most influential books is *Renewing American Compassion* (1996), which lays out a program for social transformation and the amelioration if not eradication of poverty through private charitable efforts. He is against government entitlement programs that, as he sees it, keep the poor locked in poverty and discourage individuals and organizations from pursuing compassionate activism on behalf of the poor.

Olasky believes most, if not all, poverty (at least in the United States) results from poor choices and government programs. He advocates the development of private "trampoline organizations" that help the poor get out of poverty by offering them job training and holding them accountable if they choose to receive aid. Olasky's views have profoundly impacted America through their influence on George W. Bush and his advisers.

The imaginary heavenly conversation that follows is meant to be somewhat playful. Perhaps one or more of the participants would not be as breezy and playful as they are portrayed here, but I hope nobody will be insulted or offended. The use of that literary style is meant to stimulate interest in all five thinkers and their ideas.

The Conversation

RAUSCHENBUSCH: Well, well, who have we here? Reinhold Niebuhr! I often wondered whether you would make it up here. That theologian Stanley Hauerwas claimed that you weren't even a Christian, you know.

NIEBUHR: Walter! It's so good to see you. Indeed I'm here. And it's quite a lovely place. But, you know, I feel kind of lost without sin. There's nothing to be pessimistic about up here! I'll bet you're happy, though.

GUTIÉRREZ: Excuse me, you two. May I introduce myself? I'm here just for a visit, to make sure that there is enough room for all the poor folks among whom I work every day. Señor Rauschenbusch, you were a great inspiration to me. I read your books in Spanish translation and incorporated some of your ideas into my theology of liberation. And you, Señor Niebuhr, I was also greatly influenced by your writings on social ethics. In many ways my theology of liberation is actually a combination of both of your ideas about justice.

YODER: May I chime in here and address all four of you? I found little that was really helpful in any of your writings. In my book *The Politics of Jesus,* I seemed to bear the burden of contradicting all of you.

OLASKY: I just arrived from New York where I just moved from Texas, ya'll. I'm here on a flying visit to check the quality of my future accommodations. Hope you don't mind if I join this little confab! Hey, you folks are all theologians, and I'm just a journalist, but I don't think any of you quite got it right about justice. I tried to set things straight in the American church and rather much turned things around from your communistic ideas and convinced good Christian folks to go back to the way things were done for the poor before you all started your big pity party.

RAUSCHENBUSCH: Well, now that the introductions are over, perhaps this would be a good time to talk about our common concern: justice. We all wrote about justice in society from a Christian perspective, but we certainly arrived at different views. I'm saddened to hear that your individualistic, competitive view is prevailing down there, Marvin. Surely that is a step backward for the kingdom of God.

NIEBUHR: Yes, let's discuss justice. Marvin, I agree with Walter. It's a pity that your so-called compassionate conservative social agenda is winning the hearts and minds of rich Americans. In my day many of the wealthy were truly compassionate and sought to redistribute wealth by restructuring society. If your social ethic is implemented, I predict that America will return to a time when homeless children wandered the streets, begging and dying.

GUTIÉRREZ: Indeed! I also agree that this will be the outcome of so-called compassionate conservatism. I picked up copies of Olasky's books at heaven's Barnes & Noble bookstore and read them while sipping a tall latte the other day. They made me gag! This program reminds me of "soup, soap, and salvation"! It's a step backward in time.

YODER: Well, I don't carry any torch for compassionate conservatism, but I must agree with Olasky about one thing. Implementing Christian justice is the church's duty and not something we Christians should try to impose on society at large. Jesus never called us to be revolutionaries or even social reformers; he called us to form an alternative society and thereby show the world the better way. We have no mandate to manage society with power. Our mandate is only to be obedient to Christ's way of living, which is self-sacrificial service and mutual submission to one another.

OLASKY: I'm glad for the support, John, but my vision of Christian social justice goes far beyond the walls of the church. Your vision of Christian social justice is thoroughly sectarian; mine is transformation of society. But not in the way Walter or Reinhold or Gustavo want to transform society. Real justice is something we do in personal relationships; it doesn't happen through governmental structures.

RAUSCHENBUSCH: Let's each explain our idea of Christian social justice and go on from there. Maybe we don't quite understand one another. To me, justice means establishing cooperative structures of society, where people have all of life's necessities without having to push anyone else down or out of the way. Competition is against the spirit of Jesus; Christians should find creative ways to adjust the economic and political structures so that they are truly democratic.

Equality is the essence of democracy. That extends into economics. We should strive to establish equality of wealth so there is no poverty. That means redistribution of wealth by means of taxes on high incomes and luxury. Government should guarantee everyone a job with a living wage. Justice will be seen only when poverty is abolished; then the kingdom of God will come on earth. This can hopefully come about by gentle persuasion and gradual reform.

NIEBUHR: How naive of you, Walter! You never did seem to grasp the sinfulness of the human heart! The powerful and wealthy aren't going to give up their power and wealth voluntarily. We have to use the tools of democracy to redistribute power first, and then redistribution of wealth will follow. One of democracy's tools is empowerment of the poor to confront the rich and make them give up some of their power and wealth. We need to achieve a balance of power in society so that no group of people has too much of it. Power corrupts and prevents justice—which is freedom and equality—from being experienced.

GUTIÉRREZ: I agree with both of you! Walter, you're right that society needs radical reform. Reinhold, you're right that such reform can probably only come about by confrontation and conflict. But neither of you seems to recognize that in some places and some situations, only revolution can establish justice. Justice will appear when differentiating wealth is abolished and there are no classes in society. This can come about only through revolution. Land must be redistributed, and major industries and natural resources must be publicly owned. The people must have power over their own destinies and not be subjected to the whims of corporations and oligarchies.

YODER: You all seem to think that Christ called us to manage history and society. Well, he didn't. Show me one place in the New Testament where Christians are called to go out and use power or even "gentle persuasion" to restructure secular society. I agree with you that justice is overcoming poverty, and only redistribution of wealth can do that. But the Bible's way is the Jubilee and not social reform or revolution. Today the only way the Jubilee can be implemented is in the church.

We should teach our Christian people to give away what they have to the poor within the church. Yes, we should help others as well. But especially in the church we should make sure that there are no inequalities of power and wealth. The church should be a separate society of equals living as servants of one another, and in subordination to the worldly powers. We should refuse to cooperate with injustice and take our punishment for that.

OLASKY: You're all missing the boat! God does want us to manage society and history, but not through radical reform or revolution. He wants us to be compassionate helpers of the poor, holding them accountable to pull themselves up by their own bootstraps—with the help of Christians, of course. By and large people are poor because the government has made them dependent on it. If we abolish all government entitlement programs that create dependency, then people will have to find work and be productive citizens. That's where they'll find their dignity.

We should pressure government to get out of the business of helping people and turn that over to the churches and other nonprofit organizations. The safety net has to go! Justice is accountability to be productive. The church should set up systems to help people become productive in society. One such system is job training.

RAUSCHENBUSCH: Oh, my goodness! What a mess! We don't agree at all about justice. Our progressive movement was making so much progress. It seems to be going down the drain with your individualistic charity and all your talk about accountability, Marvin. You talk as if the poor are slothful and indolent people who prefer to live off the public dole rather than work. In fact, most of the poor are children who *can't* work. What's your solution for them?

OLASKY: We need to stop encouraging welfare mothers to have more babies, which is what some entitlement programs do; instead, we need to urge them to get married so there won't be so many poor children! The present system is in crisis. There are too many poor, and the only way to fix this broken-down welfare system—which you are partly responsible for, Walter—is to abolish it completely. Once that happens, I'm sure that good Christians will step in and take care of the poor children and the disabled living around them.

NIEBUHR: You are too optimistic, Marvin. And I heard that you are a Calvinist! Don't you believe in total depravity—the first letter of the TULIP system? You seem to believe in it for the poor but not for the rich. The poor are poor by their own fault. But the rich are just chomping at the bit to help them get out of poverty by giving away some of their wealth and establishing big charitable organizations to provide job training and day care for children. Right? What makes you think the rich will do that? They're sinners too, you know.

GUTIÉRREZ: *Sí, sí!* You are too optimistic about the rich, Marvin. What we need is to liberate the rich from their wealth, which is corrupting them.

YODER: No, what we need is for Christians to start showing the world the better way of living, which is self-sacrifice, the way of the cross. The causes of poverty lie in the corrupt and evil powers of the world, which Jesus disarmed on the cross. We are to continue his work by bearing our own crosses of self-giving for others through servanthood. I agree with Marvin's solution except that he wants Christians to impose this on the world. Let the world go its own way; we Christians will demonstrate how much better it is to belong to a separate and voluntary community of servants who put others before themselves.

RAUSCHENBUSCH: But you are too sectarian, John Howard! You know that we two agree about pacifism—against these other men who are still not grasped by Jesus's vision of peace. But don't you want to transform the world around you? You talk about the evil, fallen powers. So do I. I wrote much about the "Kingdom of Evil," which is the same thing: structures of society that are corrupted by power and self-interest.

But we can't be content to sit in our separate, alternative Christian communities and let the world go to hell in a handbasket. We need to step out and pressure society through persuasion in the public square. We need to preach to Christians holding positions of power in corporations and politics, telling them that they need to put Jesus's teachings into practice through reform of society.

NIEBUHR: Well, that's true, Walter. But "gentle persuasion" isn't going to accomplish much. Yet I don't advocate violence, either—except as a last resort to oppose extreme oppression. I think Brother Gustavo here jumps to play the violence card too soon. Rather, we need to organize all concerned citizens to demonstrate and go to the polls and throw the big, bad bullies out of office. We can use boycotts of corporations to force them to practice justice for the poor. That's a kind of violence, though. It may not be bloody, but it is certainly confrontational and may lead to bloodshed.

GUTIÉRREZ: In Latin America it always does, Reinhold. So don't accuse me of resorting to violence too quickly! Violence is already there; the rich and powerful are using violence against the poor every day. They organize and pay death squads to put down any demonstrations and boycotts. We have the right to fight back.

YODER: Would Jesus fight back? Did he tell his followers to go into the streets to force social change? No. He went to the cross. So should we.

OLASKY: I think I hear heaven's dinner bell ringing, and I'm really looking forward to my first meal in heaven before I fly back to New York. So I'll put in my last two cents' worth here and let you all decide whether to join me in the dining room or keep up this debate. You all simply don't realize that much, if not most, of poverty is voluntary. For the most part, people are poor because they don't want to work.

Justice means holding the poor accountable to work and be productive citizens. Wealth is something that people create; it's not a zero sum game

or limited pie. Whoever really wants to work can get ahead. At least that's
so here in America. But the church should help people help themselves.
RAUSCHENBUSCH: But the children and the disabled . . .
(The heavenly dinner bell drowns him out.)

Analysis

The issue is "justice," a notorious slippery concept. What does it mean when
Christians apply justice to the social order? The justice under discussion or
debate here is distributive justice, not retributive justice. In other words, it isn't
about punishing offenders but about helping the poor. What is the Christian
obligation to the poor? What is society's obligation to the poor, if any? What
should Christians do to get secular society to help the poor, if anything? These
are questions that Christian ethicists debate today.

The five participants in this imaginary conversation agree on some things
and disagree about others. For example, they all clearly agree that Christians
should be very concerned about the poor. Not one of them says, "Ignore the
poor." They are not social Darwinists, who view helping the poor as against
nature because the law of nature is survival of the fittest.

Beyond helping the poor, however, they diverge in their views. What is the
best way to help the poor? How should the Christian churches help the poor?
Rauschenbusch sees the churches' obligation to the poor as including pressuring
the government to redistribute wealth through social welfare programs if not
socialism. He was an advocate of Christian socialism, but "socialism" meant
something different to him than it means to many people today.

Rauschenbusch certainly never envisioned Cuban-style socialism for America
or anywhere else. But he did think that the social order needs to be transformed
to lessen cutthroat competition and increase cooperation. For him, the best
businesses are those that do not exist to make a profit but those that exist
cooperatively (cooperative businesses) to benefit society, customers, workers,
and everyone. These businesses are owned by the employees and perhaps also
by the customers.

For Rauschenbusch, love should be the determining motive in all Christian
social relationships, and the churches should try to inject love into the order
of society so that the kingdom of God may come on earth. Love translates
socially into cooperation.

Niebuhr was much more pessimistic about the possibilities of love in the social
order than was Rauschenbusch. Yet Niebuhr interpreted Jesus's command to
"love your enemies" literally and didn't think that it admits of any exceptions.
Therefore, if a nation, for example, were to love its enemies, it would unilaterally disarm itself and allow itself to be taken over by the enemy. But, Niebuhr
argued, this would play into the hands of evil nations like Nazi Germany. Instead,
Christians should seek to incarnate love in justice, which means freedom and

equality to the extent possible under the conditions of sin. And justice includes calculation of rights, including one's own, and sometimes conflict and confrontation. He thought the whole idea of a social order ruled by love was at best an impossible ideal; it cannot be achieved under the conditions of sin.

For Niebuhr, then, the Christian's social responsibility is to seek justice even if that means compromising the strict teachings of Jesus about love and resisting evil. Only by resisting evil can we love our neighbor who is under attack. The world we know and live in is full of tensions and paradoxes. Christians want to establish justice, which indeed may mean redistributing wealth, but that can only be done by pressuring the powerful and wealthy to give up some of their power and wealth so that a rough equilibrium or balance of power can exist. That's the nature of justice. Love serves as a purifying ideal that keeps justice from running aground on the shores of retribution and violence. But it should not keep justice from compelling government, for example, to enforce a rough equality on everyone.

Gutiérrez agrees with both Rauschenbusch and Niebuhr at certain points. With Rauschenbusch, he agrees that love and justice cannot be separated or pitted against each other. And he agrees that a cooperative society of equals, devoid of cutthroat competition and great gaps between the poor and the rich, is the goal of Christian social justice. But with Niebuhr he agrees that force may be necessary to overthrow injustice and establish justice. Gutiérrez is even more open to the possibility of Christian justification of revolution than is Niebuhr.

Niebuhr did not believe that any act of justice is ever perfect; even the best efforts to establish justice are tainted by egoism and pride. Gutiérrez doesn't dwell on that. Instead, he holds forth a vision of a future utopia: a classless society of perfect justice, love, and peace. For that to happen, capitalism will have to go and be replaced by socialism.

Yoder believes that Jesus was a social radical even if not a revolutionary. His main mission was to establish the kingdom of God on earth by creating an alternative social order in the church. That alternative order should be as uninvolved with the evil of the world as possible and show the world a better way to live through love, cooperation, mutual submission, and peace. But the church has no mandate to impose any of this on society. For him, justice means everyone sharing what they have with everyone else. But that is really only a possibility in the church. A substantial number of Anabaptists form intentional Christian communities where that lifestyle of sharing is practiced.

Olasky is against any withdrawal of the church or Christians from social responsibility and involvement. But he opposes socialism and believes that the key to human fulfillment (beyond spiritual salvation) is work. The way to establish justice is to hold everyone accountable to work productively, and those who cannot work should be cared for by the church and other nonprofit organizations rather than by government.

For Olasky, justice is a combination of compassion and accountability. The outcome is universal employment, but not through government entitlement programs. It should happen through job training offered by nonprofit organizations plus withholding help from those who are able to work but won't.

Although they overlap somewhat, these are five radically divergent views of Christian social justice. Of them all, only Yoder rejects the whole idea of Christianizing the social order (unless the church is the social order). Of the rest, only Olasky rejects Christian pressure put on government to redistribute wealth. Only Gutiérrez advocates revolution, although Niebuhr holds open the possibility of that as a necessary evil in extreme cases of oppression. Only Niebuhr thinks that love is an impossible ideal. Only Rauschenbusch believes that the church can usher in the kingdom of God through social salvation.

These five visions of Christian social justice are major influences in contemporary Christianity. By and large, the so-called Religious Right is inspired by Olasky's vision and program of "compassionate conservatism." There also is a Religious Left (not often mentioned by the media) inspired by Rauschenbusch. Many politicians claim to be inspired by Niebuhr's Christian realism. Many experiments in intentional Christian communal living are inspired by Yoder. So are many individual pastors and writers who call for Christians to be uninvolved in the political machinations of society and focus on helping the church be all that it can be. Liberation theology is extremely influential in Latin America and has its adherents in North America as well. It appears wherever Christians call for radical social change that involves a transfer of power from the rich and powerful to the poor and oppressed.

For Further Reading

Gutierrez, Gustavo. *A Theology of Liberation*. Maryknoll, NY: Orbis, 1988.

Niebuhr, Reinhold. *An Interpretation of Christian Ethics*. New York: Seabury, 1979.

Olasky, Marvin, *Compassionate Conservatism*. New York: Free Press, 2000.

Rauschenbusch, Walter. *Christianizing the Social Order*. Whitefish, MT: Kessinger, 2008.

Yoder, John Howard. *The Politics of Jesus*. Grand Rapids: Eerdmans, 1994.

25

Twentieth-Century Theologians
Bultmann and Pannenberg Debate
Faith, Myth, and Jesus's Resurrection

Setting

The year is 1975, and in Germany the world's oldest and longest-living theological giant, Rudolf Bultmann, is on a train, traveling from his Marburg home to Munich to attend a theological conference. He's quite ancient now and long retired from teaching and writing. But his radical approach to New Testament interpretation is still widely discussed and quite controversial, even though it was launched in 1941 with his bombshell essay on "The New Testament and Mythology."

Bultmann was born in 1887 and died in 1976. He was an early collaborator with Karl Barth and Emil Brunner in the formation of what came to be known as neoorthodoxy, or dialectical theology. (See conversations 21 and 22 for information about Barth and Brunner.) But unlike them, he never shed his liberal tendencies and gradually alienated himself from their movement by arguing that the New Testament (to say nothing of the Old Testament) is largely mythological.

In "The New Testament and Mythology" the German New Testament scholar introduced his program of "demythologizing the New Testament." But it's not what it sounds like. Bultmann never wanted to discard myths from the Bible; he wanted to recognize them for what they are and then interpret them nonliterally as stories and symbols about transcendent realities and human existence.

Like Paul Tillich (see conversation 23), Bultmann was deeply influenced by existentialism. Thus his main concern was always human existence rather than human essence (i.e., human nature). What does it mean to live a human life before God when one did not ask to be born, is simply thrown into a world that is crazy, and is tossed about by all kinds of forces beyond one's control? The focus of existentialism is on self-understanding as either authentic or inauthentic.

Authentic existence is the correct self-understanding, and it involves coming to terms with the apparent absurdity of much of life and determining to live a meaningful life in spite of it all. For Christian existentialists, in contrast to atheistic existentialists, authentic existence comes from relying on God alone for security and eschewing all attempts to ground one's security, thus avoiding despair by putting oneself or the "crowd" in the place of God.

Bultmann believed the Bible (and he dealt mainly with the New Testament) to contain the gospel of authentic existence through Jesus Christ in mythological form. For him, any supernatural story that communicates a truth about human existence is a myth. By "myth" he did not mean fable or fiction; he meant a story that is not literally true but communicates a truth about human existence that cannot be communicated as well in any other way. His program of demythologizing the New Testament did not intend to strip the New Testament of myth but to interpret the myths of the New Testament as gospel about human existence.

Bultmann did not believe that God acts supernaturally; thus he did not believe in miracles. He thought modern people could not be expected to believe in miracles. Yet he also thought that the miracle stories of the Bible say something extremely important about God and humanity. A prime example is the resurrection of Jesus Christ, which will be the subject of much of the following conversation.

Wolfhart Pannenberg was born in 1928 at Stettin, Prussia, Germany (now Szczecin, Poland). He studied theology at various German universities and taught at the University of Chicago Divinity School in the 1960s. Pannenberg spent most of his theological career teaching in the Protestant faculty of the University of Munich in Germany. Together with Jürgen Moltmann, he formed what came to be known as the "theology of the future," or "eschatological theology." Often this theology went under the name of Moltmann's book *The Theology of Hope* (1964), but Pannenberg preferred eschatological theology. His most influential book was *Jesus: God and Man* (1968).

Pannenberg made a name for himself by publicly opposing Bultmann's existentialized interpretation of the New Testament and especially his view of the resurrection as myth. Pannenberg believes that the resurrection of Jesus is a historically verifiable fact. And in contrast to Bultmann, he regards universal history as divine revelation. In other words, God reveals himself in the very fabric of history and through historical events that are unique and unrepeatable. He does not shy away from miracles or the supernatural although he does not revel in them, either.

In many ways Pannenberg is Bultmann's opposite. On the one hand, Bultmann subjectivized the gospel, making it a message about human existence: at its center stands the individual and one's self-understanding. It is about "inner history," the history of the person (Bultmann's *Geschichte*) that is not studied by historical science (*Historie*). On the other hand, Pannenberg objectifies the gospel; it is a message about God's self-revelation in and through outer history (both *Geschichte* and *Historie*). Thus the gospel is a matter of public record and not merely a matter of faith.

The Conversation

BULTMANN: Excuse me, young man, but I thought I might have this compartment all to myself; I planned to read a little and then sleep on my journey to Munich. Are you sure you have a ticket for this compartment?

PANNENBERG: Indeed I do, Herr Professor Bultmann. I recognize you. After all, I've seen your picture many times during my theological studies, and I've read all of your books and many of your essays. It would be my privilege to sit here with you, and I'll try not to disturb you. I do have a ticket for this compartment, you see.

BULTMANN: *Ja, ja.* I see. Oh, well, I guess I'll nap at my hotel in Munich when we arrive. It's not far from the Hauptbahnhof. So, young man, you know who I am? You've studied theology? What kind of theology?

PANNENBERG: Mostly systematic theology. I've written a few books. Perhaps you've seen one of them? My most recent volume is *The Apostles' Creed in the Light of Today's Questions*. But my most popular book so far is *Theology and the Kingdom of God*.

BULTMANN: *Ach du Liebe!* Now I know who you are. You're that young Turk Pannenberg everyone has been talking about lately.

PANNENBERG: Well, I don't know about "young Turk," but I am Wolfhart Pannenberg. I apologize for not introducing myself more formally.

BULTMANN: So you and your friends are building a reputation by trying to refute my existentialist theology and demythologizing of the New Testament, right? You're swimming against the stream of twentieth-century theology. Barth, Brunner, Bultmann—we're all influenced by existentialist philosophy, which is the good-luck piece of modern theology. It rescues us from constant conflicts with science and historical studies.

PANNENBERG: Perhaps, although I doubt that Barth or Brunner would want to be included with you in that. Both of them believed that faith and history connect at certain points. Neither one of them removed faith entirely from outer history as you do. Your existentialist theology subjectivizes faith so much that it is irrelevant to the world at large; you remove faith from the public realm into a private sphere of subjective experience and self-understanding.

BULTMANN: But that's what the apostles did! I'm only continuing their project. Haven't you read my writings on the Gospel of John? Already there he or his followers were demythologizing the oral traditions about Jesus in order to bring out the kerygma communicated in the myths that surround it.

PANNENBERG: Admittedly the Gospel of John is an enigma, but I don't see it as a precursor to your existentialized theology at all. It expresses the gospel of Jesus Christ in some ways influenced by Greek thought, but it is not only about human existence and self-understanding.

BULTMANN: Well, that's your opinion. What do you think it's about?

PANNENBERG: The whole Bible is about the future and anticipatory events of history that bring the ultimate future of God's kingdom into our present. It is about promise and fulfillment and the mighty acts of God.

BULTMANN: Ah, stop right there. Mighty acts of God? You talk as if you really believe God has acted in history. That just flies in the face of everything we know about reality. The universe is a closed system of natural causes and effects ruled by natural laws. Modern people simply cannot view it any other way. The Bible presupposes a premodern worldview in which heaven is literally "up there" and hell is literally in the center of the earth or below the earth's flat crust. "Act of God" is a complicated concept. If by it you mean that God violates the natural course of events, then it's incomprehensible and unbelievable to modern people.

PANNENBERG: Well, there goes the whole gospel. If God doesn't act, then what is the revelation about? I think I know your answer, but tell me anyway.

BULTMANN: God acts in the individual's inner history, not in the world's outer history. Revelation is the story of the cross as the decisive act of God. That's actually all we really need out of revelation: the cross of Jesus Christ and its meaning.

PANNENBERG: Explain "inner history" and "outer history" and how you can talk about God acting when you've just denied that God acts.

BULTMANN: No, I didn't deny that God acts. I denied that God acts by using miracles to interrupt the course of nature. But God most certainly does act. God was in Christ and thereby reconciling the world to himself. But that was invisible to all but eyes of faith. It had nothing to do with miracles or the supernatural.

PANNENBERG: So in what sense was the cross an act of God?

BULTMANN: In that perfectly natural event, explainable by science and history, God was secretly and invisibly acting to reconcile sinners to himself by offering up his Son as a sacrifice for sins. But there was no miracle involved.

PANNENBERG: Then what about the resurrection? Surely you can't even believe in it. Yet Paul said that if the dead are not raised, we are of all people most miserable because our hope is in vain.

BULTMANN: I surely do believe in the resurrection of Jesus. I'm a Christian. But I don't see it as a miracle.

PANNENBERG: What? A resurrection of a dead body is not a miracle?

BULTMANN: That's right. The resurrection as the resuscitation of a corpse and as an empty tomb is myth. The spiritual reality to which it witnesses is the rise of faith in the hearts and lives of the disciples, their faith in the message of Jesus. The resurrection is part of *Geschichte*, not *Historie*.

PANNENBERG: Those words are usually synonyms for history. What do you mean by distinguishing them in that way?

BULTMANN: *Historie* is the series of events in time and space studied by historians. There's a uniformity to it. All is governed by natural laws. As such, it has no meaning. *Geschichte* is the hidden history of God's activity in events; it contains the significance of events like the cross. God acts in that realm but not in *Historie*. *Geschichte* is full of meaning because it is there that God is at work.

PANNENBERG: Well, if I may be so bold, I think this is all Horse*geschichte*. Nonsense! Utter and outrageous nonsense! You remove God's activity for us into a hidden and esoteric realm of subjectivity, where science and historical study cannot touch it. I think you do that just to avoid conflicts between faith and the sciences.

BULTMANN: Well, think whatever you like. I know why I do it. I do it because the true meaning of the New Testament kerygma is obviously not about events in *Historie*, although the cross is the one such event that is necessary to the kerygma. But even there, it isn't the outer event of crucifixion that is important to the gospel; its meaning for us is what counts. The cross says that God loves us and forgives us if we repent and trust him entirely for our security.

PANNENBERG: Wrong! The true meaning of the New Testament kerygma is obviously about God's future kingdom breaking into the present. It is about God and his rule as the subject of history. It is about the cross and resurrection of Jesus as the guarantee that God will make all things new and reconcile all to himself in the great *eschaton*, the consummation of his plan and purpose.

BULTMANN: And you think that's going to fly with university-educated people of the twentieth century? You're mad.

PANNENBERG: The resurrection of Jesus as an event and fact is central to the whole Christian message, and historical investigation can show that it is more probable that it actually occurred than that it did not. It is true beyond a reasonable doubt. Once they are shown the evidence, rational people will believe.

BULTMANN: What evidence? No, wait—there can't be any evidence. Miracles simply do not happen. Whatever evidence you manufacture has to be illusion. But even more important, you are yanking faith out of the center and replacing it with evidence. That's not what faith is all about. Faith is believing what cannot be seen. It is receiving a new self-understanding from the God of Jesus's cross.

PANNENBERG: Okay, I'll take the bait. What's this new self-understanding, and how does it happen?

BULTMANN: I'm glad you finally asked. Now we're getting somewhere. You see, our human predicament is that we are faced with despair because of our anxiety about the foundation of our security. We fear death and every threat that surrounds us. We feel the meaninglessness of life and face the absurd. So we search for something to give us security outside ourselves. We escape from despair by embracing pleasure or pride or even politics. These become our idols. Our self-understanding, then, is inauthentic.

Authentic existence is found only in Jesus Christ and his cross; it is found only in the resurrection, which is the rise of faith in Christ as the foundation of our security. By faith in him we are made secure by a right standing with God. We find acceptance and meaning in our relationship with him. We trust God to take care of our otherwise insecure and uncertain future.

PANNENBERG: What existential nonsense! You've been drinking too deeply at the wells of existentialist philosophy—Heidegger and Jaspers, to be specific. It's an escape from reality. It's Gnostic in its pure spirituality and depth psychologizing of faith. What does it have to do with public proclamation of truth? You sacrifice truth for the advantage of making theology immune to criticism from science and history.

BULTMANN: And you make faith depend on historical research; that's not faith at all.

PANNENBERG: Faith is believing what reason shows to be true. Many people do not want to believe even when the evidence is there in front of them. Faith is submitting one's whole life to the facts even when they demand self-sacrifice and submission to God.

BULTMANN: No, faith is believing in spite of no evidence at all. It is a venture, a risk. Jesus said that those who believe without seeing are blessed.

PANNENBERG: And the author of Hebrews says that faith is the evidence of things hoped for. Evidence, Bultmann, evidence! Of things hoped for. Faith is reaching out and taking hold of the promises of God made sure by historical events such as the resurrection and living toward the future, when God's kingdom will be manifest to everyone. Here and now God's rulership over history is still debatable, but in the future God's deity and sovereignty will be seen and acknowledged by all. Right now we have a guarantee of it in Jesus's resurrection, which is that future consummation of God's plan and his sovereign kingdom happening proleptically, ahead of time. We have faith in the God of the future because he has already appeared as Lord in Jesus Christ and in his triumphant resurrection, conquering death.

BULTMANN: I'm beginning to think you actually believe that Jesus Christ will return to establish his kingdom over all the earth in outer history. That's mythology. It's an ancient and primitive way of expressing God's lordship in lives. When we have faith in the act of God in Jesus's cross, reconciling the world to himself, then the parousia—Christ's second coming—happens within us. All that apocalyptic symbolism in the New Testament is just a way of expressing the war between flesh and spirit that takes place inside us as we struggle to overcome doubt and anxiety and to receive the gift of eternal life from God.

PANNENBERG: Eternal life? Eternal life? What are you talking about? Do you even believe in life after death?

BULTMANN: There is so much we cannot know, and I have no interest in metaphysical speculation about the furniture of heaven or the temperature of hell. But I do believe that death is not the end of the person. Beyond that I dare not speculate. The biblical imagery is not about a literal heaven or hell after death; it is about this life and authentic versus inauthentic existence.

PANNENBERG: If I should happen to die before you do, as unlikely as that seems, please stay away from my funeral. Your words bring no hope. And hope is what our Christian faith is all about.

BULTMANN: Wrong! I, too, believe that hope is what our faith is all about. But hope is not in events of time and space, but hope in God, who changes us inwardly and rescues us through Jesus Christ from despair.

PANNENBERG: That's it? Hope is only about psychology?

BULTMANN: I didn't say that. No, even a depressed person can have hope in God and overcome despair. It's not about psychology; it's about self-understanding.

PANNENBERG: That sounds like psychology to me. You know, Bultmann, you've simply taken neoorthodoxy to its logical conclusion. I used to be enamored with Barth and dialectical theology, but that whole project was too subjective. The Word of God was separated from real history. A special line of history was seen as hidden within history and constitutes God's mighty saving acts. But historians can't study it or find it. Such escapism! All you dialectical theologians lack nerve. You are afraid of the facts of science and historical research.

BULTMANN: Well, at least we don't have to wait for the latest issue of *Archaeology Today* to find out if we can still be Christians!

PANNENBERG: Except for one thing! You're inconsistent when you insist that the entire kerygma depends on the historical fact of the cross event. Why don't you demythologize that too?

BULTMANN: Now you're sounding like some of my so-called left-wing disciples. They want me to demythologize the kerygma and reduce everything to existentialist philosophy. Never. The cross is the one absolutely necessary act of God in time and space. But it's not a miracle, so it doesn't need to be demythologized.

PANNENBERG: And where do you get this belief in naturalism? You seem to start with a naturalistic philosophy dictating that miracles cannot happen, and then you dissect the New Testament to fit that philosophy.

BULTMANN: Wrong, again. Science and philosophy help us rediscover the true meaning of the New Testament. Let me ask you something, young man. Take the ascension of Jesus from the Mount of Olives as recorded in Acts 1. Do you believe that he literally rose up from the earth and went into a spatially located heaven straight up from there?

PANNENBERG: Certainly not.

BULTMANN: But you admit that's what the disciples and New Testament authors thought, right?

PANNENBERG: Probably.

BULTMANN: No probably about it. Most certainly. But we know that heaven is not "up" from the Mount of Olives. So science has forced us to deliteralize and reinterpret the ascension of Jesus. Now we regard it as a myth that says something about the ongoing reality of Jesus among us.

PANNENBERG: Well, I don't think I'd want to reduce it to that! But we don't interpret it literally because "up" from the Mount of Olives would be "down" from the other side of the globe. First-century people didn't generally know that.

BULTMANN: Just as they didn't know that dead people cannot rise.

PANNENBERG: Oh, I think they knew that. It's not as though resurrection from death was an everyday occurrence even then. And the New Testament reports that some who saw the risen Christ didn't believe. That's because even then people knew that it takes a miracle to bring the dead to life. And as for your ascension illustration, well, the ascension isn't even in the same category of importance as the resurrection. Nothing of the gospel is lost if the ascension didn't even happen.

BULTMANN: That's not my point. You accused me of allowing science and philosophy to dictate what we can believe. I just proved that you do the same.

PANNENBERG: With the ascension, not with the resurrection. We're comparing apples and oranges.

BULTMANN: So what evidence do you find for the bodily resurrection of Jesus and the empty tomb? I don't see any.

PANNENBERG: The evidence is in the existence of the early church and the Christian mission. If Jesus did not rise and if the tomb was not empty, the early disciples would never have become a force that turned the world upside down as they did. Only an encounter with the risen and living Christ could do that.

BULTMANN: What about the conflicting resurrection accounts in the Gospels?

PANNENBERG: They actually support the reality of the event itself. If they were absolutely the same, we would suspect that someone contrived them. Real events are always reported differently by witnesses.

BULTMANN: The train is slowing down. I see the outskirts of Munich. There are the twin towers of the Frauenkirche. I can't wait to get to my favorite *Bierstube* and drink a pint of *Dunkelbier*. I'd invite you to join me, but since you're a fundamentalist, I doubt that you drink beer, right?

PANNENBERG: Now, c'mon. That's uncalled for. You know I'm no fundamentalist! I heartily embrace higher-critical methods of biblical study.

BULTMANN: Well, whatever you are, you're not a modern man. I pity you and
your followers because you have to believe in the gospel on the basis of
probability rather than certainty, and you have to watch your backs to
see if science is creeping up to falsify your faith. At least my faith is immune to that.

PANNENBERG: Immune at the cost of throwing out everything distinctive and
really important about the Christian faith!

Analysis

As offensive as it may be to many conservative Christians, Bultmann's existentialist, demythologized version of New Testament Christianity made it possible
for many scientifically minded twentieth-century people to become or remain
Christians (in some sense of the word). For Bultmann, as for many liberal
Protestants of the modern Western world, God is like the hand in the glove of
nature. Nature operates by inexorable laws of physics, and God's activity is
invisible to the investigative eye and mind. But to the believer, all of nature is
God's activity. Yet no single event is God's activity in the traditional, supernatural
sense. God does not intervene in nature or break the laws of nature. After all,
why would God do that if he is the Creator? If he created the laws of nature,
why would he violate them?

So Bultmann's foundational assumption is the uniformity of nature. There
are no miraculous breaks in it, and that includes the resurrection. However,
the resurrection is real as an existential event in the lives of Jesus's disciples.
But it is an event of revelation and not an event of outer, observable history. It
became an event of outer, observable history during the development of the
oral tradition of the gospel and was eventually written that way by the Gospel
writers. According to Bultmann, however, our task as modern interpreters is to
discover the true meaning of the myth, which is a message about the significance
of the cross of Jesus Christ for our salvation. By it we are reconciled to God
through faith, and our faith in the cross establishes a new self-understanding
and a new mode of being in the world, a mode called authentic existence. It is
a mode of being or way of existence completely open to the future that God
has for us and hence without anxiety or despair.

Bultmann's demythologizing project was enthusiastically embraced by many
university-educated Christians in Europe and North America who thought it
impossible to believe in miracles but who still wanted to believe in God's action in our lives.

Pannenberg's fame came about as he collaborated with some colleagues to
oppose Bultmann's existentialized, subjectivized interpretation of the New
Testament. Pannenberg is deeply influenced by German idealism and rational-

ism. He believes that God is revealed in and through history and that reasonable investigation of historical evidence can lead to belief in the bodily resurrection of Christ as true beyond a reasonable doubt. This came as quite a shock after years of Bultmann's dominance in European and American New Testament scholarship. Here was and is a university-trained German theologian with strong academic credentials who clearly believes in the resurrection as an event in outer history and as verifiable.

Evangelicals flocked to Pannenberg's books, and not a few traveled to Germany to study with him (this author included). They quickly found out that he is not what they assumed. True, he does believe in the historically verifiable event of the resurrection, including the empty tomb, but he does not believe in the verbal inspiration of the Bible, to say nothing of its inerrancy or infallibility, and he believes the virgin birth did not happen. He is also no pietist. He is a high-church Lutheran who believes in sacramental spirituality and not what he calls "decisionism." Conversional piety, in other words, is not his thing.

Some evangelicals were disappointed with him after they found out these things. Others, however, found in him an ally in opposing Bultmannian skepticism and existentialized faith. However, those who looked deeply into his theology realized that, for him, faith assertions are always at best hypotheses to be tested. Their proof and even their truth, in some sense, is eschatological. Only when Christ returns will it turn out to be true that he was God's self-revelation in person all along. Until the end arrives, belief in Christ remains a thesis to be debated and tested by reason and evidence.

Bultmann and Pannenberg represent bookends of twentieth-century Christian thought. Bultmann is the giant of New Testament scholarship who merged existentialism with Christianity, to the delight of liberals and dismay of conservatives. Pannenberg is the giant of systematic theology who rejected existentialism and introduced a strong element of rationalism into theology, much to the delight of many conservatives and dismay of most liberals.

For Further Reading

Grenz, Stanley J. *Reason for Hope: The Systematic Theology of Wolfhart Pannenberg*. New York and Oxford: Oxford University Press, 1990.

Roberts, Robert C. *Rudolf Bultmann's Theology: A Critical Interpretation*. Grand Rapids: Eerdmans, 1976.

26

Twentieth-Century Theologians Henry and Ramm Dispute Evangelical Theology, Modernity, and the Enlightenment

Setting

During the second half of the twentieth century, something called "evangelical theology" (known early in its history as "neoevangelical theology") came into existence and matured. It evolved out of Protestant fundamentalism, which began in the late nineteenth and early twentieth centuries as a militant and often separatistic assertion of quite conservative Protestant doctrines, such as the inerrancy of the Bible. Some fundamentalists insisted that any deviation from the strictest possible orthodoxy—as they defined it—led inevitably to liberal theology, if not to outright apostasy. During the 1920s to 1940s, Protestant fundamentalism became increasingly isolationist and anti-intellectual, cutting itself off from the larger culture and from mainline denominations.

Certain fundamentalist ministers and theologians became weary of the movement's sectarian and even cultish attitude. One of them, E. J. Carnell of Fuller Theological Seminary, defined fundamentalism as "orthodoxy gone cultic." He was referring to the manner in which fundamentalists held their doctrines and not so much to the doctrines themselves. Other fundamentalists, such as Harold John Ockenga and Carl F. H. Henry, helped to found the National Association of Evangelicals (NAE) in 1941. The NAE became an umbrella group for fellowship and cooperation among relatively conservative, conversionist denominations and churches that did not want any longer to be identified with the older fundamentalism.

During the 1950s the evangelist Billy Graham (b. 1918) became the figurehead of this neoevangelical movement as he journeyed out of fundamentalism and closer to the mainstream of American religious life. Carl F. H. Henry (1913–2003) emerged as the leading theological spokesman for the movement. Together they founded the magazine *Christianity Today* (in 1956), which became the major voice of the new evangelicalism.

Henry was a member of the American Baptist Churches, U.S.A. (formerly known as the Northern Baptist Convention), but he came to be somewhat critical of its leftward theological drift. Even though he resisted the narrowness, mean-spiritedness, and anti-intellectualism of fundamentalism, he always remained conservative in his doctrines. He was the first editor of *Christianity Today* and wrote numerous books, including a massive six-volume set titled *God, Revelation, and Authority* (1976–1983). He taught at several evangelical seminaries, including Fuller Theological Seminary at Pasadena and Trinity Evangelical Divinity School near Chicago.

By the 1980s Henry was the unrivaled, acknowledged "dean" of evangelical theologians. He was the voice of evangelical theology to culture, the mainstream denominations, and evangelicalism. Fundamentalists considered him to be too ecumenical; liberals considered him to be too conservative. He fought against the inroads of neoorthodoxy—the theology of Barth and Brunner (see conversations 21 and 22)—into evangelical thought because he thought its rejection of propositional revelation made it a Trojan horse for liberal theology. Although he would hold dialogue with liberal theologians, he clearly despised that human-centered theology. For him, being evangelical meant having a certain attitude toward the Bible as both human and divine and verbally inspired in the whole and in the part. To his dying day, he strongly believed in inerrancy.

Bernard Ramm (1916–1992) was the other leading theological voice of evangelicalism from the 1950s to 1990s. Like Henry, he also was a Baptist who saw the wider evangelical movement as his context. He wrote numerous books, including *The Christian View of Science and Scripture* (1954), that attacked an overly literalistic interpretation of the Bible and argued that evangelical Christians must come to terms with the material facts of the Enlightenment and scientific revolutions.

Ramm wrote on biblical interpretation, apologetics, and doctrine. During his later years he wrote a book extolling the virtues of Karl Barth's theology: *After Fundamentalism* (1983). He did not entirely agree with Barth's theology, but he saw it as a good model for evangelicals who need to move beyond an overly anti-Enlightenment mind-set and come to terms with the Enlightenment without capitulating to its secularism.

Henry was the hero of the more conservative crowd within evangelicalism. Those who wanted to stick fairly close to their fundamentalist roots looked to him for leadership. As he grew older, he became alarmed by what he saw as defection from belief in inerrancy among those in the evangelical ranks; he strongly asserted inerrancy as the only consistent evangelical view of Scripture.

Ramm became the hero of the more progressive evangelicals. Those who wanted to shed their fundamentalism looked to him for leadership. As he grew older, he moved further away from conservative beliefs such as the inerrancy of the Bible while at the same time upholding orthodox doctrines such as original sin and the deity of Christ.

These two are chosen for this evangelical conversation because they represent the best of the movement's theology. There is unity and diversity. They agree on much while disagreeing about some things. Probably their biggest disagreement was over the proper evangelical attitude toward the Enlightenment and its aftermath, called "modernity." Imagine that they visit just outside the men's room of a large hotel where the Evangelical Theological Society has gathered at the same time as the National Association of Baptist Professors of Religion. Henry is there for the former meeting; he is a big gun in that society. Ramm is there for the latter meeting; he is a heavyweight in that society.

The Conversation

HENRY: This hotel's restrooms are quite fancy, aren't they? I mean, do we really need to meet in such a swanky hotel? Marble countertops and cloth napkins for wiping one's hands! It goes a little overboard. Since I became a lecturer at large with World Vision, I am more aware than ever of how rich we Americans are compared to our third-world counterparts.

RAMM: I agree. And it's nice to see you again, Carl. It's been some years. I guess you're here for the annual meeting of the ETS, right? I'm here for the annual meeting of the NABPR. They're honoring me for my years of service to the Baptist community and to the evangelical movement.

HENRY: And a well-deserved honor it is! Your production of volumes is, indeed, prodigious. And for the most part, your work has been positive.

RAMM: You always were given to big words, Carl. I don't know that my output of books has been prodigious, especially compared to yours! And I will pay you the same slightly backhanded compliment: most of your work has been positive.

HENRY: As soon as we're both finished washing our hands here, let's go and find a corner out in the hallway or a meeting room where we can sit and talk without interruption. From your own mouth I'd like to hear how you think any of my work has been less than positive. And if you want to know, I'll be happy to tell you what I think of your theology.

RAMM: Good. Yes, let's do that.

HENRY: Okay, so let's sit there by the window overlooking Lake Michigan and talk. I don't think we'll be interrupted here. I don't know about you, but I am constantly besieged by admirers wanting me to sign one of my books.

RAMM: Well, no, that doesn't happen to me so much. You're much more famous than I am. After all, you were in *Time* magazine! Picture and all!

HENRY: I hated the title of that article: "Theology for the Revival" or something like that. Whoever wrote the title didn't understand my theology at all. I'm not against tent revivals, but I don't think my theology is particularly consistent with much that goes on in those meetings.

RAMM: Indeed. One might even say that your theology is the opposite of that heard in tent revival meetings. There the appeal is to emotion; your appeal has always been to the intellect.

HENRY: That's because so much of evangelicalism, to say nothing of fundamentalism, has been all about emotions and feelings. Too many evangelicals go by what makes them feel comfortable or excited spiritually. I believe our theology needs to be firmly controlled by the objectively given revelation of God in inspired Scripture and not influenced by emotions or experiences or feelings.

RAMM: I know that you feel that way. But don't you think sometimes you go a little overboard in emphasizing the "objectively given revelation of God in inspired Scripture" to the neglect of the personal revelation of God in Jesus Christ?

HENRY: Not at all, Bernard. We know Jesus Christ only through Scripture.

RAMM: True enough. But we also believe in the authority of Scripture only because we experience Jesus Christ and the Holy Spirit witnessing to us that Scripture is the Word of God. Can the objective and the subjective be separated so neatly? I'm not so sure.

HENRY: Subjectivism is the poison of modern theology; the emphasis on feelings introduced by Schleiermacher has led to a plethora of heresies. I prefer to tie our theological work solely and tightly to the mighty mast, the anchoring pole of Scripture, and that only works if we view it as the objectively given and verbally inspired, inerrant Word of God.

RAMM: I'm inclined to agree with you that movement away from the *sola scriptura* principle is the disease of modern theology. But I'd prefer not to limit revelation to Scripture. I know that sounds somewhat contradictory, but please hear me. Revelation is a larger concept than Scripture. After all, there was revelation before there was Scripture, and there has been revelation after Scripture. We can't chase the Holy Spirit into a book, you know. At the same time, when we are trying to examine or construct doctrine, we have to go by the written Word. But the Holy Spirit can and must guide us, and we must use Jesus Christ as the interpretive key to all of Scripture.

HENRY: I don't see why. Scripture interprets itself. It's God's propositionally given revelation, and it is quite clear so long as one follows the objective rules of interpretation. The moment you introduce the Holy Spirit into biblical interpretation and Jesus Christ into Scripture as its necessary interpretive key, you've opened the door to neoorthodoxy.

RAMM: I think that's a bit of an overstatement. Anyway, you're way too afraid of neoorthodoxy. Look at Barth and how highly he regarded Scripture while at the same time elevating Jesus Christ above Scripture as revelation itself.

HENRY: But he said that the Bible "becomes" the Word of God; that's existentialism, and it leads right into liberal subjectivism.

RAMM: It didn't in his case.

HENRY: But it has for many of his followers. We must not relativize the Bible in any way. It must always be the mine from which we dig our doctrines, and to be that, it has to be God's inspired Word written and not just an instrument of revelation or a witness to revelation. The moment you call it that, as did Barth and Brunner, you open the door to doctrinal drift. The Bible must be seen as a book of propositional revelation; it reveals facts about God that appeal to the mind. Revelation is a mental activity; it conveys information about God to the intellect.

RAMM: I certainly agree that revelation speaks to the mind, but it does more than that. The main purpose of revelation is relationship, and the main purpose of relationship is transformation. God reveals himself to change us by drawing us into a relationship with himself.

HENRY: Yes, yes. I agree that the main point of revelation is transformation, but how can there be transformation without information? Revelation is of facts that transform us when we grasp them.

RAMM: It's a matter of which comes first: the chicken or the egg. But if I had to choose, I'd say that facts of revelation are secondary to the personal revelation of God in Jesus Christ and through the Holy Spirit in our lives.

HENRY: Sometimes I get the distinct impression that you have drunk too deeply at the wells of neoorthodoxy if not of the Enlightenment itself.

RAMM: And sometimes I get the distinct impression that you are a bit paranoid about those two subjects. Everything you disagree with or find pernicious stems from the Enlightenment and/or the theology of Karl Barth. Actually, I think evangelicals need to come to terms with the Enlightenment and can learn much from Barth's theology.

HENRY: How can you say such things? Look at the harm both have done to our Christian faith. The Enlightenment has produced nothing but naturalism, scientism, and skepticism. The religion of the Enlightenment stands in stark contrast with the gospel; it is human-centered and not God-centered. Barth removed revelation from history and made it nonpropositional. By doing so, he opened the door to all kinds of heresies. Why, he even denied the historical nature of the resurrection of Jesus!

RAMM: No, I think you're wrong there, Carl. Did you read all of *Church Dogmatics* or only some of it? After the first volume he made crystal clear his belief in the bodily nature of the resurrection, and this was against Bultmann. And he affirms that it happened in time and space. He just didn't think it was historically verifiable.

HENRY: If it isn't historically verifiable, then how is it historical? No, I think you're too generous to Barth. He did have some good points, but for the most part he is a danger to evangelical faith.

RAMM: Well, I can see we're not going to agree. But just let me say that something can be historical without being historically verifiable. Barth's point is that the resurrection is an event of revelation and not of ordinary history. It happened in time and space, but it has no natural cause, and it is totally unique. Historians study the ordinary and repeatable, not the miraculous and unique. I tend to agree with Barth about that point, although I think there's evidence for that event of the resurrection as well.

HENRY: But somehow I suspect that you and I don't see eye to eye about the nature of the Bible. You say that revelation's main point is transformation and not information. Do you believe that the Bible is the verbally inspired and inerrant Word of God? That affirmation lies at the very heart of our evangelical faith.

RAMM: No, I don't agree. At its very heart lies Jesus Christ and his cross. The Bible is inspired, but it can't be an object of worship. I know you don't worship it, but your emphasis on it makes it almost an idol. Emil Brunner described your view of the Bible as a "paper pope." I think that's harsh, but I can see why someone might say that. Yes, the Bible is inspired, but without the Holy Spirit guiding us, we would never know it is God's Word or be able to understand it.

HENRY: Now just wait. When you say "without the Spirit we would never be able to understand the Bible," you come dangerously close to making its revelation something esoteric. The Bible's truth is public truth; anyone with a working mind can understand it.

RAMM: Then why don't people understand it?

HENRY: Because they're sinful and obstinate and don't want to understand it. It requires them to change, and they don't want to change. But our task is to keep showing them its truth and calling on them to submit to what reason shows to be true.

RAMM: I think you turn our belief in the Bible into a matter of fact and not at all a matter of faith.

HENRY: Well, to a certain extent I do. I plead guilty. That the Bible is authoritative for all of life is a proper presupposition; we don't have to prove it to believe it. But there's plenty of reason to believe it. Every worldview has some presupposition with which it begins. We begin with the Bible. Then our faith in it turns out to be the very best revelation there can ever be. Our worldview explains the facts of life better than any other view.

RAMM: I agree that it does that, but surely we must have faith in order to grasp it as God's Word and understand it. Many reasonable people do not see its authority or understand it, and that's because they lack the faith given by the Holy Spirit.

HENRY: So let's talk about inerrancy. The Bible is the inerrant Word of God. It communicates truth about God without any admixture of error. Don't you agree?

RAMM: I agree that the Bible is infallible; it never fails to communicate truth about God. It never fails to bring us into encounter with Jesus Christ if we approach it with faith. But I don't particularly like the word "inerrant," which implies that there are not even minor mistakes in the Bible. I'm not sure about that.

HENRY: Well, you know the Bibles we have contain errors, but when we ascribe inerrancy to the Bible, we mean the original autographs. If we had them, we'd see that there are no errors of any kind in the Bible as it was first written by the prophets and apostles.

RAMM: But what good is that?

HENRY: If the Bible isn't inerrant, then it lacks authority.

RAMM: But if only the original autographs were inerrant, then there's no authoritative Bible in existence! What good is that?

HENRY: I think you must know the answer to that question. The whole point of textual criticism, the attempt to reconstruct the original autographs of the Bible, is to establish an authoritative text. Through textual criticism we can get back quite close to the original autographs. So the most authoritative translation of the Bible is the one closest to the inerrant autographs.

RAMM: Yes, yes. But even our best textual reconstructions and translations of the Bible fall short of the autographs. Therefore, if authority is inextricably tied to inerrancy and only the autographs of the Bible were inerrant, we will always lack a completely authoritative Bible. I would rather make the Bible's authority depend on the Spirit, who inspired it and illumines us as we read and study it.

HENRY: Well, I fear your approach will lead down the slippery slope to subjectivism in theology.

RAMM: It didn't in the case of John Calvin, who also taught that the authority of the Bible rests in the Spirit and not in the letter.

HENRY: But he also believed in its inerrancy.

RAMM: There's where the Enlightenment forces us to diverge from our theological ancestors. We cannot do theology as if the rise of critical thinking didn't happen. We now know that the worldview of the Bible was cultural and, by modern standards, seriously flawed. We evangelicals must learn to adjust our theology to the material facts of the modern world lest we become like the Catholic church in Galileo's day and appear to be obscurantists, who simply refuse to acknowledge what is manifestly known.

HENRY: We can acknowledge that the biblical authors' view of the universe was primitive without giving up inerrancy. Inerrancy allows for phenomenological language about nature. They were simply expressing what they saw.

That's no more error than when we say that the sun rose in the morning. Of course it didn't. But nobody considers that an error.

RAMM: Oh, but it goes much deeper than that. The Bible not only reports what appears but also asserts what is the case, and sometimes it asserts things that simply cannot be true by modern standards, such as the "four corners of the earth." That's not phenomenological language; nobody "sees" four corners of the earth. There the biblical writer was simply wrong. But I agree with you: that should not affect the Bible's authority because its authority does not lie in its delivering a flawless view of nature. It lies in its delivery of truth necessary for our salvation.

HENRY: Well, I can't see how you distinguish between these two kinds of truth. If the Bible is flawed in any way in anything it asserts or teaches, it cannot be trusted.

RAMM: That seems like a fairly extreme statement; I think you're setting too high a standard. Or maybe not high enough. Too high because no human book, and let's not forget that the Bible is both human and divine, can live up to it. Not high enough because it seems too focused on the Bible as a book of facts whereas it is really a book of poetry, parables, wisdom sayings, and many other genres as well as facts.

HENRY: But it is possible and necessary to derive propositional truths even from the poetic expressions of God's Word.

RAMM: Why do that? Can't truth be communicated by means of stories, symbols, and poetry?

HENRY: Only if they can be translated into propositions.

RAMM: Well, that seems rather one-dimensional to me. Surely truth is more than just facts. After all, Jesus said, "I am the way, and the truth, and the life." Surely he didn't mean that he was a proposition or set of propositions.

HENRY: But unless we can translate who Jesus is into propositions, he remains but an enigma to our minds.

RAMM: I'm not sure we're ever going to agree about this. I think our main difference is that you think being evangelical is primarily having a certain attitude—yours—toward Scripture. I think being evangelical is about adhering to the gospel of Jesus Christ and spreading that gospel to the whole world. The Bible is important because it brings the gospel to us, but it isn't the centerpiece of evangelical faith. That would be Jesus Christ and salvation.

HENRY: You're right. We're poles apart. I place the Bible at the center of evangelical faith not because I worship it but because I can know nothing about Jesus Christ or the gospel without it.

RAMM: Oops. I think we've gone over our time for the break between sessions. I've got to run to the meeting of the NABPR in the ballroom upstairs. I hope we can continue our conversation sometime in the future.

HENRY: I'm not sure what profit that would bring, but perhaps we can if you want to learn more about the truth of evangelical faith from me.

Analysis

Evangelicalism is a diverse movement. Evangelical theology is often quite different from the grassroots beliefs and practices of evangelicals. Henry and Ramm stand out as far from the stereotype of evangelical revivalism. Both were highly intellectual men of letters. Ramm studied science before becoming a theologian. Henry earned two PhDs, including one from Boston University.

The two were chosen for this conversation because they represent the best of twentieth-century evangelical theology and because they represent its two wings: one more conservative and the other more progressive. Followers of Henry continue to insist that biblical inerrancy is crucial to a consistent evangelical view of the Bible. (Henry himself did not believe it is necessary to being an evangelical, but he did believe it is necessary to being a consistent evangelical.) Followers of Ramm continue to view the Bible as more and other than a propositional revelation (although it certainly contains propositions); they have gone on to explore narrative theology and the intersections between postmodernity and an evangelical view of the Bible as "theodrama," rather than as a not-yet-systematized system of doctrinal beliefs.

In this conversation some of the enduring tensions between evangelical theologians appear. Henry views divine revelation as a mental activity; when God reveals himself, he reveals truths about himself that can be translated into factual statements. Henry was a rationalist. He believed that Christianity is true because it can be demonstrated to be the most coherent worldview and life view on the basis of its internal consistency and its explanatory power. But he was not a rationalist when it came to Christianity's foundations. He believed that two axioms form those foundations: the God axiom and the Bible axiom.

According to Henry, there is no proof of the God of the Bible, and there is no proof of the Bible's authority. Both must simply be presupposed. But every philosophy of life begins with unprovable assumptions, which then must be rationally tested by the coherence of the worldview that stems from them.

Henry's critics, including many evangelicals, worried that he tended to reduce Christianity to a rational system of beliefs. Although Ramm never attacked Henry, his response to Henry's approach to evangelical theology is not difficult to discern. In 1972 Ramm published a small volume of evangelical apologetics, *The God Who Makes a Difference: A Christian Appeal to Reason*. There he turned away from presuppositionalism and evidentialism toward a modest appeal to reason that avoids rationalism. His case for the truth of Christianity rested more on a holistic view of life experience and how Christian revelation satisfies life's ultimate questions better than competing worldviews do. In other words, he was neither a fideist (belief by blind faith) nor a rationalist.

Ramm's approach to divine revelation was laid out in *Special Revelation and the Word of God* in 1961. There he acknowledged the inspiration and authority of Scripture while avoiding the usual conservative evangelical appeal to inerrancy. It's safe to say that he believed the Bible to be infallible even if not inerrant. In short, he also held a high view of Scripture. Postconservative evangelicals tend to regard Ramm as their mentor and model; conservative evangelicals look to Henry for guidance.

For Further Reading

Carpenter, Joel. *Revive Us Again: The Reawakening of American Fundamentalism*. New York: Oxford University Press, 1997.

Dorrien, Gary. *The Remaking of Evangelical Theology*. Louisville: Westminster John Knox, 1998.

27

Twentieth-Century Roman Catholic Theologian Rahner Is Interviewed about His Controversial but Influential Theories

Setting

By many accounts, Karl Rahner was the most influential Catholic theologian of the twentieth century. He was born in 1904 and died in 1984. His theological production was both profound and prolific. Rahner wrote numerous books and articles in German, soon translated. His best-known works were *Spirit in the World* (1936) and *Hearers of the Word* (1941). In 1976 he published *Foundations of Christian Faith*, which summarized his life's work in theology. The twenty-three volumes of *Theological Investigations* present his collected essays and articles.

Rahner was a subtle theologian; his ideas are difficult to master. Yet certain themes are relatively clear and run throughout his works. These will be brought out in the interview. Like Paul Tillich, Rahner was an apostle to the intellectuals. He was trying to make Catholic faith intelligible to educated twentieth-century people, and Europe was his context; yet his books have been translated into many languages and are read and studied around the world, especially in Catholic seminaries. He engaged in dialogue with atheists and agnostics and tried to demonstrate to them that faith in God is not unreasonable but actually makes more sense of human experience than unbelief.

Although Rahner was a faithful son of the Catholic church, he was not afraid to take risks in theology. Rather than beginning with either Scripture or tradition, he based his theological investigations on human experience. His theological method is known as "the transcendental method": trying to ascertain what must be true in reality to explain what we experience of ourselves and the world around us. Catholic theology traditionally begins with natural theology: proofs of the existence of God and such. In place of natural theology, Rahner substituted what he called "fundamental theology" (some prefer "foundational theology," to avoid confusion with fundamentalism). Fundamental theology is laying the foundation upon which doctrines will be constructed. Rahner believed that any person with a normally working mind and senses can understand, perhaps with help, that God is the necessary "horizon" of all basic human experience. By horizon he meant that toward which we must look and toward which we are moving.

Rahner was not interested in traditional natural theology and the proofs of God's existence. For Catholic theologians, however, the theology of Thomas Aquinas is considered normative, and Thomas strongly emphasized natural theology. For that and other reasons, the Vatican opened a file on Rahner in the 1970s. He had been a mover and shaker of the Second Vatican Council, which met in Rome from 1962 to 1965; but after John Paul II became pope in 1978, Rahner was placed under suspicion as a revisionist of traditional Catholic thought. However, nothing ever came of investigations by the CDF (Congregation for the Doctrine of the Faith, the Inquisition renamed); he was always eventually exonerated of charges of heresy. Nevertheless, conservative Catholic theologians and bishops, "integralists," tend to view him as accommodating too much to modern philosophy. He was influenced by existentialism, but so were almost all Christian theologians of Europe and North America in the aftermaths of the two World Wars.

Rahner has been compared with both Karl Barth and Paul Tillich (see conversations 21–23). His theological production was as prolific as theirs if not more so. And Rahner did for Catholic theology what Barth and Tillich did for Protestant theology in different ways: making it relevant to the twentieth century. In this imagined conversation, Rahner is near the end of his life. He is living near the University of Munich, in Germany. A leading Vatican Catholic newspaper sends a reporter to interview him. This imaginary paper is quite conservative.

The Conversation

INTERVIEWER: Father Rahner, as you know, our readers are traditional Catholics, and they want to know what makes you tick. The word on the street in Rome is that you are a closet liberal, a revisionist of doctrine. Is that true?

RAHNER: I'm glad you came right to the source instead of to some of my critics.

INTERVIEWER: Oh, don't worry. We'll interview some of your critics as well.

RAHNER: If you do, please keep in mind what I say here and now. I am not a doctrinal revisionist. I am certainly no modernist, as some of them charge.

INTERVIEWER: But you do use atheistic philosophies in your theological speculations, right?

RAHNER: And some of the greatest church fathers appropriated ideas from pagan philosophers of Greece and Rome, didn't they? And our own beloved Angelic Doctor, Thomas Aquinas, borrowed heavily from the Greek philosopher Aristotle, didn't he?

INTERVIEWER: And your point is?

RAHNER: My point, my dear man, is that theology has always been in conversation with philosophy and not always necessarily Christian or even theistic philosophies. I'm not doing anything new.

INTERVIEWER: Well, what about the existentialist philosophers and especially Martin Heidegger, whose work you use quite heavily? Isn't there a danger of corrupting the pure truth of our faith by using ideas from an atheist like him?

RAHNER: I use his ideas and every philosopher's ideas critically; I don't allow any of them to influence my theological constructions unduly. You called my work "theological speculations." I prefer "constructions."

INTERVIEWER: Please explain to our readers how you use existentialist philosophy critically.

RAHNER: Twentieth-century existentialist philosophers investigate the human condition and uncover its predicament of being thrown into a world without being asked. And they demonstrate how we humans live toward death and how our lives are marked by anxiety if not despair because of our inability to find a solid ground for security, meaning, and hope. I use these ideas about our human condition to raise questions that point toward God as the only source of security, meaning, and hope. But I don't settle for despair or self-determining meaning as the atheists do.

INTERVIEWER: Okay, but why don't you just begin with Catholic tradition or with natural theology? You know, the proofs for God's existence.

RAHNER: Because those things don't speak into the lives of twentieth-century people who are inclined toward atheism and nihilism. We need to begin where they are and with their questions if we want them to listen.

INTERVIEWER: I'm sure our readers will sympathize with your good intentions, Father Rahner, but some of them, perhaps including our Holy Father, will wonder if those intentions lead to compromise with secularism. You know what the road to perdition is paved with!

RAHNER: Yes, yes. Good intentions. Well, let me tell you something. And please explain this clearly to your readers: I am a faithful son of the church.

INTERVIEWER: But wasn't your first attempt at a doctoral dissertation turned down by the faculty because it was too heavily influenced by secular philosophy?

RAHNER: Yes, but the priests and theologians who did that failed to understand that we Catholics must come to terms with the modern age and its ways of thinking without capitulating to secularism.

INTERVIEWER: So please explain to us how you approach Catholic theology if not with our time-honored natural theology or tradition.

RAHNER: I call it the "transcendental method." That's my method of doing fundamental, or foundational, theology. It takes the place of traditional natural theology. The basic axiom is that where the actuality exists, there must also be the possibility. In other words, when we observe a certain phenomenon, we must suppose that the conditions for its existence also exist even if they are unseen. When we investigate human existence, we see that to be human means to be a questioner. Humans differ from animals in that we ask life's ultimate questions. We seek truth and knowledge. And we know that we will die, so we ask about life beyond death.

What is the source of our ability to ask, seek, and fundamentally alter our own condition by discovering new knowledge through science and philosophy? I say that it is the infinite horizon of being itself that surely is God. In all our asking, we presuppose answers. Our questioning shows us to be hearers of a word from beyond ourselves. And that Word comes from God; our ability to hear it and live by it shows that we are more than merely matter that is conscious of itself. We are spirits in the world, being tugged forward by Spirit itself toward our destiny in God.

INTERVIEWER: Wow! Now that's deep stuff. So what you're saying is that atheism is inconsistent with what we know about ourselves.

RAHNER: Fundamentally, yes. I don't claim to be able to prove God's existence directly, but my investigations into human existence point toward God as the only answer to our most basic questions. Without God we must fall into nihilism.

INTERVIEWER: But this God you speak of seems rather vague. How is He or It related to the Christian God of revelation and tradition?

RAHNER: He is the same God, but to know him personally, we need his historical revelation and not merely his revelation of himself to us as a question in our human condition. Hence, the answers we find in Christian revelation fit with the questions raised by human existence. Historical revelation in Jesus Christ speaks to the need uncovered by the transcendental examination of humans in the world.

INTERVIEWER: Now, this all seems to presuppose that a human is capable of knowing God without anything supernatural, right? I mean, we don't have to have a direct Word from God to know that God exists and even cares for us, right?

RAHNER: What I believe is that every person is human by virtue of the power to hear and obey the Word of God. This power is inherent within each of us. It is part of our natural equipment. But by itself it doesn't deliver a personal knowledge of God or salvation. Yet God in his mercy graces every person with what I call the "supernatural existential."

INTERVIEWER: Now you'll have to explain that to our readers. It sounds contradictory. An "existential" is something that belongs intrinsically to a person. But "supernatural" indicates something from beyond, something from God that adds to nature.

RAHNER: Right. It's both. It is supernatural because it is a gift from God. It is an existential because every person has it. But it isn't part of every person's natural equipment.

INTERVIEWER: What does this supernatural existential do?

RAHNER: It elevates our humanity above itself toward God. It gives us a special ability to know and respond to God personally.

INTERVIEWER: In other words, we are all more than merely human?

RAHNER: Right. By God's grace no human is merely human. We all have a special power given to us by God to transcend our mere humanity and reach out to God and receive the gift of his saving grace. I believe philosophy itself points to this in its quest to know and understand the deeper meanings of things.

INTERVIEWER: So does every human already have a relationship with God?

RAHNER: Absolutely.

INTERVIEWER: Oh, watch out now! Isn't that the heresy of universalism?

RAHNER: Not at all. Having a relationship with God does not mean being already saved. Everyone stands before God and is enabled by God's grace to receive his salvation. But we have to accept it by faith and works of love.

INTERVIEWER: Oh, okay, I see. So how does this differ from traditional Catholic theology?

RAHNER: Only in form, not in substance. Except that I believe even unbaptized persons have the ability to know God truly as they follow the light of the supernatural existential on a journey toward God. Somewhere and sometime on that journey, they will be encountered by the historical revelation of God in Jesus Christ.

INTERVIEWER: So unbaptized persons may be saved? What about the belief that outside the church there is no salvation? As you know, our church father Cyprian said, "Whoever does not have the church as mother cannot have God as father."

RAHNER: But who is to say where the boundaries of God's church lie? Can't someone without formal membership be mysteriously attached to the body of Christ by God's grace and mercy?

INTERVIEWER: Well, perhaps we can't rule that out. But if you say that unbaptized persons can be saved, then what is our motive to evangelize and bring people into the one true church?

RAHNER: Would you rather say that millions of people are going to hell just because they've never had the opportunity to be baptized and join Christ's visible and institutional church?

INTERVIEWER: I see what you mean. That is a concern of many modern people. So you have an answer to it, do you?

RAHNER: Yes. I make room in my theology for "anonymous Christians."

INTERVIEWER: Yes, we've heard of that over in Rome. I think that idea is why the Vatican is investigating you.

RAHNER: It is? I hadn't heard that.

INTERVIEWER: Yes, the CDF has opened a new file on you.

RAHNER: So, I'm an object of investigation by the Inquisition again, am I?

INTERVIEWER: Yes, so I've heard.

RAHNER: Then I'm in good company.

INTERVIEWER: So please explain "anonymous Christians."

RAHNER: Gladly. These are persons whose lives of love demonstrate implicit faith in Christ such that they are Christ's followers even without being members of Christ's church.

INTERVIEWER: Even someone who explicitly rejects the gospel can be an anonymous Christian?

RAHNER: Yes. Even an atheist might be one.

INTERVIEWER: An atheist? Really?

RAHNER: Certainly. What makes persons into Christians is their following the light of the supernatural existential within and making use of the ability it gives to live in love toward fellow beings. Anyone who does that is fulfilling Christ's command and will be recognized by Christ as one of his own at the judgment.

INTERVIEWER: That's quite radical stuff. No wonder the CDF is after you!

RAHNER: You're making me nervous. Stop saying that.

INTERVIEWER: Well, they don't burn people at the stake anymore, you know.

RAHNER: Very funny. But they can declare someone like myself not a Catholic theologian and forbid Catholic students to study under me.

INTERVIEWER: As has happened in another famous case.

RAHNER: Yes. But he deserved it. I don't.

INTERVIEWER: Let's hope the CDF can see that fine distinction.

RAHNER: Let's go back to the interview, please.

INTERVIEWER: Yes, certainly. So an atheist can be a Christian. Wow! Who would have guessed it?

RAHNER: Please!

INTERVIEWER: So, let's see. Oh, yes. Jesus Christ. We hear that you believe his deity is just a symbol.

RAHNER: Oh, my goodness. There is no such thing as "just a symbol." At least not if you mean a "real symbol." Such a symbol is not merely a sign that points but also something that participates in the reality it symbolizes. Jesus is the real symbol of the Christ and of God. He is truly man, but at the same time he participates in the reality of God because he perfectly represents God.

INTERVIEWER: Is that really Chalcedonian Christology? Confessing the two natures' idea of Christ?

Rahner: Well, I don't reject that, but having two natures doesn't speak to most people today. We need a better way to communicate the message of who Christ is to people now. The old language of substance doesn't resonate with them.

Interviewer: And this language of real symbol does?

Rahner: Yes. We live in a world of symbolic reality. Educated people today understand that a symbol has power; it is not merely a cipher that stands for something else. In a sense a symbol, if it is really a symbol and not merely a sign, brings into our field of experience a transcendent reality. That's what Jesus Christ does; he brings God into our historical experience as the symbol of God among us. God's representation, you might say.

Interviewer: So is Christ still our Savior?

Rahner: Certainly. He truly is the absolute Savior. All human wishes, dreams, and aspirations for wholeness find their fulfillment in him.

Interviewer: So let's tie this all together. You are saying that you can move smoothly from philosophy to Jesus Christ without making any leap where an honest secular seeker cannot follow?

Rahner: Well put.

Interviewer: So Christ is the answer to life's existential questions?

Rahner: Absolutely.

Interviewer: Why don't you just say that?

Rahner: And how would that make me famous?

Analysis

That last response by Rahner is meant tongue in cheek. He was often asked about his philosophically oriented theology and why it was so subtle. Rahner would just shrug and say, "That's the way it is when you're trying to do serious, academic theology. Some people just won't understand." But his audience was the doubting Thomases of his day, the intellectual intelligentsia, and the academic elites of Europe. Secular philosophies had convinced many people that despair is the only authentic conclusion to careful examination of the absurdity of existence in this world.

Rahner wanted to show that there is an escape from despair and that philosophy itself points toward it. The very ability to ask life's ultimate questions indicates a "horizon" of answers, toward which we are faced. All we have to do is to keep following the signals of transcendence embedded in our own spiritual quest for meaning, and we will arrive at an awareness of God. Actually, in some sense everyone already has a preconscious awareness of God that even represents a presence of God to and in them.

As a good Catholic, Rahner certainly did not think that the mere presence of God in the form of a question and a preconscious awareness is salvific. But it is a starting point, and anyone who follows that path faithfully and lives a life of love will meet the Savior as anticipated, either in this life or the next.

So why was the Vatican suspicious of Rahner? First, because he was so positive about secular and even atheistic philosophers like Heidegger, who was quite hostile to traditional Catholic faith. But as he pointed out, he did not embrace them completely or uncritically. Second, because he did not work enthusiastically with Catholic tradition. He didn't reject it, but neither did he wallow in it. And he didn't speak its language. He gave every traditional doctrine a new face, as it were. And often that face was philosophical. Third, many people, including his critics, simply didn't understand him. They mistook his new formulations of doctrine and his philosophical approach for modernistic compromise of the true faith. Yet he seems to have been a rather conservative theologian when it came to doctrine except that he used new and unfamiliar expressions.

Rahner's idea of anonymous Christians caught on among progressive Catholic thinkers and eventually led to a new attitude toward non-Christian religions. For the most part, the Catholic hierarchy now believes and teaches that salvation is available to those outside the Christian fold. God will judge them by the light they have. And if they are people of love, they are somehow mysteriously connected to Christ's church even if they don't know it and even if they reject it.

Is this universalism? Not at all. It's inclusivism. That's the idea, held by many Protestants as well, that God's will to save includes many more than just those who explicitly respond to the preached gospel. Others who never hear still have some hint of divine revelation in nature and conscience; they will be saved if they respond to that hint by faithfully living a life marked by a habit of faith. The Protestant writer C. S. Lewis was an inclusivist even if he wouldn't like the term "anonymous Christians."

The investigation of Rahner by the CDF (the Inquisition renamed) never turned up any evidence of heresy. But it put him under a shadow of suspicion just because he used nontraditional language. After all was said and done, he gladly affirmed the Nicene Creed and the traditional Catholic confessions of faith and dogmas. He just preferred to explain them to his contemporaries by using their concepts and terms.

For Further Reading

Marmion, Declan, and Mary E. Hines. *The Cambridge Companion to Karl Rahner*. Cambridge: Cambridge University Press, 2005.

Kelly, Geffrey B. *Karl Rahner: Theologian of the Graced Search for Meaning*. Minneapolis: Fortress, 1992. This book contains excerpts from Rahner's works with a lengthy interpretive essay on Rahner's theology.

28

Three Liberation Theologians Debate about Humanity's Worst Oppression and How Liberation Should Happen

Setting

I have met Gustavo Gutiérrez and Rosemary Ruether and have read most of their writings. I have not met James Cone, but I have read most of his books. This imaginary conversation does not pretend to tell exactly what these three would say to one another; it purports only to deliver an imaginary but educated guess at that. At the time of this writing, all three of them are still alive and actively writing and speaking. Here I try to do justice to each of them while admitting that I am putting words into their mouths and hoping those words are consistent with what they would say.

Rosemary Ruether was born in 1936 in Georgetown, Texas, near Austin, and eventually become the leading voice of Christian feminism. She is a Roman Catholic who taught much of her career at Garrett Evangelical Divinity School of Northwestern University in Illinois. Ruether is a visiting professor at Claremont School of Theology at Claremont Graduate University. Her best-known book is *Sexism and God-Talk* (1983), where she lays out a program for feminist interpretation of the Bible and feminist theology. Her book *Liberation Theology: Human Hope Confronts Christian History and American Power* (1972) was one of the first books about liberation theology written in English.

James Cone was born in 1938 in Arkansas. His childhood and youth in the rural South contributed to his later interest in the Black Power movement. He has taught theology at Union Theological Seminary in New York City since

1970 and is the Charles Augustus Briggs Distinguished Professor of Systematic Theology at that venerable institution. His best-known books include *Black Theology of Liberation* (1970) and *God of the Oppressed* (1975).

Cone is known for his strong interest in Black Power and lack of interest (at least early in his career) in racial reconciliation. His voice caused many American Christians to rethink their racial attitudes and especially their uncritical acceptance of white privilege. Cone's influence on the African-American churches was recognized during the 2008 presidential campaign season when Democratic candidate Barack Obama's pastor, Jeremiah Wright, was put under media scrutiny for comments he had made in various sermons that reflected many of Cone's themes.

Gustavo Gutiérrez was born in Lima, Peru, in 1928 and has been a Catholic parish priest in that city for most of his adult life. During his later years he has taught at various North American universities as well. He is often considered the "father of liberation theology" because of his groundbreaking book *A Theology of Liberation: History, Politics, Salvation* (Spanish, 1971; English, 1972). It is still widely considered the "Bible of liberation theology." Gutiérrez believes that poverty in most Latin American countries is planned and sustained through violence, and he has called for the Catholic church to take the side of the poor in their struggle for liberation from dehumanizing poverty.

Liberation theology comes in many flavors, but all have some themes in common. All assume that theology is best done contextually and locally; liberation theologians resist universal theology imposed on every culture by some magisterial power in Europe or North America or by white people or men. All assume that God has a preferential option for the poor and oppressed and that the oppressed have a privileged insight into God. They all argue that salvation includes identifying with the oppressed as they struggle to be liberated from imposed injustice. All also believe that theological reflection arises out of praxis, which is defined as the struggle for liberation from oppression. Theology, then, is never neutral or objective. It is either for or against the oppressed.

Some critics and observers of liberation theology consider it to be a theology of protest. In other words, it is not meant to replace systematic theologies or dogmas. It is meant to speak into them and beyond them, with normally unheard voices calling for attention to the problems of political, economic, and social oppression and for radical reform, if not revolution.

Liberation theology of all kinds has been and is extremely controversial. The Roman Catholic hierarchy has pressured liberation theologians to cease their calls for radical change in the structures of church and society. Some Latin American liberation theologians have been silenced by the Vatican. Conservative Protestants generally despise and condemn liberation theology as heresy because it highlights the social dimensions of salvation and often calls for abolition of capitalism, separation of African-Americans from dominant white cultures, and the full freedom of women to be self-determining subjects of their own lives apart from men.

This imaginary conversation is set at a professional society of theologians meeting in Chicago in 1990. It didn't happen, but it could have. These three notable liberation theologians constitute a panel discussing liberation theology before an audience of professors of religion and theology from universities around the world.

The Conversation

RUETHER: Well, well, well. It's good to see you two gentlemen here. I've been looking forward to our panel presentations and our conversations. But Jim, you don't usually associate with us while folks, do you? Hey, I'm just joking. I know you're not like that. And Gustavo, it's good to see you again. You've certainly come a long way to be here. All the way from Lima, Peru. Do you still live in that little one-room apartment above a printshop in the barrio?

CONE: Well, excuse me, madam prosecutor! You know very well that I don't shun white folks. Especially ones like you who have done so much to promote our cause. Yes, I know you're just kidding. But tell me, would I be welcome in one of your Women-Church meetings? Hah!

GUTIÉRREZ: Thanks for that very kind welcome, Rosemary. It's so good to be here with both of you. I've looked forward to this for a long time. But please, let's not give the audience a wrong impression. We're friends here. We're all together in this struggle against oppression. So even jousting jokingly may not be the best thing.

RUETHER: James, you're always welcome at my Women-Church meetings! I can't speak for others. We are autonomous congregations, you know. But please come and visit mine here in Chicago tomorrow. I'll be happy to give you a map and a special welcome. As for you, Gustavo, yes, you're right. We need to be careful to present a united front so that the enemies of liberation don't think we're divided against one another. You know what they say about a divided house.

CONE: Um, yeah. That's in the Bible.

RUETHER: Oh, yes. So it is! Thanks for reminding me.

CONE: Don't mention it. I would like to visit your Women-Church sometime. I don't know about tomorrow. But hey, have you visited one of our African-American congregations lately?

RUETHER: All the time, James.

GUTIÉRREZ: And both of you are more than welcome to come down to Lima and worship with our base communities.

CONE: I've heard of them, but what are they?

GUTIÉRREZ: Since many of the established churches are closed to talk of liberation and revolution, we have established small groups of oppressed Christians to study the Bible and support one another as we decide how best to live and work in a revolutionary situation.

RUETHER: Sounds kind of like our Women-Churches. Most of us are Catholics or former Catholics who don't feel comfortable in the mainstream churches because they don't allow women to perform the sacraments. So we meet together to talk about how to change things, and if we can't change things, we'll just keep meeting separately and develop our own liturgies.

CONE: And likewise, I've been saying for years that African-Americans in this country need to stop talking about integration with white churches and white religious organizations because they always co-opt us into their ways of doing things. We have our own ways of worshiping and our own issues to discuss, so we should stay separate.

GUTIÉRREZ: I know we want to emphasize what we have in common. And I urge that we do that when the session begins and our microphones are turned on. But we have a few minutes left just to chat among ourselves; so I'd like to ask you two what you think our differences are. I mean our theological differences. We all agree that God is on the side of the oppressed and that the oppressed have a privileged insight into God. And we all agree that salvation is integral: it includes social change and not just individual salvation to heaven. But are we completely on the same page, or are there areas where we need to come together more?

RUETHER: What do you have in mind, Gustavo?

CONE: Yeah, what's up with your question? I don't know if we do have any significant differences except that we're two men and a woman, and you two are white and I'm black.

GUTIÉRREZ: Okay, how about this. Rosemary, I get a little nervous when I hear you talking about God as "God/ess" and "divine Mother" and "matrix of being." Those names for God are so far outside of anything recognizably Christian that I have to wonder if you're being unduly influenced by paganism in the form of Wicca or goddess worship? I'm all for equality of men and women in both church and society, but I really don't think we have to change all our beliefs and language about God to achieve that.

RUETHER: With all due respect, Gustavo, that's just the trouble with you Latin American theologians of liberation. You're not radical enough. You think you can leave the basic structures of Christian theology the same, just add on some ideas about mission as "integral liberation," and then rescue Christianity from being oppressive. It's as if you think oppression is just something added on to traditional Christianity, and all we have to do is strip it away. Well, we believe Christianity itself is oppressive to women. Nothing less than a complete resymbolizing of God and the church and salvation can bring liberation to women.

CONE: Aren't you forgetting the problem of racism? Everything's about race, you know. At least that's so here in the good old USA. It doesn't matter whether we call God "our Father" or "Mother" or "God/ess" or whatever so long as God is pictured as white and used to prop up white, middle-class values. In my opinion you are both too timid. We have to say that

God is black. Nothing less than that will liberate us in this context, where slavery has not been completely left behind yet.

GUTIÉRREZ: But isn't poverty the most basic problem for both African-Americans and women? Wouldn't both groups be liberated if poverty were overcome with a socialist revolution? I don't mean a violent revolution, but a bloodless yet radical change in the structures of society.

RUETHER: First let me address your concern, James. I think black women are the most oppressed group in society, and that's why some African-American feminists have developed what they call "Womanist theology." They say that even within the African-American communities of this county, it's being female that pushes them down more than being black. They suffer oppression even from fellow blacks—men, that is. The most basic form of oppression is sexism. Let's liberate all women from patriarchy and misogyny first, and then other forms of oppression will tend to fall. And to you, Gustavo, I have to say that I know some affluent women who are more oppressed than poor men because of their absolute dependence on men and the male-dominated society. Just being a man gives you special privileged status in this society, and I'm sure that's true in yours as well.

CONE: I'm sorry to hear you say that black women are oppressed by black men, Rosemary. But I agree; it's true. At least in some cases. But the solution is to liberate all black people from racism. African-American men struggle under such a load of suspicion and even hatred in this society that their lives are almost impossible. That's why they lash out at other people, including their own women. If we liberate them from the white racism, which holds them down, they'll treat all of their own people better.

GUTIÉRREZ: No, no, no. To both of you, I say that poverty is the worst form of oppression. Black men in this country, as in many other racist societies, struggle mostly with poverty. When they have equal economic opportunity, they will have pride in who they are and shake off whatever controlling and oppressive attitudes and actions they may have toward women. Poverty is what keeps both African-American men and white women from achieving their full human potential. What we need first and foremost is a social structure that guarantees a human living for every person.

RUETHER: Both of you are just saying these things because you are men and not women. If you were women, you'd know that sexism is the worst social evil of all. What we need is not so much economic equality or racial equality, as desirable as they are, but gender equality. And that must begin in the churches and church-related institutions and then spread out from there into society as a whole. It can begin with churches openly condemning all those Scripture passages that demean women and then changing our liturgical language so that God is addressed as Mother. And we need to re-conceive of God as inseparable from the earth. All hierarchies must go!

GUTIÉRREZ: So feminism is not just about equality of men and women?

CONE: It appears not. Please explain, Rosemary.

RUETHER: I hoped that you two would already understand this. What we women want is what Jesus was all about: tearing down all hierarchies. Hierarchies oppress. They even oppress those at the top because then they are trapped in their dominating power over others and cannot be fulfilled in community. I would even go so far as to say that God is not "over" creation. God is completely with creation, as its soul. God is the soul of the creation and not its master.

GUTIÉRREZ: I don't know what to say about that. I just can't fully wrap my mind around it. God is not our Lord but our servant? Is that what you're saying?

CONE: I think all this talk about radical, deep ecology among the feminists can be a distraction from the real issues we face. Yes, we need to take better care of the environment, but to do that, we don't have to tear down all hierarchies, especially the God-over-world hierarchy. I prefer Barth's emphasis on God's transcendence because only if God is both transcendent and black can we count on God to be our liberator.

RUETHER: James, would you please explain what you mean when you say God is black? You don't mean her skin color is black, do you?

CONE: Certainly not. God doesn't have skin. I'm talking about God's identification with the oppressed. In this struggle against white racism, God is on our side.

GUTIÉRREZ: Yes, I agree that God is on the side of the oppressed. So I could say that God is poor. And you, Rosemary, could say that God is a woman, and I guess you do. But we need to be careful not to humanize God too much. We need a warrior God capable of overthrowing the systems that oppress people, capable of protecting the powerless. Perhaps we are called to keep peace, as Jesus said, but we can trust God to fight for us only if he is powerful and strong.

RUETHER: That's really a testosterone-driven image of God, I'm afraid. No, we need to think of God as our friend and lover and strong companion on the journey toward full freedom. Fighting is a man thing. Well, for the most part. But Jesus showed us how to speak truth to power without fighting. And he bowed to no hierarchy. He even said that he was equal with God the Father.

CONE: Let's be realistic. Evil is not going to be overcome with love and peace. We need to be prepared to fight oppression. If the white establishment of America won't listen to reason and let us African-Americans be self-determining subjects of our own history, then we might just have to take matters into our own hands. At least I can't condemn those who do pick up the rock and throw it when all attempts to be freed by talk fail.

GUTIÉRREZ: I agree, James. There's a time for violence as a last resort when we are faced with deadly violence. In Latin America we have death squads, which go around killing people who criticize their governments. Some of our base communities have been wiped out by government death squads who fear our talk of liberation. Violence is never a good thing, but some-times it is the lesser of two evils.

RUETHER: Well, I'm not promoting pacifism here, guys. I'm just saying that in our struggle for liberation from oppression, we should be careful that we don't become like our oppressors. Power corrupts. We don't want power. We want freedom to be ourselves.

GUTIÉRREZ: I'm not sure either one of you can fully understand the evil of poverty in Latin America unless you come over to our countries and experience it firsthand. Then you, Rosemary, may be more open to overthrow of the status quo. And you, James, may realize that poverty is worse than racism when it comes to deadening our very humanity.

CONE: And I suggest that both of you change your skins to black and go to live in a ghetto for a while. And then walk or drive out into the suburbs to see what it feels like to be stared at and have the police call on you for no reason at all except your skin color. You'll soon discover what it's like to be black in America. It's bad even if you're affluent. Every black man I know who drives an expensive car gets pulled over by a police officer about once a week for absolutely no reason except being black.

RUETHER: I wish both of you could be women for just one week and see what it's like. You enjoy male privilege, and so you don't understand what we women suffer. But that's one reason why we women need to have our own churches: men just can't understand the evil of sexism. You can't become a woman. You just have to take our word for it that it's the major cause of oppression in America. Women have to watch their backs constantly lest they be mugged or worse. Men can go virtually anywhere without fear. We women can't.

GUTIÉRREZ: Hey, our moderator is at the microphone, and ours have been turned on. It's been nice talking with you, but now we have to answer questions from the audience. Oh, oh. Look at all the hands up in the air. Were our microphones on this whole time?

Analysis

So, for many feminist theologians, sexism is the most oppressive form of oppression, and the only solution is to abolish all hierarchies. In her book *Gaia and God: An Ecofeminist Theology of Earth Healing* (1992), Ruether even argues that belief in human life after death is oppressive because it elevates humans over other parts of creation. She and many other feminist theologians favor panentheism over classical theism in any form. God and the world must be equal, or else all kinds of abusive hierarchical patterns of authority and power are justified. Feminist theology, then, is marked by an emphasis on a radical immanence of God. God is not male or female, but like women, God is a lover, nurturer, and intimate companion who cares, not a powerful controller, like many men.

Feminist theology has been deeply influenced by the theology of Paul Tillich (see conversation 23), who called God the "ground of being" and "being itself." Ruether calls God the "matrix of being," among other things. For her, then, God is like the infrastructure of creation: more than anything else, God wants absolute equality and mutual affirmation among his creatures. But "s/he" (a popular pronoun for God among feminists) will not impose it unilaterally. That would be against the character of God as revealed in Jesus Christ, who is the ultimate liberator of women and men.

Many people wonder if Christian feminists like Ruether hate men. Not at all. Ruether is married and has children and grandchildren. But feminists detest the pattern of social relationships that men have built and defend, relationships that encourage dominating power over others and things. Women are typically better at collaboration and nurture. That's like God, according to Ruether and many other feminists. God is the liberating Spirit of equal power, who nurtures us and encourages rather than controls.

Latin American liberation theologians typically view institutionalized, structural poverty and the violence engendered by such poverty as the worst form of oppression, at least in their societies. Until it is abolished, they argue, other forms of oppression must not set the agenda. And when it is abolished, other forms of oppression will tend to cease. Their view of God is not as radical as feminist theology's view of God. For liberation theologians, God is the triune Father, Son, and Holy Spirit of traditional orthodoxy, but they view God as siding with the poor against the rich and powerful in the historical struggle for self-determination and full humanity. Some, if not most, liberation theologians of Latin America picture the Trinity as a community of equals, without domination or power over.

But more important, these liberation theologians picture the coming kingdom of God as a society of equal wealth, with no differentiating wealth. They believe that the church should not acquiesce in a system that contradicts kingdom-of-God values. Their solution is some form of socialism in which the means of production are publicly owned and used for the public interest.

Black theologians like James Cone talk about God being black, but they make clear that they do not mean skin color or even culture. In this sense "black" means "oppressed in America," and who is more oppressed in America than African-Americans? Well, someone might argue (and a few have) that Native Americans are the most oppressed group in America. Does that mean that God is "red" (to use a rather politically incorrect term but only for the sake of parallelism with "black")? Cone would probably say yes. But Native Americans will have to develop their own liberation theology, and some have begun to do it. Cone speaks for the African-American community in America and allows other oppressed communities to speak for themselves. That is not in any way to say that he is unconcerned about them. But it's enough to be a spokesperson for African-Americans in a society obsessed with race and controlled by racism.

Liberation theology suffered some severe blows in the 1980s and 1990s and is struggling to regain its footing and momentum in the early part of the twenty-first century. An African-American middle class is emerging in the United States and adopting middle-class values, such as economic upward mobility. One of the two main political parties in the United States recently nominated a black man as its candidate for the presidency, and he won the election in 2008. A woman was chosen by the other party as its candidate for vice president. Socialism has suffered severe setbacks around the world. Some of the most socialistic countries have turned toward capitalism. Nicaragua, which was supposed to be the new society where oppression would be absent, turned out to be a basket case under the Sandinistas. It has turned away from socialism toward democratic capitalism.

The future of liberation theology is in question. But as long as there is oppression in society, there will be some form of liberation theology. Today, in the first decade of the twenty-first century, new forms of liberation theology are arising, including gay liberation theology and animal rights theology. But a worldwide shift toward conservatism has challenged all forms of liberation theology. It will be interesting to see where liberation theology goes in the next decades.

For Further Reading

Clifford, Ann M. *Introducing Feminist Theology*. Maryknoll, NY: Orbis Books, 2001.

Gutiérrez, Gustavo. *Essential Writings*. Edited by James B. Nickoloff. Minneapolis: Fortress, 1996. This book contains a compilation of excerpts from Gutiérrez's writings, with a lengthy interpretive essay.

Hopkins, Dwight. *Introducing Black Theology of Liberation*. Maryknoll, NY: Orbis Books, 1999.

29

Two Postmodern Theologians Discuss the Meaning of Theology in Postmodern Culture

Setting

Does anyone really know what "postmodern" means? The term has been around since 1925 and in frequent use for about fifty years, yet there's still no consensus about its meaning beyond "after modernity." Most people who know a little about the postmodern condition define "postmodern" as an attitude of incredulity toward all metanarratives. That comes from the postmodern philosopher Jean-François Lyotard (1924–1998). A metanarrative is an all-encompassing story that purports to explain everything. Lyotard and other postmodern thinkers encourage doubt in the face of all such totalizing worldviews.

That only scratches the surface of what it means to be postmodern. And some self-identified postmoderns do not doubt all metanarratives. They just think that none should be imposed on everyone and that we should hold our own worldviews with humility, being open to correction. But one thing is clear. Postmoderns are disillusioned with modernity, which is the culture that grew out of the Enlightenment. Modernity prizes absolute certainty and objectivity; it elevates reason to authoritative status. It tends toward rationalism.

Postmoderns do not discard reason; they just doubt its omnicompetence. And they doubt the very possibility of objective reasoning. All knowing is local and particular; perspective colors all investigations of truth. Some radical postmoderns argue that truth claims are nothing more than masks for will to power and should be deconstructed to show their hidden motives. But not all postmoderns are deconstructionists; many believe truth is "out there" but doubt that anyone can arrive at a complete, objective grasp of it, especially by scientific reason alone.

Postmodernity started to affect Christian theology in the 1990s as theologians began to converse with postmodern philosophers. Some theologians embrace postmodernism; others reject it entirely. Many are somewhere in the middle, seeing some truth in postmodernity while rejecting its more extreme forms. Some Christian theologians who have engaged with postmodern thought in some way include Stanley Hauerwas (b. 1940), Mark C. Taylor (b. 1945), and Stanley Grenz (1950–2005). These are quite different Christian thinkers, but in their own ways each has made some use of postmodern thought and culture to construct or reconstruct Christian theology and doctrine for the postmodern age.

What are the typical marks of a postmodern theologian? Generalizing about this is risky; postmoderns don't have much in common beyond being disillusioned with the culture of modernity and not wanting to go back to a premodern culture. One thing is safe to say: postmodern theologians, like all postmodern people, reject the idea of anything "mainline." They object to the notion that some particular religious expression is normative for everybody. That doesn't necessarily mean that there's no truth; what they are objecting to is the elevation of one particular version of truth to a special status as socially and culturally normal while others are marginal.

But what about postmodern theology? What makes a Christian theology postmodern? Self-identified postmodern (critics call them "pomo") theologians are all over the place in theory; there's very little about which they all agree. But one thing stands out: they all wish to escape the traditional right-versus-left spectrum of theologies determined by the Enlightenment, or modernity, and responses to it. In other words, since at least the late nineteenth century, it has been the habit of commentators and critics to try to place every Christian theologian somewhere on a spectrum between "extremely conservative" (reacting against the Enlightenment and modernity) and "extremely liberal" (accommodating to the Enlightenment and modernity).

Postmodern theologians deplore this habit because, for them, the Enlightenment should not be the criterion of anything in theology. In their view the Enlightenment, with its foundationalist approach to knowledge, is dead. Foundationalism is the idea that a statement is true to the extent that it arises logically from an indubitable, rational fact. The classical foundationalist is philosopher René Descartes's "I think, therefore I am." According to Descartes, his own existence formed the foundation from which all other ideas must be derived by logic in order to be considered true.

Postmodern theologians, like postmodern philosophers, eschew foundationalism in favor of a more holistic approach to knowledge, in which truth is determined by coherence with a web of beliefs. Truth, then, is a function of coherence. Every person has some kind of web of beliefs; individual beliefs are justified by their consistency with the total web. A web, in this case, is somewhat like a metanarrative. For radical postmoderns, webs or metanarratives are to be questioned and doubted insofar as they claim to be absolute; they are to be deconstructed insofar as they try to be totalizing to the exclusion of other ones. For moderate postmoderns, webs or metanarratives are to be embraced, tested for coherence, and held somewhat lightly because none is absolute or totalizing.

Take the truth claim that God exists. All postmoderns would agree that this statement, like all truth claims, is an expression of a particular worldview, metanarrative, web of beliefs. It is true insofar as it coheres with the web of which it is a central part. Whether it is true outside that web is impossible to prove. A radical postmodern would probably say no: it is not true outside that web. A moderate postmodern would definitely say yes, God is real outside the home web, but that affirmation is made from within the web itself. A person who doesn't participate in the form of life that gives rise to the web of belief will probably not be able to affirm that God is real. If one does, then the question becomes whether that affirmation fits with the rest of what the person (or tradition-community) believes and affirms.

These are fairly deep waters. People socialized in modernity (most public schools in America still teach that) tend to think that truth claims are straightforward statements of fact, to be tested by objective methods. Postmoderns reject objectivity. What counts as evidence and perhaps even logic is determined by a web of beliefs.

That's enough for now. Listen to these two postmodern theologians as they discuss and debate these and other issues of postmodern theology.

Here two unnamed contemporary (2008) postmodern Christian thinkers meet at a conference on postmodern theology. They are at a table in a hotel restaurant, eating lunch between conference sessions.

The Conversation

RADICAL POSTMODERN (RP): Good morning. Or should I say "good noon"? May I sit here with you? We seem to have a lot in common, and I'd like to talk about that.

MODERATE POSTMODERN (MP): By all means. Here, let me move my pile of books that I just bought in the publishers' showroom. Sit here, please.

RP: Hey, I see you purchased a copy of my latest book, *Theology's Only Job*. Have you had a chance to look at it yet?

MP: No, but I read a review of it in *Books and Culture*, and it sounds like something I should read. At first I thought it was a commentary on the book of Job in the Bible, but . . .

RP: Yeah, that's funny. I've heard that a lot.

MP: Seriously, though. The review was not very complimentary, but I thought I'd buy the book at 40 percent off and look into it anyway. I'm always interested in postmodern theology of any kind, and the subtitle is certainly intriguing: *Deconstructing Itself*. A century ago liberal theologians such as Henry Churchill King said that theology's job is to reconstruct Christian doctrines in the light of modernity. Now you're saying that theology's job is to deconstruct itself. Quite interesting. Care to explain?

RP: I hate to rob you of the joy of reading my book by giving it all away over lunch! But, okay, yes—I'll tell you my basic thesis, and then let's talk about it. I've read your book on *Postmodernizing Theology* so I know you have a strong interest in postmodern theology.

MP: Don't let that keep you from eating, though. Oh, here's our waiter. Shall we order first?

RP: By all means. I'll have the totally mixed-up salad and the vegetarian wrap.

MP: And I'll have the green eggs and ham. I didn't have breakfast. They aren't really green, are they?

RP: No. I had them for breakfast, and they're just jealous. Hah!

MP: So, please explain theology's only job to me.

RP: For centuries we've thought that theology was about examining doctrines and teachings of the churches and constructing and reconstructing doctrines. Now in the postmodern age, we know that all truth claims are power plays intended to protect the claimers' vested interests and oppress others.

MP: Really? We know that, do we? Is that a truth claim? If so, isn't it also a mask for the will to power?

RP: Please. Don't interrupt me just yet. Let me finish. In light of the postmodern suspicion of all truth claims, theology's new and only task is to deconstruct itself. We have to turn our magnifying lens on ourselves and ask how our theological assertions oppress others and protect us from them.

MP: Example, please?

RP: Yes, well, let's see. Christians say that all people everywhere need to accept Jesus as Savior and Lord and become Christians in order to be saved.

MP: Really? I haven't heard that in a liberal Protestant church in ages.

RP: Please. Let me finish. So our task as theologians now is to examine such a claim and expose its power play. Here's what I see. We Christians say things like that so that our missionaries will go around the world making more of us and less of them.

MP: Who's "them"?

RP: Non-Christians. We who send missionaries and create theologies to justify that expansion care only about making more of us, Westerners and Christians, and less of them. We abhor the "other." That's why we create a theology that wipes them out. It's just a new form of the medieval crusades.

MP: That's rather pessimistic about "us," isn't it?

RP: That's our job, to be critical of ourselves.

MP: Isn't it one thing to be self-critical and another thing to accuse ourselves and everyone like us of having sinister ulterior motives?

RP: Not at all. We all have ulterior motives, and theology's job is to uncover and expose them.

MP: Give another example, please.

RP: Okay. Here's one. Most Christian theologians have portrayed God as male whether they actually say it or not. God is immutable and impassible. God is transcendent and "wholly other." Our job now is to expose the traditional Christian view of God as patriarchal and oppressive to both men and women. Men have created the Christian doctrine of God in order to oppress women by portraying God in typically male terms. The whole scheme is to protect men's vested interest in dominating women.

MP: Interesting. But does your method of suspicion and deconstruction work on feminist theology?

RP: Don't muddy the waters. You're only raising that question because you're a man and you want to defend your male, hierarchical theology.

MP: Oh, really? So what's good for the gander isn't good for the goose?

RP: Again, you have no right to try to deconstruct a theology other than your own.

MP: But do you claim traditional male-created theology as your own?

RP: Yes. I and people like me created it to oppress women and keep them in their place. I may not agree with it now, but I stand within the oppressive tradition that created it.

MP: So you expect feminists to deconstruct their theology themselves, right?

RP: That's their business, if they want to do it. But I regard their theology as already a deconstructed theology. Their whole project is to expose the power moves made by traditional, patriarchal theology.

MP: But what about their truth claims for God as "God/ess" and the "matrix of being"? Aren't those truth claims and therefore masks for will to power? Isn't their theology just traditional theology turned upside down? What about their Women-Church movement? Aren't men oppressed there?

RP: No, not at all. So far as I know, men are welcome. I've visited two or three Women-Churches. I don't see any oppression there at all.

MP: Well, I also visited one, and I felt like there should be an altar call for men to come forward and repent of their misogyny.

RP: And what would be wrong with that?

MP: Well, maybe nothing. But I felt oppressed in that context.

RP: Then don't go back.

MP: But you're missing my point. Oppression always takes place within a context. It's true that in many and maybe most contexts in North America, women are oppressed. But in the context of a Women-Church, men might be oppressed.

RP: Oppression requires power over. Feminists explicitly reject power over.

MP: But you haven't answered my question about truth claims. If all truth claims are but masks for will to power, aren't the feminists' claims about God/ess also masks for will to power? And what about your own deconstructing truth claims? Aren't you engaging in a power play when you assert that the traditional doctrine of God is a mask for men's will to power?

RP: See. This is what always happens when the oppressed rise up against their oppressors. The oppressors try to turn the tables on the rebels and say that they too are oppressive. It just isn't so.

MP: I don't see why you won't answer my question. Is it because you don't really believe in truth claims at all? Perhaps you only recognize two kinds of assertions. All of them are speech acts, but some are oppressive speech acts, and others are liberating speech acts. Neither is saying something about truth itself.

RP: And how would we have access to this "truth itself"? We are all locked up within our language games. Truth itself "out there" is beyond our grasp. So our task is to liberate people from the whole concept of "truth itself." Even the concept of truth is oppressive.

MP: So that's not a truth claim but a speech act, right? And what makes it a right speech act while the claim "God is immutable," for example, is a wrong speech act?

RP: Because the claim "Truth itself is beyond our grasp" is liberating rather than oppressive.

MP: I can't buy into all that, partly because it's circular and has to end up deconstructing itself, and partly because it isn't theology. You're just turning theology into politics. I mean politics in the broadest sense, but still politics.

RP: And your point is?

MP: Why don't you just quit calling it theology and call it politics?

RP: Because it's about the word "God." Politics doesn't use that word. Theology is one language game, and politics is another one.

MP: But you're just destroying the whole language game of theology. In fact, I don't think you're doing theology at all. Theology is about truth.

RP: I thought you were postmodern.

MP: I have sympathies with some postmodern perspectives. But not your kind of postmodernism. I'm not into deconstructing theology although I certainly have some sympathies with exposing real power plays in theology and every other discipline. But I can't agree that all truth claims are only power plays.

RP: Then I don't think you're really postmodern at all.

MP: And who are you to decide who is and who isn't postmodern? Isn't that quite un-postmodern of you? Aren't you being oppressive with that?

RP: I don't think so. But please, go on; explain what kind of postmodern theologian you are.

MP: I believe that truth is out there, but no human can claim to have a complete or perfect grasp of it. And there's no "view from nowhere." We are all biased. Not necessarily in favor of our own vested interests, but because of our locations.

RP: Right. Our social locations determine our theologies.

MP: No. If that were true, your social location would be the whole cause of your deconstructing theology. So please, let me continue. Our social location doesn't determine our theology, but it does influence it. In theology we do make truth claims that can't be reduced to politics. We are after the truth about God. But we all work from within some tradition of discourse; we are all working from within some story-shaped community. There's no neutral ground for anyone to stand on. The so-called secularist is not more neutral than the Christian. Even the secularists' truth claims are biased because of their tradition and the story that creates and shapes it.

RP: Ah, so you're postmodern in that you reject all metanarratives?

MP: Well, I am suspicious of all metanarratives especially insofar as they try to be totalizing by defeating all other metanarratives.

RP: Isn't that exactly what the Christian metanarrative does?

MP: No, actually. The true Christian metanarrative is the only one that by its nature cannot be totalizing.

RP: Tell that to the Jews and Muslims slaughtered by the crusaders past and present!

MP: Well, I would say that those so-called Christians who go out and oppress people in the name of Jesus are false Christians because they are doing what is against the Christian metanarrative, which is Jesus centered.

RP: Just talking about the Christian metanarrative as true is oppressive.

MP: But claiming to know what is and isn't oppressive isn't oppressive?

RP: You keep dodging the main point, which is to liberate the oppressed. You are playing games with words.

MP: Actually, that's what I think you do. But please, let me continue. I'm postmodern in that I don't believe in totalizing metanarratives. And I acknowledge that all truth claims arise from within a story about reality. I'm a Christian because I explicitly embrace the Christian story as my own and work from within it while at the same time acknowledging that it is not objectively true for all people.

RP: That sounds relativistic to me. But I certainly agree!

MP: No, it's not relativistic. I'm not saying there is no truth or that all metanarratives are equally true. I'm saying that there is no objective truth; by that I mean that no truth claim can be made outside of some story, and stories are not falsifiable or verifiable except from within themselves. Truth is not a function of neutral observation of evidence or of logical deduction from unquestionable and undoubtable foundations. Truth is a function of coherence within a story.

RP: So there's no way to bridge from one story to another and convince a person working out of another story that yours is truer?

MP: Not in the way modernity tried to do that. Modernity created a whole new story that pretended to be objective and the judge of every other story. Objective reason, foundationalism, became the allegedly sole path to truth. Even a lot of Christians bought into that and tried to prove Christianity true by appealing to the modern story of objective facts verified by evidence, as offered up by modernity itself. I'm postmodern because I think evidence itself is largely determined by a story. Each metanarrative decides what is evidence and what isn't.

RP: But what about the bridges between stories? Can people of different stories communicate meaningfully, or are we locked into our language games?

MP: I wouldn't say we're locked into our language games, but at the same time I deny that there is any overarching language game that is neutral and does not arise out of a story-shaped form of life. Christianity is first and foremost a form of life shaped by a story: the Jesus story of God. Secondarily it gives rise to reflection on that story. The moment that happens, a language game appropriate to the story is created. Doctrines are expressions of the culture of the community that lives by the story of Jesus and expresses itself by means of the language game appropriate to that culture.

No overarching story, culture, or language game has the right or ability to dominate all others and make them bow to it by bringing their beliefs to its bar of reason for verification. But we can discover common ground with other cultures, communities, and language games. Rarely are they so disparate that they cannot find some common ground.

RP: Give an example, please.

MP: Well, questions about God arise from within most story-shaped communities and their traditions. We can try to show that the answers in our story and tradition are better than the answers found in other ones.

RP: Better? In what sense? Doesn't that assume some neutral, objective standard?

MP: No, it doesn't. All I'm saying is that I can try to show a person with a different worldview than mine that my worldview, partial as it is, provides more satisfying answers to life's ultimate questions. I can try to lead that person to see the world "as" what I see it to be. Not by proving it true but by showing a gestalt, or pattern, that better explains life experience. But in the end, if a person switches life views and worldviews, it means a conversion and not just a change of mind about some facts.

RP: I'm sorry, but I just don't get it at all. Your very belief in truth "out there," outside of our own minds, is not postmodern at all. It's actually quite modern. That's what we postmoderns are trying to get away from. I take it that you're a critical realist, someone who believes truth is out there but inaccessible to our minds, right?

MP: Yes, something like that. Except that I believe it is not totally inaccessible. Through revelation, for example, truth can enter into our world and into our minds even though never perfectly or completely. What do you think truth is?

RP: Truth is what liberates people from oppression. When people are being oppressed, truth is whatever will liberate them from that.

MP: That's just circular. Who defines liberation? One person's liberation is another person's oppression, and vice versa. Surely if I'm going to speak truth to power, I have to assume that I have at least a partial grasp of what really is the case. For example, I have to assume that I have some idea of what justice really is. How do you think about justice? Isn't it just your creation?

RP: Like everything else, justice is a tool for defeating power.

MP: But doesn't the very idea of "defeating" assume your own power? Like I said, you talk in circles. But I see everyone moving toward the Great Hall to hear our plenary speaker. Who is it this time?

RP: I'm certainly going to hear her. You should too, although I doubt that you're going to agree with much of what she says. Her topic is "God and Her Survival in an Age of Environmental Crisis." She argues that we must become God's saviors through deep ecology.

MP: What does she mean by "God"?

RP: What kind of question is that? She doesn't claim to know anything about God. For her, "God" is a cipher for nature. C'mon. You should hear this.

MP: No thanks. I think I'll go and read your book and start writing my review of it.

Analysis

Confused? Well, postmodern thought is meant to confuse you! To a certain extent, anyway. It's a repositioning of all thought. In theology it calls for new ways of thinking outside the "box" of modernity. Postmodern thinkers are convinced that we are still living within the suffocating confines of the Enlightenment, which elevated objective reason almost to the status of a god. Postmodernists believe that kind of all-encompassing account of truth and knowledge is oppressive; it lacks flexibility and permission for local philosophies and theologies to thrive and flourish.

Mr. Radical Postmodern expresses the common view among postmodernists that all truth claims are oppressive; for him, as for many postmoderns, truth itself is a chimera, a mirage, a false god. The task of theology is to destroy the idols, including truth itself. Repeatedly throughout history, truth has been used to crush enemies and oppress the victims and outsiders of the dominant society. For him, then, theology's main job is to unmask itself and expose its oppressive tendencies.

Mr. Moderate Postmodern has little in common with Mr. Radical Postmodern except that they both reject the hegemony of the Enlightenment and modern culture or "modern thought." Neither of them believes in "mainstream" culture, religion, or philosophy. All cultures, religions, and philosophies are local. There is no universal truth that can be discovered and imposed on everyone everywhere.

But the two postmodern theologians disagree strongly about whether there is any truth at all. When Mr. Moderate Postmodern denies the reality of "objective truth," he does not mean, as some critics assert, that truth does not exist. He means that nobody can claim to have and to hold "objective truth," as if that person's grasp of truth is unbiased while everybody else's grasp of truth is biased. Moderate postmoderns believe that the postmodern age is opening new doors for Christian theology. No longer can a self-appointed elite of intellectuals and academics pretend that they have a firm hold on objective truth, to the detriment of everyone else. Truth is not what can be proved; very little can be proved. After all, we now know that what counts as evidence depends on one's perspective on life and the world.

Moderate postmoderns believe that story precedes facts; all facts are "interprefacts": they are someone's interpretation of reality, and they are colored if not determined by a story in which the one asserting truth finds oneself. Even the scientist conducts research within a paradigm of thought shaped by the scientific revolutions of the seventeenth through the twentieth centuries. Nobody is totally objective; none can claim to be free of a local story that greatly influences what he or she thinks.

Christian doctrines, then, are attempts to put the Christian story into speech, and to make sure that all assertions of truth made by Christians are consistent with that story and with one another. Coherence is the key to truth even though truth itself is something that only God knows objectively and completely.

Radical postmoderns agree that we all work from within some story, but they are not optimistic about achieving any real grasp of truth itself. They aren't even sure that truth exists "out there." What they are sure of is that oppression exists and that worldviews or metanarratives tend to oppress. Metanarratives are unconsciously designed to marginalize others while placing the believers at the center of power. All metanarratives must be doubted, and the factual assertions based on them must be deconstructed.

The problem with radical postmodernism is its circularity. It says that all truth claims are but masks for will to power and then deconstructs them. But why not deconstruct that initial truth claim that all truth claims are masks? A lot of special pleading is going on there. Radical postmoderns seem to think that all others except they themselves are making power plays in asserting something as true. In the end, what is really going on is politics and not theology. Theology serves politics and is "true" only insofar as it works to liberate the oppressed.

Moderate postmoderns have trouble with apologetics and evangelism. How can the truth of the gospel be made known to the nations when people are seemingly locked inside their local narratives and language games? Christian moderate postmoderns fall back on the Holy Spirit to work through the message of Jesus and thereby draw people into the Christian metanarrative. There is no rational way from one metanarrative to another. Lots of conservative evangelical theologians blast that strategy as essentially relativistic while ignoring the fact that their own approaches to evangelism and apologetics depend on an Enlightenment-shaped paradigm of truth and knowledge.

For Further Reading

Tilley, Terrence. *Postmodern Theologies*. Eugene, OR: Wipf & Stock, 2001.
Vanhoozer, Kevin J., ed. *The Cambridge Companion to Postmodern Theology*. Cambridge: Cambridge University Press, 2003.

Conclusion

As in the introduction, I feel the need in this conclusion to apologize for the liberties I have taken in composing these imaginary conversations. I confess that I have injected a good deal of playfulness into the dialogues in order to entertain readers. But some of the playfulness may not be as imaginary as you might think; theologians and philosophers of the past were much more likely to hurl insults at their critics and opponents than they are today. According to contemporary reports, when Luther heard that Zwingli, his Swiss counterpart and debate partner, was killed in battle defending Zurich against Catholic armies, he said, "Serves him right for wearing a sword as a priest and for having wrong opinions about the Lord's Supper." Today we cringe at such invectives, but throughout much of Christian history theology was taken much more seriously and argued more vehemently.

If you've reached the conclusion, presumably you've read the book, or at least most of it. You might be a little confused after reading all those theological opinions and arguments. Perhaps you want to know "Who's right?" in each "conversation." Well, the purpose of this book is not to indoctrinate or convince but to inform and hopefully delight. As a result of reading (and perhaps performing some of) these "conversations," you should understand some of the diversity of Christian thought through twenty centuries. But if you're still obsessed with knowing who's right in each "conversation," I will tell you I left clues in each one about which person I agree with and think you should agree with as well. They are subtle clues, however, so as not to overwhelm anyone with my views. The hope is that you make up your own mind.

Hopefully this project doesn't end here but continues with some of you, the readers, writing your own imaginary conversations. I couldn't include every important Christian voice in this book. Who was left out? Perhaps the early Christian bishop and theologian John Chrysostom (347–407), also known as "Golden Mouth" because of his great preaching, would make a great conversation partner with Billy Graham (b. 1918). They could meet in heaven and talk about the preaching task and the preacher's relationships with powerful political figures. (Anyone who knows about Chrysostom's and Graham's involvements with emperors and presidents gets the idea!)

Perhaps someone could write a "conversation" between medieval philosopher/theologian William of Ockham (1287–1347) and nineteenth-century Christian existentialist Søren Kierkegaard (1813–1855). They might discuss the nature of universals, such as truth, beauty, and goodness, and whether God has a nature. Finally, a reader might want to write an imaginary "conversation" between twentieth-century Catholic theologian Hans Küng (b. 1928) and Joseph Cardinal Ratzinger (b. 1927), who became Pope Benedict XVI. When Ratzinger was head of the Vatican's Sacred Congregation for the Doctrine of the Faith (Inquisition), he investigated Küng and contributed to his being declared not a Catholic theologian.

I hope this book grows as others add imaginary conversations to it, but my main hope is that it makes theology come alive to many students, pastors, and lay people.